PET WELCOMe!

1996

The Animal Lovers' Holiday Guide

35th Edition 1996
ISBN 1 85055 205 3 © FHG Publications Ltd.

Cover design: Sheila Begbie
Cover photograph: Rex Features

Cartography by GEO Projects, Reading

Maps are based on Ordnance Survey Maps with the permission of the
Controller of Her Majesty's Stationery Office, Crown copyright reserved.

Set by Keyset Composition, Colchester.
Printed and bound in Great Britain by Guernsey Press, Guernsey

Published by FHG Publications Ltd,
Abbey Mill Business Centre, Seedhill, Paisley PA1 1TJ
(Tel: 0141-887 0428. Fax: 0141-889 7204).

Distribution. **Book Trade**: WLM, Downing Road, West Meadows Ind Est., Derby DE21 6HA
(Tel: 01332 343332. Fax: 01332 340464).
News Trade: United Magazine Distribution Ltd, 16–28 Tabernacle Street, London EC2A 4BN
(Tel: 0171-638 4666. Fax: 0171-638 4665).

FHG Publications

Abbey Mill Business Centre, Seedhill, Paisley PA1 1TJ
Tel: 0141 887 0428.   Fax: 0141 889 7204

PETS WELCOME!
1996

HERE IS another super selection of holiday accommodation choices for pets and their owners. Lots of old favourites and new prospects from Tain to Truro, from Bosherton to Broadhaven with a warm welcome for your short break or holiday. As usual we include a small selection of Kennels and Catteries as an extra option and we have started what we hope might be a growing section of accommodation contacts for Horses, with or without owners, and travelling perhaps for Shows or Trials as well as holidays. Pet-Friendly Pubs is now an established feature and who knows what other pet-related topics will be useful in future.

Health and holidays are often discussed together and most people, especially when travelling abroad make some kind of provision for illness or accidents. In Britain we can expect reasonably prompt and professional care when we are away from home – but would this also be true of our pets? With older pets or those who may be subject to recurring conditions it's probably a good idea to check in advance that there is a local vet and that they'll be willing to be called in an emergency. Fortunately that's not likely to be a common problem and you should be able to look forward to a happy holiday with your pet when you contact the advertisers on the pages which follow in PETS WELCOME! for 1996.

Some proprietors offer fuller facilities for pets than others. In the *Classified* entry which we give each advertiser we try to indicate by symbols whether or not there are special facilities and if additional charges are involved. However, we suggest that you raise any queries or requirements when you make enquiries and bookings.

Most of our entries are of long standing and are tried and tested favourites with animal lovers. However as publishers we do not inspect the accommodation advertised in *Pets Welcome!* and an entry does not imply our recommendation. If you have any problems or complaints about accommodation, please raise them on the spot with the owner or his representative in the first place. We will follow up complaints if necessary but we regret that we cannot act as intermediaries nor can we accept responsibility for details of accommodation and/or services described here. Happily, serious complaints are few.

Finally, if you have to cancel or postpone a holiday booking, please give as much notice as possible. This courtesy will be appreciated and it could save later difficulties.

Please let us know if you have any unusual or humorous experiences with your pet on holiday. This always makes interesting reading! And we hope that you'll mention *Pets Welcome!* when you make your holiday enquiries and bookings.

Peter Clark
Publishing Director

CONTENTS

4

The fascinating story of farming and country life with working watermill, gardens, collections of bygones, farm and nature trails. Excellent for young children. Campers and Caravanners welcome.

DIRECTIONS: off A47, 8 miles west of Peterborough.

OPEN: daily all year.

FHG PUBLICATIONS, ABBEY MILL BUSINESS CENTRE, PAISLEY PA1 1TJ

Railway Museum and operating centre

DIRECTIONS: adjacent to Safeway supermarket in town centre; follow brown-and-white tourist signs.

OPEN: daily 10am to 4pm (21st February to 21st December 1996).

FHG PUBLICATIONS, ABBEY MILL BUSINESS CENTRE, PAISLEY PA1 1TJ

Europe's leading marine animal rescue centre, dedicated to the rescue and release of pups found around the coastline; also home to a colony of adult seals and sealions.

DIRECTIONS: from Helston follow A3083, past RNAS Culdrose turn left at roundabout and follow tourist signs to Gweek (approx. 5 miles).

OPEN: daily (except Christmas Day) from 9am.

FHG PUBLICATIONS, ABBEY MILL BUSINESS CENTRE, PAISLEY PA1 1TJ

Britain's premier farm attraction - milking parlour, Heritage Centre, Farmpark and playground. Daily events include bottle feeding, "Pat-a-Pet" and rally karts.

DIRECTIONS: 4 miles from Newquay on the A3058 Newquay to St Austell road.

OPEN: from early April to end October 10.30am to 5pm. Also open from early December to Christmas Eve 12-5pm daily.

FHG PUBLICATIONS, ABBEY MILL BUSINESS CENTRE, PAISLEY PA1 1TJ

Relax, escape and enjoy a great day out - Carp, Rudd, Tench, Bream, Crucians, Ide, Roach and (for fly) Rainbow and Brown Trout

DIRECTIONS: from Kirkoswald follow signs for Staffield, turn right (signposted Dale/Blunderfield); Crossfield is 200m up narrow road via cattle grid.

OPEN: April to November open daily; November to April weekends only

FHG PUBLICATIONS, ABBEY MILL BUSINESS CENTRE, PAISLEY PA1 1TJ

READERS' OFFER 1996   **VALID** during 1996

THE CUMBERLAND TOY AND MODEL MUSEUM

Banks Court, Market Place, Cockermouth, Cumbria CA13 9NG Tel: 01900 827606

One person **FREE** per full paying adult

NOT TO BE USED IN CONJUNCTION WITH ANY OTHER OFFER

FHG   **READERS' OFFER 1996**   **VALID** April to September 1996

Lowther Leisure and Wildlife Park

Hackthorpe, Penrith, Cumbria CA10 2HG Tel: 01931 712523

£2 off standard admission price (per person) up to maximum of 5 persons

NOT TO BE USED IN CONJUNCTION WITH ANY OTHER OFFER

FHG   **READERS' OFFER 1996**   **VALID** to end October 1996

HEIGHTS OF ABRAHAM

Matlock Bath, Derbyshire DE4 3PD Telephone: 01629 582365

FREE child entry with one full paying adult

NOT TO BE USED IN CONJUNCTION WITH ANY OTHER OFFER

FHG   **READERS' OFFER 1996**   **VALID** during 1996

National Tramway Museum

Crich, Matlock, Derbyshire DE4 5DP Telephone: 01773 852565

Admit one child **FREE** with full paying adult (not valid for Santa Specials)

NOT TO BE USED IN CONJUNCTION WITH ANY OTHER OFFER

READERS' OFFER 1996   **VALID** Easter to October 1996

TOTNES MOTOR MUSEUM

Steamer Quay, Totnes, Devon TQ9 5AL Telephone: 01803 862777

One child **FREE** when accompanied by full-paying adult

NOT TO BE USED IN CONJUNCTION WITH ANY OTHER OFFER

100 years of mainly British toys including working tinplate Hornby trains,
Scalextric cars, Lego etc. Free quiz.

DIRECTIONS: just off the market place in Cockermouth

OPEN: daily 10am to 5pm from 1st February to 30th November

FHG PUBLICATIONS, ABBEY MILL BUSINESS CENTRE, PAISLEY PA1 1TJ

Attractions, rides, adventure play areas, circus and wildlife - all set in undulating parkland
amidst beautiful scenery - make Lowther the Lake District's premier all-day attraction.

DIRECTIONS: travelling North leave M6 at J39, follow brown signs; travelling South
leave at J40, follow brown signs. A6 Shap Road, 6 miles south Penrith.

OPEN: March/April to September 10am to 5/6pm.

FHG PUBLICATIONS, ABBEY MILL BUSINESS CENTRE, PAISLEY PA1 1TJ

Cable car return journey plus two famous show caverns. Tree Top Visitor Centre with
restaurant, coffee and gift shops; nature trails and children's play areas.

DIRECTIONS: signposted from all nearby major trunk roads.On A6 at Matlock Bath.

OPEN: daily Easter to end October 10am to 5pm (later in High Season).

FHG PUBLICATIONS, ABBEY MILL BUSINESS CENTRE, PAISLEY PA1 1TJ

Outdoor action with indoor attractions! Unlimited vintage tram rides through period
street to open countryside, plus video theatre, exhibition hall, cafe, picnic areas, shops.

DIRECTIONS: 15 miles north of Derby, 6 miles from Matlock,
8 miles from Junction 28 M1

OPEN: April to October 10am to 5.30pm daily (6.30pm weekends and Bank Holidays);
March and November Sundays only

FHG PUBLICATIONS, ABBEY MILL BUSINESS CENTRE, PAISLEY PA1 1TJ

Vintage, sports and racing cars, motorbikes, bicycles; 1920s picnic, 1930s garage;
video showing old racing film. Something for everyone!

DIRECTIONS: Totnes town centre. Follow brown tourist signs.

OPEN: Easter to October 10am to 5.30pm

FHG PUBLICATIONS, ABBEY MILL BUSINESS CENTRE, PAISLEY PA1 1TJ

READERS' OFFER 1996

VALID during 1996

THE BIG SHEEP

Bideford, Devon EX39 5AP   Telephone: 01237 472366

Admit one **FREE** with each paid admission

NOT TO BE USED IN CONJUNCTION WITH ANY OTHER OFFER

FHG

READERS' OFFER 1996

VALID Easter to end Oct. 1996

Dorset Heavy Horse Centre

Edmondsham, Verwood, Dorset BH21 5RJ   Telephone: 01202 824040

Admit one adult **FREE** when accompanied by one full-paying adult

NOT TO BE USED IN CONJUNCTION WITH ANY OTHER OFFER

FHG

READERS' OFFER 1996

VALID April to October 1996

Killhope Lead Mining Centre

Cowshill, Upper Weardale, Co. Durham DL13 1AR   Tel: 01388 537505

Admit one child **FREE** with full-paying adult

NOT TO BE USED IN CONJUNCTION WITH ANY OTHER OFFER

FHG

READERS' OFFER 1996

VALID during 1996

Cotswold Farm Park

Guiting Power, Near Stow-on-the-Wold, Gloucestershire GL54 5UG   Tel: 01451 850307

Admit one child **FREE** with an adult paying full entrance fee

NOT TO BE USED IN CONJUNCTION WITH ANY OTHER OFFER

FHG

READERS' OFFER 1996

VALID during 1996

NATIONAL WATERWAYS MUSEUM

Lllanthony Warehouse, Gloucester Docks, Gloucester GL1 2EH   Tel: 01452 318054

20% off all tickets (Single, Family or Shopper).

NOT TO BE USED IN CONJUNCTION WITH ANY OTHER OFFER

"England for Excellence" award-winning rural attraction combining traditional rural crafts with hilarious novelties such as sheep racing and duck trialling.

DIRECTIONS: on A39 North Devon link road, 2 miles west of Bideford Bridge

OPEN: daily all year, 10am to 6pm

FHG PUBLICATIONS, ABBEY MILL BUSINESS CENTRE, PAISLEY PA1 1TJ

Heavy horse and pony centre, also Icelandic riding stables. Cafe, gift shop. Facilities for disabled visitors.

DIRECTIONS: signposted from the centre of Verwood, which is on the B3081

OPEN: Easter to end October 10am to 5pm

FHG PUBLICATIONS, ABBEY MILL BUSINESS CENTRE, PAISLEY PA1 1TJ

Britain's best preserved lead mining site - and a great day out for all the family, with lots to see and do

DIRECTIONS: alongside A689, midway between Stanhope and Alston in the heart of the North Pennines.

OPEN: April 1st to October 31st 10.30am to 5pm daily

FHG PUBLICATIONS, ABBEY MILL BUSINESS CENTRE, PAISLEY PA1 1TJ

The home of rare breeds conservation, with over 50 breeding flocks and herds of rare farm animals. Adventure playground, pets' corners, picnic area, farm nature trail.

DIRECTIONS: M5 Junction 9, off B4077 Stow-on-the-Wold road. 5 miles from Bourton-on-the-Water.

OPEN: daily 10.30am to 5pm April to September (to 6pm Sundays, Bank Holidays and daily in July and August).

FHG PUBLICATIONS, ABBEY MILL BUSINESS CENTRE, PAISLEY PA1 1TJ

The history of 200 years of inland waterways by means of interactive exhibits, working engines, and two quaysides of floating exhibits. Special school summer holiday activities.

DIRECTIONS: Junction 11 or 12 off M5 - follow brown signs for Historic Docks. Railway and bus station 10 minute walk.

OPEN: Summer 10am to 6pm; Winter 10am to 5pm. Closed Christmas Day.

FHG PUBLICATIONS, ABBEY MILL BUSINESS CENTRE, PAISLEY PA1 1TJ

READERS' OFFER 1996

VALID 1st Jan to 30th Oct. 1996

Marwell Zoological Park

Colden Common, Winchester, Hampshire SO21 1JH Telephone: 01962 777407

Admit up to **TWO** Adults at party rates (current saving £2)

NOT TO BE USED IN CONJUNCTION WITH ANY OTHER OFFER

READERS' OFFER 1996

VALID during 1996 and 1997

Isle of Wight Rare Breeds and Waterfowl Park

St Lawrence, Ventnor, Isle of Wight PO38 1UW Tel: 01983 852582

Admit one child **FREE** with full-paying adult

NOT TO BE USED IN CONJUNCTION WITH ANY OTHER OFFER

READERS' OFFER 1996

VALID during 1996

SNIBSTON DISCOVERY PARK

Ashby Road, Coalville, Leicestershire LE67 3LN Telephone: 01530 510851

Admit one child **FREE** with full-paying adult

NOT TO BE USED IN CONJUNCTION WITH ANY OTHER OFFER

READERS' OFFER 1996

VALID during 1996 except Bank Holidays

Southport Zoo and Conservation Trust

Princes Park, Southport, Merseyside PR8 1RX Telephone: 01704 538102

Admit one child **FREE** with two full paying adults

NOT TO BE USED IN CONJUNCTION WITH ANY OTHER OFFER

FHG

READERS' OFFER 1996

VALID March to October 1996

HEXHAM HERBS

Chesters Walled Garden, Chollerford, Hexham, Northumberland NE46 4BQ Tel: 01434 681483

One adult **FREE** with paid adult entry

NOT TO BE USED IN CONJUNCTION WITH ANY OTHER OFFER

The No.1 Zoological Park in the South, dedicated to breeding endangered species. 1000 animals in 100 acres of parkland - ideal for all ages.

DIRECTIONS: 6 miles south-east of Winchester, clearly signposted from M3 and M27.

OPEN: daily from 10am (closed Christmas Day).

FHG PUBLICATIONS, ABBEY MILL BUSINESS CENTRE, PAISLEY PA1 1TJ

One of the UK's largest collections of rare farm animals, plus deer, llamas, miniature horses, waterfowl and poultry in 30 beautiful coastal acres.

DIRECTIONS: on main south coast road A3055 between Ventnor and Niton.

OPEN: Easter to end October open daily 10am to 5.30pm;
Winter open weekends only 10am to 4pm

FHG PUBLICATIONS, ABBEY MILL BUSINESS CENTRE, PAISLEY PA1 1TJ

Award-winning science and industry museum. Fascinating colliery tours and "hands-on" displays including a robot, holograms, tornado and virtual reality.

DIRECTIONS: 10 minutes from Junction 22 M1 and Junction 13 M42/A42.
Well signposted along the A50.

OPEN: April to Oct.10am to 6pm; Nov. to March 10am to 5pm. Closed 25/26 Dec.

FHG PUBLICATIONS, ABBEY MILL BUSINESS CENTRE, PAISLEY PA1 1TJ

Lions, snow leopards, chimpanzees, penguins, reptiles, aquarium and lots more, set amidst landscaped gardens.

DIRECTIONS: on the coast 16 miles north of Liverpool; follow the brown tourist signs.

OPEN: daily except Christmas Day. Summer 10am to 6pm; Winter 10am to 4pm.

FHG PUBLICATIONS, ABBEY MILL BUSINESS CENTRE, PAISLEY PA1 1TJ

Beautiful walled garden with nearly 900 types of herbs, woodland walk, nursery, shop. Guide dogs only.

DIRECTIONS: 6 miles north of Hexham, next to Chesters Roman Fort.

OPEN: daily March to October/November.

FHG PUBLICATIONS, ABBEY MILL BUSINESS CENTRE, PAISLEY PA1 1TJ

FHG

READERS' OFFER 1996

VALID during 1996

WHITE POST MODERN FARM CENTRE

Farnsfield, Near Newark, Nottinghamshire NG22 8HL Tel: 01623 882977

TWO child admissions for the price of one

NOT TO BE USED IN CONJUNCTION WITH ANY OTHER OFFER

FHG

READERS' OFFER 1996

VALID during 1996

Perry's Cider Mills

Dowlish Wake, Near Ilminster, Somerset TA19 0NY Telephone: 01460 52681

10% OFF all shop goods excluding cider, cider brandy and stone jars. SAE for leaflet for free entry

NOT TO BE USED IN CONJUNCTION WITH ANY OTHER OFFER

FHG

READERS' OFFER 1996

VALID until March 1997

Wookey Hole Caves and Papermill

Wookey Hole, Wells, Somerset BA5 1BB Telephone: 01749 672243

£1.00 per person **OFF** full admission price (up to maximum 5 persons)

NOT TO BE USED IN CONJUNCTION WITH ANY OTHER OFFER

FHG

READERS' OFFER 1996

VALID 1996 except Bank Hols and Special Events

Wilderness Wood

Hadlow Down, Near Uckfield, East Sussex TN22 4HJ Tel: 01825 830509

One **FREE** entry with full-paying adult (only one voucher per group).

NOT TO BE USED IN CONJUNCTION WITH ANY OTHER OFFER

FHG

READERS' OFFER 1996

VALID during 1996

PLANET EARTH AND DINOSAUR MUSEUM

Garden Paradise, Avis Road, Newhaven, East Sussex BN9 0DH Tel: 01273 512123

Admit one **FREE** adult or child with one adult paying full entrance price

NOT TO BE USED IN CONJUNCTION WITH ANY OTHER OFFER

A modern working farm with over 3000 animals including ducklings, deer, bees, rheas, piglets, snails, lambs (all year). New pet centre.

DIRECTIONS: off the A614 at Farnsfield, 12 miles north of Nottingham. From M1 Junction 27 follow "Robin Hood" signs for 10 miles.

OPEN: daily all year round.

FHG PUBLICATIONS, ABBEY MILL BUSINESS CENTRE, PAISLEY PA1 1TJ

Traditional cider made on the premises (Oct/Nov) on sale all year- sample before you buy. Shop with pottery and gifts; garden section; museum of farm tools, wagons and photos.

DIRECTIONS: approx. 2 miles from Ilminster off A303, 3 miles from Cricket St Thomas.

OPEN: all year except Sunday afternoons.

FHG PUBLICATIONS, ABBEY MILL BUSINESS CENTRE, PAISLEY PA1 1TJ

---

* Britain's most spectacular caves * Traditional paper-making * Fairground Memories *
* Penny Arcade * Magical Mirror Maze *

DIRECTIONS: from M5 Junction 22 follow brown-and-white signs via A38 and A371. Wookey Hole is just 2 miles from Wells.

OPEN: Summer 9.30am to 5.30pm; Winter 10.30am to 4.30pm. Closed 17-25 December.

FHG PUBLICATIONS, ABBEY MILL BUSINESS CENTRE, PAISLEY PA1 1TJ

See woodland with new eyes at this family-run working wood; fascinating and fun for all the family. Trails, adventure playground, exhibition, picnic areas, BBQs for hire, teas.

DIRECTIONS: on main A272 in Hadlow Down village, 5 miles north-east of Uckfield.

OPEN: daily all year.

FHG PUBLICATIONS, ABBEY MILL BUSINESS CENTRE, PAISLEY PA1 1TJ

World of Natural History including World of Dinosaurs and Fossil Museum.

DIRECTIONS: signposted "Garden Paradise" off A26 and A259

OPEN: all year, except Christmas Day and Boxing Day.

FHG PUBLICATIONS, ABBEY MILL BUSINESS CENTRE, PAISLEY PA1 1TJ

READERS' OFFER 1996
VALID during 1996

STORYBOOK GLEN

Maryculter, Aberdeen, Aberdeenshire AB1 0AT   Telephone: (01224) 732941

10% Discount on all entry fees on production of voucher.

NOT TO BE USED IN CONJUNCTION WITH ANY OTHER OFFER

READERS' OFFER 1996
VALID April to October 1996

SCOTTISH MARITIME MUSEUM

Harbourside, Irvine, Ayrshire KA12 8QE Telephone: (01294) 278283

One adult FREE with each paid adult entry

NOT TO BE USED IN CONJUNCTION WITH ANY OTHER OFFER

READERS' OFFER 1996
VALID during 1996

MYRETON MOTOR MUSEUM

Aberlady, East Lothian EH32 0PZ Telephone: 01875 870288

One child **FREE** with each paying adult

NOT TO BE USED IN CONJUNCTION WITH ANY OTHER OFFER

READERS' OFFER 1996
VALID April 1996 to April 1997

EDINBURGH CRYSTAL VISITOR CENTRE

Eastfield, Penicuik, Midlothian EH26 8HB   Telephone: 01968 675128

OFFER: Two for the price of one (higher ticket price applies).

NOT TO BE USED IN CONJUNCTION WITH ANY OTHER OFFER

READERS' OFFER 1996
VALID during 1996

HIGHLAND FOLK MUSEUM

Duke Street, Kingussie, Inverness-shire PH21 1JG Tel: 01540 661307

One **FREE** child with accompanying adult paying full admission price

NOT TO BE USED IN CONJUNCTION WITH ANY OTHER OFFER

28 acre landscaped park with over 100 life-sized models of nursery rhymes.

DIRECTIONS: 5 miles west of Aberdeen on the B9077

OPEN: 1st March to 31st October: daily 10am to 6pm.
1st November to end February: Saturday and Sunday only 11am to 4pm

FHG PUBLICATIONS, ABBEY MILL BUSINESS CENTRE, PAISLEY PA1 1TJ

Historic vessels open to the public including a "puffer" and a steam yacht; "There Is A Cow In My Cabin" exhibition, plus world's oldest clipper "Carrick" under restoration.

DIRECTIONS: follow signs to Irvine and then signposts for harbourside.

OPEN: 1st April to 31st October - 10am to 5pm

FHG PUBLICATIONS, ABBEY MILL BUSINESS CENTRE, PAISLEY PA1 1TJ

Motor cars from 1896, motorcycles from 1902, commercial vehicles from 1919, cycles from 1880, British WWII military vehicles, ephemera, period advertising etc.

DIRECTIONS: off the A198 near Aberlady.

OPEN: daily October to Easter 10am to 5pm; Easter to October 10am to 6pm.
Closed Christmas Day and New Year's Day.

FHG PUBLICATIONS, ABBEY MILL BUSINESS CENTRE, PAISLEY PA1 1TJ

Visitor Centre with Exhibition Room, factory tours, Crystal Shop, gift shop,
coffee shop. Facilities for disabled visitors.

DIRECTIONS: 10 miles south of Edinburgh on the A701 Peebles road;
signposted a few miles from the city centre.

OPEN: Visitor Centre open daily; Factory Tours weekdays all year,
plus weekends April to October.

FHG PUBLICATIONS, ABBEY MILL BUSINESS CENTRE, PAISLEY PA1 1TJ

One of the oldest open air museums in Britain! A treasure trove of Highland life and culture. Live events June to September.

DIRECTIONS: Easily reached via the A9, 68 miles north of Perth and 42 miles south of Inverness.

OPEN: Easter to October: open daily. November to March: open weekdays.
Closed Christmas and New Year.

FHG PUBLICATIONS, ABBEY MILL BUSINESS CENTRE, PAISLEY PA1 1TJ

READERS' OFFER 1996

VALID until 30th September 1996

LLANGOLLEN RAILWAY

The Station, Abbey Road, Llangollen, Clwyd LL20 8SN Tel: (01978) 860979

One child **FREE** with each full fare-paying adult

NOT TO BE USED IN CONJUNCTION WITH ANY OTHER OFFER

READERS' OFFER 1996

VALID during 1996

Big Pit Mining Museum

Blaenafon, Gwent NP4 9XP Telephone: (01495) 790311

Admit one child **FREE** per voucher with two full-paying adults.
(not to be used with family ticket).

NOT TO BE USED IN CONJUNCTION WITH ANY OTHER OFFER

READERS' OFFER 1996

VALID March to October 1996

PILI PALAS - BUTTERFLY PALACE

Menai Bridge, Isle of Anglesey, Gwynedd LL59 5RP Tel: 01248 712474

One child **FREE** with each adult paying full entry price

NOT TO BE USED IN CONJUNCTION WITH ANY OTHER OFFER

READERS' OFFER 1996

VALID during 1996

Llanberis Lake Railway

Llanberis, Gwynedd LL55 4TY Telephone: 01286 870549

One child travels **FREE** with two full fare-paying adults

NOT TO BE USED IN CONJUNCTION WITH ANY OTHER OFFER

READERS' OFFER 1996

VALID during 1996

CENTRE FOR ALTERNATIVE TECHNOLOGY

Machynlleth, Powys SY20 9AZ Telephone: 01654 702400

One child **FREE** when accompanied by paying adult (one per party only)

NOT TO BE USED IN CONJUNCTION WITH ANY OTHER OFFER

Preserved railway with steam and diesel engines, diesel multiple units and coaching stock; cafes and shops.

DIRECTIONS: A539 on left past river bridge in Llangollen; A5 turn right at traffic lights and left across river bridge - station is immediately on left.

OPEN: 10am to 6pm

FHG PUBLICATIONS, ABBEY MILL BUSINESS CENTRE, PAISLEY PA1 1TJ

Underground tours of original colliery workings by experienced miners. On the surface: exhibitions, forge, stables, craft shop and licensed cafeteria.

DIRECTIONS: M4 Junction 6, then A4042/3 to Pontypool and Blaenafon. From M50, A449 to Raglan, then A40 to Abergavenny and A4246 to Blaenafon.

OPEN: daily March to November. Phone for Winter opening times.
Last admission 3.30pm

FHG PUBLICATIONS, ABBEY MILL BUSINESS CENTRE, PAISLEY PA1 1TJ

Visit Wales' top Butterfly House, with Bird House, Snake House, Ant Avenue, Creepy Crawly Cavern, shop, cafe, adventure playground, picnic area, nature trail etc.

DIRECTIONS: follow brown-and-white signs when crossing to Anglesey; one-and-a-half miles from the Bridge.

OPEN: March to end October 10am to 5pm daily; November/December 11am to 3pm.

FHG PUBLICATIONS, ABBEY MILL BUSINESS CENTRE, PAISLEY PA1 1TJ

A 40-minute ride on a quaint historic steam train along the shore of Llyn Padarn. Spectacular views of the mountains of Snowdonia.

DIRECTIONS: just off the A4086 Caernarfon to Capel Curig road. Follow the "Padarn Country Park" signs.

OPEN: most days March to October. Free timetable available from Railway.

FHG PUBLICATIONS, ABBEY MILL BUSINESS CENTRE, PAISLEY PA1 1TJ

Europe's leading Eco-Centre. Water-powered cliff railway, interactive renewable energy displays, beautiful organic gardens, animals; vegetarian restaurant.

DIRECTIONS: two-and-a-half miles north of Machynlleth on the A487 towards Dolgellau.

OPEN: From Easter to October inclusive: open daily 10am to 5pm; times may vary in Winter.

FHG PUBLICATIONS, ABBEY MILL BUSINESS CENTRE, PAISLEY PA1 1TJ

HOSEASONS HOLIDAYS, LOWESTOFT NR32 2LW (01502 501010). For your widest choice of hand-picked cruiser, yacht and traditional narrowboat holidays throughout Britain. Short Breaks too! Call for free brochure (quote B68).

HOSEASONS HOLIDAYS, LOWESTOFT NR32 2LW (01502 501501). Lodges, cottages and caravans – your widest choice of self catering holidays from seaside to countryside. Short Breaks too! Phone for brochure (quote H58).

AVON

AVON *Bath*

The Old Malt House Hotel
Radford, Timsbury, Near Bath BA3 1QF
Tel: 01761 470106 Fax: 01761 472726

Between Bath and Wells in beautiful country surroundings. A relaxing, comfortable hotel, built in 1835 as a brewery malt house, now a hotel of character, with log fires in cooler months. Car park, gardens, lawns and 12 acres for you to explore. Owned/managed by the same family for over 20 years. All 10 bedrooms en suite. Extensive menus, restaurant and bar meals served every evening. Fully licensed including draught Bass.

♣ ♣ ♣ Commended
Minotels   Logis
Ashley Courtenay
Recommended
Bargain Breaks All Year

Bath

The best-preserved Georgian city in Britain, Bath has been famous since Roman times for its mineral springs. It is a noted centre for music and the arts, with a wide range of leisure facilities.

THE OLD MALT HOUSE HOTEL, RADFORD, TIMSBURY, NEAR BATH BA3 1QF (01761 470106). A relaxing, comfortable hotel, in beautiful surroundings between Bath and Wells. Gardens, lawns and 12 acre grounds to explore. All bedrooms en suite. Restaurant and bar meals. 3 Crowns Commended *[Pets £1 per night.]*

Bristol

Busy University city on River Avon (spanned by Brunel's famous suspension bridge). SS Great Britain, Brunel's iron ship, is moored in the old docks. Many historic buildings including cathedral and Theatre Royal. Gloucester 35 miles, Bath 13.

ALANDALE HOTEL, 4 TYNDALL'S PARK ROAD, CLIFTON, BRISTOL BS8 1PG (0117 973 5407). An elegant, warm and friendly hotel, centrally situated with car park. Colour TV, telephone and tea/coffee making facilities in all bedrooms. All pets welcome. ETB 2 Crowns. *[🐕]*

MRS C. B. BERRY, CLEVE HILL FARM, UBLEY, NEAR BRISTOL BS18 6PG (01761 462410). Family-run dairy farm in beautiful countryside. Self-catering accommodation in "The Cider House". Fully equipped except towels and linen. £1 electricity meter. One double, one twin room, one double bed settee. Terms from £95 to £200 per week. Obedient pets welcome.

Churchill

Village convenient for the Mendips, the sea and the historic city of Bristol. Associations with the Marlborough family. Bristol 13 miles.

MARION SHERRINGTON & JILL GREEN, WINSTON MANOR HOTEL, CHURCHILL BS19 5NL (01934 852348). Pets and well-trained owners most welcome! Secluded walled garden for emergency night-time outings! Close to Wells, Glastonbury, Bath and Cheddar. Excellent walking country. Our guests tell us the food is excellent too!! Special break rates available. [🐾]

BERKSHIRE

BERKSHIRE   *Compton*

COMPTON SWAN HOTEL ❀❀❀
Near Newbury, Berkshire RG20 6NQ

Situated in the heart of the Berkshire Downlands the Hotel has 5 bedrooms with en suite bathrooms, Satellite TV, beverage facilities and telephones. There is an extensive menu with traditional, exotic, vegetarian and special diets catered for. Our homecooked meals are a speciality. Downlands Healthy Eating Award winner. Large walled garden where we have *Al Fresco* eating; B.B.Q's. We are near the famous ancient Ridgeway National Trail and are an ideal base for walking, horseriding and golf. Stabling and horsebox available. Real Ales and Bar Meals available. Entry in CAMRA Good Beer Guide & Good Pub Guide.

Phone **Liz** or **Garry Mitchell FHCIMA** on 01635 578269

Compton

Village 5 miles/7 km west of Streatley where Georgian houses are one of the notable sights on the banks of the Thames.

COMPTON SWAN HOTEL, NEAR NEWBURY RG20 6NQ (01635 578269). Situated in the heart of the Berkshire Downlands; 5 rooms en suite with Satellite TV, beverage facilities and telephones. Extensive menu with special diets catered for. Large walled garden. ETB 3 Crowns.

Lambourn

Small town 12 miles north west of Newbury. Racehorse training centre.

ALVESTOKE. Ranch-type house on the Downs, with panoramic views. Large garden. Double and twin bedroom, bathroom, two toilets. B&B or self catering. Evening meal/packed lunches by arrangement. MRS RUTHERFOORD, ALVE-STOKE, SHEEPDROVE ROAD, LAMBOURN RG17 7XA (01488 71737). [🐾]

CAMBRIDGESHIRE

Huntingdon

Town on River Ouse, 15 miles north-west of Cambridge. Famous for its medieval bridge and links with Oliver Cromwell.

GLYNNE AND JUNE HEWLETT, THE ELEPHANT & CASTLE, THE GREEN, WOOD WALTON PE17 5YN (01487 773337). Country Inn with motel, six miles Huntingdon, and within easy travelling distance Peterborough and Cambridge, Wood Walton Fen and Nature Reserve. Pets very welcome. *[🐾]*

St Ives

Town on River Ouse 5 miles east of Huntingdon.

ST IVES MOTEL, LONDON ROAD, ST IVES, HUNTINGDON PE17 4EX (Tel & Fax: 01480 463857). RAC & AA 2 Stars. 16 rooms, all en suite, overlooking orchards and garden. Close to Cambridge and A14. Licensed bar and restaurant. *[Pets £2–£5 per night depending on type of animal.]*

CLEVELAND

Saltburn-by-the-Sea

Family resort with 5-mile stretch of sand, rock pools, cliffs. Lovely gardens. Good sporting facilities. Whitby 19 miles, Middlesbrough 13, Redcar 5.

MR & MRS BULL, WESTERLANDS GUEST HOUSE, 27 EAST PARADE, SKEL-TON, SALTBURN-BY-SEA (01287 650690). Situated alongside Cleveland Way, Westerlands is a quiet, modern detached house with beautiful views. Ideal base for touring Moors and East Coast resorts. Evening meals by arrangement; special meals available. All bedrooms with private bathrooms and/or showers. Open March until end September. *[🐾]*

NOTE

All the information in this book is given in good faith in the belief that it is correct. However, the publishers cannot guarantee the facts given in these pages, neither are they responsible for changes in policy, ownership or terms that may take place after the date of going to press. Readers should always satisfy themselves that the facilities they require are available and that the terms, if quoted, still apply.

CORNWALL

CORNWALL *Bissoe*

CLASSY COTTAGES
POLPERRO to FOWEY

We are the proud owners of 3 SUPERB coastal cottage locations
Our cottages are of the highest standard

★ Dishwashers, microwaves & washing machines   ★ Open fires and heating

★ Telephone and Fax available   ★ Cleaning/maid services

We have farm pets for our visitors to enjoy: goats, Vietnamese pot-bellied black pigs, hens and ducks.

★ Daily feeding of farm pets   ★ We are animal lovers.

You are very welcome to arrange to bring your pets

INDOOR PRIVATE POOL 85°F

★ Sauna, spa solarium and games room

SWIMMING   GOLF COURSES

Isolated with 3 acres of gardens and sea views

Please contact FIONA and MARTIN NICOLLE on 01720 423000

COURTYARD FARM & COTTAGES
Lesenewth, Nr Boscastle, Cornwall
Tel: 01840 261256 Fax: 01840 261794

A warm welcome awaits you at a group of delightful 17th Century traditional stone cottages, converted original cornmill and buildings. Cottages sleep 2–8 and are furnished and equipped to a very high standard, including colour TV, microwave etc. Secluded, and overlooking the Valency Valley. Dogs welcome. Open all year round. Short Breaks out of season. Colour Brochure available.

Hedley Wood
Caravan & Camping Park
Bridgerule, Holsworthy,
Devon EX22 7ED
Tel & Fax 01288 381404

16 acre woodland family-run site with outstanding views, where you can enjoy a totally relaxing holiday with a 'laid-back' atmosphere, sheltered & open camping areas. Just 10 minutes' drive from the beaches, golf courses, riding stables & shops.

On-Site facilities include: Children's adventure areas, Bar, Clubroom, Shop, Laundry, Meals and all amenities. Free Hot showers and water. Nice dogs/pets **are** welcome. Daily kennelling facility. Dog walks/Nature trail. Clay pigeon shoot. Static caravans for hire, **caravan storage** available.

Open all year.

THE EDGCUMBE HOTEL
Summerleaze Crescent, Bude, Cornwall EX23 8HJ
Tel: (01288) 353846 Fax: (01288) 355256

★Superb location overlooking sea, sandy beach and downs★All 15 rooms have colour TV, tea/coffee making facilities and radio/intercoms★Most rooms en-suite★Excellent and varied food using fresh produce and home-made sweets with a choice of menu for breakfast and 5 course dinner★Children's menu and vegetarian meals★Attractive bar with pool table★Sun lounge with panoramic view of breakwater and beach★2 minute walk to town centre and golf course★Baby listening service★Private parking★Generous reductions for children★Special out-of-season breaks★Open all year except Christmas.
Dinner, Bed and Breakfast from £157.25 – £189.50 (incl. VAT) per week.
Please write or telephone for colour brochure

Gunnedah
Crackington Haven, Near Bude EX23 0JZ
Telephone: 01840 230265
Superior self-contained Bungalows and Cottages with balcony and/or patio with individual entrance for each unit. Electricity by meter. 2–4 bedrooms. Comfortable lounge with dining area. Colour TV. All with fully equipped kitchens and bathrooms. All bed linen provided. Garage/parking on the premises. Launderette. All units but one overlook the sea with sandy beach only 200 yards away. Wonderful views and scenery. Suitable for occupation all year round Special out-of-season terms.

Send for brochure and terms to Resident Proprietors:
John and Ann Connell

The **MORNISH** *Hotel*
SUMMERLEAZE CRESCENT
BUDE · EX23 8HJ
Telephone (01288) 352972

★ All rooms en-suite and well furnished with colour T.V. and tea/coffee making facilities
★ Special rates for Short Breaks
★ Full central heating
★ Residents Bar
★ Dinner, Bed and Breakfast from £167 per week.

Ideally situated - only 2 minutes walk away from the Town Centre, Golf Course & Open Air Swimming Pool

Stamford Hill Hotel
"A Country House Hotel"
Set in five acres of gardens and woodland overlooking open countryside yet only a mile from the sandy beaches of Bude. Our spacious Georgian Manor House with 15 en-suite bedrooms with TV and tea/coffee making facilities, outdoor heated pool, tennis court, badminton court, games room and sauna is the ideal place for a relaxing holiday or short break. Daily Bed and Breakfast from £23.50, Three-day Break Dinner, Bed and Breakfast from £95.00. Pets welcome.

Contact: Ian and Joy McFeat, Stamford Hill Hotel, Stratton, Bude EX23 9AY Tel: (01288) 352709.

The Liscawn Inn
Charming, family-run 14th century Hotel. Close to Coastal Path in the forgotten corner of Cornwall. En suite accommodation. Bar meals available. Cask ales a speciality. *OPEN ALL YEAR.*
Crafthole, Near Torpoint, Cornwall PL11 3BD Tel: 01503 230863

FREE and REDUCED RATE Holiday Visits!
Don't miss our Readers' Offer Vouchers on pages 5 to 18.

CORNWALL *Helston, Lamorna, Liskeard*

Mr & Mrs Donald, "Halwyn", Manaccan, Helston TR12 6ER
Tel: 01326 280359/565694
Situated in an area of outstanding natural beauty, near the Coastal Footpath, "Halwyn" is an ancient Cornish farmstead. The original old farmhouse and former farm buildings have been converted to a choice of holiday homes. There are two acres of delightful gardens with an indoor heated swimming pool, sauna and solarium. A perfect "away from it all" holiday retreat. Open all year with special low rates, log fires and storage heaters out of season.
Terms from £95 per week inclusive.

TREMENETH HOTEL
Lamorna, Penzance, Cornwall, TR19 6XL.
Tremeneth is situated in the heart of the beautiful Lamorna Valley, in an area of outstanding natural beauty. Ideal for people looking for a quiet relaxing holiday, a short walk to the cove, Merry Maidens and coastal path. Fresh local home cooking and personal service at all times. Most rooms are en suite, centrally heated with tea & coffee facilities, Colour TV. Pets are welcome FREE.
Tel: (01736) 731367 for brochure

Mrs Northcott, Pendower, East Taphouse, Liskeard, Cornwall PL14 4NH
Tel: Liskeard (01579) 320332
Bed and Breakfast   Evening Meal optional
H/C in all rooms. Good touring area. Television. All comforts. Central heating.
Good Food. Main Road. Open all year. Moderate terms.

Cornish Dream
"For those who enjoy the comfort of a high quality hotel but prefer the freedom of a cottage" ...The Good Holiday Cottage Guide

Idyllic Old World Country Cottages in the beautiful Looe River Valley. Your own delightful private garden with roses round the door. Breathtaking views. Heated

swimming pool. Full linen. Delicious home cooked meal service. Beautifully furnished with Antiques. Dishwashers, Microwaves, log fires, Colour TVs and videos. Wonderful walks from your cottage gate. Golf, riding, fishing, sea, coastal walks, all nearby. Looe 3 miles. Heated: really warm and cosy in winter. Pets welcome. Personal attention and colour brochure from:

B. Wright, Treworgey Cottages, Duloe, Liskeard, Cornwall, PL14 4PP. TEL: 01503 262730

Mrs L. F. Arthur, **ROSECRADDOC LODGE**, Liskeard PL14 5BU
Tel or Fax: 01579 346768
Enjoy a peaceful holiday in beautiful South East Cornwall in one of our modern but traditionally built two/three bedroom bungalows. Each bungalow is furnished and equipped to a high standard. Two bungalows specially adapted for disabled. Ideally situated for fishing, golf, walking, beaches, touring Cornwall and Devon. Terms from £120 – £330 per week. Please write or telephone for brochure. **Up to ✧✧✧✧ Commended.**

31

JANET AND MALCOLM BARKER

RIVERMEAD FARM

Twowatersfoot, Liskeard, Cornwall PL14 6HT
Telephone: (01208 821464)

Self Catering Apartments and Farm Cottage

nestling in the beautiful, wooded Glynn Valley amidst 30 acres of meadows and water-meadows kept as a Nature Reserve.
* Convenient for both Coasts and Moors
* A mile of Trout and Salmon fishing on River Fowey
60% of our visitors return
PETS WELCOME

Woodlay Farm Holidays

Herodsfoot, Liskeard PL14 4RB
Tel: 01503 220221 Fax: 01503 220802

200 ACRES OF PETS PARADISE
Luxury accommodation set in landscaped gardens amidst 200 acres of beautiful Cornish countryside. Converted 16th century barn and cottage to accommodate between 2–6 people.

Tastefully modernised to a very high standard to include fitted carpets, colour TV, central heating, electric blankets, etc.
Short drive to Looe, Polperro, Mevagissey and many lovely secluded beaches. Golf, riding, sea fishing all available close by. Woodlay also offers free coarse fishing to residents only in 6 well-stocked lakes.

AA, West Country Tourist Board Listed.
Colour brochure available – stamp appreciated.

32

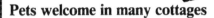

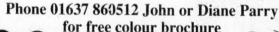

CORNWALL *Newquay, Padstow, Penryn, Penzance*

Minerva Hotel
The Crescent, Newquay, Cornwall TR7 1DT
Tel: 01637 873439

Friendly licensed family-run hotel, quietly situated in town centre overlooking Towan Beach.
* Close to shops, bus station and all amenities
* 18 en suite rooms with colour TV and tea making
* Full central heating * Open March to November * Mid week bookings
* Child FREE offers * Spring/Autumn Breaks.

B&B from £95 – £177 weekly; BB&EM from £115 – £197 weekly

Cy and Barbara Moore **THE RANCH HOUSE** Tel: 01637 875419
TRENCREEK, NEWQUAY TR8 4NR
Detached bungalow 1½ miles Newquay in Trencreek village. Lovely gardens, views of sea and countryside. Lounge, dining room with separate tables. Parking. Children welcome, cot/high chair/reduced rates. Good home cooked food. Bed, Breakfast and Evening Meal from £99 per week. Phone or send stamp only for Brochure.

"WHISTLERS"
Treyarnon Bay, Padstow PL28 8JR Tel and Fax: 01841 520228
MRS WATTS

Pleasant Victorian House. Well converted to 3 fully equipped apartments.
Sleep 4/6. Large garden. Car park. **Dogs love us!**

GLENGARTH
Burnthouse, St Gluvias, Penryn, Cornwall
TR10 9AS

Ideally situated for touring Cornwall and furnished to a high standard. Centrally heated first-floor flat in a delightful detached house. Two double bedrooms and one with full-size bunk beds; comfortable lounge with colour TV; fully equipped kitchen/diner; bathroom; shower room with toilet. Hot water, electricity, bed linen and towels included in tariff. Garden and ample parking.
Mrs B. Newing Pets welcome. Families and couples only please. **Tel: 01872 863209**

PENWITH COTTAGES
Chyandour Office,
Penzance,
CORNWALL TR18 3LW
Tel: (01736) 741112

WCTB Approved

Carefully selected, high quality Cottages and Farmhouses all registered with Tourist Board. Set in beautiful Cornish countryside within easy reach of sea and with freedom to walk your dogs in surrounding fields and woods. Sleeping 3/8 and very well equipped. Most properties have lawned gardens.
Send SAE for brochure to above address, or telephone for friendly help and advice to choose your perfect holiday.

ETB 3 CROWNS **EDNOVEAN HOUSE** AA QQQ
Perranuthnoe, Penzance, Cornwall TR20 9LZ

Our small family-run 9-bedroom hotel is situated in one acre of gardens, with lovely views overlooking St.Michael's Mount and Mount's Bay. Mostly en suite. Licensed bar and restaurant. Car park. 9-hole putting green. 5 minutes' stroll to safe beach and lovely coastal walks. Pets welcome free. For brochure ring **Val & Arthur Compton on 01736 711071.**

40

POLZEATH

Overlooking golden sands – Flats, Chalets and Cottages.

Many guests, their children and pets return regularly to relax in 2½ acres of Pinewood grounds.

The 12 self-contained units all have colour television. Table tennis, a launderette and baby-sitting are available (cots and highchairs too). Own path to beach (surfing and rock pools), shops, tennis, crazy golf and children's playground (4–5 minutes' walk). Sea-fishing trips, golf, riding, sailing and wind-surfing are within 3–4 miles. Superb coastal walks start right at the door, so a car is not essential. Spring and autumn are kindest for your pets. Prices from £60 per week for two.

Interested? Please phone or write for colour brochure to:
D. & L. SHARPE, Pinewood Flats, Polzeath, Wadebridge, Cornwall PL27 6TQ
or Tel: (0120–886) 2269 for availability.

Headlands Hotel

AA**

Port Gaverne, Port Isaac PL29 3SH
Tel: 01208 880260 Fax: 01208 880885

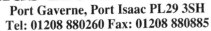

Standing alone on the clifftop, Headlands offers a peaceful haven just half a mile from the picturesque fishing village of Port Isaac. Ideal for walking or touring the Heritage Coast. Comfortable bedrooms, all en suite with magnificent sea views. We offer a personal welcome, efficient and friendly service and delicious international cuisine. Short breaks all year. Dogs accepted.

BB&EM from £250 weekly; Short Breaks from £75 (2 nights)

G U L L R O C K   C O T T A G E S
Port Gaverne   Port Isaac   North Cornwall

Personal attention from resident owners ensures your home from home comfort in a tranquil setting just yards from the sea at bygone Port Gaverne.
Tel: Carole & Malcolm Lee (01208) 880106

CASTLE GOFF FARM
Lanteglos, Camelford PL32 9RQ Tel: 01840 213535

Centrally located cottages sleeping 6/8. Approximately 5 miles of beautiful beaches, moors, golf course and bike trails. Please send for a brochure.

Rosemundy House Hotel

AA **RAC**
★★ ★★

St Agnes · Cornwall
TR5 0UP

ETB
♛ ♛ ♛
Commended

Rosemundy House Hotel is an elegant Queen Anne residence set in its own informal garden and woodland, sheltered and secluded, in the pretty, unspoilt village of St Agnes, and within easy reach of spectacular North Cornish coast with its magnificent sandy beaches.

Rosemundy offers the perfect combination for a holiday with your pet. Our comfortable bedrooms have their own individual charm and are all centrally heated and provided with colour TV and tea and coffee making facilities. Our 45ft heated swimming pool, games room, badminton court, putting and croquet lawn are here for your pleasure.

There is much to do and much to see in beautiful Cornwall. There are magnificent walks along cliff tops, historic houses and gardens to visit, and many quaint fishing villages with their stone-built harbours to explore.

From only £155 per week for dinner, bed and breakfast in May to £250 in August.
Why not come and see for yourself? Write or 'phone for your full colour brochure and tariff.

Tel: (01872) 552101

Holiday bungalows, caravans and a fully-serviced touring park; all with country views and within easy reach of the sea. No bar or gaming machines, but a swimming pool, tennis court and fishing lakes etc. We provide a supervised Kids' Club in the main season and the park is safely situated a quarter of a mile off the main road, down our own private lane.

SPECIAL OFFERS: Easter to mid-July:
Self catering: second week half price; **Touring:** £35 per pitch, per week, including electricity, awning and up to 6 people.

Trencreek Farm Holiday Park
Hewaswater, St Austell PL26 7JG Tel: 01726 882540

ST MARGARET'S HOLIDAY PARK
Polgooth, St Austell PL26 7AX

Family owned and run with 27 Bungalows and Chalets set in 6 acre sun trap wooded valley 2½ miles from safe sandy beaches.
500 yards to Golf, Village Inn and Shop.
NO BINGO, NO DISCOS.
Children and pets welcome.
We have a playing field and separate dog walking area.
Colour brochure from **MRS M. KING**
Chalets from **£85** per week.
Tel: (01726) 74283; Fax: (01726) 71680

BOSINVER COTTAGES FARM HOUSE AND BUNGALOWS

• Quality SELF CATERING on 35 acre RURAL ESTATE (18 only)

• Relax in quiet seclusion away from the crowds.

• Sleeps 2, 3, 4, 5, 6, 11 (one suitable for a wheelchair).

Special discounts given
"Bosinver is the best value for money" (quote from visitor)
• Solar heated swimming pool • Sauna and solarium • Tennis court
• Lake Trout fishing • Games room • Pay phone
• Children's swings and clock golf • Book and jigsaw library
• Washing and drying machines • Bed linen included, cots and barbecues available.
Close to golf course, village with Post Office/Stores and Old World Pub. Short drive to many safe beaches, town, wet weather attractions, National Trust coast and properties, Recreation centre and horse riding. Colour brochure from:

P. W. Milln, Bosinver Farm,
St. Austell PL26 7DT Tel: (01726) 72128

Dalswinton Country House Hotel
ST MAWGAN-IN-PYDAR, NR NEWQUAY, CORNWALL TR8 4EZ
Tel: St. Mawgan (01637) 860385

Approached by its own 200 yard drive, Dalswinton is an old Cornish house of immense character, standing in 9½ acres of secluded grounds overlooking the beautiful wooded Vale of Lanherne, with views to the sea. Ideally situated between Newquay and Padstow with many picturesque beaches and coves, superb woodland and coastal walks. The family-run hotel has been completely refurbished and offers excellent cooking with a varied choice of menu in a relaxed friendly atmosphere.

* All rooms en-suite with colour TV and tea/coffee facilities
* Full central heating *Log fires in bar and lounge.
*Heated swimming pool * Residential licence

PETS VERY WELCOME, AT NO EXTRA CHARGE, IN ALL AREAS OF THE HOTEL EXCEPT THE DINING ROOM.

Dinner, Bed and Breakfast from £155.00 per week. Bed and Breakfast from £110.00 per week. Bargain Breaks available.

COLOUR BROCHURE ON REQUEST

CORNWALL *St Ives, St Mellion, Tintagel*

The LINKS
HOLIDAY FLATS
Lelant, St Ives, Cornwall TR26 3HY
Tel: 01736 753326

Situated just 3 miles from St Ives, adjoining West Cornwall Golf Club, with panoramic views from each flat. Residents' bar; games room; ample parking. All flats are self-contained with fully equipped kitchens, colour TV; en suite shower/bath and toilet for almost every bedroom. Small charge for linen (if required).

* Safe play area for children * Cots/high chairs available
* Pets welcome (under control) * Many superb walks

CARLYON GUEST HOUSE
18 The Terrace, St Ives, Cornwall TR26 3BP
Tel: 01736 795317

* Comfortable, attractive bedrooms, all with colour TV and tea/coffee facilities; most with showers * Separate tables in dining room * Good English cooking * Panoramic sea views * Warm, friendly atmosphere * Children welcome

BED AND BREAKFAST WITH 4-COURSE EVENING MEAL (OPTIONAL)
SAE for terms and further details

KERNOCK COTTAGES

S.E. Cornwall – between Bodmin Moor and Dartmoor
3 traditional stone cottages for 2/6/8 set in 28 acres. Safe and quiet for pets and the family. Personal attention from the resident owners.
For brochure: call or fax Richard Steel on 01579 350435

BOSSINEY FARM CARAVAN AND CAMPING PARK TINTAGEL PL34 0AY 01840 770481

- Family-run park renowned for cleanliness and hospitality.
- Two ranges of Caravans:
- Semi-serviced, toilet, fridge etc
- Fully-serviced, H & C with shower, room heater
- All with TV
- On the Coast at Tintagel, ideal touring

SEND FOR OUR COLOUR BROCHURE TODAY!

The Penallick Hotel
Tintagel, Cornwall PL34 0EJ   Tel: 01840 770296

A small comfortable family-run licensed hotel with magnificent cliff-top position. Superb cliff walks. All rooms have colour TV and tea-makers; most en suite sea views. Restaurant overlooks outstanding coastal and sea views. Excellent home cooking. Regret no children under 12 years old.

* Christmas Breaks * Bargain Breaks * Short Breaks
NICE DOGS VERY WELCOME AT NO EXTRA CHARGE

Colesent Cottages **St Tudy, Bodmin, Cornwall PL30 4QX Tel: 01208 850112**
Recently converted farm cottages in a quiet situation with superb outlook over the countryside and Camel Valley. Ideally situated for walking, cycling and touring Cornwall and North Devon. These cottages are furnished to a high standard with log fires, storage heating, washing machines etc, and own gardens.   3 Keys Approved.
Electricity and linen included   Personally supervised. Sleep 2/7 + cot   Dogs by arrangement

WELCOME COTTAGE HOLIDAYS. Hundreds of properties in wonderful locations at welcoming low prices. Pets, linen and fuel mostly included. For FREE colour brochure telephone 01756 702201.

CORNISH TRADITIONAL COTTAGES, LOSTWITHIEL PL22 0HT (01208 872559). A fine selection of self-catering cottages on both coasts of Cornwall and on Scilly. Write or telephone for free brochure. [£10 per week.]

POWELLS COTTAGE HOLIDAYS. Your choice of cottage in Cornwall, Devon, Somerset, Avon, Cotswolds, Wye Valley, Gower and Pembrokeshire in our full colour brochure. [Pets £10 per week.] FREEPHONE 0800 378771 or apply: 61 High Street, Saundersfoot, Pembrokeshire SA69 9EJ or (24 hrs) 01834 813232.

Your choice of four Premier Holiday Villages. St Ives* Hayle* Penzance* Tamar*: acres of walks, beaches; indoor pools; FREE leisure clubs. Lodges sleeping 2/10. Ben Bowers Self Catering Holidays, c/o 4 Park Drive, The Park, Nottingham NG7 1DA (Freephone 0500 026222).

CLASSIC COTTAGES (25), HELSTON, CORNWALL TR13 8NA (24 HOUR DIAL-A-BROCHURE 01326 565555). Choose your cottage from 300 of the finest coastal and country cottages throughout the West Country. [Pets £9 weekly.]

Bissoe

Village four miles south-west of Truro.

IVY COTTAGE, BISSOE, CORNWALL. 200-year-old country cottage 5 miles from Truro. Kitchen/dining room, lounge, 2 bedrooms. All facilities incl. TV and microwave. Terms £103–£295. For brochure phone 01872 70768. [🐾]

Bodmin

Quaint county town of Cornwall, standing steeply on the edge of Bodmin moor. Pretty market town and touring centre. Plymouth 31 miles, Newquay 20, Wadebridge 7.

COOMBE MILL, ST. BREWARD, BODMIN PL30 4LZ (01208 850344). Superb cottages and beautiful log cabins set in an idyllic 30 acre farm park. Barbecues, fishing, woodland walks, gardens. Linen provided. Free colour brochure. [Pets £10 per week.]

Boscastle

Picturesque village in tiny harbour. Rocky beach, some sand, fine scenery. Tintagel 4 miles.

Boscastle/Crackington-Haven area. Modern bungalow sleeping 2–6, heating, ETB 3 Keys Approved. Near sandy beaches, cliff and valley walks. Beautiful scenery, walking distance local store and Inn. Spring and Autumn £80–£180 per week. MRS PROUT (01840 250289). [pw! £8 per week.]

MRS M. CONGDON, TREMORLE, BOSCASTLE PL35 0BU (01840 250233). Peaceful, spacious self-catering bungalow in own grounds with views. Comfortable, heated and well equipped for 2–8. Lovely cliff, valley walks. Spring and autumn £80–£225 per week. Short breaks from £70. /pw!★/ ETB 3 Keys Approved.

MRS D. HANCOCK, PARADISE FARM COTTAGE, BOSCASTLE PL35 0BL (01840 250 528) ETB 4 Keys Commended. National Trust harbour village. Antiques. Log fires. Sleeps 3–5, £115–£340 weekly. Also nearby cosy COTTAGES FOR TWO. From £98 weekly. Secluded village location. Peaceful gardens. Suntrap patios. Parking.

THE WELLINGTON HOTEL, THE HARBOUR, BOSCASTLE PL35 0AQ (01840 250202). Historic 16th-century Coaching Inn in glorious National Trust area offers 21 bedrooms (16 en suite) with colour TV, tea/coffee making facilities. Anglo-French restaurant; Free House with real ale. Log fires. Pets always welcome. 10 acres woodland walks. Free brochure. /★/

COURTYARD FARM COTTAGES, LESNEWTH, NEAR BOSCASTLE (01840 261256). Picturesque group of seven 17th century cottages, sleep 2–8. Fully furnished, microwave, colour TV. Launderette. Set in acres of fields; lovely walks nearby. Open all year. /Pets £15 per week./

Bude

Popular seaside resort overlooking a wide bay of golden sand flanked by spectacular cliffs. Ideal for surfing; seawater swimming pool for safe bathing.

JOHN AND JULIA HILDER, MORNISH HOTEL, 20 SUMMERLEAZE CRESCENT, BUDE EX23 8HL (01288 352972). Homely and friendly with comfortable, well-equipped rooms. All en-suite with tea/coffee making facilities and television. Central heating. Residents' bar. /Pets £2 per day./

JOHN AND ANN CONNELL, "GUNNEDAH", CRACKINGTON HAVEN, NEAR BUDE EX23 0JZ (01840 230265). Self-contained Bungalows and Cottages. All with fully equipped kitchens, bathrooms. Launderette. Pets by prior arrangement. /Pets £5 per week./

STAMFORD HILL HOTEL, STRATTON, NEAR BUDE EX23 9AY (01288 352709). Elegant Georgian manor, 5 mins from beaches, 15 en suite rooms, all with colour TV, tea/coffee makers. Heated pool, tennis court, badminton etc. Ideal for golf, fishing, walking. /pw! £2 per night./

HENTERVENE PINE LODGE CARAVAN AND CAMPING PARK, CRACKINGTON HAVEN, NEAR BUDE EX23 0LF (01840 230365. Fax: 01840 230514). 1½ miles unspoilt sandy beach. Area of ouistanding natural beauty. Luxury caravans to let. First-class facilities for families and pets. Open all year. AA 3 Pennants. Short breaks. /pw! Pets £10 per week, 70p per night camping./

HEDLEY WOOD CARAVAN AND CAMPING PARK, BRIDGERULE, NEAR BUDE EX22 7ED (Tel and Fax: 01288 381404). Superb 16-acre site amidst lovely countryside, 10 minutes from sandy beaches. All modern facilities. Licensed bar, club room, separate children's play area. /★pw!/

EDGCUMBE HOTEL, SUMMERLEAZE CRESCENT, BUDE EX23 8HJ (01288 353846; Fax: 01288 355256). Overlooking sea and downs. All rooms colour TV, most with en suite, tea/coffee facilities, radio/intercom. 2 minutes town centre, golf course. Dinner, Bed and Breakfast from £157.25 to £189.50 including VAT per week. Private parking. *[pw]*

Cawsand

Quaint fishing village with bathing beach; sand at low tide. Ideal for watersports. Plymouth (car ferry) 11 miles, (foot ferry) 3.

MR AND MRS A. FIDLER, RAME BARTON GUEST HOUSE, RAME, CAWSAND PL10 1LG (01752 822789). Old Country House standing in own grounds on beautiful Rame Peninsula. Lovely coastline/beaches. Pets, children very welcome. Bed and Breakfast. Licensed. *[pw! Pets £0.30p nightly.]* Extensive exercise area. SAE please.

Crackington Haven

Small coastal village in North Cornwall set amidst fine cliff scenery. Small, sandy beach. Launceston 18 miles, Bude 10, Camelford 10.

BREMOR HOLIDAY BUNGALOWS AND COTTAGES, CRACKINGTON HAVEN, NEAR BUDE EX23 0JN (01840 230340). Delightfully furnished and equipped bungalows for 6. Linen provided. Enclosed garden. Pets free. Also cottage for two, recently renovated. Open beams, idyllic setting. 3 Keys. *[🐴]*

Crafthole

Village near sea at Portwrinkle. Fine views over Whitsand Bay and River Lynner. Golf course nearby. Torpoint 6 miles.

THE LISCAWN INN, CRAFTHOLE, NEAR TORPOINT PL11 3BD (01503 230863). Charming, family-run 14th century Hotel. Close to Coastal Path in the forgotten corner of Cornwall. En suite accommodation; bar meals available; cask ales a speciality. Open all year. *[🐴]*

Falmouth

Well-known port and resort on Fal estuary, ideal for boating, sailing and fishing; safe bathing from sandy beaches. Of interest is Pendennis Castle (16th century). Exeter 97 miles, Newquay 26, Penzance 26, Truro 11, Redruth 10.

Ideally situated, spacious self-catering bungalow with garden. Full heating. Ample parking. Children and dogs welcome. Sleeps 1–6. Low Season: £115 to £165; High Season: £190 to £265. Apply MRS J. A. SIMMONS, 215A PERRY STREET, BILLERICAY, ESSEX CM12 0NZ (01277 654425). *[Pets £5 weekly.]*

Fowey

Historic town, now a busy harbour. Regatta and Carnival Week in August.

OLD FOWEY INN, BODINNICK-BY-FOWEY PL23 1LX (01726 870237; Fax: 01726 870116). Family-run Inn, ideal for many varied walks. Excellent à la carte restaurant; bar meals available. Comfortable bedrooms with colour TV and tea/coffee. B&B from £30pppn. *[Pets £1.50 per night]*

CLASSY COTTAGES – Three superb coastal cottages, locations between Polperro and Fowey. Willy Wilcox cottage is just 11 feet from beach over smugglers' cave. Log fires, dishwashers, washing machines etc. Indoor Private Swimming Pool. Contact FIONA & MARTIN NICOLLE (01720 423000).

Gorran Haven

Coastal village, 3 miles from Mevagissey.

Self catering apartments sleeping 2–7. Beautiful rural area, 600 yards from sandy beach and harbour. Colour TV, cooker, microwave, fridge freezer. Secluded garden, private parking. Open all year. KEN AND SALLY PIKE, TREGILLAN, TREWOLLOCK LANE, GORRAN HAVEN PL26 6NT (01726 842452 24 hours). *[🐕]*

Hayle

Resort, shopping centre and seaport with excellent sands and dunes. Helston 10 miles, Redruth 10, Penzance 8, Camborne 5.

MR A. JAMES, ST IVES BAY HOLIDAY PARK, 73 LOGGANS ROAD, UPTON TOWANS, HAYLE TR27 5BH (01736 752274). Park in sand dunes adjoining huge sandy beach. Choice of bars, free entertainment. Chalets, Caravan and Camping. Large indoor pool. *[Pets £14 per week.]*

Helford

Creek-side village straight from a picture postcard with thatched roofs, whitewashed walls and gardens bright with flowers. Ferry link to Helford Passage has operated since Middle Ages.

TREGILDRY HOTEL, GILLAN, MANACCAN, HELSTON TR12 6HG (01326 231378). Peaceful and elegant small hotel in 4 acres enjoying a spectacular setting overlooking Helford River. Excellent restaurant and spacious lounges. 3 Crowns Commended.

Helston

Ancient Stannary Town and excellent touring centre. Noted for the quaint annual "Furry" Dance. Nearby is Loe Pool, separated from the sea by a bar. Truro 17 miles, St. Ives 15, Falmouth 13, Lizard 11, Redruth 11.

GILLAN, HELFORD RIVER. Enjoy a relaxing holiday in one of two quiet, comfortable cottages to suit two/three. Old stone buildings originally used by Parish Monks as cattle houses and hayloft. Lovely country/coastal views; nearby boating; beaches and walking in an area of natural beauty. MRS UNA HARVEY, MENIFTERS, GILLAN, MANACCAN, HELSTON TR12 6ER (01326 280711).

MR & MRS DONALD, HALWYN, MANACCAN, HELSTON TR12 6ER (01326 280359/565694). Ancient Cornish farmstead converted to a choice of holiday homes. 2 acres of gardens with indoor swimming pool, sauna and solarium. Perfect for an "away from it all" holiday. Open all year. Terms from £95 per week. [🐾]

Holywell Bay

Faces west with extensive sands, cliffs, rocks, 5½ miles Newquay.

Two self-catering Bungalows 2 minutes from beach. Colour TV, private gardens. Pets welcome. £100–£290 per week. APPLY – M. DEVONSHIRE, WHITE SURF, PENTIRE, NEWQUAY TR7 1PP (01637 871862). [🐾]

Lamorna

Village beside steep-sided valley running down to Lamorna Cove, 4 miles south of Penzance.

TREMENETH HOTEL, LAMORNA, PENZANCE TR19 6XL (01736 731367). Situated in an area of outstanding natural beauty, a short walk from the cove, Merry Maidens and the coastal path. Most rooms en suite with central heating and tea/coffee; colour TV. Brochure on request. [🐾]

Liskeard

Pleasant market town and good centre for exploring East Cornwall. Bodmin moor and the quaint fishing villages of Looe and Polperro are near at hand. Plymouth 19 miles, St Austell 19, Launceston 16, Fowey (via ferry) 15, Bodmin 13, Looe 9.

MRS V. M. NORTHCOTT, "PENDOWER", EAST TAPHOUSE, LISKEARD PL14 4NH (01579 320332). All comforts. Open all year. Main road. Good food. Moderate terms. [🐾]

B. WRIGHT, TREWORGEY COTTAGES, DULOE, LISKEARD, CORNWALL PL14 4PP (01503 262730). Old World Country Cottages. Private garden. Heated summer swimming pool. Full linen. Home cooking. Colour TV, videos, dishwashers, micro-waves and log fires. Golf, riding and fishing nearby. Looe 3 miles. Colour brochure available. [pw! £11 per week.]

Gorgeous old world country cottages for 2, 4, 6 near Looe and Polperro. Open all year. Everything from nightstore heating and log fires in the winter to heated summer pool. Meals service, colour TV, linen, own private garden, plenty of country walks. O. SLAUGHTER, ST MARY MANOR, TREFANNY HILL, DULOE, LISKEARD PL14 4QF (01503 220622). [One pet free, others £10 weekly.]

MRS L. F. ARTHUR, ROSECRADDOC LODGE, LISKEARD PL14 5BU (Tel or Fax: 01579 346768). Modern two/three bedroom bungalows set in lawned gardens and woodland, in countryside at the foot of Bodmin Moor. Many have microwave ovens and videos. Suitable for disabled visitors. From £120–£330 per week. [Pets £10 per week].

MR AND MRS M. BARKER, RIVERMEAD FARM, TWOWATERSFOOT, LISKEARD PL14 6HT (01208 821464). Self-catering Apartments and Farm Cottages convenient for both coasts and moors. Fishing on River Fowey. Pets welcome! [🐾]

Luxury accommodation in converted 16th century barn, tastefully modernised to a high standard, accommodating 2–6 people. Set in 200 acres near secluded beaches, towns, sporting amenities. AA/WCTB Listed. APPLY – ANN HAWKE, WOODLAY FARM HOLIDAYS, HERODSFOOT, LISKEARD PL14 4RB (01503 220221; Fax: 01503 220802). *[Pets £17.50 per week.]*

MRS E. COLES, CUTKIVE WOOD CHALETS, ST. IVE, LISKEARD PL14 3ND (01579 362216). Self-catering chalets in 41 acres of woodland. 2/3 bedrooms; fully equipped inc. linen, colour TV, fridge, cooker and microwave. On site shop. Pets corner for children. Dogs welcome. *[🐾pw!]*

Lizard

The most southerly point in England. Fine coast scenery and secluded coves. Sandy beach at Housel Bay. Truro 28 miles, Falmouth 22, Helston 11.

PARC BRAWSE HOUSE, PENMENNER ROAD, THE LIZARD TR12 7NR (01326 290466). Small Georgian-style hotel in superb coastal position offers every comfort. Home cooking, including vegetarian. Sea views. Cosy bar. En-suite available. Tea making facilities and radio/alarms, colour TVs. Open all year. RAC Acclaimed. ETB 2 Crowns Commended. *[Pets £1 per night.]*

Looe

Twin towns linked by a bridge over the River Looe. Capital of the shark fishing industry; nearby Monkey Sanctuary is well worth a visit.

TRADITIONAL CORNISH HOLIDAY COTTAGES for 2, 4, 6, 8. 250 yards Polperro harbour, 5 miles Looe. Either magnificently situated directly overlooking harbour, fabulous outlook, 14 miles sea views; or nicely positioned in the quaint old village centre, by river, gardens, parking, 2 minutes shops, beach, cliff walks. GRAHAM WRIGHT, THE MILL, POLPERRO, CORNWALL PL13 2RP (01579 344080).

FIONA AND MARTIN NICOLLE, CLASSY COTTAGES (01720 423000). Three superb coastal cottages equipped to highest standards: dishwashers, microwaves, washing machines. Farm pets for visitors to enjoy. Indoor private pool, sauna, solarium and games room.

MRS JOY RYDING, APPLE TREES, PORTUAN ROAD, HANNAFORE, LOOE PL13 2DN (01503 262626). Well-furnished, self-contained bungalow flat. Sleeps 2/4. 150 yards sea. Dogs welcome, no charge. Open all year. SAE please. *[🐾]*

HENDRA FARM COTTAGES, PELYNT, LOOE PL13 2LU (01503 220701). Three quality cottages peacefully set in 120 acres of beautiful countryside on working farm. A hidden retreat only four miles Looe, Polperro, Coastal Path and coves. Excellent locality for walking. Cottages sleep 2 to 5 persons. Heating, electricity and bed linen included in price. 4 Keys Highly Commended.

TALLAND BARTON CARAVAN PARK, TALLAND BAY, LOOE PL13 2JA (01503 272429). Caravans with electricity and running water, some with showers, flush toilets on family-run farm site close to beaches. Some available from Friday to Friday. Site has shop, licensed club, toilet and shower block, swimming-pool, laundry room. Ideal touring centre. Pets welcome. SAE for colour brochure.

ALLHAYS COUNTRY HOUSE, TALLAND BAY, LOOE PL13 2JB (Tel: 01503 272434, Fax: 01503 272929). Come and discover what makes a perfect holiday for you and your pet. En suite rooms (ground floor available). Award winning food; 2 acres of secluded gardens; coastal paths nearby. ETB 3 Crowns Commended. *[pw! 🐾]*

55

CORNWALL

TRENANT PARK COTTAGES. Four delightful cottages sleep from 2 to 7 persons. Each has spacious lounge with colour TV, fully equipped kitchen, private garden. Ample room to relax. APPLY: MRS E. M. CHAPMAN, TRENANT LODGE, SANDPLACE, LOOE PL13 1PH (01503 263639/262241). *[Pets £15 per week.]*

Gorgeous old world country cottages for 2, 4, 6. Near Looe and Polperro. Open all year. Everything from nightstore heating and log fires in the winter to heated summer pool. Meals Service, Colour TV, Linen. Own Private Garden. Plenty of country walks. O. SLAUGHTER, ST MARY MANOR, TREFANNY HILL, DULOE, LISKEARD PL14 4QF (01503 220622). *[One pet free, others £10 weekly.]*

First floor double bedroom apartment with large verandah overlooking sea. Not suitable children. Well behaved pet accepted. Available all year. Reasonable rates. APPLY: R. MILLER, 320 OLD LAIRA ROAD, PLYMOUTH PL3 6AQ (01752 661915). *[Pets £7 per week.]*

JOHN & NANCY JOLLIFF, TREMAINE GREEN, PELYNT, NEAR LOOE PL13 2LS (01503 220333). Dogs love our cosy and comfortable character cottages, Cornish countryside and coastal walks. Accompanying humans also welcome if well behaved. Send for our free colour brochure. *[Pets £16.00 per week.]*

MR J. R. A. STORER, KANTARA LICENSED GUEST HOUSE, 7 TRELAWNEY TERRACE, WEST LOOE PL13 2AG (01503 262093). A family-run Guest House noted for its warm and informal atmosphere. Convenient for amenities and beach. All rooms 24-hour access, with washbasins, Sky TV and videolink, tea/coffee. Bar lounge with 28'' TV. Children and pets welcome. Many additional facilities available. AA QQ Recommended, ETB One Crown Commended.

Lostwithiel

Charming town on River Fowey 5 miles south-east of Bodmin. A medieval bridge spans the river and there is a 14th century church.

Fal Estuary/River Fowey – choice of 10 Apartments and Cottage, all personally owned and run with good friendly Cornish hospitality. See Display Advertisement in this guide. For brochure contact: MR P. W. EDWARD-COLLINS, LANWITHAN FARM, LOSTWITHIEL PL22 0LA (01208 872444). *[Pets £10 per week.]*

Mawgan Porth

Modern village on small, sandy bay. Good surfing. Inland stretches the beautiful Vale of Lanherne. Rock formation of Bedruthan Steps is nearby. Newquay 6 miles W.

MR C. E. & MRS H. ROBINSON, SEAVISTA HOTEL, MAWGAN PORTH, NEAR NEWQUAY TR8 4AL (01637 860276). Small nine-roomed Hotel, family run, with some en-suite accommodation. All fresh food used whenever possible. Terms: B & B £16 Low Season, £18 High Season; D, B & B £25.00. Three- and four-day Breaks. Phone Carl or Hazel. [🐕]

THE MALMAR HOTEL, TRENANCE, MAWGAN PORTH, NEWQUAY TR8 4DA (01637 860324). Small licensed hotel. Reputable sea-fishing coast. Two good golf courses nearby. Good English cooking. Rooms with tea-making facilities, some en-suite. *[🐕]*

WHITE LODGE HOTEL, MAWGAN PORTH BAY, NEAR NEWQUAY TR8 4BN (01637 860512). Give yourselves and your dogs a quality holiday break at this family-run hotel overlooking beautiful Mawgan Porth Bay. Bedrooms en-suite, all rooms with washbasins, shaver points, heaters etc. Lounge bar, games room, sun patio, dining room. Car park. Phone for free brochure. 2 Crowns Approved. AA. RAC. *[🐕pw!]*

Mevagissey

Pretty little resort and fishing village. Interesting harbour, narrow streets. Sandy coves nearby. Bodmin 17 miles. Truro 17, St Austell 6.

Small family Park. Chalets, Caravans at Carnmoggas Holiday Park, Cornish Riviera; Cottage for 8; heated indoor pool, indoor bowls, Clubhouse. Pets welcome. WCTB; ETB; 3 ticks. APPLY: c/o 14 RYSDALE ROAD, BRISTOL, AVON BS9 3QU (0117 962 3792 or 01275 849248). *[Pets £12 per week.]*

Mousehole

Picturesque fishing village with sandy and shingle beach. Penzance 3 miles.

Four s/c flats, two with full sea view, at entrance to unspoilt fishing village. Fully equipped, bedding supplied, colour TV. Open all year. From £70.00 per week. Pets welcome. MR A. G. WRIGHT, 100 WENSLEY ROAD, WOODTHORPE, NOTTINGHAM NG5 4JU (01159 201275; Fax 01159 639279). *[🐕]*

Newquay

Popular family holiday resort surrounded by miles of golden beaches. Semi-tropical gardens, zoo and museum. Ideal for exploring all of Cornwall.

ROSEMERE HOTEL, WATERGATE BAY, NEAR NEWQUAY TR8 4AB (01637 860238). Relaxed, informal, family-run Hotel; large grassed area, beach and Coastal Footpath all within 100 yards. 44 rooms, 36 en suite. Licensed bar, entertainment. Open all year. *[🐕]*

FORT WAYNE HOTEL, HENVER ROAD, NEWQUAY (FREEPHONE 0800 445546). Central for beaches, gardens, town. 27 modern bedrooms, many en suite. Heated pool and sun terrace. Licensed bar. Fine food, varied menu, full English breakfast. Well-behaved pets welcome.

WHITE LODGE HOTEL, MAWGAN PORTH BAY, NEAR NEWQUAY TR8 4BN (01637 860512). Give yourselves and your dogs a quality holiday break at this family-run hotel overlooking beautiful Mawgan Porth Bay. Bedrooms en-suite, all rooms with washbasins, shaver points, heaters etc. Lounge bar, games room, sun patio, dining room. Car park. Phone for free brochure. 2 Crowns Approved. AA. RAC. *[🐕pw!]*

MINERVA HOTEL, THE CRESCENT, NEWQUAY TR7 1DT (01637 873439). Friendly licensed family-run hotel overlooking Towan Beach. 18 en suite rooms with colour TV. Close to shops and all amenities. Spring/Autumn Breaks, free child offers. Open March to November.

CORISANDE MANOR HOTEL, PENTIRE, NEWQUAY TR7 1PL (01637 872042). A Hotel of unique turreted Austrian design, quietly situated and commanding an unrivalled position in three-acre secluded landscaped gardens. Private foreshore. 17 en suite bedrooms with TV, tea-making facilities. Same chef proprietors since 1968. DB&B weekly £165–£205 pp inc. VAT. For brochure and menus telephone David and Anne Painter. AA**RAC, ETB Three Crowns Commended, Les Routiers. *[🐕]*

PARADISE BEACH HOTEL, WATERGATE BAY, NEWQUAY (01637 860273). Superb location 200 yards from beach (dogs allowed); beautiful cliff walks. En suite rooms; sauna, solarium. Excellent choice meals. Licensed. ETB Two Crowns. *[🐕]*

CY AND BARBARA MOORE, THE RANCH HOUSE, TRENCREEK, NEWQUAY TR8
4NR (01637 875419). Detached bungalow with lovely gardens and superb views.
Shower rooms; lounge. Parking. Children and pets welcome. Bed, Breakfast and
Evening Meal from £99 per week. *[Pets £10 per week.]*

Padstow

*Bright little resort with pretty harbour on Camel estuary. Extensive sands. Nearby is Prideaux
Place (Eliz). Launceston 35 miles, Truro 24, Bodmin 15, Newquay 15, Wadebridge 8.*

Pleasant Victorian House. Well converted to 3 fully equipped apartments. Sleeps 4/6.
Large garden. Car park. Dogs love us! MRS WATTS, "WHISTLERS", TREYARNON
BAY, PADSTOW PL28 8JR (Tel and Fax: 01841 520228). *[🐕]*

**RAINTREE HOUSE HOLIDAYS, WHISTLERS, TREYARNON BAY, PADSTOW
PL28 8JR (Tel and Fax: 01841 520228). We have a varied selection of
accommodation. Small or large, houses and apartments, some by the sea. All
in easy reach of our lovely beaches. Please write or phone for brochure.** *[🐕]*

Penryn

Creekside town with small harbour, adjacent to Falmouth. Truro 9 miles, Redruth 8.

Ideally situated for touring Cornwall. 3 bedrooms (one with bunk beds); lounge with
colour TV, kitchen/diner; bathroom, shower room with toilet. Hot water, electricity,
bed linen incl. Garden. MRS B. NEWING, GLENGARTH, BURNTHOUSE, ST
GLUVIAS, PENRYN TR10 9AS (01872 863209). *[🐕]*

Penzance

*Well-known resort and port for Scilly Isles. Sand and shingle beaches. Bodmin 48 miles, Truro 27,
Falmouth 26, Redruth 18, Helston 13, Land's End 10, St Ives 8.*

EDNOVEAN HOUSE, PERRANUTHNOE, PENZANCE TR20 9LZ (01736 711071).
Small friendly 9-bedroomed hotel situated in one acre of gardens. Lovely views
overlooking Mount's Bay. Car park. 9-hole putting green. ETB 3 Crowns, AA QQQ.
Phone for brochure. *[🐕]*

GLENCREE PRIVATE HOTEL, 2 MENNAYE ROAD, PENZANCE TR18 4NG (01736
62026). Just off seafront with comfortable friendly atmosphere. Spacious rooms with
colour TV and teamaking. Most rooms are en suite, some with good sea views.
Unrestricted parking. Good home cooking. All well-behaved pets welcome and their
owners too! WCTB 2 Crowns. B&B from £12 nightly, £72 weekly. *[🐕]*

MRS HOOD, TRENANT PRIVATE HOTEL, ALEXANDRA ROAD, PENZANCE TR18
4LX (01736 62005). Comfortable, friendly Hotel near seafront. Colour TV, teamaker,
B&B from £15 nightly, £100 weekly. En-suite, fourposter bedrooms and ground floor
twin available. Dinner optional. Licensed. Early Breakfasts. All welcome from stick
insects to elephants! AA Recommended QQQ, Cornwall Tourist Board. *[🐕]*

PENWITH COTTAGES, CHYANDOUR OFFICE, PENZANCE TR18 3LW (01736
741112). Holiday Cottages, Farmhouses set in beautiful Cornish countryside. Well
equipped. SAE for brochure. *[pw! Pets £10 per week.]*

Perranporth

Popular family resort with wide sands and cliffs. Surf-bathing. Of interest is St Piran's Church (6th cent). Redruth 10 miles, Truro 10, Newquay 9.

Up to 8-berth Caravans, two and three bedrooms. Bungalow. Colour TV, showers, WC. Sea views. Club and swimming pool with flume slide available. Sandy beach. Apply: MR P. W. ABRAM, 1 CROW HILL, BOLINGEY, PERRANPORTH TR6 0DG or telephone (01872) 572385 anytime. *[Pets £15 weekly.]*

Polperro

Picturesque and quaint little fishing village, harbour. Of interest is the "House of the Props". Fine coast scenery. Fowey 9 miles, Looe 5.

POLPERRO. 250 yards harbour, holiday cottages sleeping 2, 4, 6 or 8. Spectacularly situated either overlooking Harbour, fabulous outlook, 15 miles sea views and terraced gardens giving Mediterranean setting or nicely positioned by river in old part of village. Gardens, private parking, 2 minutes' shops, beach, quay, NT cliff walks. Well furnished, colour TV. Open all year. Competitive rates. Children welcome. Ring or write NOW GRAHAM WRIGHT, THE MILL, POLPERRO, CORNWALL PL13 2RP (01579 344080). [🐕]

Gorgeous old world country cottages for 2, 4, 6. Near Looe and Polperro. Open all year. Everything from nightstore heating and log fires in the winter to heated summer pool. Meals Service, Colour TV, Linen. Own Private Garden. Plenty of country walks. O. SLAUGHTER, ST MARY MANOR, TREFANNY HILL, DULOE, LISKEARD PL14 4QF (01503 220622). *[One pet free, others £10 weekly.]*

CLASSY COTTAGES – Three superb coastal cottages, locations between Polperro and Fowey. Willy Wilcox cottage is just 11 feet from beach over smugglers' cave. Log fires, dishwashers, washing machines etc. Indoor Private Swimming Pool. Contact FIONA & MARTIN NICOLLE (01720 423000).

CLAREMONT HOTEL, THE COOMBES, POLPERRO PL13 2RG (01503 272241). All rooms en suite with colour TV and tea-making facilities. Bar. Restaurant. Ideally located for walking and touring Cornwall. Short breaks. Open all year. ETB 3 Crowns, AA/RAC 1 Star. Logis. [🐕]

Polzeath

Small, friendly resort on cliffs near Padstow. Fine sands, good bathing, surfing. Sheltered by Pentire Head (N.T.) to the north. Wadebridge 8 miles.

D. & L. SHARPE, PINEWOOD FLATS, POLZEATH PL27 6TQ (0120-886 2269). Flats, Chalets and Cottage. Table tennis, launderette, baby-sitting. Superb touring centre. *[🐕]*

Port Gaverne

Hamlet on east side of Port Isaac, near Camel Estuary.

HEADLANDS HOTEL, PORT GAVERNE, PORT ISAAC PL29 3SH (01208 880260; Fax: 01208 880885). A peaceful haven, ideal base for walking or touring Heritage Coast. Comfortable en suite bedrooms. Warm welcome, friendly service and delicious cuisine. Dogs accepted.

Homes from home around our peaceful courtyard garden 100 yds from sea in bygone fishing hamlet. Each sleeps six and has full CH, fridge-freezer, washer-dryer, dishwasher, microwave, video. £140 (February) £480 (August) weekly. Daily rates off-season. Resident owners. APPLY:- CAROLE & MALCOLM LEE, GULL-ROCK, PORT GAVERNE, PORT ISAAC PL29 3SQ (01208 880106). [🐕]

Port Isaac

Attractive fishing village with harbour. Much of the attractive coastline is protected by the National Trust. Camelford 9 miles, Wadebridge 9.

Cottages sleep 6/8. Central location. Approximately 5 miles beautiful beaches, moors, golf course and bike trails. Brochure. MRS S. STEPHENS, CASTLE GOFF, LANTEGLOS, CAMELFORD PL32 9RQ (01840 213535).

LONG CROSS HOTEL & VICTORIAN GARDENS, TRELIGHTS, PORT ISAAC PL29 3TF (01208 880243). Set in magnificent public gardens with tavern in the grounds. Pets' corner. Perfect base for touring. Excellent food served all day. Bargain Spring/Autumn Breaks. [Pets £1 per night.]

Portscatho

Tiny cliff-top resort on Roseland Peninsula overlooking beach of rocks and sand. Harbour; splendid views. Falmouth 5 miles.

PETER AND LIZ HEYWOOD, TREWINCE MANOR, PORTSCATHO, NEAR TRURO TR2 5ET (FREEPHONE 0500 657861). Georgian Manor house estate with luxury lodges, cedarwood cabins, cottage, small touring site. Lounge bar and restaurant; launderette. Superb walking and sailing. Dogs welcome.

ROSEVINE HOTEL, PORTHCURNICK BEACH, PORTSCATHO, TRURO TR2 5EW (01872 580206; Fax: 01872 580230). A friendly, family-managed country house hotel in a peaceful setting with delightful sea views. Top class cuisine, fresh local fish a speciality. Four Crowns Highly Commended. AA/RAC***, Ashley Courtenay Highly Recommended. [pw! Pets £3 per night.]

Poundstock

Attractive village with interesting frescoes on church wall. Nearby Penfound Manor is mentioned in Domesday Book. Bude 4 miles.

Two cottages in an area of outstanding natural beauty. Sleep 6 and 8. 100 yards from unspoilt beach. Open all year. Pets and children welcome. [£8 per pet per week.] APPLY – MR AND MRS H. CUMMINS, MINESHOP, CRACKINGTON HAVEN, BUDE EX23 0NR (01840 230338). [Pets £9 per week.]

Praa Sands

Magnificent stretch of sands and dunes. Nearby is picturesque Prussia Cove. Penzance 7½ miles, Helston 6.

Superb Bungalows sleeping 6 and 8, plus cot. One overlooking sea at Praa Sands. One 2 miles Praa Sands, secluded situation. Well furnished and large gardens all round. All breeds welcome. Terms from £100. APPLY – MRS J. LAITY, CHYRASE FARM, GOLDSITHNEY, PENZANCE TR20 9JD (01736 763301). [Pets £10 per week.]

Redruth

Market town 8 miles west of Truro.

GLOBE VALE HOLIDAY PARK, RADNOR, REDRUTH TR16 4BH (01209 891183). "In the Countryside, near the Sea." Perfect for pets and owners, with unlimited trails to explore and near "Dogs Allowed" beaches. Shop, play area, launderette, bar and games room. Caravans, tourers and tents welcome. *[pw!* 🐕*]*

Ruan High Lanes

Picturesque hamlet convenient for Veryan and Philleigh. Beautiful surrounding countryside.

POLSUE MANOR HOTEL, RUAN HIGH LANES, TRURO TR2 5LU (Tel/Fax: 01872 501270). Tranquil secluded manor house in 4 acres. All rooms en suite. Close to sandy coves, coastal paths and country walks. Pets very welcome. *[Pets £2 per night, pw!]*

St. Agnes

Patchwork of fields dotted with remains of local mining industry. Watch for grey seals swimming off St. Agnes Head.

SUNHOLME HOTEL, GOONVREA ROAD, ST AGNES TR5 0NW (01872 552318). Enjoy some of the finest views in the South West. Ideal for touring; cliff walks and beaches. Good food and service. All bedrooms en suite. Write or phone for brochure. *[Pets £1.50 per night.]*

MARC WATTS, TREVAUNANCE POINT HOTEL, ST AGNES TR5 0RZ (01872 553235; Fax: 01872 553874). Old world clifftop Hotel, ships timbered rooms, sea views, candlelight cuisine. Sea-food specialities. Open all year. Winter breaks. *[*🐕 *pw!]*

ROSEMUNDY HOUSE HOTEL, ST AGNES TR5 0UF (01872 552101). An elegant Queen Anne residence set in 4 acres of informal garden and woodland. Swimming pool, games room, croquet, putting. Half board from £155. Send or telephone for colour brochure. *[*🐕*]*

THE DRIFTWOOD SPARS HOTEL, TREVAUNANCE COVE, ST AGNES TR5 0RT (01872 552428). Take a deep breath of Cornish fresh air at this comfortable Hotel ideally situated for a perfect seaside holiday. Wonderful food, traditional Cornish home cooking. Children and pets welcome.

St Austell

Old Cornish town and china clay centre with small port at Charlestown (1½ miles). Excellent touring centre. Newquay 16 miles, Truro 14, Bodmin 12, Fowey 9, Mevagissey 6.

TRENCREEK FARM HOLIDAY PARK, HEWASWATER, ST AUSTELL PL26 7JG (01726 882540). Holiday bungalows, caravans and fully serviced touring park, all within easy reach of sea. Swimming pool, tennis court and fishing lakes. Supervised Kids Club. Special offers Easter to mid-July.

ST MARGARET'S HOLIDAY PARK, POLGOOTH, ST AUSTELL PL26 7AX (01726 74283; Fax 01726 71680). Family-run 27 Bungalows and Chalets in sunny wooded valley. Village inn, shop, golf 500 yards. Children and pets welcome. From £85 per week. *[pw! £8 per week.]*

P. W. MILLN, BOSINVER FARM, ST AUSTELL PL26 7DT (01726 72128). Quality self-catering Cottages and Bungalows on small estate. Sleep 2, 3, 4, 5, 6, 11 – one suitable for a wheelchair. Children and dogs welcome. Personally supervised by owners. Colour brochure. *[pw! £7 per week.]*

St. Ives

Picturesque resort, popular with artists, with cobbled streets and intriguing little shops. Wide stretches of sand.

CARLYON GUEST HOUSE, 18 THE TERRACE, ST IVES TR26 2BP (01736 795317). Warm, friendly atmosphere with good English cooking. All bedrooms with TV and tea/coffee facilities; most with showers. Bed and Breakfast, with Evening Meal optional.

THE LINKS HOLIDAY FLATS, CHURCH LANE, LELANT, ST IVES TR26 3HY (01736 753326). Self-catering Holiday Flats on 2-acre site 5 minutes from beach, dogs allowed. All flats are self-contained with colour TV. Write or phone for brochure. *[🐕]*

Country Cottages at Hellesveor, one mile St Ives Harbour. Sleep 4–6. Luxuriously equipped; sheets, central heating; garden, parking; farm views, cliff walks. Children welcome. Available all year. Terms £200–£390; includes sheets and heating. Tourist Board Category 3. APPLY: MRS P. H. SEABROOK, 30 NEWCOMBE STREET, MARKET HARBOROUGH, LEICESTERSHIRE LE16 9PB (01858 463723).

St Mawgan

Delightful village in a wooded river valley. Ancient church has fine carvings.

DALSWINTON COUNTRY HOUSE HOTEL, ST MAWGAN, NEAR NEWQUAY TR8 4EZ (01637 860385). Old Cornish house standing in nine and a half acres of secluded grounds. All rooms en-suite, colour TV, tea/coffee facilities. Heated swimming pool. Open all year including Christmas and New Year. ETB 3 Crowns, AA 2 Stars. *[🐕]*

St Mellion

Village 3 miles south east of Callington.

KERNOCK COTTAGES. Three traditional stone cottages for 2/6/8 set in 28 acres between Bodmin Moor and Dartmoor. Safe and quiet for pets and the family. Personal attention from resident owners. For brochure call/fax RICHARD STEEL on 01579 350435. *[🐕]*

Tintagel

Attractively situated amidst fine cliff scenery. Small rocky beach with some sand. Famous for associations with King Arthur, whose ruined Castle on Tintagel Head is of interest. Also worthy of note is Barras Head and Glebe Cliff (N.T.), Church and Old Post Office. Bodmin 20 miles, Bude 19, Wadebridge 16, Camelford 6.

CHILCOTTS, BOSSINEY, TINTAGEL PL34 0AY (Tel/Fax: 01840 770324). Friendly old sixteenth century listed cottage with beamed ceiling and stonework. In National Trust countryside overlooking the sea. Adjoining cliff and Bossiney Beach. Magnificent walks. Small number of guests. B&B. En suite rooms. TV, coffee/tea maker. From £14.00. Open all year. Self catering cottages available. Brochure with pleasure. [Pets £1.50 per night.]

BOSSINEY FARM CARAVAN AND CAMPING PARK, TINTAGEL PL34 0AY (01840 770481). BGHP √ √ √ √. Family-run park. Two ranges of caravans – semi-serviced with toilet, fridge etc. Fully serviced with H&C, shower and room heater. All with TV. On the coast at Tintagel. Colour brochure available. [🐕]

THE PENALLICK HOTEL, TINTAGEL PL34 0EJ (01840 770296). Comfortable, family-run licensed hotel, magnificent cliff top position. All rooms colour TV, tea-makers; most en suite/sea views. Open all year. [🐕]

MILL HOUSE INN, TREBARWITH STRAND, TINTAGEL PL34 0HD (01840 770200/770932). Picturesque 17th century inn set in 7 acres of woodland with stream running alongside. Ideal for walking, quarter-mile from beach. Seven letting bedrooms, mostly en suite. TV, tea/coffee making facilities, hairdryers. Restaurant, ample parking. Friendly atmosphere. Pets welcome. [Pets £2 per night.]

MRS M. LEEDS, WILLAPARK MANOR HOTEL, BOSSINEY, TINTAGEL PL34 0BA (01840 770782). Beautiful character house amidst 14 acres and only minutes from the beach. All en suite rooms. Children and pets welcome. Open all year. SAE for brochure. ETB 3 Crowns Commended. [🐕]

Tregony

Good touring centre for south coast and Roseland Peninsula. St Austell 8 miles, Truro 8.

TREGONY HOLIDAY PARK, TREGONY, NEAR TRURO TR2 5RW (01872 530257). An exclusive award-winning park with fully self-contained bungalows and caravans set in beautifully landscaped surroundings in the centre of Tregony village. Free brochure. [Pets £13 per week.]

Treknow

Village near north coast of Trebarwith Strand. Camelford 4 miles.

MRS S. M. ORME, "HILLSCROFT", TREKNOW, TINTAGEL (01840 770551). Comfortable accommodation near surfing beach in beautiful National Trust countryside. Walks, riding, sea-fishing all nearby. Car parking. Good home cooking. All rooms tea/coffee facilities. Pets welcome. Bed and Breakfast. Non smoking. [🐕]

Truro

Pleasant cathedral city. An excellent touring centre with both north and south coasts within easy reach. Many tourist attractions including fine shops. There are numerous creeks to explore and boat trips may be made across the estuary to Falmouth. Penzance 27 miles, Bodmin 25, Helston 17, St. Austell 14, Falmouth 11, Redruth 8.

MRS TRESEDES, MARCORRIE HOTEL, 20 FALMOUTH ROAD, TRURO TR1 2HX (01872 77374 or Fax: 01872 41666). Victorian town house, five minutes' walk from city centre. Ideal touring base. All rooms en suite with central heating, colour TV, telephone, tea-making facilities. Ample parking. Outdoor swimming pool. Major credit cards accepted. Open all year. Bed and Breakfast from £19.50 per person per night. 3 Crowns Approved.

Wadebridge

Town on River Camel six miles N.W. of Bodmin. Oldest working roadbridge in Britain, dates from 1485. Piers said to be built on woolpacks.

Recently converted farm cottages in quiet situation, ideally situated for walking, cycling and touring. Furnished to high standard with log fires, storage heating; own gardens. Sleep 2/7 +cot. Dogs by arrangement. COLESENT COTTAGES, ST TUDY, BODMIN PL30 4QX (01208 850112). *[🐕]*

DINHAM FARM COURTYARD COTTAGES. Three luxury cottages for 2/4/6; bed linen and electricity included. Use of swimming pool in summer months. Near lovely beaches and cycle paths. For colour brochure phone **01208 880927**.

Whitsand Bay

Bay running north-west from Rame Head on south coast to the Long Stone between Downderry and Portwrinkle.

MRS KATHY RIDPATH, FIR COTTAGE, LOWER TREGANTLE, ANTONY, TORPOINT PL11 3AL (01752 822626). On coastal path between Rame Head and Looe. Warm, comfortable accommodation. H&C, colour TV in each room. Surrounded by beautiful countryside. Beach and golf close by. *[Pets £5 per week.]*

Widemouth Bay

Small resort, 3 miles Bude. Good sands and cliffs.

CORNWALL, NEAR WIDEMOUTH BAY. Luxury family caravan, also deluxe flatlet to suit couples. Both have excellent facilities and lead into 1.5 acre secluded grounds. Beaches nearby, two minutes to shops. Reasonable rates. Pets very welcome. Brochure telephone 01566 781493. *[🐕]*

CUMBRIA

CUMBRIA   *Alston, Ambleside*

Welcome COTTAGE HOLIDAYS

HUNDREDS OF PROPERTIES
IN WONDERFUL LOCATIONS AT WELCOMING LOW PRICES.
MOST LESS THAN £150 PER WEEK FROM OCTOBER TO APRIL.
HUNDREDS LESS THAN £300 PER WEEK IN JULY AND AUGUST.
PETS, LINEN AND FUEL MOSTLY INCLUDED.

FREE COLOUR BROCHURE **01756 702208**

GATEWAY TO THE LAKE DISTRICT

★ On the Furness & Cartmel Peninsula (Holiday Destination Winner 1994)
★ Luxury Holiday Homes for 2 - 8 people   ★ Heated Indoor & Outdoor Swimming Pools
★ Bowling, Putting, Tennis & Horseriding on park   ★ Bradley Bear Kids Club and Teen Club
★ Restaurants - Bars   ★ Live Family Evening Entertainment   ★ TOURERS/TENTS

Call now for your free colour brochure

LAKELAND

24 hours a day - 7 days a week
015395 58556
or see your local travel agent

★ A BRITISH HOLIDAYS PARK

NENT HALL COUNTRY HOUSE HOTEL
ALSTON, NORTH PENNINES,
CUMBRIA CA9 3LQ
Tel: 01434 381584 Fax: 01434 382668

The peace and tranquillity of the North Pennines offers a superb setting
for Nent Hall. Escape from the world and let us care for you with consideration and that personal touch.
We offer 18 en suite bedrooms with all facilities and elegant dining with freshly prepared cuisine and a
range of specially selected wines for the discerning guest. From this beautiful central location visit such
historic sites as Hadrian's Wall and Durham Cathedral or enjoy the landscape of the North Lakes &
Scottish Borders. £45.00 per person per night for D, B&B.

4 Crowns Highly Commended   **RAC & AA ***   **PETS WELCOME**

WANSLEA GUEST HOUSE
Lake Road, Ambleside LA22 0DB Tel: 015394 33884

Spacious family-run guest house just a stroll from village and lake. We offer a friendly
welcome and comfortable rooms, most en suite. Relax in our licensed residents'
lounge with a real fire on winter evenings. B&B from £16.00pp; Evening Meal also
available. Pets welcome by arrangement (please bring bedding).

KINGSWOOD

OLD LAKE ROAD
AMBLESIDE. TEL. 015394 34081

Near town centre yet off main road. Ample car parking. Comfortable, well-equipped
bedrooms with washbasins, tea/coffee making facilities. Colour TV. Central heating. Non-
smoking. Pets welcome. Bargain Breaks off season. Phone for rates and details.

THE BRITANNIA INN
ELTERWATER
TEL: 015394 37210
FAX: 015394 37311

Commended

The Britannia Inn is a genuine olde-worlde, 400-year-old inn, overlooking the village green in the delightful unspoilt village of Elterwater in the beautiful Langdale Valley. There are seven double rooms, six of which have en suite shower and toilet and two twin-bedded rooms both of which have en suite shower and toilet. All have colour TV, telephone, hair dryer, central heating and tea & coffee making facilities. The inn is renowned for its fine bar meals, excellent real ales and extensive wine list. The bars, lounge, dining room and bedrooms are furnished to give a homely atmosphere to accompany the warm welcome. This is a superb centre from which to walk and enjoy the Lakeland hills and valleys without motoring or equally for the less energetic from which to tour by car or coach. Dogs are welcome.

The Britannia Inn, Elterwater, Ambleside, Cumbria LA22 9HP

FHG PUBLICATIONS LIMITED publish a large range of well-known accommodation guides. We will be happy to send you details or you can use the order form at the back of this book.

CUMBRIA *Buttermere, Caldbeck, Carlisle*

Buttermere – beautiful at any time of the year.

* 22 Bedrooms, all with private bathroom
* Four-Poster Beds available
* Direct Dial Telephones
* Drying Room
* Log Fires
* Afternoon Tea Free to Residents
* Daily changing menus
* Carefully chosen wines
* Two Fully Licensed Bars and Patio
* REAL ALES
* Self Catering Apartments available
* Maid Service
* Large Car Park
* Dogs Welcome
* Superb, unrestricted walking
* Free golf

BRIDGE HOTEL
Buttermere, Cumbria CA13 9UZ
Tel & Fax: 017687 70252

SPECIAL BREAKS ALL YEAR

ETB 🏆🏆🏆🏆
Highly Commended

ETB ♣♣♣♣♣
Highly Commended

AA**RAC, CAMRA, RELAIS ROUTIERS, BHA
Painting–Photography–Fishing–Birdwatching

PARKEND RESTAURANT
Parkend, Caldbeck, Cumbria CA7 8HH
Tel: 016974 78494   3 Crowns Commended
A charming old world restaurant where you can enjoy a quality traditional meal made from the finest fresh local produce. There is a varied à la carte menu with vegetarian choices and three-course traditional lunches. Excellent en suite accommodation available.

🏆🏆🏆 COMMENDED   Tel: 01228 577308   4 Keys Commended

NEW PALLYARDS, HETHERSGILL, CARLISLE CA6 6HZ
One modern bungalow, 3/4 bedrooms, sleeps 8; 2 lovely cottages on farm. Bed and Breakfast, Half Board. En suite double/family, twin/single rooms. Disabled welcome. We are proud to have won the National Award for the Best Breakfast in Britain and have been filmed for BBC TV.
Bed and Breakfast £17.50–£19.50, Dinner from £12.00
Dinner, Bed and Breakfast weekly rate £160.00–£170.00. Self Catering £80–£360.

CHARACTER COTTAGES AND PINE LODGES
Fringe of Lake District, National Park. 3 Lodges peacefully situated in our grounds in picturesque hamlet.
Views over farmland to Caldbeck Fells, 30 minutes Lake Ullswater, Keswick or Gretna Green.
* 1/2/3 Bedrooms (sleep 2/7) * Shower/bath, second WC in 3-bedroom properties
* Heaters in all properties * Colour TVs * Laundry * Microwaves
* Three cottages, 1 heavily beamed, with wood-burning stove * Open all year, winter breaks
* Warm for your arrival * Excellent quality throughout * Direct-dial telephones
* 4 Keys/5 Keys up to Highly Commended
Featured in Good Holiday Cottage Guide. Terms £140–£440. For details and brochure:

Mrs Ivinson (SCF), Green View, Welton, Near Dalston, Carlisle CA5 7ES.
Tel: 016974 76230 Fax: 016974 76523.

SELF CATERING COTTAGES

In an undiscovered corner of Cumbria two lovely cottages with 320 tranquil acres of flora and fauna to explore (maps provided). Use of swimming pool from May to September. Central for Hadrian's Wall and Gretna Green. 5 Keys Highly Commended. Barn conversion sleeps 8. Detached cottage sleeps 2/4.

Apply: MRS J. JAMES, MIDTODHILLS FARM, ROADHEAD,
CARLISLE CA6 6PF. Tel & Fax: 016977 48213

LAKESHORE LODGES Scandinavian pine Bungalows beautifully situated amongst 50 acres of English woodland designated an 'Area of Special Scientific Interest'. Perfect base for touring Lake District, Scottish Borders and Yorkshire Dales National Park. Dream location for Fly Fishing Holiday with Brown and Rainbow Trout, Boats and tackle available. For brochure and fishing details: *Mrs Sheelagh Potter, Lakeshore Lodges, The Lough Trout Fishery, Thurstonfield, Carlisle CA5 6HB*
Telephone: 01228 576552 Fax: 01228 576761 ☂ ☂ ☂

ETB ☙ ☙ ☙ Commended **CRAIGBURN FARM** AA Recommended
Catlowdy, Penton, Carlisle CA6 5QP

One of the best farmhouses for delicious food. Distinction in Cookery held.
Cosy and friendly atmosphere. Beautiful bedrooms—some with four poster beds. All rooms have en suite bathrooms, tea/coffee facilities, colour TV and central heating.
A working farm, some rare breed animals – Pets Corner. Stop over and go to and from Scotland & Northern Ireland.
Bargain Breaks, 20% off weekly bookings.
Bed & Breakfast from £19.

Mrs Jane Lawson Tel and Fax: (01228) 577214

Hundith
Hill
Hotel

Our period hotel is in the quiet part of the Lakes, with splendid views over Lorton Vale and Fells – ideal for long peaceful walks with the dog, or as a base for touring. We offer you comfort, tranquillity, an informal atmosphere and good food. We can also accommodate disabled/wheelchair users. If you want to see the Lakes unspoilt and prefer a gentle pace, whether for your holiday or a break away, send or telephone for our brochure now.

HUNDITH HILL HOTEL
Lorton Vale, Cockermouth, Cumbria
CA13 9TH. Telephone: (01900) 822092 Fax: (01900) 828215

TEL MRS J. HALL (01946 723319)

SELF CATERING IN STYLE
Luxury Pine Lodges and Stone Cottages
Colour TVs, Telephone
Microwaves, Dishwashers
Central Heating, Open fires, Laundry
Sports Hall, Games Room, pond & rafts
Adventure playground, Miniature railway
Brochure on request.
ETB 4 Keys COMMENDED
PARADISE FOR KIDS & PETS

FISHERGROUND FARM ESKDALE CUMBRIA CA19 ITF

THE GRASMERE HOTEL
BROADGATE
GRASMERE
NEAR AMBLESIDE
CUMBRIA LA22 9TA

ETB ♛♛♛♛ Highly Commended

AA**   RAC**

A family-run 12 bedroomed licensed Hotel. All rooms with bath or/and showers. Quietly situated in the picturesque village of Grasmere. Restaurant overlooking large, secluded garden, river and surrounding hills. Superb four-course dinners and carefully chosen wine list. Award winning restaurant. Bar with log fire in winter. Special breaks throughout the year. For brochure and tariff
TEL/FAX: (015394 35277)

BETTY FOLD
HAWKSHEAD HILL
AMBLESIDE
LA22 0PS
015394 36611

Situated between Ambleside and Coniston, set in spacious grounds with magnificent views, this small Guest House (2 Crowns Highly Commended) with self catering Flat and Cottage (ETB 3 Keys Approved) for 2–6 people is ideally located for walkers and families with pets. Special self-catering Winter Breaks. Please write or telephone for brochure and tariff.

Woodlands Country Guest House and Cottage

Ireby, Cumbria CA5 1EX   **Tel: 016973 71791 Fax: 016973 71482**

Former Victorian vicarage in private wooded grounds on the edge of quiet village. Bassenthwaite 4 miles. All bedrooms en suite with colour TV and tea making facilities. Our small family run guest house offers good home cooking and a warm welcome.

• Residential Licence • Ample Parking
• Drying room • Suitable for wheelchair users
• Children and pets welcome • Nearest main road A591/A595

Superb 2 bedroom stable conversion self-catering cottage also available.

B&B from £20. DB&B from £32.50. Special terms on request.
Please send for brochure.
Pauline and John Bibby

FREE and REDUCED RATE Holiday Visits!
Don't miss our Readers' Offer Vouchers on
pages 5 to 18.

"YOUR PET(S)–YOUR HOLIDAY"
Combine COMFORT, PEACE & QUIET, RELAX, FISH, STROLL OR WALK:
(SECLUDED COTTAGES AND PRIVATE FISHING).

Tranquil quality cottages overlooking small lake amid Lakeland's beautiful Eden Valley countryside, only 30 minutes' drive from Ullswater, North Pennines, Hadrian's Wall and Scottish Borders.

* Well fenced areas for pets' freedom & exercise
* Guaranteed clean * Well equipped and maintained
* Linen provided * Beds freshly made for your arrival
* Centrally located * Exceptional wildlife and walking area
* Laundry area * Trout & Coarse Fish too–11lb weight caught *
* **Pets welcome** * Honest brochure–clear prices
* Open all year–breaks/weeks

Relax & escape to "YOUR" home in the country, why settle for less...

Tel: 01768 896275 (Fax available).

24hr Brochure line 01768 898711
(manned most Saturdays).

SAE CROSSFIELD COTTAGE, KIRKOSWALD,
PENRITH, CUMBRIA CA10 1EU
RING NOW! It's never too early or too late!
PETS – NO PROBLEM!

No silly rules

KIRKWOOD

Prince's Road, Windermere LA23 2DD
Tel: 015394 43907

KIRKWOOD occupies a quiet spot betwixt Windermere and Bowness, offering guests a warm and friendly atmosphere with an individual personal service. Rooms are large and all en suite with TV and tea/coffee making facilities; some have four-poster beds. Your hosts will be pleased to help plan tours or walks with maps provided. Three-night special breaks available.

ETB ♚♚ Commended   RAC Highly Acclaimed   AA QQQQ   *B&B £19–£26*

Try us! You won't be disappointed

Our attractive self-catering holiday homes are in a variety of good locations – well equipped and carefully managed by friendly pet-loving staff.

🐾 🐾 🐾- 🐾 🐾 🐾 🐾 🐾 **UP TO DE LUXE**

Lakelovers
Holiday Homes

Tel (015394) 88855   Fax (015394) 88857
Lakelovers, The Toffee Loft, Ash Street, Windermere LA23 3RA

GREENRIGGS GUEST HOUSE

Small, family run guest house situated in a quiet cul-de-sac close to park, with easy access to shops, lake and all transport. B&B from £15.00; BB & EM from £24.75. **Open all year.**
8 Upper Oak Street, Windermere, Cumbria LA23 2LB
Tel: 015394 42265/45874
♚♚ Commended

DALES HOLIDAY COTTAGES offer a selection of superb, self catering, holiday properties in beautiful rural and coastal locations from the Lakes and Fells that inspired Wordsworth and Beatrix Potter to Cumbria's Borders. Cosy cottages for 2, to a country house for 15, many open all year. For FREE Brochure contact Dales Holiday Cottages, an English Tourist Board Registered Agency, Carleton Business Park, Skipton, North Yorkshire BD23 2DG. Telephone (01756) 799821 & 790919.

LAKELAND LEISURE (015395 58556). Gateway to the Lake District. Luxury Holiday Homes for 2–8 people. Heated indoor and outdoor swimming pools. Bowls, Putting, Tennis and Horseriding on park. Restaurant – Bars. Live family Evening Entertainment. Call now for free colour brochure. *[Pets £2.50 p.n.]*

WELCOME COTTAGE HOLIDAYS. Hundreds of properties in wonderful locations at welcoming low prices. Pets, linen and fuel mostly included. For FREE colour brochure telephone 01756 702208.

Allonby

Small coastal resort with sand and shingle beach, 5 miles north-east of Maryport across Allonby Bay.

EAST HOUSE GUEST HOUSE, ALLONBY, MARYPORT CA15 6PQ (01900 881264 or 881276). Overlooking Solway Firth, two minutes sea. Central Lakes. Riding, tennis, golf near. Bed and Breakfast from £12 nightly, en suite Bed and Breakfast £15 nightly; EM, Bed and Breakfast £15 nightly, £95 weekly; en suite EM, Bed and Breakfast £18 nightly, £110 weekly.

Alston

Said to be England's highest market town at an altitude of nearly 1,000 feet.

NENT HALL COUNTRY HOUSE HOTEL, ALSTON, NORTH PENNINES CA9 3LQ (01434 381584 or Fax: 01434 382668). Let us care for you with consideration and that personal touch. 18 en suite bedrooms with all facilities; elegant dining with freshly prepared cuisine. Visit Hadrian's Wall and Durham Cathedral. 4 Crowns Highly Commended.

Ambleside

Popular centre for exploring Lake District at northern end of Lake Windermere. Picturesque Stock Ghyll waterfall nearby, lovely walks. Associated with Wordsworth. Penrith 30 miles, Keswick 17, Kendal 13, Windermere 5.

NANNY BROW COUNTRY HOUSE HOTEL & RESTAURANT, AMBLESIDE, CUMBRIA LA22 9NF (Tel: 015394 32036; Fax: 015394 32450). Set in five acres of gardens and woodland with stunning views over the fells and River Brathay, you can access the local fells and woodlands from the hotel grounds and walk dogs in safety. For full brochure telephone. *[pw! £4.50 per night.]*

MRS EDITH PEERS, FISHERBECK FARMHOUSE, OLD LAKE ROAD, AMBLESIDE LA22 0DH (015394 32523). Comfortable 16th century Farmhouse (not working farm). Singles, doubles/twins, family rooms. Washbasins, tea/coffee making facilities, parking. Tourist Board 2 Crowns.

MR E. M. C. SCOTT, CROW HOW HOTEL, RYDAL ROAD, AMBLESIDE LA22 9PN (015394 32193). Country house with 2 acre garden, wonderful Fell views. Ideal walking/touring. ½ mile from Ambleside. Spacious rooms, private parking. Special breaks, also S/C apartment. AA 2 Stars, ETB 3 Crowns Commended. *[🐕]*

THE OLD VICARAGE, VICARAGE ROAD, AMBLESIDE LA22 9DH (015394 33364). "Rest awhile in style." Tranquil wooded grounds in heart of village. Car park. All rooms ensuite. Kettle, clock/radio, TV, hair dryer. Quality B&B from £19pp/pn (low season). Reductions for longer stays. Friendly service where your pets are welcome. Phone Ian or Helen Burt.

WANSLEA GUEST HOUSE, LAKE ROAD, AMBLESIDE LA22 0DB (015394 33884). Spacious family-run guest house with walks beginning at the door. Comfortable rooms, most en suite. Licensed lounge. B&B from £16; Evening Meal available. Pets welcome by arrangement. *[Pets £1 per night.]*

AMBLESIDE AREA – IVY HOUSE, HAWKSHEAD. Small family-run hotel located in the centre of this picturesque village – sensibly priced, no charge for dogs. Write or telephone David or Jane Vaughan for brochure (015394 36204). *[🐕]*

CUMBRIA

MRS RUSS, CROYDEN HOUSE, CHURCH ST, AMBLESIDE LA22 0BU (015394 32209). Croyden House offers a warm friendly welcome – comfortable, tastefully furnished rooms (all en suite), all with colour TV, tea/coffee tray and washbasin. Central location. Private car park. Open all year. B&B from £16.50–£20. Special rates for children.

KIRKSTONE FOOT HOTEL, KIRKSTONE PASS ROAD, AMBLESIDE, CUMBRIA LA22 9EH (015394 32232). Country house hotel with luxury self-catering Cottages and Apartments sleeping 2/7. Set in peaceful and secluded grounds. Adjoining lovely Lakeland fells, great for walking. Special winter breaks. *[pw! Pets £2.50 per night.]*

SKELWITH BRIDGE HOTEL, NEAR AMBLESIDE LA22 9NJ (015394 32115; Fax: 015394 34254). Traditional 17th Century Lakeland Inn has well-appointed en suite bedrooms which offer every comfort including colour TV, radio, tea/coffee facilities. Children welcome. Sun terrace and gardens. *[Pets £3 per night.]*

BRITANNIA INN, ELTERWATER, AMBLESIDE LA22 9HP (015394 37210). 400-year-old inn renowned for fine food and excellent cellar. All bedrooms with colour TV, tea/coffee facilities etc; most en suite. Fishing, sailing, pony trekking nearby. *[🐕]*

"KINGSWOOD", OLD LAKE ROAD, AMBLESIDE LA22 0AE (015394 34081). Near town centre yet off main road. Ample parking. Rooms have washbasins, tea/coffee making facilities. Colour TV; central heating. Pets welcome. Phone for rates and details. *[Pets £1/£1.50 per night.]*

Appleby

Pleasant touring centre on River Eden, between lofty Pennines and Lake District. Of historic note are the Castle (12th and 17th cent.) and Moot Hall (16th cent.). Good trout fishing, swimming pool, tennis, bowls. Kendal 24 miles, Penrith 13, Brough 8.

"JUBILEE COTTAGE." Sleeps 5/6. 18th century cottage situated between North Lakes and Pennines. Car essential; off road parking for two cars in front of cottage. Well-behaved pets welcome. Terms £125–£160. MISS L. I. BASTEN, DAYMER COTTAGE, LEE, NEAR ILFRACOMBE, DEVON (01271 863769). *[🐕]*

APPLEBY MANOR COUNTRY HOUSE HOTEL, ROMAN ROAD, APPLEBY-IN-WESTMORLAND CA16 6JB (Tel: 017683 51571; Fax: 017683 52888). Enjoy the comfort of Cumbria's highly commended Country House Hotel with superb meals, relaxing lounges, indoor leisure club and breathtaking scenery all around. Phone for a full colour brochure. *[🐕 pw!]*

MILBURN GRANGE COTTAGES are quality properties sleeping 2–7, set in beautiful location at foot of Pennines. Excellent facilities throughout. Ideal for Lakes/Dales/Borders/walking. Breaks from £80.00. Weekly from £140 to £350. Dogs £10.00. Low season Bargains. Contact: MARGARET BURKE, MILBURN GRANGE, APPLEBY CA16 6DR (Tel/Fax: 017683 61768 or 0836 547130).

Askam-in-Furness

Coastal village on the Cartmel and Furness Peninsula. ETB "Holiday Destination of the Year" Award 1994. Fine sandy beaches. Many tourist attractions. Ulverston 4 miles.

MRS C. DOWLE, 1 FRIARS GROUND, KIRKBY-IN-FURNESS LA17 7YB (01229 889601). "Owl Cottage." Self catering. Two bedrooms. Sleeps 4/6. Garden. Garage. 5 minutes sea/sandy beaches. Coniston/Windermere within easy reach. Ideal fell walking. Open all year. *[🐕]*

Borrowdale

Scenic valley of River Derwent, splendid walking and climbing country.

MARY MOUNT HOTEL, BORROWDALE, NEAR KESWICK CA12 5UU (017687 77223). Set in 4½ acres of gardens and woodlands on the shores of Derwentwater. 2½ miles from Keswick in picturesque Borrowdale. Superb walking and touring. All rooms en suite with colour TV and tea/coffee making facilities. Licensed. Brochure on request. 3 Crowns. *[🐕]*

ROYAL OAK HOTEL, ROSTHWAITE, KESWICK CA12 5XB (017687 77214). Traditional Lakeland hotel with friendly atmosphere. Home cooking, cosy bar and comfortable lounge. Winter and Summer discount rates. Brochure and Tariff available. ETB 3 Crowns Commended. *[🐕]*

STAKIS LODORE SWISS HOTEL, BORROWDALE, NEAR KESWICK CA12 5UX (017687 77285; Fax: 017687 77343). Luxury Hotel with fabulous views overlooking Derwentwater and fells. Facilities include 70 bedrooms, restaurant and lounge, bar and leisure club. 4 Crowns Highly Commended. *[Pets £2 per night.]*

Bowness-on-Solway

Village on Solway Firth four miles north of Kirkbride. Roman sites in vicinity, at west end of Hadrian's Wall.

WALLSEND GUEST HOUSE, THE OLD RECTORY, BOWNESS ON SOLWAY, CARLISLE CA5 5AF (01697 351055). Former Rectory, standing in own grounds on the fringe of this quiet village, 25 minutes from Carlisle. Hadrian's Wall walk; Cumbria Cycle/Coastal Way; birdwatching. Non-smoking. ETB 1 Crown, AA QQ. *[🐕]*

Burton-in-Kendal

A small village five minutes from M6 Junctions 35 and 36. Five miles from Kirkby Lonsdale, 10 miles from Kendal on the A6070 road.

ANNE TAYLOR, RUSSELL FARM, BURTON-IN-KENDAL, CARNFORTH, LANCS. LA6 1NN (01524 781334). Bed, Breakfast & Evening Meal offered. Ideal centre for touring Lakes and Yorkshire Dales. Good food, friendly atmosphere on working dairy farm. Modernised farmhouse. Guests' own lounge. *[🐕]*

Buttermere

Between lake of same name and Crummock Water. Magnificent scenery. Of special note is Sour Milk Ghyll waterfall and steep and impressive Honister Pass 2½ miles S.E. Golf course. Keswick 15 miles, Cockermouth 10.

BRIDGE HOTEL, BUTTERMERE CA13 9UZ (Tel & Fax: 017687 70252). 22 bedrooms, all with private bathrooms; four-posters available. Daily freshly prepared menus, large selection wines; real ales. Superb walking and fishing. Dog welcome. Self catering apartments available. *[Pets £3.20 per night.]*

Caldbeck

Village 7 miles south-east of Wigton. River-powered woollen mills once produced grey cloth for John Peel's famous hunting coats.

PARKEND RESTAURANT, PARKEND, CALDBECK CA7 8HH (016974 78494). A charming old world restaurant where you can enjoy a quality traditional meal made from the finest local produce. Weddings, anniversaries, Christmas Dinners and Buffet. 3 Crowns Commended. *[🐕]*

Carlisle

Important Border city and former Roman station on River Eden. The Cathedral (12–14th cent.) has famous East window. 12th cent. Castle is of historic interest, also Tullie House Museum and Art Gallery. Good sports facilities inc. football and racecourse. Kendal 45 miles, Dumfries 33, Penrith 18.

NEWPALLYARDS, HETHERSGILL, CARLISLE CA6 6HZ (01228 577308). ETB 4 KEYS COMMENDED. Relax and see beautiful North Cumbria and the Borders. Self-catering accommodation in one Bungalow, 3/4 bedrooms; two lovely Cottages on farm. Also Bed and Breakfast or Half Board – en suite rooms. [🐈]

GREEN VIEW LODGES, WELTON, NEAR DALSTON, CARLISLE CA5 7ES. Luxury self-catering lodges and cottages, sleeping 2–7 – two/three bedroomed. Peaceful setting. Central heating, microwave, telephone, linen and towels, bath/shower. Lake Ullswater, Keswick, Gretna Green nearby; golf 5 miles. Terms £140–£440 per week. 4/5 Keys (up to Highly Commended). *[Pets £15 per week.]* Telephone: MRS IVINSON (016974 76230).

In an undiscovered corner of Cumbria two lovely cottages with 320 tranquil acres of flora and fauna to explore (maps provided). Use of swimming pool from May to September. Central for Hadrian's Wall and Gretna Green. 5 Keys Highly Commended. Apply: MRS J. JAMES, MIDTODHILLS FARM, ROADHEAD, CARLISLE CA6 6PF (016977 48213). *[Pets £10.00 per week.]*

MRS SHEELAGH POTTER, LAKESHORE LODGES, THE LOUGH TROUT FISHERY, THURSTONFIELD CA5 6HB (01228 576552; Fax: 01228 576761). Scandinavian pine Bungalows with verandahs overlooking 30 acre lake surrounded by unspoilt English woodland. 3 Keys. Dream location for fishing holiday. Boats and tackle available. *[Pets £20 per week.]*

MRS JANE LAWSON, CRAIGBURN FARM, CATLOWDY, PENTON, CARLISLE CA6 5QP (Tel & Fax: 01228 577214). Beautiful countryside, superb food, friendly atmosphere. All bedrooms en suite with tea-making facilities and colour TV. Residential licence. Games room. Pets most welcome. 3 Crowns Commended. [🐈]

DALSTON HALL CARAVAN PARK, DALSTON HALL, DALSTON, NEAR CARLISLE CA5 7JX (01228 710165). √√√√ Exit 42 off M6, follow signs for Dalston. Small family-run park set in peaceful surroundings. Electric hook-ups, shops, playground, launderette, fly-fishing, nine-hole golf course. *[pw!]*

Carnforth

Small town 6 miles north of Lancaster. Steamtown Railway Centre offers train rides, model and miniature railways and other memorabilia.

MRS MARGARET HOLMES, KILN CROFT, MAIN STREET, WARTON, CARNFORTH, LANCS LA5 9NR (01524 735788). Small, family-run hotel where you can relax by a log fire or wander round the animal garden. Licensed restaurant serving home-produced organic vegetables and own meat when available. Well placed for touring the Lakes, Dales and historic Lancaster; five minutes from J25 M6. B&B £18 en suite.

Cockermouth

Market town and popular touring centre for Lake District and quiet Cumbrian coast. On Rivers Derwent and Cocker. Fine fell scenery to the east. Birthplace of Wordsworth. The ruined Norman Castle is of interest. Penrith 30 miles, Carlisle 26, Whitehaven 14, Keswick 12, Workington 8, Maryport 7.

HUNDITH HILL HOTEL, LORTON, COCKERMOUTH CA13 9TH (01900 822092; Fax: 01900 828215). Comfortable, quiet family Hotel. Ideal centre for Lakes. We can accommodate disabled/wheelchair users. Dogs welcome. Bed and Breakfast from £20 *[Pets £2.00 each per night.]*

Elterwater

Beautifully situated at entrance to Great Langdale. Ambleside 4 miles.

MRS M. JONES, ROSEGATE, ELTERWATER, NEAR AMBLESIDE LA22 9HW (015394 37605). Comfortably furnished three-bedroom house. Pretty garden, pets welcome. Charming Lakeland village, ideal for exploring the beautiful Lake District. Ambleside, Windermere and Hawkshead all nearby. *[🐕]*

Eskdale

Lakeless valley, noted for waterfalls and ascended by a light-gauge railway. Tremendous views. Roman fort. Keswick 35 miles, Broughton-in-Furness 10 miles.

MRS J. P. HALL, FISHERGROUND FARM, ESKDALE CA19 1TF (01946 723319). Self-catering to suit everyone. Scandinavian Pine Lodges and Cottages – on a delightful traditional farm. Adventure playground. Sports Hall and games room. Pets' and children's paradise. Brochures available. ETB 4 Keys Commended. *[🐕]*

Grange-over-Sands

Quiet resort at the north of Morecambe Bay. Well known for its fine gardens. Convenient centre for the Lake District. Sporting facilities include golf, boating, fishing, tennis and bowls; galas are held at the swimming pool. Lancaster 25 miles, Ambleside 20, Windermere 16, Kendal 14.

HAMPSFELL HOUSE HOTEL, HAMPSFELL ROAD, GRANGE-OVER-SANDS LA11 6BG (015395 32567). 3 Crowns Commended, AA**, Ashley Courtenay Recommended. Peaceful country house hotel in two wooded acres close to sea and fells. Ideal for walking dogs. All rooms en suite with colour TV and tea/coffee making facilities. Ample safe parking. *[🐕]*

Grasmere

Village famous for Wordsworth associations; the poet lived in Dove Cottage (preserved as it was), and is buried in churchyard. Museum has manuscripts and relics.

GRASMERE HOTEL, GRASMERE, NEAR AMBLESIDE LA22 9TA (015394 35277). 12-bedroomed licensed Hotel set in the centre of the Lakes. Ideal for walking or sightseeing. All rooms have en suite facilities, TV etc. Gourmet food and interesting wines. *[pw! Pets £2.50 per night.]*

Hawkshead

Quaint village in Lake District between Coniston Water and Windermere. The 16th century Church and Grammar School, which Wordsworth attended, and the Old Court House (N.T.) are of interest. Ambleside 5 miles.

BETTY FOLD GUEST HOUSE, HAWKSHEAD HILL, AMBLESIDE LA22 0PS (015394 36611). Guest house with self-catering Flat and Cottage. Set in peaceful and spacious grounds. Ideal for the walker and dog. Open all year. 2 Crowns Highly Commended, 3 Keys Approved. *[Pets £2 per night.]*

Ireby

Quiet Cumbrian village between the fells and the sea. Good centre for the northern Lake District. Cockermouth 11 miles, Bassenthwaite 6.

WOODLANDS COUNTRY GUEST HOUSE AND COTTAGE, IREBY CA5 1EX (016973 71791). In private wooded grounds four miles from Bassenthwaite, ideal for Lakes and Borders. All bedrooms en-suite with tea making facilities. Children welcome. Residential licence. B&B from £20. 3 Crowns Highly Commended. *[🐾]*

Kendal

Market town and popular centre for touring the Lake District. Of historic note is the Castle (Norm.), birthplace of Catherine Parr. Quaint streets. Sizergh Castle (14th–18th cent.) 3 miles S. Penrith 25 miles, Ulverston 24, Lancaster 22, Grange-over-Sands 14, Ambleside 13.

MRS V. SUNTER, HUGHES HOUSE FARM, OXENHOLME LANE, NATLAND, KENDAL LA9 7QH (015395 61177). 17th Century beamed farmhouse. Double and twin rooms with private bathrooms. Four-poster bed. Residents' lounge. Central heating. Overlooking Lakeland Fells. Golf, riding, historic visits nearby. Bed and Breakfast from £18; Evening Meals and Light Suppers available. Pets and children welcome. AA QQQ.

MRS HELEN JONES, PRIMROSE COTTAGE, ORTON ROAD, TEBAY CA10 3TL (015396 24791). Excellent location for North Lakes and Yorkshire Dales. Rural village adjacent M6. Superb facilities, very friendly; pets welcome with well-behaved owners. One acre woodland garden. *[🐾]*

Keswick

Famous Lake District resort at north end of Derwentwater. Of interest are Crosthwaite Church (11th cent. and later) and museum. Carlisle 30 miles, Penrith 18, Ambleside 17, Cockermouth 12.

THE COTTAGE IN THE WOOD, WHINLATTER PASS, KESWICK CA12 5TW (017687 78409). Small comfortable Hotel, once a 17th century coaching inn, in a remote and beautiful situation with superb views. All rooms en suite, with central heating and tea/coffee facilities. Excellent traditional food. 3 Crowns. Highly Commended.

OVERWATER HALL, OVERWATER, NEAR IREBY, KESWICK CA5 1HH (017687 76566). Elegant Country House Hotel in spacious grounds. Dogs very welcome in your room. Mini breaks from £48.50 per person per night, Dinner, Room and Breakfast. Any 4 nights from £160 per person Dinner, Bed and Breakfast. 2 AA Rosettes for excellent food. 3 Crowns Commended. *[🐾pw!]*

JOHN & JEAN MITCHELL, 35 MAIN STREET, KESWICK (Tel and Fax: 017687 72790; Home Tel. No: 016973 20220). Luxurious Lakeland flats and cottages located in one of Keswick's most desirable areas. All gas central heating. Some with two bathrooms (one en suite). From £99 weekly.

ALLAN AND VIVIENNE CAIRNS, SWAN HOTEL, THORNTHWAITE, KESWICK CA12 5SQ (017687 78 256). Bed, Breakfast and Evening Meal in quiet country hotel in beautiful surroundings. Keswick 4 miles. Fully licensed. Pets welcome. RAC Merit Award. *[pw! £1.25 per night.]*

MARION AND IAN ROBINSON, THELMLEA COUNTRY GUEST HOUSE, BRAITH-WAITE, KESWICK CA12 5TD (017687 78305). Set in 1¾ acre grounds with private parking and garden area for guests' use. Ideal base for touring/walking. Superb views. Bedrooms have full facilities including tea/coffee, TV & radio alarm. Full central heating, drying facilities. Bed and Breakfast from £15 to £19.50. Reductions weekly bookings. Brochure. *[pw!]*

J. A. GRANGE, LAKELAND COTTAGE HOLIDAYS, KESWICK CA12 5ES (017687 71071; Fax: 017687 75036). Warm, comfortable homes welcoming your dog, in Keswick and beautiful Borrowdale. ETB inspected and quality graded.

Wide choice of self-catering Cottages, Chalets, Apartments and Holiday Home Caravans in and around the Northern Lake District. APPLY – GREY ABBEY PROPERTIES, DEPARTMENT PW, COACH ROAD, WHITEHAVEN CA28 9DF (01946 693346/693364) 24 hours.

Threlkeld village (Keswick 4 miles). Tourist Board 4 Keys Commended. Delightful Bungalows. Sleep 4/6. All amenities, fridge, electric cooker, night storage heaters, colour TV, telephone. Laundry room. Own grounds with ample parking. £153 minimum to £350 maximum. Bargain breaks low season. Children and pets welcome. APPLY – MRS F. WALKER, THE PARK, RICKERBY, CARLISLE CA3 9AA (01228 24848). [🐾pw!]

AYSGARTH, CROSTHWAITE ROAD, KESWICK. Situated on the outskirts of Keswick 10 minutes from town centre. Furnished to high standard with 3 bedrooms sleeping up to 6. Garden and private parking. APPLY: MRS J. HALL, FISHER-GROUND FARM, ESKDALE CA19 1TF (019467 23319). [🐾]

GORDON AND MARIAN TURNBULL, RICKERBY GRANGE, PORTINSCALE, KESWICK CA12 5RH (017687 72344). Delightfully situated in quiet village. Licensed. Imaginative home-cooked food, attractively served. Open almost all year. [Pets £1 per night.]

A traditional 17th-century farmhouse, one acre grounds with lovely garden. Ideal for numerous walks. Good home cooking. Pets and children welcome and catered for. Open all year. 3 Crowns Approved. MURIEL BOND, THORNTHWAITE HALL, THORNTHWAITE, NEAR KESWICK CA12 5SA (Tel. and Fax: 017687 78424). [🐾]

HARNEY PEAK, PORTINSCALE, NR KESWICK. We offer you the best in S/C accommodation in our spacious well equipped apartments in the quiet village of Portinscale. Glorious lake views. Ideal for disabled. [Pets £10 per week.] Apply: MRS J. SMITH, 55 BLYTHWOOD ROAD, PINNER, MIDDLESEX HA5 3QW (0181-429 0402 or 0860 721270).

Kirkby Lonsdale

Small town on River Lune, 14 miles north-east of Lancaster. Of interest – the motte-and-bailey castle, mid-19th century Market House and the 16th century Abbots Hall.

MRS PAT NICHOLSON, GREEN LANE END FARM, LUPTON, KIRKBY LONS-DALE, CARNFORTH LA6 2PP (015395 67236). Bed and Breakfast from £14 per person in 17th-century farmhouse with oak beams, fine old staircase. In peaceful area of Lakeland ideal for touring Lakes and Dales. Pets by arrangement.

Kirkby Stephen near (Mallerstang)

5 miles south on B6259 Kirkby Stephen to Hawes road.

COCKLAKE HOUSE, MALLERSTANG CA17 4JT (017683 72080). Charming, High Pennine Country House B&B in unique position above Pendragon Castle in Upper Mallerstang Dale offering good food and exceptional comfort to a small number of guests. Two double rooms with large private bathrooms. Three acres riverside grounds. Dogs welcome.

Kirkoswald

Village in the Cumbrian hills, lying north west of the Lake District. Ideal for touring. Penrith 7 miles.

SECLUDED COTTAGES AND LEISURE FISHING, KIRKOSWALD CA10 1EU (01768 896275; Fax available). 24 hr brochure line 01768 898711 (manned most Saturdays). Tranquilly secluded quality cottages, guaranteed clean, well equipped and well maintained. Centrally located for Lakes, Pennines, Hadrian's Wall, Borderland. Enjoy the Good Life in comfort. *[Pets £12 per week; reductions for more than 2.]*

Little Langdale

Hamlet 2 miles west of Skelwith Bridge. To west is Little Langdale Tarn, a small lake in course of River Brathay.

HIGHFOLD COTTAGE, LITTLE LANGDALE. A well-equipped cottage, ideally situated for walking and touring. Superb mountain views. Sleeps 5. ETB 3 keys commended. Pets and children welcome. Weekly £175–295. MRS C. E. BLAIR, 8 THE GLEBE, CHAPEL STILE, AMBLESIDE LA22 9JT (015394 37686). *[🐾]*

Lorton

Village 4 miles south east of Cockermouth.

NEW HOUSE FARM, LORTON, COCKERMOUTH CA13 9UU (Tel and Fax: 01900 85404). New House Farm has 15 acres of fields, woods, streams and ponds which guests and dogs can wander around. Comfortable en suite accommodation and fine traditional food. Off season breaks. ETB 3 Crowns Highly Commended. *[🐾 🏠]*

Loweswater

Hamlet at end of Lake Loweswater (owned by National Trust). Beautiful hilly scenery.

LOWESWATER HOLIDAY COTTAGES, LOWESWATER, COCKERMOUTH, CUMBRIA CA13 9UX (01900 85232). Nestling among the magnificent Loweswater/ Buttermere fells, our luxury cottages are available all year. They have open fires, colour TV, central heating, a four poster and gardens. Colour Brochure. *[🐾, 🏠]*

Mungrisdale

Small village ideal for touring. Keswick 8 miles.

NEAR HOWE FARM HOTEL AND COTTAGES, MUNGRISDALE, PENRITH CA11 0SH (Tel or Fax: 017687 79678). Quiet, away from it all. Within easy reach of Lakes walking. Good food. Bar, log fire in cold weather. 5 Bedrooms en suite. B&B from £16. *[Pets – Hotel £1 per day, in Cottages £10 per week.]*

Near Sawrey

This beautiful village on the west side of Windermere has many old cottages set among trees and beautiful gardens with flowers. The world-famous writer Beatrix Potter lived at Hill Top Farm, behind the Tower Bank Arms. When she died in 1943 she left the house and much of the surrounding land to the National Trust. A ferry travels across the Lake to Hawkshead. Hawkshead 2 miles, Far Sawrey ½ mile.

SAWREY HOUSE COUNTRY HOTEL, NEAR SAWREY, HAWKSHEAD LA22 0LF (015394 36387; Fax: 015394 36010). Elegant family-run hotel in three acres of peaceful gardens with magnificent views across Esthwaite Water. Excellent food, warm friendly atmosphere. Lounge, separate bar. Children and pets welcome. 3 Crowns Highly Commended. RAC Highly Acclaimed. *[Pets £2.50 per night.]*

Penrith

Historic market town and centre for touring Lake District. Of particular interest is the ruined Castle (14th cent.), Gloucester Arms (dated 1477) and Tudor House, believed to have been the school attended by Wordsworth. Excellent sporting facilities. Kendal 27 miles, Windermere 27, Carlisle 18, Keswick 18.

MRS MARY TEASDALE, LISCO, TROUTBECK, PENRITH CA11 0SY (017687 79645). Open all year for Bed and Breakfast, optional Evening Meal. Good Home Cooking. All rooms tea/coffee facilities. Lounge, Dining room, TV. Children welcome. Ideally placed for Lake District. Moderate terms. *[pw!]*

SECLUDED COTTAGES AND LEISURE FISHING, KIRKOSWALD, PENRITH CA10 1EU (01768 896275; Fax available). 24 hr brochure line (01768 898711 (manned most Saturdays). Tranquilly secluded quality cottages, guaranteed clean, well equippped and well maintained. Centrally located for Lakes, Pennines, Hadrian's Wall, Borderland. Enjoy the Good Life in comfort. *[Pets £12 per week; reductions for more than 2.]*

MOUNTAIN LODGE HOTEL, ORTON, PENRITH CA10 3SB (015396 24351). AA/RAC*** friendly hotel in glorious hillside setting, midway between Kendal and Penrith, central for walking, ideal for motoring north and south. Conservatory restaurant, bars, 30 comfortable en suite bedrooms. 4 Crowns*[🐾]*

JENNYWELL HALL COTTAGES, CROSBY RAVENSWORTH, NEAR PENRITH CA10 3JP (01931 715288). Eden Valley. Four 18th Century courtyard cottages in picturesque valley. Sleeping 2/5. Children and pets welcome. Write or phone for a colour brochure. *[Pets £8 per week.]*

LOW GARTH GUEST HOUSE, PENRUDDOCK, PENRITH CA11 0QU (017684 83492). Tastefully converted 18th century barn in peaceful surroundings with magnificent views, offering a warm welcome and Aga-cooked meals. En suite facilities. *[🐾]*

LAKE DISTRICT NATIONAL PARK. Miles of breathtaking scenery. 16th century cruck barn conversion. Fully equipped by caring owners. A real treat for your dog. Phone SUE 017684 83859. *[🐾]*

Silloth

Solway Firth resort with harbour and fine sandy beach. Mountain views. Golf, fishing. Penrith 33 miles, Carlisle 23, Cockermouth 17.

MR AND MRS G. E. BOWMAN, TANGLEWOOD CARAVAN PARK, CAUSEWAY HEAD, SILLOTH CA5 4PG (016973 31253). Friendly country site, excellent toilet and laundry facilities. Tourers welcome or hire a luxury caravan. Telephone or send stamp for colour brochure. *[🐾]*

Thornthwaite

Peaceful village, 3 miles north-west of Keswick.

THWAITE HOWE HOTEL, THORNTHWAITE, NEAR KESWICK CA12 5SA (017687 78281). Country hotel in own grounds. All bedrooms en-suite, with colour TV etc. Excellent base for touring. Regret no children under 12. Brochure available. *[pw! Pets £2 per night.]*

Windermere

Famous resort on lake of same name, the largest in England. Magnificent scenery. Car ferry from Bowness, 1 mile distant. Kendal 9 miles.

Many attractive self-catering holiday homes in a variety of good locations, all well equipped and managed by our caring staff. Pets welcome. For brochure, contact: LAKELOVERS, THE TOFFEE LOFT, ASH STREET, WINDERMERE LA23 3RA (015394 88855; Fax: 015394 88857). *[Pets £12.50 per week.]*

JENNIFER WRIGLEY, UPPER OAKMERE, 3 UPPER OAK STREET, WINDERMERE LA23 2LB (015394 45649). Built in traditional Lakeland stone and situated close to park. Warm, clean and very friendly. Single people welcome. Pets preferred to people. B&B £14.50 per person per night, en suite family rooms £15.50; children half price. Dinner optional. *[🐾]*

YORKSHIRE HOUSE, 1 UPPER OAK STREET, WINDERMERE LA23 2LB (015394 44689). A warm Scottish welcome, good food and clean, comfortable rooms. En suite rooms available. Licensed. B&B from £12, DB&B from £21. *[🐾]*

GREENRIGGS GUEST HOUSE, 8 UPPER OAK STREET, WINDERMERE LA23 2LB (015394 42265/45874). Small, family-run guest house situated in a quiet cul de sac close to a park, with easy access to shops, lake and all transport B&B from £15.00. *[🐾, pw!].*

BOWNESS LEISURE LTD, BURNSIDE HOTEL, KENDALE ROAD, BOWNESS-ON-WINDERMERE LA23 3EP (015394 42211). Self catering cottages sleeping six persons and luxurious hotel set in 3 acres of gardens. All residents have full use of all-weather leisure club. Freephone 0800 220688 for bookings.

LOW SPRINGWOOD HOTEL, THORNBARROW ROAD, WINDERMERE LA23 2DF (015394 46383). Fashion and Twiggy (Boxers) and Treacle (Heinz 57) would like to welcome you to their peaceful Hotel in its own secluded gardens. Lovely views of the Lakes and Fells. All rooms en suite with colour TV etc. Some four-posters. Brochure available. ETB 3 Crowns. [pw! 🐾]

KIRKWOOD, PRINCE'S ROAD, WINDERMERE LA23 2DD (015394 43907). A warm friendly atmosphere with individual personal service. En suite rooms with colour TV and tea/coffee making. Hosts pleased to help plan tours and walks. Two Crowns, RAC Highly Acclaimed, AA QQQQ.

APPLEGARTH HOTEL, COLLEGE ROAD, WINDERMERE LA23 1BU (015394 43206). An elegant Victorian mansion house, with individually designed bedrooms and four-poster rooms. All rooms with private facilities, most with Lake and fell views. Lounge bar and car park. Restaurant (please pre-book). Ideally situated for shops, restaurants, walking and touring. Free use of private leisure club. Close to bus and rail stations. ETB 3 Crowns. AA**. [🐾]

DERBYSHIRE

DERBYSHIRE *Ashbourne, Buxton*

DERBYSHIRE *Buxton*

THORN HEYES PRIVATE HOTEL
137 London Road, Buxton SK17 9NH

A former gentleman's residence of 1860, owner managed and retained as close to the original as possible, this small detached hotel offers seven en suite bedrooms; colour TV, hairdryers, trouser press and tea/coffee making facilities. Full choice breakfast available including the energy-packed Derbyshire Grill. Every assistance given on where to eat for evening meals. Pets welcome, open countryside opposite. Also three self catering apartments. **Tel: 01298 23539**

THE CHARLES COTTON HOTEL
Hartington, Near Buxton SK17 0AL

The Charles Cotton is a small, comfortable hotel with a starred rating for the AA and RAC. The hotel lies in the heart of the Derbyshire Dales, pleasantly situated in the village square of Hartington, with nearby shops catering for all needs. It is renowned throughout the area for its hospitality and good home cooking. Pets and children are welcome; special diets catered for. The Charles Cotton makes the perfect centre to relax and explore the area, whether walking, cycling, brass-rubbing, pony trekking or even hang gliding.
TEL: 01298 84229

PRIORY LEA HOLIDAY FLATS

Beautiful situation adjoining woodland walks and own meadows. Cleanliness assured; comfortably furnished and well equipped. Colour TV. Bed linen available. Sleep 2/8. Ample private parking. Close to Poole's Cavern Country Park. Brochure available from resident owner. Open all year. 1996 terms from £75 to £190. Short Breaks available. ⌀⌀ / ⌀⌀⌀ Keys Approved.

Mrs. Gill Taylor, 50 White Knowle Road, Buxton SK17 9NH. Tel: (01298) 23737 or 71661

WELCOME COTTAGE HOLIDAYS. Hundreds of properties in wonderful locations at welcoming low prices. Pets, linen and fuel mostly included. For FREE colour brochure telephone 01756 702215.

Ashbourne

Market town on River Henmore, close to its junction with River Dove. Several interesting old buildings. Birmingham 42 miles, Sheffield 34, Nottingham 29, Stafford 26, Buxton 21, Burton-on-Trent 19, Derby 13.

TONY & LINDA STODDART, CORNPARK COTTAGE, UPPER MAYFIELD, NEAR ASHBOURNE DE6 2HR (01335 345041). Self-catering barn conversion set by pond surrounded by fields. Ideal walking for pets. Sleeps 2–5. Close to all Peak District beauty spots. Open March–November. Telephone for brochure. *[⌑]*

MRS M. A. RICHARDSON, THROWLEY HALL FARM, ILAM, ASHBOURNE DE6 2BB (01538 308202/308243). Self-catering accommodation in Farmhouse for up to 12 and cottage for seven people. Also Bed and Breakfast in Farmhouse. Central heating, washbasins, tea/coffee facilities in rooms. Children and pets welcome. Near Alton Towers and Stately Homes. Tourist Board 2 Crowns/4 Keys Commended.

MRS A. M. WHITTLE, STONE COTTAGE, GREEN LANE, CLIFTON, ASHBOURNE, DERBYSHIRE DE6 2BL (01335 343377). Charming 19th Century cottage near quiet village of Clifton. Ideal touring base. Reductions for children under 10. Bed and Breakfast from £16.00. Pets by arrangement.

MRS M. M. STELFOX, DOG AND PARTRIDGE, SWINSCOE, ASHBOURNE DE6 2HS (01335 343183). 17th century inn offering ideal holiday accommodation. Many leisure activities available. All bedrooms with washbasins, colour TV, telephone and private facilities. *[pw!]*

DERBYSHIRE COTTAGES. In the grounds of a 17th century Inn, close to Peak District, Alton Towers and Ashbourne. Each has own patio, fully fitted kitchen, colour TV. Children and pets welcome. Phone MARY (01335 300202) for further details.

BERESFORD ARMS HOTEL, STATION ROAD, ASHBOURNE DE6 1AA (01335 300035; Fax: 01335 300065). Situated in the centre of Ashbourne and offering a warm welcome, especially to pets and children. It makes a perfect starting point to explore the area or visit Alton Towers. 3 Crowns. *[⌑]*

Bakewell

Old market town on River Wye 7 miles north-west of Matlock. Saxon cross in churchyard.

WHEEL COTTAGE, FENNEL STREET, ASHFORD-IN-THE-WATER, NEAR BAKEWELL DE45 1QH (01629 814339). Two double and one single rooms with colour TV and tea/coffee making facilities. Special diets catered for. Bed and Breakfast from £13. Evening Meal by arrangement. Open all year.

Buxton

Well-known spa and centre for the Peak District. Beautiful scenery. Good sporting amenities and entertainments. Leeds 50 miles, Stafford 37, Derby 34, Sheffield 28, Stoke-on-Trent 24, Matlock 20, Macclesfield 12.

BUXTON VIEW, 74 CORBAR ROAD, BUXTON SK17 6RJ (Tel and Fax: 01298 79222). Attractive house very near moors and 10 minutes from town centre. En suite rooms. Bed and Breakfast from £16 pppn; Evening Meal available. Pets very welcome. 3 Crowns Commended, AA QQQ Recommended.

CANDLEMAS COTTAGE, DAMSIDE LANE, PEAK FOREST, BUXTON SK17 8EH. Secluded Bed and Breakfast accommodation in the central Peak District – great for walks and drives. TV, and tea making facilities in bedrooms; lounge; terrace; sheltered garden. Excellent evening meals 250 yards. PHIL KNELLOR (01298 24853). *[pw! 50p to £1 per night.]*

THORN HEYES PRIVATE HOTEL, 137 LONDON ROAD, BUXTON SK17 9NH (01298 23539). This former gentleman's residence of 1860 offers seven en suite bedrooms with colour TV, hairdryers and tea/coffee making facilities. Full choice breakfast. Self catering available. Pets welcome.

PRIORY LEA HOLIDAY FLATS. Close to Poole's Cavern Country Park. Fully equipped. Sleep 2/8. Cleanliness assured. Terms £75–£190. Open all year. Short Breaks available. 2–3 Keys Approved. MRS GILL TAYLOR, 50 WHITE KNOWLE ROAD, BUXTON SK17 9NH (01298 23737/71661). *[Pets £1 per night.]*

MRS LYNNE P. FEARNS, HEATH FARM, SMALLDALE, BUXTON SK17 8EB (01298 24431). Farm in Peak District, 4½ miles from Buxton. Quiet location. Many activities locally. Cot and babysitting available. Car essential. Bed and Breakfast from £14.50, reductions children and weekly stays.

THE CHARLES COTTON HOTEL, HARTINGTON, NEAR BUXTON SK17 0AL (01298 84229). Small hotel, AA & RAC star rated. Good home cooking and hospitality. In heart of Derbyshire Dales. Special diets catered for. Ideal for relaxing walking, cycling, hang gliding.

Matlock

Inland resort and spa in the Derwent Valley. Chesterfield 9 miles.

TUCKERS GUEST HOUSE, 48 DALE ROAD, MATLOCK DE4 3NB (01629 583018). Victorian home in central but secluded position. Spacious, well-equipped, cosy rooms. Wonderful scenery and walks; lots to see and do. Pets welcome to stay in rooms. Bed and English/Vegetarian Breakfast £16–£17. Evening Meals by arrangement. Open all year. *[pw!* 🐾*]*

DERBYSHIRE

MRS G. PARKINSON, DIMPLE HOUSE, DIMPLE ROAD, MATLOCK DE4 3JX (01629 583228). 19th Century house close to Matlock. Large garden. Ideal for visiting Chatsworth and Peak Park. TV and teamaking in all rooms. EMTB Listed/Approved. B&B from £15. [🐶]

LANE END HOUSE, GREEN LANE, TANSLEY DE4 5FJ (01629 583981). A non-smoking Georgian farmhouse close to Chatsworth and Haddon. Lovingly refurbished by caring owners who serve delicious food at yesterday's prices. Walk in nearby fields or explore the wonderful countryside that surrounds us. EMTB 2 Crowns Highly Commended, AA Selected QQQQ Award and "Staying off the Beaten Track". [🐶].

Winster

Charming village 4 miles west of Matlock steeped in history.

MRS D. MACBAIN, BRAE COTTAGE, EAST BANK, WINSTER DE4 2DT (01629 650375). Spacious, B&B detached cottage annexe. En-suite, TV, tea/coffee facilities. Breakfast area. Garage. Patio. Picturesque Peak village. Double/Twin, Family. £14 per person. 1 Crown Commended. [🐶pw!]

DEVON

DEVON

93

DEVON *Appledore*

94

DEVON *Berrynarbor*

PETS STAY FREE

Sandy Cove Hotel stands in 20 acres of cliff, coast and garden. The hotel restaurant overlooks the sea and cliffs with spectacular views of the bay. You will probably wonder how we can do it for the price when we offer a FIVE COURSE MEAL including sea food platters with lobster, smoked salmon and steak. Every Saturday a Swedish Smorgasbord and Carvery carved by the chef and followed by dancing 'till late. Live entertainment weekly from Whitsun until September. All bedrooms have colour TV, telephone, teamaking and are en suite. The cocktail bar overlooks the bay and you have the use of the hotel's 80°F heated indoor pool and recreation centre with sauna, sunbed, gym equipment and whirlpool, ALL FREE OF CHARGE.

Please return this advertisement to qualify for 'Pets stay free' offer. Bargain Breaks and weekly rates available all year.

Including 5 course evening meal and coffee. Children – free accommodation. Please send for free brochure pack. Children under 8 years old completely free, inc. meals.

Sandy Cove Hotel,
**Combe Martin Bay,
Devon EX34 9SR
Tel: (01271) 882243 & 882888**

Indoor pool heated to 80°F with rolling back sides to enjoy the sun.

98

DEVON *Bucks Mills, Budleigh Salterton, Chittlehamholt, Combe Martin*

Rosemary & Ray Newport **THE OLD MILL, Bucks Mills, Bideford, North Devon EX39 5DY (Tel: 01237 431701).** Comfortable 17th century cottage/tea rooms. Warm and friendly atmosphere, good home cooking, log fires. Situated in quiet coastal village, with beach and woodland walks. Open all year round.

TIDWELL HOUSE COUNTRY HOTEL
Knowle, Budleigh Salterton EX9 7AG *Telephone Chris on* **01395 442444**
A peaceful haven one mile from sea. With its friendly atmosphere, guests feel at home in this lovely Georgian house. You can relax and enjoy the wonderful home-cooked food knowing that your pets are genuinely welcome. With 3 acres of gardens and large en suite rooms there is plenty of space. We have a TV lounge, Cellar Bar with darts, bar bowls etc, and a car park. Open all year.

SNAPDOWN FARM CARAVANS
Chittlehamholt, Umberleigh, North Devon EX37 9PF (01769) 540708
12 ONLY-6 berth CARAVANS in two sheltered paddocks. Flush toilets, showers; colour TVs, fridges; gas cookers and fires. Laundry room. Outside seats and picnic tables in peaceful unspoilt countryside; site sheltered by trees, lots of space, well away from busy roads. Field and woodland walks. No commercialisation. Sea and Moors within easy reach. Well behaved pets welcome. Terms (two types) £70–£195 and £75–£210 inc. gas and electricity in caravans.

Rone House Hotel
AA★★

KING STREET, COMBE MARTIN, N. DEVON EX34 0AD
Telephone: 01271 883428
Props: Graham and Elspeth Cottage
A small comfortable Hotel with the personal touch, set in the centre of Combe Martin village, within walking distance of the sea. Ideal resting spot for touring, rambling and family holidays with a happy and relaxed atmosphere.

* Colour TV in all bedrooms
* Welcome bar
* Good traditional English cooking
* Full central heating
* Private facilities in most bedrooms
* Children and pets welcome
* Tea/coffee making facilities
* Large private car park
* Reduced rates Special Short Breaks
* Family run Hotel
* Heated swimming pool

Miramar Hotel
COMBE MARTIN
NORTH DEVON EX34 0JS
Telephone Mike and Pam
on (01271) 883558
Friendly family Hotel on the edge of Exmoor and coast. Heated outdoor pool in secluded setting. Magnificent views. Reductions for children sharing. Residents' Bar. Some en-suite bedrooms.
● Central heating ● Car park
● Games Room ● Open all year.

FHG PUBLICATIONS LIMITED publish a large range of well-known accommodation guides. We will be happy to send you details or you can use the order form at the back of this book.

 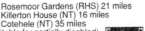

SYMBOLS

🐾	Indicates no charge for pets.
£	Indicates a charge for pets: nightly or weekly.
pw!	Indicates some special provision for pets: exercise, feeding etc.
🏠	Indicates separate pets accommodation.

Peaceful woodland setting next to the River Walkham in the Dartmoor National Park. Ideally placed to explore the beauty of Devon. Purpose-built lodges available all year round, sleeping 2-7, tastefullly blending into the surroundings. Interior specification and furnishings to a very high standard – including fully-fitted kitchen with oven, hob, microwave and dishwasher.

- 2 golf courses a short drive away.
- Easy walk to village and shops. • Scenic walks.
- Fishing. • Dogs accepted. • Horseriding nearby.
- Small, select touring area for caravans, tents and motor caravans. • Launderette. • New modern toilet block with washing-up facilities.
- On A386 Plymouth–Tavistock road.

Free brochure: Dept PW, Dartmoor Country Holidays, Magpie Leisure Park, Horrabridge, Yelverton, Devon PL20 7RY. Tel: 01822 852651

MAGPIE LEISURE PARK

A warm family **WELCOME** *is here for you!*

One of the finest choices for your holiday in South Devon, *Welcome Family* offers all the facilities and atmosphere of a large holiday centre, but with the friendly, personal service of a small park. Situated in a very picturesque part of South Devon, only a short level walk to the famous safe sandy dunes and wildlife areas. Only 15 minutes from the M5, a half hour drive from a host of attractions, including Dartmoor, Torbay or Exeter.

WELCOME FAMILY HOLIDAY PARK
DAWLISH WARREN SOUTH DEVON EX7 0PH
Reservations 01626 862070 — Dial a Brochure 01626 888323

- Stylish **DOLPHIN CLUB** & Entertainment Centre
- Super Indoor Heated **NEPTUNE TROPICANA** Water Leisure Complex – four Feature-packed Pools, Solarium, Sauna, spectator viewing.
- **CRUISERS** adult Cocktail bar
- Children's **JOLLY ROGER** Club with Disco, Cinema & large Games arcade
- Short, level walk to safe sandy beach
- Great *Value - for - money* prices
- **FREE** Electricity, Linen, Colour TV
- Welcome T.V. – great films, local attractions, and more
- 2 Shops   Cafe
- 2 Takeaways
- Crazy Golf
- Adventure Playground
- Laundrette
- Hire Service with computer games
- Pets *Welcome* (at small charge)
- Choose from economy 4-berth to luxury 8-berth caravans.

WEST LYN FARM   *Self Catering*

Secluded working sheep/beef farm overlooking Lynmouth Bay and Bristol Channel.
Farmhouse sleeps 8/9; Cottage sleeps 4. Peaceful surroundings, scenic walks: adjoining
Coastal Path and National Trust woodlands.

For brochure and tariff tel: **01598 753618**

Hedley Wood Caravan & Camping Park
Bridgerule, Holsworthy, Devon EX22 7ED
Tel & Fax 01288 381404

16 acre woodland family-run site with outstanding views, where
you can enjoy a totally relaxing holiday with a 'laid-back'
atmosphere, sheltered & open camping areas. Just 10 minutes'
drive from the beaches, golf courses, riding stables & shops.
On-Site facilities include: Children's adventure areas, Bar,
Clubroom, Shop, Laundry, Meals and all amenities. Free Hot showers and water. Nice
dogs/pets **are** welcome. Daily kennelling facility. Dog walks/Nature trail. Clay pigeon
shoot. Static caravans for hire, **caravan storage** available.
Open all year.   RAC   AA▷

The Belfry Country Hotel

Yarcombe, Near Honiton, East Devon EX14 9BD

Victorian village school converted to small luxury
Hotel. Beautifully appointed en suite rooms. Lovely
views over Blackdown Hills and Yarty Valley. Cosy
Bar/Restaurant serving AA Rosette-awarded
scrumptious home cooking. Log fire, comfy lounge. Ideal
walking and touring area. Free entry to Classic Gardens.

Phone 01404 861234 or Fax 01404 861579 for brochure and information
AA** 74% Rosette   ETB ♚ ♚ ♚ ♚ Commended

Lower Luxton Farm, Upottery, Honiton, Devon EX14 9PB

Get away from the toil of everyday life at Lower Luxton Farm, where a
warm welcome awaits you in an area of outstanding natural beauty.
Peaceful walks; ideal base for touring. Carp fishing. Good home cooking
using fresh farm produce. Reductions early and late season. Pets
welcome. *Weekly terms from £105, 6 Dinners and Bed and Breakfast.*

SAE for brochure and terms Mrs Elizabeth Tucker Tel: 01823 601269

HOPE COVE: HOPE BEACH HOUSE

Seven luxury two and three-bedroomed Apartments, set 50 yards from safe sandy beach (Seaside
Award Winner 1994), in old-world fishing village nestling under Bolt Tail National Trust headland.
All apartments furnished and equipped to a very high standard. Night storage heating, electric fires in
all rooms. Colour TV, kitchen with electric cooker, microwave, fridge/freezer, dishwasher, washing
machine, dryer etc. Linen and towels supplied FREE. Magnificent coastal walks with golf at nearby
Bigbury and Thurlestone. Open all year. Children and pets welcome.

ETB ♪ ♪ ♪ ♪ Commended. Full details from:
Mr and Mrs P. G. Pedrick, Hope Beach House, Hope Cove,
Nr. Kingsbridge, S. Devon TQ7 3HH
Tel: 01548 560151

St. Brannocks House Hotel
St. Brannocks Road, Ilfracombe EX34 8EQ

RAC Acclaimed   ETB

A friendly Hotel offering good food, relaxing atmosphere and service with a smile. Stay one night or as long as you like. Licensed Bar. Large car park. Some rooms en-suite, all with TV and tea making. Children and pets welcome.

OPEN ALL YEAR
INCLUDING
CHRISTMAS

**Short breaks from £46 for 2 nights DB & B
7 nights DB & B £150–£185
TEL: (01271) 863873**

The Darnley Hotel
Proprietors: Val Marston & Reg Jenner
**BELMONT ROAD, ILFRACOMBE, DEVON EX34 8DR
TEL: (01271) 863955**

Enjoy a holiday in the tranquil setting of The Darnley Hotel. Quietly situated at the foot of the famous Torrs and coastal walks yet only 5 minutes' walk from the main shopping area and sea front. Friendly personal service and good food. All rooms have central heating, coffee/tea making facilities and colour TV. En suite rooms available. Ample parking, garden, TV lounge and bar. Pets welcome. Open all year including Christmas.

CAIRN HOUSE HOTEL (01271) 863911 RAC*

Set in own grounds. Noted for good food and personal service. All 10 rooms en suite, colour TV, tea-makers. Bar. Car Park. Adjacent to plenty of dog walking areas. Bed and Breakfast from £18 incl; with Dinner £28 per person per day. ❤ ❤ ❤ Approved
ST. BRANNOCKS ROAD, ILFRACOMBE, DEVON EX34 8EH

TIDES' REACH COTTAGE
Instow – Sleeps 6 + cot

Ideal for traditional family beach holidays, Instow offers estuary sailing, fishing and walking all year round; the Coastal Footpath goes right through the village, and both Tarka Country and Exmoor are easily reached. With gas central heating the cottages (which are open all year) are warm and cosy for autumn or spring breaks. Photograph shows view from the main bedroom of Tides' Reach , one of the three comfortable cottages we have in Instow. All are close to the long sandy beach, and have two or three bedrooms, well fitted kitchens (with washing machines, fridge/freezers etc.), fitted carpets and colour TVs. Please send stamp or SAE for colour brochure.

Mr P.W. Baxter, Huish Moor Farm, Instow, Bideford, North Devon EX39 4LT (01272 861146)

FREE and REDUCED RATE Holiday Visits!
Don't miss our Readers' Offer Vouchers on
pages 5 to 18.

DEVON *Kingsbridge*

WOODLAND VIEW
GUEST HOUSE
Stokenham, Kingsbridge, S. Devon TQ7 2SQ
Tel: (01548) 580542

 COMMENDED

Set in picturesque village one mile from the sea and a short distance from many beaches. Superb country and coastal walks. Comfortable rooms, some on the ground floor, also en suite. Tea/coffee making facilities. Licensed. **As animal lovers we hope you will bring your pets and enjoy our hospitality.** No guard dogs. Children welcome.
Telephone or send SAE for our brochure to Ann & John Cadman

CHALLABOROUGH BAY, KINGSBRIDGE,
SOUTH DEVON TQ7 4JB
TEL: KINGSBRIDGE (01548) 810089

Delightful cedarwood chalets just 250 yards from a safe, sandy beach. Gardens and children's play areas on peaceful 2½ acre site. Experience stunning cliff walks on South Devon's Heritage Coast. A haven for surfing, windsurfing and diving enthusiasts. Heated pool and golf nearby.
Dartmoor National Park 30 mins.
Pets welcome. Colour brochure available.
Contact NICKY FAULKNER for details.

ETB 3 KEYS APPROVED

JOURNEY'S END INN
Ringmore, Near Kingsbridge TQ7 4HL

Historic inn set in a beautiful and unspoilt thatched village amidst rolling South Hams countryside. An extensive and inviting food menu is served in the oak-panelled bar and dining room, complemented by a wide range of real ales. The comfortable bedrooms are en suite and have colour TV. Golf, fishing, coves and beaches, and places of interest are within easy reach. Open all year except Christmas.

Tel: 01548 810205

HALLSANDS HOTEL, North Hallsands, Kingsbridge, Devon
Tel: Chivelstone (01548) 511264
 Family hotel on the sea edge. Children and doggie terms.
Bed, Breakfast and Evening Meal. Fully licensed. Good food.
Fishing and bathing. Compressed air available.

Readers are requested to mention this guidebook when seeking accommodation (and please enclose a stamped addressed envelope).

110

PETS STAY FREE

Your pets are welcome to stay free if you return this advert with your booking.

👑 👑 👑

The Exmoor Sandpiper Inn

A fine old coaching Inn, reputedly dating in part from the 13th and 15th centuries. It is in a beautiful setting amidst rolling moors, high above Lynmouth on the coastal road with the dramatic backdrop of Exmoor. Let us spoil you on arrival with a **free cream tea** and then be shown up to a beautiful character bedroom with teamaking, colour TV and bathroom en suite, designed for your every comfort. A warm bath then a 5-course dinner including smoked salmon, seafood platters with lobster, steaks and a delicious selection of sweets. Sit in the character bars and sample our real ales or watch the late film in your bedroom.

After a traditional English breakfast set off to discover the magic of Exmoor whether in the car or on foot, along Doone Valley following the River to the majestic Watersmeet, or further to the Valley of Rocks and up over to Glenthorne and beyond to the Devon/Somerset Borders.

We have 7 circular walks around the area and the Inn can provide a packed lunch.

Please write or ring for FREE colour brochure to:-

The Exmoor Sandpiper Inn, Countisbury, Lynmouth, N. Devon EX35 6NE Tel: (01598) 741263

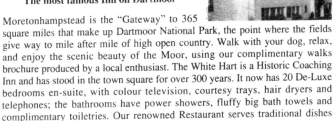

DEVON

ROSELANDS HOLIDAY CHALETS
Totnes Road, Ipplepen, Newton Abbot, Devon TQ12 5TD Tel: 01803 812701

Three detached, completely self contained chalets situated within a peaceful garden and within easy reach of South Devon amenities. Near golf course. Accommodation for 3/5 people.
PETS MOST WELCOME. Safe parking.

Fox and Hounds Hotel
Bridestowe, Okehampton EX20 4HF
Tel: 01822 820206

ON THE EDGE OF THE MOOR
Fully Licensed Free House – Open all day
Central for touring Devon and Cornwall, only 45 mins drive from either coast. Family-run hotel, specialising in home cooking, using fresh vegetables as often as possible. Rooms are centrally heated and en suite. Full bar snack menu. A la carte restaurant menu served lunchtime and evening. Games room with pool, bar billiards, darts, games machines and full-length skittle alley. Beer garden and children's play area. Ideal for pets – large field at rear; garage with kennels. Bunkhouse accommodation and Caravan and Camping site. *Please phone for further details.*

FLUXTON FARM HOTEL

Ottery St Mary, Devon
EX11 1RJ
Tel: 01404 812818

LICENSED

AA Listed; ETB ♛ ♛ ♛

Cat lovers' paradise in charming 16th century farmhouse set in lovely Otter Valley. Two acres of beautiful gardens with trout pond and stream. Garden railway. Putting green. Five miles from beach at Sidmouth. Enjoy fresh local produce, superbly cooked in the beamed candle-lit dining room. Log fires. All double rooms en suite, TV and Teasmaids. Central heating, two colour TV lounges, one non-smoking. Peace and quiet; all modern conveniences. Pets welcome free of charge. Plenty of dog-walking space. The cats will welcome your dogs; we welcome you. Brochure available.

Dinner, Bed and Breakfast from £210 per person per week.
SAE please to Anne and Maurice Forth.

SYMBOLS
🐕 Indicates no charge for pets.
£ Indicates a charge for pets: nightly or weekly.
pw! Indicates some special provision for pets: exercise, feeding etc.
🏠 Indicates separate pets accommodation.

Readers are requested to mention this guidebook when seeking accommodation (and please enclose a stamped addressed envelope).

HETB Four Keys Highly Commended
Charming character cottage and barn conversion for 4/6 persons. Both provide every facility for comfort and convenience. TV, dishwasher, microwave, linen. Delightful quiet village, six miles from Torquay and Teignmouth; ideal base whether touring/walking or just resting.
Beaches two miles; moors 20 miles.
Mrs J. A. Rees, "Congdons", Stoke-in-Teignmouth, Newton Abbot
Tel: 01626 872433/872505

AA**   🏵🏵🏵 **COMMENDED**
Small Victorian Country House Hotel in 5 acres of gardens and paddocks, with direct access onto Dartmoor. All rooms en suite, with TV etc.
Excellent menu changed daily, plus vegetarian menu. Children and pets welcome. Riding, fishing, golf nearby. Personal attention at all times from resident proprietors.

Moorland Hall Hotel
Brentor Road, Mary Tavy,
Nr Tavistock, Devon PL19 9PY

Tel: 01822 810466

Mrs P. G. C. Quinton,
Higher Quither, Milton Abbot, Tavistock, Devon
Edge of Dartmoor
Modern self-contained, very comfortable open-plan barn conversion. Own garden. TERMS from £195 per week, inc. linen, coal and logs.
Children and pets welcome. Tel: 01822 860284

Springfield Holiday Park
Tedburn Road, Tedburn St Mary, Exeter EX6 6EW
In a superb 9 acre setting; Exeter 5 miles, Dartmoor 3 miles. * Heated swimming pool * Licensed shop
* Launderette * Children's play area * Pets welcome.
LUXURY STATIC CARAVANS FOR HIRE: CARAVANS, MOTOR HOMES, TENTS WELCOME.
ETB ✓✓✓✓   *AA Campsite of the Year 1993/4 (S.W. Region)*   **TEL: 01647 24242**

LYME BAY HOUSE HOTEL
Den Promenade, Teignmouth, South Devon TQ14 8SZ Tel: 01626 772953
On the level sea front within sight of station. Quiet atmosphere. Licensed. Comfortable rooms. Pleasing outlook across Lyme Bay. En suite rooms available.
Lift. No steps.

A warm welcome awaits you at Silver Birches, a comfortable bungalow on the edge of Dartmoor. Good centre for birdwatching, forest walks, golf, riding; free salmon/trout fishing nearby for residents. Three twin/double bedrooms, all with own bath/shower, toilet. Guest lounge with TV, dining room, sun lounge. Bed and Full English Breakfast from £22 nightly.
Silver Birches, Teign Valley, Trusham, Newton Abbot, Devon TQ13 0NJ   **Tel: 01626 852172**

SYMBOLS
🐾   Indicates no charge for pets.
£   Indicates a charge for pets: nightly or weekly.
pw!   Indicates some special provision for pets: exercise, feeding etc.
🏠   Indicates separate pets accommodation.

DEVON   *Woolacombe*

LITTLE BEACH HOTEL

AA** RAC

Elegant, spacious and friendly family-run hotel. Superb seafront location with magnificent views of sea and countryside. Early season bargain breaks. AA Red Rosette for Food. RAC Merit Award for Hospitality and Service.

The Esplanade, Woolacombe,
Devon EX34 7DJ
Tel: 01271 870398

ETB ♛ ♛ ♛ Highly Commended.
An Ashley Courtenay
Highly Recommended Hotel.

WEST COUNTRY COTTAGES. From Land's End to the New Forest, from South Hams to the Cotswolds. ETB Graded and Commended cottages; video available. For free brochure apply: WEST COUNTRY COTTAGES, THE GEMINDS (PW), ABBOTSKERSWELL, DEVON TQ12 5PP (01626 333679). *[£9 per pet per week.]*

POWELLS COTTAGE HOLIDAYS. Your choice of Cottage in Cornwall, Devon, Somerset, Avon, Cotswolds, Wye Valley, Gower and Pembrokeshire in our full colour brochure. *[Pets £10 per week.]* FREEPHONE 0800 378771 or apply: 61 High Street, Saundersfoot, Pembrokeshire SA69 9EJ or (24 hrs) 01834 813232.

WELCOME COTTAGE HOLIDAYS. Hundreds of properties in wonderful locations at welcoming low prices. Pets, linen and fuel mostly included. For FREE colour brochure telephone 01756 702203.

TOAD HALL COTTAGES. 100 outstanding waterside and rural properties in truly beautiful locations in Devon. Call for our highly acclaimed brochure. Video also available **TEL: 01548 853089.**

CLASSIC COTTAGES (25), HELSTON, CORNWALL TR13 8NA (24-HOUR DIAL-A-BROCHURE 01326 565555). Choose your cottage from 300 of the finest coastal country cottages throughout the West Country. *[Pets £9 weekly.]*

Appledore

Unspoilt resort and small port on estuaries of Taw and Torridge. Sandy beach, good bathing. Bideford 3 miles.

OTTER COTTAGE. Traditional fisherman's cottage. Totally equipped – 2 TVs, VCR, microwave, autowasher etc. Also unique harbourside apartments and bungalow. Brochure from B. H. SMITH, 26 MARKET STREET, APPLEDORE EX39 1PP (01237 476154). *[Pets £8 per week.]*

SEA BIRDS, pretty Georgian cottage facing directly out to the open sea. Spacious cottage with large lounge, colour TV, dining room, modern fitted kitchen and 3 double bedrooms. Other cottages available. SAE to P. S. BARNES, BOAT HYDE, NORTHAM, BIDEFORD, DEVON EX39 1NX (01237 473801). *[pw! Dog £5 per week.]*

DEVON

MARINERS COTTAGE, IRSHA STREET, APPLEDORE. Elizabethan fisherman's Cottage at sea edge. Extensive views of sea and boats. Enclosed garden. Sleeps 6: three bedrooms, lounge, dining room, children's play house. Good fishing, coastal walks. SAE please to MRS P. A. BARNES, BOAT HYDE, NORTHAM, BIDEFORD EX39 1NX or phone 01237 473801 for prices and vacancies. *[Dog £5 per week.]*

Ashburton

Delightful little town on southern fringe of Dartmoor. Centrally placed for touring and the Torbay resorts. Plymouth 24 miles, Exeter 20, Kingsbridge 20, Tavistock 20, Teignmouth 14, Torquay 14, Totnes 8, Newton Abbot 7.

PARKERS FARM HOLIDAYS, HIGHER MEAD FARM, ASHBURTON, NEWTON ABBOT TQ13 7LJ (01364 652598). Farm Cottages and Caravans to let, also level touring site with toilet/shower block and electric hook-ups. Central for touring; 12 miles Torquay. Pets welcome.

MRS A. BELL, WOODER MANOR, WIDECOMBE-IN-THE-MOOR, NEAR ASHBURTON TQ13 7TR (01364 621391). Cottages on family farm. Surrounded by unspoilt woodland and moors. Clean and well equipped, colour TV, central heating, laundry room. One property suitable for disabled visitors. Brochure available. 4 Keys Commended. *[Pets £10 per week.]*

Aveton Gifford

Village on River Avon, 3 miles from lovely Bigbury Bay. Good fishing. Salcombe 8 miles, Kingsbridge 4.

MISS E. M. BALKWILL, LITTLECOURT, AVETON GIFFORD, KINGSBRIDGE TQ7 4LE (01548 5509362). Guest House, opposite family farm, 3 miles from sea. Television lounge. Car space. Dogs welcome. Tea making facilities.

Axminster

Agricultural town in the Axe river valley, famous for carpets. Cattle and street market.

LILAC COTTAGE. A beautifully renovated cottage. Oil-fired central heating. All electric kitchen. Inglenook fireplace; beamed ceiling. Sleeps six plus cot. Colour TV. Garden. Garage. SAE please. APPLY – MRS J. M. STUART, HUNSCOTE HOUSE, WELLESBOURNE, WARWICKSHIRE CV35 9EX (Tel/Fax: 01789 840228) or Mrs Young (01769 573788). *[Pets £5 per week.]*

Aylesbeare

Quiet village set in beautiful countryside within easy reach of M5 motorway. Exeter and south-east Devon resorts. Exeter 8 miles, Sidmouth 8, Ottery St Mary 5.

MRS H. BALE, GREAT HOUNDBEARE FARM, AYLESBEARE, EXETER EX5 2DB (01404 822771). In the heart of the countryside yet only minutes from Exeter, M5 and coast. B&B: all rooms en suite, colour TV, tea/coffee; or self-catering: cottage sleeps up to 14. Secure stabling/grazing and kennels if required.

Barnstaple

The largest town in Devon, once an important centre for the wool trade, now a lively shopping centre with thrice weekly market, modern leisure centre etc.

COASTAL EXMOOR HIDEAWAYS. House with indoor pool and jacuzzi; house on beach; riverside cottages in 80-acre valley; plus many more properties. Dogs welcome. Breaks from £98. TELEPHONE 01598 763339. *[pw!]*

BEACH AND BRACKEN EXMOOR HOLIDAYS, BRATTON FLEMING, BARNSTAPLE EX31 4TJ (01598 710702). Comfortable self-catering cottages; farmhouse accommodation with food. Short notice all-season breaks. Telephone anytime.

NORTH DEVON HOLIDAY HOMES, 19 CROSS STREET, BARNSTAPLE EX31 1BD (01271 76322 24 hours). Send for guide to 500 of best value Cottages around Devon's National Trust coast. All regularly inspected and guaranteed to offer first class value. *[Pets £10 per week.]*

MRS C. M. WRIGHT, FRIENDSHIP FARM, BRATTON FLEMING, BARNSTAPLE EX31 4SQ (01598 763291 evenings). Comfortable three-bedroom Bungalow, sleeps 6 plus cot. Linen provided. Situated on edge of Exmoor, near coast (Combe Martin). From £100 Low Season, £220 High Season. *[🐾pw!]*

MRS V. M. CHUGG, VALLEY VIEW, MARWOOD, BARNSTAPLE EX31 4EA (01271 43458). Bungalow on 300 acre farm. Bed and Breakfast accommodation. Near Marwood Hill Gardens and Arlington Court. Children most welcome, free baby-sitting. Dogs by arrangement. Terms from £12. *[pw!]*

Berrynarbor

This peaceful village overlooking the beautiful Sterridge valley, has a C17th pub and even older church and is a half-mile from the coast road between Combe Martin (1½ miles) and Ilfracombe (3 miles).

Detached 18th century cottage overlooking this pretty village with "dog welcoming" pub. Near coast and Exmoor. Four bedrooms (two en suite), central heating, log fire, electric blankets, garden. Enquire for Short Breaks discount. From £195 (for two) Low Season, to £575 (for seven) High Season. ETB 5 Keys Commended. (One pet £15 per week, £25 for two.) NUT COTTAGE – MRS PAM PARKE, NUT COTTAGE, HAGGINTON HILL, BERRYNARBOR, NEAR ILFRACOMBE EX34 9SB (Tel/Fax: 01271 883758).

SANDY COVE HOTEL, BERRYNARBOR EX34 9SR (01271 882243 or 882888). Hotel set amidst acres of gardens and woods. Heated swimming pool. Children and pets welcome. A la carte restaurant. All rooms en-suite with colour TV, tea-making. Free colour brochure on application. *[🐾]*

Bigbury-on-Sea

A scattered village overlooking superb coastal scenery and wide expanses of sand.

MR SCARTERFIELD, HENLEY HOTEL, FOLLY HILL, BIGBURY-ON-SEA TQ7 4AR (01548 810240). Edwardian cottage-style hotel, spectacular sea views. Near good beach, dog walking. En-suite rooms with telephone, tea making, TV etc. Home cooking. No smoking establishment. Licensed. 3 Crowns Commended. AA 1 Star. *[Pets £1.00 per night.]*

PAT CHADWICK, "MARINERS", RINGMORE DRIVE, BIGBURY-ON-SEA, KINGS-BRIDGE TQ7 4AU (01548 810454). 2 large flats with extensive sea views. Sandy beaches within yards. Golf nearby. Dogs welcome. [🐕]

Bondleigh

Small, sleepy hamlet on the River Taw in mid-Devon.

CROSS PARK COTTAGE, BONDLEIGH. Picturesque thatched 16th century cottage with beautiful views in peaceful hilltop hamlet close to River Taw and Tarka Trail. Good walks nearby, ideal centre for exploring Devon. Sleeps 8. Large enclosed garden, perfect for dogs. From £150 weekly. Contact: MRS M. KNIGHT, GRUB-WOOD, CADMORE END, HIGH WYCOMBE, BUCKS HP14 3PL (01494 881825). [🐕]

Bovey Tracey

Little town nestling on southern fringe of Dartmoor. Fine scenery including Haytor Rocks (4 miles) and Becky Falls (3½ miles). The 14th cent. Church is of interest. Exeter 14 miles, Torquay 13, Teignmouth 12, Ashburton 8, Newton Abbot 6, Chudleigh 4.

BLENHEIM COUNTRY HOUSE HOTEL, BOVEY TRACEY TQ13 9DH (01626 832422). Family Hotel on edge of Dartmoor National Park. RSPCA member. Open all year. All pets free. 2 Crowns. [🐕]

Braunton

Ideally placed for sea and country holidays. Surrounded by rich farmland, yet close to the sands at Saunton, Croyde and Putsborough. The sand dunes at Braunton Burrows are noted for their plant and bird life, also of interest is the 13th century Church. Barnstaple 6 miles.

MRS J. RABEY, "SON GAL", ASH LANE, BRAUNTON EX33 2EF (01271 816835). Self catering detached house – luxury accommodation in unspoilt village, near sheltered flat sandy beach. Three bedrooms, one en suite. Lounge with TV and video. All modern facilities. [🐕]

Brixham

Lively resort and fishing port, with quaint houses and narrow winding streets. Ample opportunities for fishing and boat trips.

ANGELA AND PETER ELLIS, WESTBURY, 51 NEW ROAD, BRIXHAM TQ5 8NL (01803 851684). Situated a short level walk from the harbour; rooms with TV and tea making; some en suite. Surrounding area is a paradise for walkers and sightseers. B&B from £16.00. Small to medium dogs accepted.

HOLIDAYS TORBAY, 26 COTMORE CLOSE, BRIXHAM TQ5 0EF (01803 854708). Harbourside cottages, houses, flats. Sea views and close to beaches, town and coastal walks. Colour TV, clean and comfortable. [🐕]

DEVONCOURT HOLIDAY FLATS, BERRYHEAD ROAD, BRIXHAM TQ5 9AB (01803 853748 24 hours). 24 self-contained flats with private balcony, colour television, heating, private car park, all-electric kitchenette, separate bathroom and toilet. Open all year. [Pets £10 per week.]

Buck's Mills

Picturesque hamlet in steeply descending coombe above Barnstaple Bay. Clovelly 3 miles.

ROSEMARY & RAY NEWPORT, THE OLD MILL, BUCKS MILLS, BIDEFORD EX39 5DY (01237 431701). Comfortable 17th century cottage/tea rooms. Warm and friendly atmosphere, good home cooking, log fires. In quiet coastal village with beach and woodland walks. Open all year. [🐕]

Bude (Cornwall)

Popular seaside resort overlooking a wide bay of golden sand flanked by spectacular cliffs. Ideal for surfing; sea water swimming pool for safe bathing.

4 Apartments & Cottage sleeping 2/6 in old country house situated in 4 acres grounds. Tremendous views and only 7 miles from beaches. Ideal for families and quiet breaks; children's play area; friendly animals. Well-behaved pets welcome. Open all year. For brochure please contact: ANNE AND DAVID OLIVANT, BENNETTS, WHITSTONE, HOLSWORTHY EX22 6UD (01288 341322).

Budleigh Salterton

South Devon resort of dignified charm. Attractive sea-front, shingle beach, pleasant walks in vicinity. Good fishing in sea and River Otter. Facilities for tennis, bowls, croquet, golf. Hayes Barton, birthplace of Sir Walter Raleigh, is 3 miles distant. Taunton 16 miles, Exeter 14, Sidmouth 7, Exmouth 5.

TIDWELL HOUSE COUNTRY HOTEL, KNOWLE, BUDLEIGH SALTERTON EX9 7AG (01395 442444). Come and unwind at this Listed Georgian house of great character set in 3 acres of gardens. Ideal centre for walking, touring, playing golf etc. Large en suite rooms. Pets and children welcome. [Pets £1 per night.]

MRS JUNE SUMMONS, CHAPTER HOUSE, 6 WESTBOURNE TERRACE, BUDLEIGH SALTERTON EX9 6BR (01395 444100). Family run. One family, one double, one twin rooms. Victorian house. All rooms colour TV, tea making facilities. Minutes from cliff path and beach. Dogs allowed on beach all year. [🐕 Please bring own bed & feeding bowls for pets.]

Chagford

Unspoilt little town on the edge of Dartmoor in an area rich in prehistoric remains. Noted for 16th-century bridge, and Tudor and Georgian houses.

I. SATOW, WEEKE BROOK, CHAGFORD TQ13 8JQ (01647 433345). Away from the tumult of the world. One mile charming small Dartmoor town. Lovely ancient thatched house. Pets welcome. Bed and Breakfast £11.00 to £15.00.

A wonderful variety of over 450 cottages, houses and apartments all over the West Country, ideal for self-catering holidays. Many accept pets. Free colour brochure from: HELPFUL HOLIDAYS, COOMBE 49, CHAGFORD, DEVON TQ13 8DF (01647 433593) 24 hours.

Chittlehamholt

Standing in beautiful countryside in the Taw Valley and just off the B3227. Barnstaple 9 miles, South Molton 5.

SNAPDOWN FARM CARAVANS, CHITTLEHAMHOLT, UMBERLEIGH, NORTH DEVON EX37 9PF (01769 540708). 12 only – 6 berth caravans with flush toilets, showers, colour TV, fridges, cookers and fires. Laundry room. Picnic tables. Unspoilt countryside – field and woodland walks. Terms (2 types) £70–£195 or £75–£210 inc. gas and electricity in caravans. *[Pets £8.75 per week.]*

Chulmleigh

Mid-Devon village set in lovely countryside, just off A377 Exeter to Barnstaple road, Exeter 23 miles, Tiverton 19, Barnstaple 18.

THE FOX AND HOUNDS, EGGESFORD HOUSE HOTEL, EGGESFORD, NEAR CHULMLEIGH EX18 7JZ (01769 580345; Fax: 01769 580262). 30 acres of countryside and forest. 7 miles River Taw salmon/trout fishing. Ideal touring centre for Dartmoor, Exmoor and coasts. 20 en-suite bedrooms. B&B from £31.50. *[Pets £3.50 per night.]*

Combe Martin

Coastal village with harbour set in sandy bay. Good cliff and rock scenery. Of interest is the Church and "Pack of Cards" Inn. Barnstaple 14 miles, Lynton 12, Ilfracombe 6.

RONE HOUSE HOTEL, KING STREET, COMBE MARTIN EX34 0AD (01271 883428). Small, comfortable family-run Hotel, close to sea. Central heating. TV in all bedrooms, private facilities in most. Heated swimming pool. Children and dogs welcome.

MIKE AND PAM CARTER, MIRAMAR HOTEL, COMBE MARTIN EX34 0JS (01271 883558). Homely Hotel with relaxed, friendly atmosphere. Licensed residents' bar, large heated swimming pool, children's playground. Good varied menu. Children at reduced rates. *[pw!]*

SAFFRON HOUSE HOTEL, KING STREET, COMBE MARTIN EX34 0BX (01271 883521). Charming farmhouse hotel in picturesque coastal village on Exmoor. Ideal for touring, lovely views. Heated swimming pool and pretty gardens. *[🐾]*

MODERN BUNGALOWS on a choice of two attractive sites. Sleep 2, 4, 6 or 8 people. Adjacent to safe beach. Lounge with free colour television. Heated swimming pool, crazy golf course. Free entertainment and dancing. JOHN FOWLER HOLIDAYS, DEPARTMENT PW, MARLBOROUGH ROAD, ILFRACOMBE EX34 8PF (01271 866766). *[Pets £12 per week.]*

1 STATTENS COTTAGES, CASTLE STREET, COMBE MARTIN (01344 780409 or 01276 681817). Cosy four-bedroomed cottage dating from 18th Century. Sleeps 7 plus cot. Two lounges with TVs. Small enclosed garden with patio and barbecue. Parking for 2/3 cars. Convenient village shops, pubs, beaches, fishing, coastal path, Exmoor and local attractions. *[🐾]*

MR M. J. HUGHES, MANLEIGH HOLIDAY PARK, RECTORY ROAD, COMBE MARTIN EX34 0NS (01271 883353). Holiday Chalets, accommodate 4/6 persons. In 6 acres. Free use of swimming pool. Dogs welcome provided they are kept under control. Also 12 luxury Caravans to let. Graded 4 ticks [Pets £14 per week.]

Crediton

Ancient small town. Chapter house with Cromwellian relics. Cidermaking. Cathedral-type church. 7 miles from Exeter.

WEST AISH FARM, MORCHARD BISHOP, NEAR CREDITON EX17 6RX (01363 877427). Relax by a log fire after a day's touring, walking or riding. Self catering cottages situated in the peaceful setting of a former cobbled farmyard. Two cottages, sleep 5. £110–£240. Short Breaks: 3 nights £85.

Croyde

Village 7 miles south-west of Ilfracombe on the Golden Coast. Gem, rock and shell museum includes giant clams from South Pacific.

JOHN AND DIANA WOODINGTON, FIG TREE FARMHOUSE, ST MARY'S ROAD, CROYDE EX33 1PJ (Tel & Fax: 01271 890204). Bed and Breakfast in a 400 year old thatched Devon Longhouse. Friendly welcome and very comfortable en suite available. Pets particularly welcome. Acre garden. Accommodation for dogs on site. Kennelling available. Dog sitting, feeding or walking by arrangement. [pw! 🐕]

MR AND MRS G. PADDISON, MANOR COTTAGE, 11 ST MARY'S ROAD, CROYDE EX33 1PE (Tel/Fax: 01271 890324). Comfortable bungalow, sleeps 5. Enclosed garden and car space. Easy walking distance to beach and village. Coastal footpath and golf course nearby. Available all year.

Croyde Bay

Charming village nestling in a sheltered combe behind Croyde Bay.

MRS JENNIFER PENNY, CROYDE BAY HOUSE HOTEL, CROYDE BAY, NORTH DEVON EX33 1PA (01271 890270). Small hotel beside beach at Croyde Bay. All rooms en-suite with tea/coffee making facilities. Good food and friendly atmosphere. AA & RAC 2 Star. 3 Crowns Highly Commended. [🐕]

Cullompton

Small market town off the main A38 Taunton–Exeter road. Good touring centre. Noted for apple orchards which supply the local cider industry. Taunton 19 miles, Exeter 13, Honiton 11, Tiverton 9.

MRS J. M. HILL, SUNNYSIDE FARM, BUTTERLEIGH, NEAR CULLOMPTON, TIVERTON EX15 1PP (01884 855322). 130-acre mixed farm, central for touring Dartmoor and Exmoor. En suite bedrooms with tea/coffee facilities. Bed and Breakfast; Evening Meal optional. Children welcome. [🐕]

FOREST GLADE HOLIDAY PARK (PW), KENTISBEARE, CULLOMPTON EX15 2DT (01404 841381). Country estate with deluxe 2/4/6 berth caravans. All superbly equipped. Many amenities on site. Mother and Baby Room. Campers and tourers welcome. SAE for free colour brochure. AA Four Pennants; 5 ticks √ √ √ √ √. [Pets 50p per night.]

Dartmoor

365 square miles of National Park, with spectacular unspoiled scenery and fringed by picturesque villages.

MRS SUSAN BOOTY, "ROGUES ROOST", POUNDSGATE, ASHBURTON TQ13 7PS (01364 631223). Dartmoor National Park. Two self-catering moorland properties sleeping 4 and 8. Children and dogs welcome. Off beaten track. *[🐾]*

THE TWO BRIDGES HOTEL, NEAR YELVERTON, DARTMOOR PL20 6SW (01822 890581; Fax: 01822 890575). Famous Olde World riverside inn. Centre Dartmoor. Log fires, very comfortable, friendly, own brewed beer, excellent food. Ideal walking, touring, fishing, riding, golf. Warning – Addictive. *[🐾]*

MAGPIE LEISURE PARK, DEPT PW, BEDFORD BRIDGE, HORRABRIDGE, YELVERTON PL20 7RY (01822 852651). Purpose-built pine lodges in peaceful woodland setting. Sleep 2–7. Furnished to very high standard (microwave, dishwasher etc.). Easy walk to village and shops. Launderette. Dogs permitted. *[Pets £12.50 per week.]*

DEVONSHIRE INN, STICKLEPATH, OKEHAMPTON EX20 2NW (01837 840626). A real country pub! Out the back door past the water wheels, cross the river by ford or footbridge and up through the woods onto the north edge of Dartmoor proper. Dogs and horses always welcome, fed and watered. 1994 Winner National Beta Petfood Golden Bowl Competition for most dog-friendly pub!

P. WILKENS, POLTIMORE, RAMSLEY, SOUTH ZEAL EX20 2PD (01837 840209). Dartmoor National Park. Self catering accommodation consisting of summer chalet, granite barn conversion and superb detached bungalow. Also pretty thatched guest house. All with direct access to the Moor. Write or phone for details. *[1st pet free, 2nd or more £7.50 each per week.]*

CHERRYBROOK HOTEL, TWO BRIDGES, YELVERTON PL20 6SP (01822 880260). Set in the heart of Dartmoor National Park. Seven comfortably furnished en suite bedrooms. Good quality home-cooked food with menu choice. Ideal for touring. 3 Crowns Commended. *[🐾]*

Dartmouth

Historic and picturesque port and resort on the estuary of the lovely River Dart. Sandy coves; pleasure boat trips up river. Car ferry to Kingswear. Of interest are St Saviour's Church (14th cent.); old houses and Butterwalk; Tudor Castle, Royal Naval College.

DARTSIDE HOLIDAYS, RIVERSIDE COURT, SOUTH EMBANKMENT, DARTMOUTH TQ6 9BH (01803 832093; Fax: 01803 835135). Comfortable holiday apartments with private balconies and superb river and harbour views. Available all year with colour TV, linen and parking. From £79–£625 per week. Free Colour Brochure on request. *[Pets £10 per week.]*

MRS S. R. RIDALLS, THE OLD BAKEHOUSE, 4 BROADSTONE, DARTMOUTH TQ6 9NR (01803 832109). 3 Cottages (one with four-poster bed). Sleep 2–6. Near river, shops, restaurant. Blackpool Sands 15 minutes' drive. TV, linen hire, baby-sitting. Open all year. ETB 3 Keys up to Commended. *[🐾]*

Dawlish

Bright resort with sandy beach and sandstone cliffs. Lovely gardens with streams, waterfalls and famous black swans. Exeter 13 miles, Torquay 12, Newton Abbot 9, Teignmouth 3.

MRS P. KITSON, 3 CLEVELAND PLACE, OFF HIGH STREET, DAWLISH EX7 9HP (01626 865053). Self-Catering "Listed" Town House. Six bedrooms, two bathrooms. Three minutes' walk beaches/shops. Also brand new two-bedroomed Cottage in grounds. Parking. Garden. Reasonable terms. *[🐶]*

MRS F. E. WINSTON, "STURWOOD", 1 OAK PARK VILLAS, DAWLISH EX7 0DE (01626 862660). Holiday Flats. Comfortable, self-contained, accommodating 2–6. Own bathroom, 1/2 bedrooms. Colour television. Garden. Parking. Full Fire Certificate. Leisure centre and beach close by. Pets welcome. *[pw!]*

Dawlish Warren

A 500 acre nature reserve with a sandy spit at the mouth of the River Exe.

WELCOME FAMILY HOLIDAY PARK, DAWLISH WARREN, SOUTH DEVON EX7 0PH (Reservations: 01626 862070, Dial a brochure: 01626 888323). Activities include the Dolphin Club and entertainment centre, indoor heated swimming pool, sauna and Jolly Roger club with disco and cinema. Free electricity, linen and colour TV. *[Pets £20 per week.]*

Dunsford

Attractive village in Upper Teign Valley with Dartmoor to the west. Plymouth 35 miles, Okehampton 16, Newton Abbot 13, Crediton 9, Exeter 8.

M. I. HARRISON, ROYAL OAK INN, DUNSFORD, NEAR EXETER EX6 7DA (01647 252256). Welcome to our Victorian country inn. We specialise in real ales and home-made food. All en suite rooms are in a 300-year-old converted barn. Each room has its own front door opening into a beautiful walled courtyard. WCTB Approved. *[🐶]*

Exeter

Chief city of the South-West, Exeter, with its cathedral and University, has a long and glorious history. Ample shopping, sports and leisure facilities.

MR CHRIS MORRIS, CLOCK TOWER HOTEL, 16 NEW NORTH ROAD, EXETER EX4 4HF (01392 424545). English Tourist Board 2 Crowns. Listed building of character in city centre 10 minutes' level walk stations, shops and Cathedral. All modern facilities including en suite rooms with baths and satellite TV. Licensed. Credit cards. Rates from £12.50 B&B. Colour brochure available. *[🐶]*

MRS D. L. SALTER, HALDON LODGE FARM, KENNFORD, NEAR EXETER EX6 7YG (01392 832312). Modern Holiday Caravan. Two bedrooms, kitchen, lounge, bathroom/toilet. TV. Farm shop, famous village Inns. Sea short distance. Private grounds near Teign Valley Forest with two Coarse Fishing lakes. Pets welcome. *[pw!]*

DEVON

MRS SALLY GLANVILL, RYDON FARM, WOODBURY, EXETER EX5 1LB (01395 232341). 16th Century Devon Longhouse on working dairy farm. Bedrooms with private or en-suite bathrooms, hairdryers, tea/coffee facilities. Romantic 4-poster. Open all year. ETB 2 Crowns Commended, AA QQQQ Selected. From £16 to £22. [🐾]

Exmoor

265 square miles of unspoiled heather moorland with deep wooded valleys and rivers, ideal for a walking, pony trekking or fishing holiday.

WEST LYN FARM, BARBROOK, LYNTON EX35 6LD. Farmhouse sleeps 8/9; cottage sleeps 4. Secluded working beef/sheep farm overlooking Lynmouth Bay and Bristol Channel. Peaceful surroundings; adjoining Coastal Path and NT woodlands. For brochure and tariff **01598 753618**.

THE STAG HUNTERS HOTEL, BRENDON, EXMOOR EX35 1PS (Tel: 01598 741222; Fax: 01598 741352). Family run village inn set in four acres of garden and paddock. 12 en-suite rooms with CH, TV and tea/coffee. Open all year. Fishing, shooting and riding. 3 Crowns Commended. [🐾]

MRS T. H. FARTHING, BRENDON HOUSE HOTEL, BRENDON, LYNTON EX35 6PS (015987 41206). Small comfortable country hotel. Licensed. Good food. Fishing permits sold. Dogs very welcome. Dinner, Bed and Breakfast from £30. [🐾]

Exmouth

Resort on the estuary of the River Exe with excellent sands and bathing.

MARGARET GRAY, "NORTHLEIGH", WEST DOWN FARM, SANDY BAY, EX-MOUTH EX8 5BU (01395 271141). Converted barn cottage. One double bedroom with TV and two single bedrooms. Kitchen equipped with cooker, fridge/freezer, microwave, washing machine. Own enclosed patio garden and garage. Half mile from beach and adjoins open countryside. Children welcome. [Pets £15 per week.]

Harberton

Small picturesque village two miles from Totnes.

M. H. & J. S. GRIFFITHS, "OLD HAZARD", HIGHER PLYMOUTH ROAD, HARBERTON, TOTNES TQ9 7LN (01803 862495). 3 miles Totnes. Attractive well-equipped self catering cottage and farmhouse flat. Convenient rural location. Open all year. Dogs welcome. Brochure on request. [Pets £7.00 per week.]

Holsworthy

Town 9 miles east of Bude.

HEDLEY WOOD CARAVAN AND CAMPING PARK, BRIDGERULE, NEAR BUDE EX22 7ED (Tel and Fax: 01288 381404). Superb 16-acre site amidst lovely countryside, 10 minutes from sandy beaches. All modern facilities. Licensed bar, club room, separate children's play area. [🐾pw!]

Honiton

Busy south Devon town now happily by-passed. Noted for lace and pottery. Excellent touring centre. Newton Abbot 31 miles, Exmouth 18, Taunton 18, Exeter 17, Budleigh Salterton 16, Lyme Regis 15, Chard 13, Sidmouth 10.

THE BELFRY COUNTRY HOTEL, YARCOMBE, NEAR HONITON EX14 9BD (01404 861234; Fax: 01404 861579). Small luxury hotel with lovely views over Blackdown Hills and Yarty Valley. Cosy bar/restaurant serving home cooking. Log fire, comfy lounge. Ideal walking and touring area. ETB 4 Crowns Commended, AA Two Stars and Rosette. [🐾]

MRS E. TUCKER, LOWER LUXTON FARM, UPOTTERY, HONITON EX14 9PB (01823 601269). Olde worlde Farmhouse in an area of outstanding natural beauty. Ideal for touring. Carp fishing. Good home cooking. Children welcome. B&B or D,B&B. Weekly terms from £105, 6 Dinners and Bed and Breakfast.

Hope Cove

Attractive fishing village, flat sandy beach and safe bathing. Fine views towards Rame Head; cliffs. Kingsbridge 6 miles.

THE PORT LIGHT, BOLBERRY DOWN, MALBOROUGH, NEAR SALCOMBE TQ7 3DY (01548 561384 or 0831 218047). A totally unique location set amidst acres of National Trust coastline. Luxury en suite rooms. Superb home-cooked fare, specialising in local seafood. Licensed bar. Pets welcome throughout the hotel. Bargain Breaks throughout the year. [🐾]

CHRIS AND JO MOON, SUN BAY HOTEL, INNER HOPE COVE, NEAR SALCOMBE TQ7 3HH (01548 561371). Licensed hotel overlooking sandy beach. Television lounge. Magnificent coastal walks. Children and pets welcome. [Pets £2 per night.]

TANFIELD HOTEL, HOPE COVE, NEAR KINGSBRIDGE TQ7 3HF (01548 561268). A warm welcome awaits you at this Ashley Courtenay recommended, licensed Hotel. Ideal for a relaxing holiday. All rooms have central heating, en suite facilities, hairdryers, colour TV, tea/coffee making. Colour brochure. Bargain breaks available. [Pets £1.50 per night.]

Seven luxury 2 and 3 bedroom Apartments, all facilities, equipped to highest standards: ETB 4 Keys Commended. Linen supplied free. Open all year. Children/ pets welcome. Apply: MR AND MRS P. G. PEDRICK, HOPE BEACH HOUSE, HOPE COVE, NEAR KINGSBRIDGE TQ7 3HH (01548 560151). [Pets £11 weekly.]

Ilfracombe

This popular seaside resort clusters round a busy harbour. The surrounding area is ideal for coastal walks.

ST BRANNOCKS HOUSE HOTEL, ST BRANNOCKS ROAD, ILFRACOMBE EX34 8EQ (01271 863873). Good food and excellent accommodation guaranteed at this friendly seaside Hotel. All rooms TV, tea making; en-suite available. Licensed bar. Parking. Children and pets welcome. 3 Crowns. [🐾]

DEVON

COMBE LODGE HOTEL, CHAMBERCOMBE PARK, ILFRACOMBE EX34 9QW (01271 864518). Pets and their owners will enjoy holidays at our licensed Hotel. En-suite rooms available, good food, total freedom and walks galore. Dogs sleep in your bedroom. [🐕]

THE OLD COACH HOUSE, WATERMOUTH, ILFRACOMBE EX34 9SJ (01271 867340). Accommodation for 2 to 6 persons in converted courtyard complex. Fully equipped, colour TV etc. Terms from £80 to £310. Colour brochure from **Peggy Dobson**.

WESTWELL HALL HOTEL, TORRS PARK, ILFRACOMBE EX34 8AZ (01271 862792). Elegant Victorian hotel in own grounds, adjacent to National Trust coastal walks. All spacious rooms en suite with colour TV and tea/coffee facilities. AA Recommended, RAC Acclaimed, ETB 3 Crowns. [🐕]

JOHN FOWLER HOLIDAYS, DEPARTMENT PW, MARLBOROUGH ROAD, ILFRACOMBE EX34 8PF (01271 866766). Modern Bungalows to sleep 2, 4, 6 or 8 people. Lounge with free colour television. Heated swimming pool, crazy golf course. Free entertainment and dancing. Sea and shops are close. [Pets £12 per week.]

THE DARNLEY HOTEL, BELMONT ROAD, ILFRACOMBE EX34 8DR (01271 863955). Enjoy a holiday in the tranquil setting of this hotel, only five minutes' walk from main shopping area. All rooms have central heating and en suite rooms are available. Pets welcome

CAIRN HOUSE HOTEL, ST BRANNOCKS ROAD, ILFRACOMBE EX34 8EH (01271 863911). Set in own grounds 5 minutes from all amenities. Good food and comfort. Choice of menu. Any day arrival. RAC One Star. [🐕]

Instow

On estuaries of Taw and Torridge, very popular with boating enthusiasts. Barnstaple 6 miles, Bideford 3.

Modern cottage-style house next to beach. Excellent views. Sleeps six people plus cot. Full central heating. Pets and children welcome. For brochure APPLY – MRS P. W. BAXTER, HUISH MOOR FARMHOUSE, INSTOW, BIDEFORD EX39 4LT (01272 861146). [🐕]

Kingsbridge

Pleasant town at head of picturesque Kingsbridge estuary. Centre for South Hams district with its lush scenery and quiet coves. Plymouth 21 miles, Dartmouth 15, Totnes 13.

LIPTON FARM, EAST ALLINGTON, NEAR TOTNES TQ9 7RN (01548 521252). Luxury 30ft. six-berth caravan on organic farm in quiet valley. Kingsbridge 5 miles. Ideal centre for beautiful beaches, coastal walks, touring Dartmoor. From £150 per week. [Pets £5 per week.]

MR & MRS H. D. IDE, FAIRFIELD, WALLINGFORD ROAD, KINGSBRIDGE TQ7 1NF (01548 852441). "Garden Flat" sleeps 2–5, £140 to £180 per week. Direct access to garden, ideal for children and/or dogs. Colour TV. Bed linen provided. Parking space. A friendly welcome and cream tea await you.

WOODLAND VIEW GUEST HOUSE, KILN LANE, STOKENHAM, KINGSBRIDGE TQ7 2SQ (01548 580542). In picturesque village one mile sea. Superb walking. Comfortable rooms. Pets very welcome. No guard dogs. [Pets 95p nightly.]

BEACHDOWN, CHALLABOROUGH BAY, KINGSBRIDGE TQ7 4JB (01548 810089). Self catering holidays for families in pleasant cedarwood bungalows 200 yards from quiet, sandy beach. Children's playground. Local shopping. Pets welcome. Fully furnished and equipped. ETB Approved 3 Keys. Contact NICKY FAULKNER for details. [pw! £12 per week.]

HALLSANDS HOTEL, NORTH HALLSANDS, KINGSBRIDGE (01548 511264). Fully licensed family Hotel offering Bed, Breakfast and Evening Meal. Good food. Fishing, bathing and compressed air available.

MRS B. KELLY, BLACKWELL PARK, LODDISWELL, KINGSBRIDGE TQ7 4EA (01548 831263). 17th century Farmhouse, 5 miles from Kingsbridge. Ideal centre for Dartmoor, Plymouth, Torbay, Dartmouth and many beaches. Some bedrooms en-suite. Bed, Breakfast and Evening Meal or Bed and Breakfast. Pets welcome free of charge. ETB 2 Crowns. [🐾]

JOURNEYS END INN, RINGMORE, NEAR KINGSBRIDGE TQ7 4HL (01548 810205). Historic inn in unspoilt setting. Extensive food menu served in bar and dining room; wide range of real ales. Comfortable en suite bedrooms with colour TV. Golf, fishing nearby.

TORCROSS APARTMENT HOTEL, TORCROSS, NEAR KINGSBRIDGE TQ7 2TQ (01548 580206). Family self-catering in our luxury apartment hotel; accommodation available in a wide range of sizes. Equipped to highest standards. Inn, Waterside Family Restaurant. Pets welcome. Brochure on request.

MRS J. TUCKER, MOUNT FOLLY FARM, BIGBURY-ON-SEA, KINGSBRIDGE TQ7 4AR (01548 810267). Cliff top position, with outstanding views of Bigbury Bay. Spacious, self catering wing of farmhouse, attractively furnished. Farm adjoins golf course and River Avon. Lovely coastal walks, ideal centre for South Hams and Dartmoor. Always a warm welcome, pets too!

Lee

Delightful seaside village in wooded valley. Beach of sand and rocks, fine coastal scenery. Ilfracombe 3 miles.

NORTH DEVON COASTAL PATH (Lee, Near Ilfracombe). Comfortable, refurbished self-catering cottage adjacent to National Trust area in peaceful setting of scenic coastal beauty. Double en suite bedroom (extra bed available for living room). Own garden. Parking. Sheep-friendly pets very welcome. Leaflet: MICHAEL & MAVIS ROGERS, THE BLUE MUSHROOM, LEE, ILFRACOMBE EX34 8LR (01271 862947). [Pets £5 per week.]

Lustleigh

Creeper-clad cottages of Dartmoor granite thick with Thatch hem in 13th century church in matching stone in this picturesque Devonshire village.

EASTWREY BARTON HOTEL, LUSTLEIGH, NEWTON ABBOT TQ13 9SN (01647 277338). Small, superbly appointed country house hotel. Relaxing breaks, good food, personal service. Ideal for exploring Dartmoor and South Devon. Non-smoking, licensed. Enjoy being cosseted. 3 Crowns Highly Commended, AA QQQQ. [🐾 pw!]

Lynton/Lynmouth

Picturesque twin villages joined by a unique cliff railway (vertical height 500 ft). Lynmouth has a quaint harbour and Lynton enjoys superb views over the rugged coastline.

THE EXMOOR SANDPIPER INN, COUNTISBURY, NEAR LYNMOUTH EX35 6NE (01598 741263). This fine old coaching inn is in a beautiful setting with good food and hotel facilities for complete comfort. All 16 rooms en-suite with colour TV, tea/coffee making. *[🐕]*

COUNTISBURY LODGE HOTEL, TORS PARK, LYNMOUTH EX35 6NB (01598 752388; Freephone 0500 0600 729). Former Victorian vicarage, peacefully secluded yet only 5 minutes to Lynmouth village. En suite rooms with tea/coffee facilities, central heating, and choice of menu. Log fires. Parking. Spring/Autumn Breaks. *[🐕]*

THE HEATHERVILLE HOTEL, TORS PARK, LYNMOUTH EX35 6NB (01598 752327). Country house hotel in peaceful setting with magnificent river and woodland views. Tea and coffee making in all rooms. Some en suite rooms with colour TV. Traditional English cooking. Licensed. Four minutes' walk to village. Parking. Bargain Breaks. Pets very welcome free of charge. *[🐕]*

SHELLEY'S COTTAGE HOTEL, WATERSMEET ROAD, LYNMOUTH EX35 6EP (01598 753219). Small family-run hotel, overlooking village and sea. Some en suite and family rooms. All rooms have colour TV and tea/coffee facilities. Write or phone for brochure.

GABLE LODGE HOTEL, LEE ROAD, LYNTON EX35 6BS (01598 752367). Grade II Listed building. Friendly and homely atmosphere. En suite rooms with TV and beverage trays. Licensed. Good home cooking. Car park and garden. *[🐕]*

DAVID BARNES AND JOHN WALLEY, COMBE PARK HOTEL, HILLSFORD BRIDGES, LYNTON EX35 6LE (01598 752356). Exmoor. Comfortable exquisite Country House Hotel near Lynton within National Trust parkland. Bedrooms with all facilities. Licensed. Dogs welcome. Bargain breaks. *[pw! £1 per night.]*

MRS V. EVELEIGH, WEST ILKERTON FARM, BARBROOK, LYNTON, NORTH DEVON EX35 6QA (01598 752310). Luxurious semi-detached S/C cottage on secluded Exmoor Hill. Livestock farm bordering open moor. Coast 3 miles, riding ½ mile. Marvellous walking and riding country. Children, dogs and horses welcome. 4 Keys COMMENDED. £120–£380 pw. Winter Breaks from £60. *[🐕pw!]*

CASTLE HILL HOUSE HOTEL, CASTLEHILL, LYNTON EX35 6JA (01598 752291). Quality small private hotel with emphasis on friendly service. Village setting, perfect for whole family. All bedrooms en suite, colour TV, tea/coffee making. Lounge, bar, restaurant. *[pw! 🐕]*

SYLVIA HOUSE HOTEL, LYDIATE LANE, LYNTON, NORTH DEVON EX35 6HE (01598 752391). A charming Georgian Hotel offering delightful rooms, most en suite, some with four-poster beds, all with colour TV and tea/coffee making facilities. Freshly prepared and cooked cuisine. *[🐕]*

MRS W. PRYOR, STATION HOUSE, LYNTON (01598 752275/752381). Holiday Flat situated in the former narrow gauge railway station closed in 1935, overlooking the West Lyn Valley. Centrally placed for Doone Valley and Exmoor. Parking available. *[🐕]*

R. S. BINGHAM, NEW MILL FARM, BARBROOK, LYNTON EX35 6JR (01598 753341). Exmoor Valley. Two cottages by stream and modern Bungalow with panoramic views of Exmoor on 86-acre farm with A.B.R.S. Approved riding stables. Free fishing. SAE for brochure. [pw! £15 per week.]

Moretonhampstead

Small market town on the east side of Dartmoor containing 17th-century Almshouses.

WHITE HART HOTEL, THE SQUARE, MORETONHAMPSTEAD, SOUTH DEVON (01647 440406). This historic Coaching Inn has stood in the town square for over 350 years and now has 20 De-Luxe bedrooms en suite with colour televisions. Traditional dishes served in the Restaurant. ETB 4 Crowns Highly Commended. [🐾]

Mortehoe

Adjoining Woolacombe with cliffs and wide sands. Interesting rock scenery beyond Morte Point. Barnstaple 15 miles, Ilfracombe 6.

LUNDY HOUSE HOTEL, MORTEHOE, WOOLACOMBE EX34 7DZ (01271 870372). Quality en suite accommodation in small, friendly hotel. Superb food, licensed bar lounge, separate TV lounges. Nadines à la carte restaurant. Write or phone for full details. [🐾]

Newton Abbot

Known as the gateway to Dartmoor and the coast, this lively market town has many fine buildings, parks and a racecourse.

ROSELANDS HOLIDAY CHALETS, TOTNES ROAD, IPPLEPEN, NEWTON ABBOT TQ12 5TD (01803 812701). Three detached, completely self contained chalets in peaceful garden. Within easy reach of South Devon amenities. Near golf course. Accommodation for 3/5 people. PETS MOST WELCOME. Safe parking. [pw! One pet free, others £5 per week.]

Okehampton

Historic market town on northern fringe of Dartmoor. Fine touring centre. Plymouth 31 miles, Bude 29, Bideford 27, Exeter 23, Launceston 19, Tavistock 16.

FOX AND HOUNDS HOTEL, BRIDESTOWE, OKEHAMPTON EX20 4HF (01822 820 206). Fully licensed, family-run hotel, ideal for touring Devon and Cornwall. All rooms en suite. A la carte restaurant and bar snacks. Large field at rear for pets. [pw!]

KATHY JONES, NORTHLAKE, STOCKLEY HAMLET, OKEHAMPTON EX20 1QH (01837 53100). Set in own grounds, clean, comfortable and friendly. Beautiful views across Dartmoor. Bed and full English Breakfast £15.00. Brand new kennel facilities with large exercise area plus walks. [pw! Pets £4.00 per night; 🏠]

Ottery St Mary

Pleasant little town in East Devon, within easy reach of the sea. Many interesting buildings including 11th-century Parish Church. Birthplace of the poet, Coleridge.

MR AND MRS M. FORTH, FLUXTON FARM HOTEL, OTTERY ST MARY EX11 1RJ (01404 812818). Charming 16th-century farmhouse with large garden. Good food superbly cooked, log fires. Peace and quiet, all modern conveniences. Teasmaids. Licensed. ETB Three Crowns, AA Listed. [🐾 pw!]

Paignton

Popular family resort on Torbay with long, safe, sandy beaches and small harbour. Exeter 25 miles, Newton Abbot 9, Dartmouth 8, Brixham 6, Totnes 6, Torquay 3.

AMBER HOUSE HOTEL, 6 ROUNDHAM ROAD, PAIGNTON TQ4 6EZ (01803 558372). Family-run licensed hotel. En-suite facilities and ground floor rooms. Good food. Highly recommended. A warm welcome assured to pets and their families. 3 Crowns. [🛏 pw!]

J. AND E. BALL, DEPARTMENT P.W., HIGHER WELL FARM HOLIDAY PARK, STOKE GABRIEL, TOTNES TQ9 6RN (01803 782289). Within 4 miles Torbay beaches and 1 mile of River Dart. Central for touring. Dogs on leads. Tourist Board graded park, 3 ticks. [pw! £8 per week in statics, free in tents and tourers.]

Plymouth

Famous and historical port and resort, impressively rebuilt after severe war damage. Large naval docks at Devonport. Beach of pebble and sand. Of particular interest is the Hoe, overlooking the Sound, old and new lighthouses and Barbican.

PATRICIA STEER, "ROOKERY NOOK", NOSS MAYO, PLYMOUTH PL8 1EJ (01752 872296). Quiet village 10 miles from Plymouth on picturesque River Yealm Estuary. River and coastal walks. TV lounge, tea/coffee facilities. Also self catering accommodation. B&B from £15.00. Dogs free. [🛏]

CRANBOURNE HOTEL, 282 CITADEL ROAD, THE HOE, PLYMOUTH PL1 2PZ (01752 263858/661400; Fax: 01752 263858). Convenient for Ferry Terminal and City Centre. All bedrooms with colour TV and tea/coffee. Ample parking. Keys provided for access at all times. Under personal supervision. Pets by arrangement. ETB 2 Crowns. [🛏]

HEADLAND HOTEL, RADFORD ROAD, WEST HOE, PLYMOUTH PL1 3BY (01752 660866). Licensed. Very friendly atmosphere. Pets welcome. Rooms with bath en suite. Two lounges. Spacious restaurant. 150 yards sea front.

CHURCHWOOD VALLEY, DEPT PW, WEMBURY BAY, NEAR PLYMOUTH PL9 0DZ (01752 862382). Quality holiday Cabins in peaceful wooded valley, 500 metres from beach. Licensed shop, launderette, riding stables. Near Plymouth and Dartmoor. Two family pets welcome free. √ √ √ √ [🛏]

Salcombe

Fishing and sailing centre in a sheltered position. Fine beaches and coastal walks nearby.

THE SALCOMBE BOAT COMPANY, WHITESTRAND, SALCOMBE TQ8 8ET (01548 843730/844224). A holiday with a difference. Unwind with a houseboat holiday on Salcombe's tranquil estuary. Write or phone for brochure. [Pets £15 weekly.]

GRAFTON TOWERS HOTEL, MOULT ROAD, SALCOMBE TQ8 8LG (01548 842882). Small luxury Hotel with wonderful views. Convenient for ferry, town. Magnificent walks. Speciality local seafood. Homemade desserts. 2 stars AA, RAC. [Pets £2.50 per night.]

MRS E. J. LONSDALE, FERN LODGE, HOPE COVE, KINGSBRIDGE TQ7 3HF (01548 561326). PETS FREE OF CHARGE. Fern Lodge offers comfort, good food and personal attention. Five rooms en-suite. Three minutes from sea. All pets accepted. ETB Two Crowns. [🐾]

SEAMARK HOLIDAY APARTMENTS, THURLESTONE SANDS, NEAR SALCOMBE TQ7 3JY (01548 561300). 5 lovely apartments adjoining coastal path. Beach 500 yards, golf one mile. Games room with darts, table tennis, snooker. Laundry room, Pay phone. Colour brochure. [Pets £10 per week.]

A. R. AND J. A. FERRIS, ROCK HOUSE MARINE, THURLESTONE SANDS, NEAR SALCOMBE TQ17 3JY (01548 561285). Sample a touch of luxury in Hotel apartments in secluded bay. Heated pool, games room, waterside bar. Full Hotel facilities except Breakfast. Restaurant serves fresh food, bar snacks. [Pets £5 per week.]

Saunton Sands

Excellent sands, about 4 km long. Barnstaple 8 miles, Croyde 3.

SAUNTON BEACH VILLAS sleep 2–8 and are fully equipped. Every amenity nearby; adjacent to unspoilt beach. Open Easter to October. Weekend and Midweek Breaks available. [Pets £15 per week.] APPLY – SAUNTON BEACH VILLAS, BROADFIELD HOLIDAYS, 1 PARK VILLAS, TAW VALE, BARNSTAPLE EX32 8NJ (01271 22033; 24 hours).

Seaton

Bright East Devon resort near Axe estuary. Shingle beach, chalk cliffs. Good bathing, many lovely walks in vicinity. Taunton 30 miles, Exeter 23, Chard 14, Sidmouth 11.

MILKBERE HOLIDAYS, MILKBERE HOUSE, 14 FORE STREET, SEATON EX12 2LA (01297 22925). Attractive self-catering Cottages, Bungalows, Apartments. Coast and Country on Devon/Dorset border. Free colour brochure. Pets welcome. [pw! £12 per week.]

MRS R. B. HALLETT, BOROLANDS FARM, AXMOUTH, SEATON EX12 4BP (01297 552680). Bed and Breakfast. Children and pets welcome. Quiet countryside, beaches, golf, pleasure parks near by. All rooms hot and cold water, television, tea/coffee facilities. [🐾]

SEATON. Self-contained Holiday Bungalows, ETB 2 Keys Approved, rural site. Fully equipped, accommodate six plus cot. Optional linen hire. Parking. Adjacent filling station and shop. Pets, children welcome. Contact: NETHERHAY HOLIDAYS, NETHERHAY, NEAR BEAMINSTER, DORSET DT8 3RH (Tel. and Fax: 01308 868872 [24 hours]). [Pets £10 per week.]

Shaldon

Delightful little resort facing Teignmouth across the Teign estuary. Sheltered by the lofty prominence of Shaldon Ness, beach-side activities are largely concerned with boats and sailing; beaches are mainly of sand. Mini-golf course. The attractions of Teignmouth are reached by a long road bridge.

GLENSIDE HOTEL, RINGMOOR ROAD, SHALDON TQ14 0EP (01626 872448). Charming, waterside cottage hotel. Level river walks to beach. En suite available. Garden, car park. B&B from £16.50; D, B&B from £24.50. Telephone for brochure. [Pets £1.50 per night.]

MRS P. O'DONNELL, THE ROUND HOUSE, MARINE PARADE, SHALDON TQ14 0DP (01626 873328). Situated right on the beach with glorious views from all apartments in this pretty, olde worlde village. Full central heating. Parking. *[£5 weekly per dog.]*

EAST CLIFF HOLIDAY APARTMENTS, MARINE PARADE, SHALDON TQ14 0DP (01626 872334). Situated on Shaldon's lovely beach with superb views over sea, river and picturesque harbour. Each beautifully furnished, self-contained Apartment has modern kitchen and bathroom. Our prices include bed linen, colour television, central heating, car parking. Laundry facilities, telephone. No smoking. [pw! Pets £5 weekly.]

Sidmouth

Charming and sheltered resort. Winner of many awards for its floral displays. Good sands at Jacob's Ladder beach.

SWEETCOMBE COTTAGE HOLIDAYS. ROSEMARY COTTAGE, WESTON, NEAR SIDMOUTH EX10 0PH (01395 512130; Fax: 01395 515680). Selection Cottages, Farmhouses and Flats in Devon and Cornwall. Televisions, gardens. Colour video available on request. Pets welcome. Please ask for our illustrated brochure.

ENID & BERT CARR, BARRINGTON VILLA GUEST HOUSE, SALCOMBE ROAD, SIDMOUTH EX10 8PU (01395 514252). A Regency Villa in beautiful gardens on the River Sid. Dog-walk riverside park nearby. Ample forecourt parking. Dogs with house trained owners most welcome. *[🐾]*

OAKDOWN CARAVAN PARKS, WESTON, SIDMOUTH EX10 0PH (01297 680387; Fax: 01395 513731). Two privately owned parks set on the East Devon Heritage Coast. Level, well drained and closely mown. Luxury Holiday Homes for hire, pitches for touring units. Colour brochure. AA Three Pennants; BGHP √ √ √ √ √. *[pw! from 70p per night.]*

LOWER KNAPP FARM, SIDBURY, SIDMOUTH EX10 0QN (01404 871438). Luxury self catering cottages sleeping 2/8 set in 16 acres. Indoor heated pool, sauna, solarium. All cottages with fully fitted kitchens; colour TV etc. Linen supplied. Colour brochure on request. Three Keys. *[Pets £15 per week.]*

South Brent

Just off the busy A38 Plymouth to Exeter road, this is a good centre on the River Avon for Dartmoor and the South Devon resorts. Plymouth 15 miles, Ashburton 8.

EDESWELL FARM COUNTRY CARAVAN PARK, RATTERY, SOUTH BRENT TQ10 9LN (01364 72177). Picturesque Park in 21 acres wooded hillside. Ideally situated for Dartmoor, Torbay, South Devon. 18 static caravans, 46 touring pitches. Indoor pool, games room; bar, shop, launderette. *[pw! £7.00 weekly static, 50p per night touring.]*

Enchanting, select site for those seeking a quiet restful holiday amidst beautiful surroundings, overlooking the Dartmoor Hills. Fully serviced luxury caravans, with colour TV, fridge, heater and shower. Separate low density site for tents/tourers. Several acres for carefree exercising. 3 ticks. APPLY – TREVOR AND JILL HORNE, WEBLAND FARM HOLIDAY PARK, AVONWICK, NEAR SOUTH BRENT TQ10 9EX (01364 73273). *[pw! £1 nightly.]*

Southleigh

Village situated 3 miles north-west of Seaton.

WISCOMBE PARK, SOUTHLEIGH, NEAR COLYTON EX13 6JE (01404 871474). Nature lovers' and children's paradise. Working farm. Beautiful walks. Trout and coarse fishing. Near Coast. Comfortable self-contained accommodation. Free brochure. *[🐾]*

South Molton

On the southern edge of Exmoor, 12 miles east of Barnstaple, a busy market town, noted for antiques and its elegant Georgian buildings.

NORTH LEE HOLIDAY LETS, NORTH LEE FARM, SOUTH MOLTON, NORTH DEVON EX36 3EH (Tel and Fax: 01598 740248). Southern edge of Exmoor. One and two bedroomed new barn conversions. Fully equipped, bed linen and towels included. Courtyard setting. Pets welcome. Easy reach of Exmoor and Coast. Open all year. Weekend and short breaks available. *[🐾pw!]*

Stoke-in-Teignhead

Quiet village, 4 miles east of Newton Abbot. 6 miles Torquay and close to sandy beaches.

Charming character cottage and barn conversion for 4/6 persons. TV, dishwasher, microwave, linen. Delightful quiet village. Six miles Torquay/Teignmouth. Ideal base for touring/walking. Beaches two miles. Moors 20 miles. MRS J. A. REES, "CONGDONS", STOKE-IN-TEIGNHEAD, NEWTON ABBOT (01626 872433/ 872505).

Tavistock

Birthplace of Sir Francis Drake, and site of a fine ruined Benedictine Abbey. On edge of Dartmoor, 13 miles north of Plymouth.

MOORLAND HALL HOTEL, BRENTOR ROAD, MARY TAVY, NEAR TAVISTOCK PL19 9PY (01822 810466). Small Victorian country house hotel in 5 acres of grounds, with direct access onto Dartmoor. All rooms en suite. Children and pets welcome. Riding, fishing, golf nearby. *[Pets £1.50 per night.]*

MRS P. G. C. QUINTON, HIGHER QUITHER, MILTON ABBOT, TAVISTOCK PL19 0PZ (01822 860284). Modern self-contained barn conversion. Own private garden. Terms from £195 inc. linen, coal and logs. Electricity metered. *[🐾]*

Tedburn St Mary

Village on the edge of Dartmoor, 7 miles west of Exeter.

SPRINGFIELD HOLIDAY PARK, TEDBURN ROAD, TEDBURN ST MARY, EXETER EX6 6EW (01647 24242). In superb 9-acre setting three miles from Dartmoor. Heated swimming pool, shop, launderette, play area. Pets welcome. Caravans for hire; tourers and tents welcome. *[Pets £1 per night (tourer), £10 per week (static).]*

Teign Valley

Picturesque area on edge of Dartmoor. The River Teign flows into the English Channel at Teignmouth.

S. & G. HARRISON-CRAWFORD, SILVER BIRCHES, TEIGN VALLEY, TRUSHAM, NEWTON ABBOT TQ13 0NJ (01626 852172). Comfortable bungalow on the edge of Dartmoor. Good centre for birdwatching, forest walks, golf, riding; fishing nearby. Three double/twin bedrooms, all with private bath/shower and toilet. B&B from £22.00 nightly.

Teignmouth

Resort at mouth of River Teign. Bridge connects with Shaldon on south side of estuary.

LYME BAY HOUSE HOTEL, DEN PROMENADE, TEIGNMOUTH TQ14 8SZ (01626 772953). Near rail and coach stations and shops. En suite facilities available. Licensed. Lift – no steps. Bed and Breakfast. *[🐾]*

Thurlestone

Picturesque South Hams village near the glorious sands of Bigbury Bay. Famous golf course, delightful cliff scenery. Plymouth 20 miles, Kingsbridge 4.

LA MER, THURLESTONE SANDS TQ7 3JY (01548 561207). Country Hotel on water's edge. Ten bedrooms with washbasins, several with showers en-suite. Residential licence. Children and pets most welcome. Please phone for details. *[Pets £0.80 per night.]*

Tiverton

Market town on River Exe 12 miles north of Exeter, centrally located for touring both North and South coasts.

MRS PRATT, MOOR BARTON, NOMANSLAND, TIVERTON EX16 8NN (01884 860325). 18th-century superior farmhouse on a 250-acre mixed farm, situated equidistant from the North and South coasts. Four double, four family and one twin-bedded rooms. Children welcome. B&B from £14 per night; DB&B £120 per week inclusive.

Torbay

The bay which extends from Hope's Nose in the north to Berry Head in the south and the location of three of Devon's most popular resorts: Torquay, Paignton, and Brixham.

THE SMUGGLERS HAUNT HOTEL, CHURCH HILL, BRIXHAM TQ5 8HH (01803 853050; Fax: 01803 858738). Friendly, private 300-year-old hotel situated in the centre of old Brixham. Quality bar and à la carte menus. Vegetarian choice; children's menu. Fully equipped en suite rooms. Children and pets welcome. ETB 3 Crowns, AA 2 Stars. *[🐾]*

SYMBOLS

🐾 Indicates no charge for pets.
£ Indicates a charge for pets: nightly or weekly.
pw! Indicates some special provision for pets: exercise, feeding etc.
🏠 Indicates separate pets accommodation.

Torquay

Premier resort on the English Riviera with a wide range of attractions and entertainments. Yachting and watersports centre with 10 superb beaches and coves.

MR AND MRS D. G. MAISEY, CROSSWAYS AND SEA VIEW HOLIDAY FLATS, MAIDENCOMBE, TORQUAY TQ1 4TH (01803 328369). Modern self-contained flats set in one-acre grounds. Sleep 2/5. Colour TV. Pets welcome – exercise field adjacent. Children's play area. *[*🐾*pw!]*

MRS M. A. TOLKIEN, FAIRMOUNT HOUSE HOTEL, HERBERT ROAD, CHELSTON, TORQUAY TQ2 6RW (01803 605446). Small licensed Hotel with en suite bedrooms, central heating. Peaceful setting; excellent coast and country walking. One mile town centre. B&B from £26.50 per person. Bargain Breaks available. *[Pets £2 per night.]*

SOUTH SANDS APARTMENTS, TORBAY ROAD, LIVERMEAD, TORQUAY TQ2 6RG (Tel: 01803 293521; Fax: 01803 293502). 18 superior self-contained ground and first floor Apartments for 1–5 persons. Central heating. Open all year. Parking. Beach 100 yards. Convenient Riviera Centre, theatre, marina. Mini Breaks except Summer season. *[pw! £1 per night.]*

CLEVEDON HOTEL, MEADFOOT SEA ROAD, TORQUAY TQ1 2LQ (01803 294260). Set in its own peaceful grounds 300 yards from beach and woods. En suite rooms with TV, radio/alarm and tea/coffee. Licensed bar and traditional home cooked meals. *[*🐾*]*

RED HOUSE HOTEL AND MAXTON LODGE HOLIDAY APARTMENTS, ROUSDOWN ROAD, CHELSTON, TORQUAY TQ2 6PB (01803 607811). Choose either the friendly service and facilities of an hotel or the privacy and freedom of self-catering apartments. The best of both worlds! 4 Keys/3 Crowns Commended. *[*🐕* or £3 p.n. in hotel.]*

MR AND MRS T. H. FISH AND FAMILY, FAIRLAWNS HALL, ST MICHAEL'S ROAD, TORQUAY TQ1 4DD (01803 328904). Delightful self-contained holiday apartments and mews cottages. Central heating available. Pets welcome. Large woods nearby, gardens and parking. Stamp for brochure. *[Pets £10 weekly.]*

Torrington

Pleasant market town on River Torridge. Good centre for moors and sea. Exeter 36 miles, Okehampton 20, Barnstaple 12, Bideford 7.

SALLY MILSOM, STOWFORD LODGE, LANGTREE, NEAR TORRINGTON EX38 8NU (01805 601540). Away from the crowds. Four luxury cottages with heated indoor pool, and two secluded period farm cottages. Sleep 4/6. Peaceful countryside, convenient North Devon coast and moors. Magnificent views and walks. ETB 4 Keys Highly Commended. Phone for brochure. *[pw! Pets £10 per week.]*

Two Bridges

Situated 8 miles from Tavistock, ideal for exploring Dartmoor National Park.

PRINCE HALL HOTEL, TWO BRIDGES, YELVERTON PL20 6SA (01822 890403; Fax: 01822 890676). Small, friendly, relaxed country house hotel with glorious views onto open moorland. Walks in all directions. Eight en suite bedrooms. Log fires. Gourmet cooking by French owner/chef. Excellent wine list. Fishing, riding, golf nearby. 3 Crowns Commended. *[*🐾*]*

Umberleigh

Quiet North Devon village on River Taw, ideal for exploring Exmoor. Barnstaple 8 miles, Torrington 8, South Molton 7.

KINGFORD HILL HOLIDAY VILLAGE, UMBERLEIGH EX37 9BN (01769 560211). Small, secluded site in glorious woodland. Chalets sleep six. Heated pool, bar, games room. Children and pets welcome. *[pw!]*

Westward Ho!

Charming village named after the novel by Charles Kingsley. Good sands; two-mile long pebble ridge to the north west.

Self-catering Bungalows, almost adjoining three miles of glorious sand. Fully carpeted, with free colour TV, bathroom, WC, H&C, electric cooker, fridge. Free colour brochure on request. APPLY – JOHN FOWLER HOLIDAYS, DEPARTMENT PW, MARLBOROUGH ROAD, ILFRACOMBE EX34 8PF (01271 866766). *[Pets £12 per week.]*

Woolacombe

A favourite resort for children, with long, wide stretches of sand. Barnstaple 15 miles, Ilfracombe 6.

PAT AND TONY WORTHINGTON, COMBE RIDGE HOTEL, THE SEA FRONT, WOOLACOMBE EX34 7DJ (01271 870321). Small, detached, family hotel facing Combesgate Beach. Open February to end October. Special Discounts offered for Senior Citizens (early/late). 3 Crowns. Ample private parking. *[Pets £1 per night/£5 per week.]*

CROSSWAYS HOTEL, SEAFRONT, WOOLACOMBE EX34 7DJ (01271 870395). Homely, family-run licensed Hotel surrounded by National Trust land. Children and pets welcome. *[🐕]*

MRS JOYCE BAGNALL, CHICHESTER HOUSE, THE ESPLANADE, WOOLACOMBE EX34 7DJ (01271 870761). Holiday apartments on sea front. Fully furnished, sea and coastal views. Watch the sun go down from your balcony. Open all year. SAE Resident Proprietor. *[Pets £8 per week.]*

LITTLE BEACH HOTEL, THE ESPLANADE, WOOLACOMBE EX34 7DJ (01271 870398). Elegant, spacious and friendly family-run hotel. Superb seafront location with magnificent views of sea and countryside. Early season bargain breaks. ETB 3 Crowns Highly Commended. *[🐕]*

EUROPA PARK, STATION ROAD, WOOLACOMBE (01271 870159/870772). Luxury bungalows, superb views. Touring caravans and tents. Full facilities. Pets welcome, 6-acre dog park. Indoor heated swimming pool. *[pw! £5 per week.]*

PEBBLES HOTEL, COMBESGATE BEACH, WOOLACOMBE EX34 7EA (01271 870426). Family-run Hotel overlooking sea and beaches. All rooms en suite, with colour TV, tea/coffee making etc. Special Short Break packages. Write or phone for colour brochure. *[🐕]*

DORSET

Ashdale Hotel

SUE and CLIFF LOGGEY invite you and your pet to join us in this delightful area of Bournemouth. Ideal location beside beautiful Alum Chine with varied walks to miles of golden sand and sea.

We offer:
* A friendly welcome in a relaxed atmosphere.
* Spacious rooms, most with private facilities, all with central heating.
* All rooms have colour TV and tea/coffee facilities.
* Residential licence.   * Open throughout the year.

Bed and Breakfast from £13.50 to £18.50. Bed and Breakfast and Evening Meal Weekly from £105.00 to £155.00. No charge for pets. Special rates for Senior Citizens, over 55s and Weekend Breaks. So why not write or phone to:

The Ashdale Hotel, 35 Beaulieu Road, Alum Chine, Bournemouth BH4 8HY. Tel: (01202) 761947

THE ALUM GRANGE HOTEL

You don't have to be an old "seadog" to visit our hotel. With its nautical flavour you can almost smell the salt air – hardly surprising as we are only 200 metres from the sea and sandy beach. For landlubber dogs, we are situated in beautiful Alum Chine with trees galore!

* Captain's Bar for residents * Menu choices * A la carte * Car park * Wheelchair access * Ground floor rooms * All bedrooms en suite * Non-smoking bedrooms * Credit cards accepted * Christmas Breaks. AA QQQ.

1 Burnaby Road, Alum Chine, Bournemouth BH4 8JF (01202 761195).

CONISTON HOTEL

27 Studlands Road, Alum Chine, Bournemouth BH4 8HZ Tel: 01202 765386

Three minutes to lovely beach through Chine walks. Pets welcome free. Small, comfortable hotel. Home cooking, licensed bar, friendly atmosphere. En suites in all rooms and TV and teamakers. B&B from £15 pppn. B&B, EM from £110–£162 pw.

CRAVEN GRANGE HOLIDAY FLATS
17 BODORGAN ROAD, BOURNEMOUTH
TEL: 01202 296234

*Self-contained flats and cottage, 2-6 persons. * Short distance to town, golf and parks. *Large garden in quiet surroundings. *Car parking. *Free Welcome Pack. *Pets Welcome.
For further details: telephone Diana Parker or send SAE

Sea Breeze Hotel

A small, peaceful hotel in a delightful location opposite beach where dogs are allowed. Superb sea views. Family atmosphere – generous home cooking. Full central heating.

* ALL rooms en suite
* Tea making facilities
* TVs in bedrooms
* Residential licence

* Children from 5 to 16 sharing with parents half price.
* Parking
* Open all year, excluding Christmas

CLOSE TO HENGISTBURY HEAD; NEW FOREST 10 MINS DRIVE
BED AND BREAKFAST FROM £16; EVENING MEAL £8.50
David & Barbara Fowler, 32 St Catherine's Road, Southbourne, Bournemouth BH6 4AB
Tel: 01202 433888

All the advertisers in PETS WELCOME! have an entry in the appropriate classified
section and each classified entry may carry one or more of the following symbols:

🐾   This symbol indicates that pets are welcome free of charge.

£   The £ indicates that a charge is made for pets. We quote the amount where
possible, either per night or per week.

pw!   This symbol shows that the establishment has some special provision for
pets; perhaps an exercise facility or some special feeding or accommodation
arrangements.

⌂   Indicates separate pets accommodation.

PLEASE NOTE that all the advertisers in PETS WELCOME! extend a welcome to
pets and their owners but they may attach conditions. The interests of other guests
have to be considered and it is usually assumed that pets will be well trained,
obedient and under the control of their owner.

BLOXWORTH HOLIDAY COTTAGES

Large Georgian Farmhouse and thatched cottages in quiet village. Purbeck beauty spots and beaches along the Dorset Coast easily accessible. Pleasant walks. Beautiful Poole Harbour 10 miles. Comfortably furnished and equipped except linen and towels. Dogs welcome. Open all year. Ideal for winter week-ends.

SAE to:

Mr and Mrs P.G. Macdonald-Smith, Bloxworth Estate, Nr Wareham, Dorset BH20 7EF
Tel/Fax: 01929 459442

WELCOME COTTAGE HOLIDAYS. Hundreds of properties in wonderful locations at welcoming low prices. Pets, linen and fuel mostly included. For FREE colour brochure telephone 01756 702204.

Abbotsbury

Village of thatched cottages in sheltered green valley. Benedictine monks created the famous Abbotsbury Swannery.

MRS JOSEPHINE PEARSE, TAMARISK FARM, WEST BEXINGTON, DORCHES-TER DT2 9DF (01308 897784). Self Catering. On Chesil Beach: two secluded Chalets and one large and two smaller Bungalows on mixed organic farm with arable, sheep, cattle, horses and market garden with vegetables on sale. Good centre for touring, sightseeing, all sports. Pets and children welcome. ETB 2/3 Keys. Terms from £105 to £410. [🐾]

Blandford

Handsome Georgian town that rose from ashes of 1731 fire; rebuilt with chequered brick and stone. Also known as Blandford Forum.

ANVIL HOTEL & RESTAURANT, PIMPERNE, BLANDFORD DT11 8UQ (01258 453431/480182). A typical old English hostelry offering good old-fashioned English hospitality. À la carte menu and bar meals. All bedrooms with private facilities. Ample parking. 3 Crowns Commended, AA and RAC **. [Pets £2.50 per night.]

Bournemouth

One of Britain's premier holiday resorts with miles of golden sand, excellent shopping and leisure facilities. Lively entertainments include Festival of Lights at the beginning of September.

SEAWAY HOLIDAY FLATS. Self contained holiday flats with exercise area in garden. Three minutes' level walk between shops and cliffs, with lift to fine sandy "Pets Allowed" beach. Most reasonable terms early and late season. EATON HOUSE, 41 GRAND AVENUE, SOUTHBOURNE, BOURNEMOUTH BH6 3SY (01202 300351). [🐾 pw!]

CORRA LINN, 13 KNYVETON ROAD, BOURNEMOUTH BH1 3QG (01202 558003). Self catering holiday flatlets. Situated on the East Cliff within easy reach of sea, shops and entertainments. Fully equipped with central heating, TV, linen and refrigerator. Children and pets welcome. Free parking. Terms from £35 pp. [Pets £5 per week.]

DORSET

BARBARA AND ANDY HOATH, ALUM GRANGE HOTEL, 1 BURNABY ROAD, ALUM CHINE, BOURNEMOUTH BH4 8JF (01202 761195). Pets and owners are assured of a warm welcome at this superbly furnished hotel, 250 yards from the beach. All rooms with colour TV and tea/coffee making. [🐾]

CAIRNSMORE PRIVATE HOTEL, 37 BEAULIEU ROAD, BOURNEMOUTH BH4 8HY (01202 763705). 4 minutes' walk through wooded glades to sea. Colour TV in all bedrooms, all en suite. Parking. B, B & ED from £22 per person per day. Residential licence. Special diets catered for. No charge for pets. 3 Crowns Commended. [🐾pw!]

MIKE AND LYN LAMBERT, AARON, 16 FLORENCE ROAD, BOURNEMOUTH BH5 1HF (01202) 304925/(01425) 474007. Modern Holiday Apartments sleeping one to 10 persons, close to sea and shops. Recently extensively renovated with new kitchens and bathrooms. Clean well-equipped flats. Car park and garages. Write or phone for colour brochure and terms. [Pets £14 weekly.]

EAST CLIFF COURT, EAST OVERCLIFF DRIVE, BOURNEMOUTH (01202 554545; Fax: 01202 557456). Luxury seafront Hotel, all bedrooms en suite. Games room, outdoor pool, sauna, solarium. Pets welcome. Send for colour brochure and menus. AA *** RAC. [Pets £5 per day.]

St George's Holiday Flats are near sea and shops; Questors overlooks quiet, wooded Pleasure Gardens; superb for you and your dog. Both properties have good car parks; pay-phones, laundry, TV, fridges in all units. Clean and fully equipped. We like dogs. Apply: SANDRA & BARRY GLENARD, 45 BRANKSOME WOOD ROAD, BOURNEMOUTH BH4 9JT (01202 763262). [Pets £12 per dog, per week.]

CRAVEN GRANGE HOLIDAY FLATS, 17 BODORGAN ROAD, BOURNEMOUTH BH2 6JY (01202 296234). Self-contained flats and cottage, 2–6 persons. Town centre, golf and parks nearby. Car parking. Free Welcome Pack. Pets welcome. Telephone or SAE for details. [🐾]

THE COUNTY HOTEL, WESTOVER ROAD, BOURNEMOUTH (01202 552385). 50 bedroomed Hotel situated in the heart of Bournemouth; en suite rooms with colour TV, central heating etc. Pets and guests can look forward to excellent attention from a well-trained staff.

BILL AND MARJORIE TITCHEN, WHITE TOPPS HOTEL, 4 CHURCH ROAD, SOUTHBOURNE, BOURNEMOUTH BH6 4BB (01202 428868). Situated in quiet position close to lovely walks and beach. Dogs welcome. Free parking. Residential licence. [🐾pw!]

SUE AND CLIFF LOGGEY, ASHDALE HOTEL, 35 BEAULIEU ROAD, ALUM CHINE, BOURNEMOUTH BH14 8HY (01202 761947). Recommended for our warm, friendly atmosphere and good, plentiful food. Delightful situation by Alum Chine. Clean, well-equipped bedrooms. Licensed. [🐾]

OVERCLIFF HOTEL, 29 BEAULIEU ROAD, ALUM CHINE, BOURNEMOUTH BH4 8HY (01202 761030). Small comfortable licensed Hotel; en suite available. Home cooking, TV lounge. Three minutes to beach. B&B from £15, BB&EM from £100–£150 weekly. Open all year. [🐾]

MRS W. HOLLAND, 12 AVONCLIFFE ROAD, SOUTHBOURNE, BOURNEMOUTH BH6 3NR (01202 426650). Self catering flatlet on Southbourne cliff top. Fully equipped, close shops, buses; car parking available. Small dogs welcome. Open all year. SAE Mrs W. Holland. [🐾]

DORSET

CONISTON HOTEL, 27 STUDLAND ROAD, ALUM CHINE, BOURNEMOUTH BH4 8HZ (01202 765386). Three minutes to lovely beach through Chine walks. Pets welcome free. Small, comfortable hotel. Home cooking, licensed bar, friendly atmosphere. B&B from £15 pppn. *[🐾]*

SEA BREEZE, 32 ST CATHERINE'S ROAD, SOUTHBOURNE, BOURNEMOUTH BH6 4AB (01202 433888). Small peaceful Hotel, opposite beach. All rooms en suite, TV, teamakers. Parking. Generous home cooking. Pets welcome. B&B from £16; Evening Meal £8.50. *[Pets £2.50 per night.]*

THE STUDLAND DENE HOTEL, ALUM CHINE, WEST CLIFF, BOURNEMOUTH BH4 8JA (01202 765445). Overlooking the beach, marvellous walks. All rooms with TV, direct-dial phone; all en-suite. A la carte restaurant, carvery. *[Pets £2 per night.]*

MR AND MRS E. A. MURRAY AND MRS B. ECTOR, "SURREY DENE", 33 SURREY ROAD, BOURNEMOUTH BH4 9HR (01202 763950). Comfortable self-contained Flats, beautifully situated adjoining Bournemouth Upper Gardens. Free private parking. SAE for brochure. *[🐾]*

THE EMBASSY HOTEL, MEYRICK ROAD, EAST CLIFF, BOURNEMOUTH BH1 3DW 01202 290751; Fax: 01202 557459. Privately owned Hotel within walking distance of town centre and amenities. En suite bedrooms; heated outdoor pool and games room. Superb service and excellent cuisine. B&B from £25 per night. ETB 4 Crowns. *[Pets £3.00 per night.]*

MR AND MRS J. JENKINS, THE VINE HOTEL, 22 SOUTHERN ROAD, SOUTH-BOURNE, BOURNEMOUTH BA6 3SR (01202 428309). Small family Hotel only 3 minutes' walk from sea and shops. All rooms en-suite. Residential licence. Pets welcome. No smoking in bedrooms and dining room *[🐾]*

3 self-contained apartments in quiet avenue, one minute from clean, sandy beaches and 5 minutes from shops. Sleep 3/6. Fully equipped including linen. All have fridge, toilet and shower room, fitted carpets, colour TV, central heating, electric meter. Parking. Terms from £75. Contact: MRS HAMMOND, STOURCLIFFE COURT, 56 STOURCLIFFE AVENUE, SOUTHBOURNE, BOURNEMOUTH BH6 3PX (01202 420698). *[Pets £5 weekly.]*

Bridport

Market town of Saxon origin, noted for rope and net making. Harbour at West Bay has sheer cliffs rising from the beach.

MR AND MRS HADDON AND MR AND MRS RICE, DURBEYFIELD GUEST HOUSE, WEST BAY, BRIDPORT DT6 4EL (01308 423307). 2 minutes from Chesil Beach. Near small harbour. Home cooking. Washbasins all rooms. Colour television. Prices from £15.50 to £25 pppn. Free parking. Dogs welcome. ETB Listed.

MRS S. NORMAN, FROGMORE FARM, CHIDEOCK, BRIDPORT DT6 6HT (01308 456159). The choice is yours – Bed and Breakfast, optional Evening Meal, in charming farmhouse, OR self-catering Cottage equipped for six plus cot, pets welcome. Brochure and terms free on request *[🐾pw!]*

SYMBOLS

🐾   Indicates no charge for pets.
£   Indicates a charge for pets: nightly or weekly.
pw!   Indicates some special provision for pets: exercise, feeding etc.
🏠   Indicates separate pets accommodation.

Super Self Catering Bungalows in old smugglers' haunt of Eype, near market town of Bridport. Beach 5 minutes' walk. Accommodation suitable for the wheelchair user. No club or disco. CONTACT: MR SPEED, GOLDEN ACRE, EYPE, NEAR BRIDPORT DT6 6AL (01308 421521).

MRS CAROL MANSFIELD, LANCOMBES HOUSE, WEST MILTON, BRIDPORT DT6 3TN (01308 485375). 4 Keys Approved. Pretty cottages in converted barns. Panoramic views to sea four miles away. Set in 10 acres, some have fenced gardens. Many walks from our land. [Pets £10.00 per week.]

MR F. LOOSMORE, MANOR FARM HOLIDAY CENTRE, CHARMOUTH, BRIDPORT DT6 6QL (01297 560226). All units for 6 people, 10 minutes' level walk to beach, many fine local walks. Swimming pools, licensed bar with family room, shops launderette. Sporting facilities nearby. Children and pets welcome. SAE. [Pets £15 per week.]

BRIDPORT ARMS HOTEL, WEST BAY, BRIDPORT DT6 4EN (01308 422994). Thatched Hotel on edge of beach in picturesque West Bay. Two character bars, real ale, wide range bar meals. A la carte Restaurant featuring local fish. 2 Crowns Approved. AA/RAC One Star. [🐾]

MRS M. CHATTIN, DOGHOUSE FARM, CHIDEOCK, BRIDPORT DT6 6HY (01297 89208). 17th-century farmhouse, comfortable and welcoming. TV lounge. Tea/coffee making facilities. Two twin rooms, one double en suite. Terms from £16. Footpath, sea and village 10 minutes. Adjoining National Trust. [🐾]

Charmouth

Small resort on Lyme Bay, 3 miles Lyme Regis. Sandy beach backed by undulating cliffs, where many fossils are found. Good walks.

DOLPHINS RIVER PARK, BERNE LANE, CHARMOUTH DT6 6RD (012975 60022). Luxury 4 and 6 berth Caravans on small, peaceful park. Licensed shop, coin-op laundry; children's play area. One mile from beach. Colour brochure available. [pw! £1.20 per night.]

NEWLANDS CARAVAN PARK, CHARMOUTH, DORSET DT6 6RB (01297 560259). Six berth caravans for hire. Many adjacent to beach. Touring caravans and tents welcome. Two swimming pools. Free colour brochure.

Christchurch

Residential town near coast. Yachting based on Christchurch Harbour, with outlet into Christchurch Bay.

Country Holiday Chalet near woods and sea. Dogs welcome, SAE. APPLY – MRS L. M. BOWLING, OWLPEN, 148 BURLEY ROAD, BRANSGORE, DORSET BH23 8DB (01425 672875). [pw! 🐾]

Crewkerne

Market town on a sheltered slope of the Blackdown Hills, 8 miles south-west of Yeovil.

MRS G. SWANN, BROADVIEW, 43 EAST STREET, CREWKERNE TA18 7AG (01460 73424). Traditionally furnished bungalow in over an acre of gardens. Three en-suite bedrooms with colour TV, central heating etc. Bed and full English Breakfast £23. [🐾pw!]

Dorchester

Busy market town steeped in history. Home of Thomas Hardy. Roman remains include Amphitheatre, Age circle and villa.

MRS JACOBINA LANGLEY, THE STABLES, HYDE CROOK (ON A37), FRAMP-TON, DORCHESTER DT2 9NW (01300 320075). A comfortable equestrian property in some 20 acres grounds. Well situated for bridleways/footpaths. Guests' TV lounge, three bedrooms with en suite and private facilities. Tourist Board 2 Crowns. *[pw! £1.50 per night.]*

CHURCHVIEW GUEST HOUSE, WINTERBOURNE ABBAS, DORCHESTER DT2 9LS (01305 889296). Beautiful 17th Century Licensed Guest House set in the heart of West Dorset, character bedrooms, delightful period dining room, two lounges, one non-smoking. B&B £18–£24pp. B&BEM £28–£35. Two Crowns, AA QQQ. *[🐾]*

LAMPERTS FARMHOUSE AND COTTAGE, 11 DORCHESTER ROAD, SYDLING ST NICHOLAS, DORCHESTER DT2 9NU (01300 341 790). 17th Century thatched listed farmhouse nestling in the Sydling valley. Choose self catering in our well-equipped farm cottage or B&B in our tastefully decorated en suite bedrooms. *[🐾]*

Piddletrenthide

Village 6 miles north of Dorchester.

THE OLD BAKEHOUSE HOTEL, PIDDLETRENTHIDE, DORCHESTER DT2 7QR (01300 348305). Family-run B&B hotel ideal for visiting Dorset's beauty spots. All bedrooms en suite. Several good walks nearby. Write or phone for brochure. Two Crowns Commended. AA QQQ, RAC Acclaimed. *[Pets £2 per stay.]*

THE POACHERS INN, PIDDLETRENTHIDE DT2 7QX (01300 348358). On B3143 in lovely Piddle Valley, this delightful Inn offers en-suite rooms with colour TV, tea/coffee making, phones. Swimming pool; residents' lounge. Restaurant or Bar meals available. Garden – good dog walks! B&B from £21. 3 Crowns. RAC; AA QQQ. *[Pets £1 per night.]*

Poole

Popular resort, yachting and watersports centre with large harbour and many creeks. Sand and shingle beaches. Salisbury 30 miles, Dorchester 23, Blandford 14, Wareham 9, Bournemouth 5.

WHISPERING PINES. Self-contained holiday flat. Fully equipped except linen. Colour TV. Within easy reach of beaches and entertainments. SAE for brochure to MRS H. LEE, 9 SPUR HILL AVENUE, LOWER PARKSTONE, POOLE BH14 9PH (01202 740585). *[🐾]*

"SEA-WITCH", 47 HAVEN ROAD, CANFORD CLIFFS, POOLE BH13 7LH (01202 707697). Small licensed Hotel, clean, comfortable, fully en suite. B&B from £23–£33; Evening Meals. Convenient for ferries. Own car park. Open all year round. *[🐾]*

TWIN CEDARS HOTEL, 2 PINEWOOD ROAD, BRANKSOME PARK, POOLE BH13 6JS (01202 761339). All dogs welcome. Marvellous freshly prepared food; licensed bar, table tennis. Own grounds. Bed and Breakfast from £19.00, Evening Meal £9.00 p.p. Bathrooms/WCs en-suite. Accommodation also available in Cottages adjoining.

Portesham

Picturesque village 6 miles north-west of Weymouth.

MILLMEAD COUNTRY HOTEL, GOOSE HILL, PORTESHAM DT3 4HE (01305 871432). Set in an Area of Outstanding Natural Beauty the Millmead is ideal for exploring the surrounding countryside. All rooms en suite. Close to Sub-Tropical Gardens. Short breaks. [🐾]

Sherborne

Town with abbey dating mainly from 15th century. Two castles; ruined 12th-century Old Castle; and Sherborne Castle built by Sir Walter Raleigh in 1594, lake and gardens by Capability Brown.

MRS R. A. DARKNELL, THE BUNGALOW, WILLOW TREE FARM, BISHOP'S DOWN, NEAR SHERBORNE DT9 5PN (01963 210400). Bed, Breakfast and Evening Meal, £65–£70 per week. Good food. Quiet. Children and dogs welcome. Senior Citizens. [🐾]

Studland

Unspoilt seaside village at south-western end of Poole Bay, 3 miles north of Swanage.

KNOLL HOUSE HOTEL, STUDLAND BN19 3AW (01929 450450; Fax: 01929 450423) Country House Hotel within National Trust reserve. Golden beach. 100 acre grounds. Family suites, six lounges. Tennis, golf, swimming, games rooms, health spa. Full board terms £55–£79 daily. See also our full-page advertisement under Studland Bay. [Pets £3.50 nightly.]

THE MANOR HOUSE, STUDLAND BAY (01929 44288). An 18th century Manor House, nestling in 20 acres of secluded grounds. All bedrooms en suite with central heating, colour TV, direct dial telephone, tea/coffee making facilities. [Pets £2.75 per night.]

Sturminster Newton

Small town on River Stour, edged by Blackmoor Vale. Blandford Forum 8 miles.

MRS S. SOFIELD, OLD POST OFFICE, HINTON ST MARY, STURMINSTER NEWTON DT10 1NG (01258 472366). Comfortable, homely and conveniently situated to explore the beautiful, varied scenery of unspoilt Dorset. We appreciate the importance of holidays and do our best to make you and your pet welcome. Brochure on request. B&B £15, optional Evening Meal £7.50. Tourist Board Listed Commended.

Swanage

Traditional family holiday resort set in a sheltered bay ideal for water sports. Good base for a walking holiday.

LIMES HOTEL, 48 PARK ROAD, SWANAGE BH19 2AE (01929 422664). Small friendly Hotel. En suite rooms; tea/coffee facilities. Licensed bar. Central heating. Children and pets welcome. Telephone or SAE for brochure.

MRS GILLIAN MACDERMOTT, THE LITTLE MANOR, 389 HIGH STREET, SWAN-AGE BH19 2NP (01929 422948). A friendly small Guest House open all year round, where pets and children are welcome. Television, tea and coffee making facilities in all rooms. [🐾]

MRS M. SMITH, 35 PROSPECT CRESCENT, SWANAGE BH19 1BD (01929 423441). Comfortable Guest House. Quiet, level position. Good food. Bed and Breakfast. TV Lounge. Pets welcome. Parking. [🐾]

MRS M. STOCKLEY, SWANAGE CARAVAN SITE, 17 MOOR ROAD, SWANAGE BH19 1RG (01929 424154). 4/5/6-berth Caravans. Pets welcome. Easter to October. Colour TV. Shop. Parking space. Rose Award Park. √ √ √ √ [🐾]

Wareham

Picturesque riverside town, almost surrounded by earthworks, considered pre-Roman. Nature reserves of great beauty nearby. Weymouth 19 miles, Dorchester 17, Bournemouth 14, Swanage 10, Poole 6.

MRS L. S. BARNES, LUCKFORD WOOD HOUSE, EAST STOKE, WAREHAM BH20 6AW (Tel. and Fax: 01929 463098). Spacious, peaceful surroundings. Bed and Breakfast available in luxurious farmhouse. Camping facilities include showers and toilets. Near Lulworth Cove, Tank Museum and Corfe Castle. Open all year. LISTED. AA QQ [🐾]

Bloxworth Holiday Cottages. Large Georgian farmhouse and thatched cottages sleeping 5/12. Well furnished and equipped except linen and towels. Quiet village in country estate. Open all year. Dogs welcome. [🐾] SAE to MR & MRS P. G. MACDONALD-SMITH, BLOXWORTH ESTATE, NR WAREHAM, DORSET BH20 7EF (Tel/Fax: 01929 459442).

West Bexington

Seaside village with pebble beach. Chesil beach stretches eastwards. Nearby is Abbotsbury with its Benedictine Abbey, Chapel and famous Swannery. Dorchester 13 miles, Weymouth 13, Bridport 6.

GORSELANDS CARAVAN PARK, DEPT PW, WEST BEXINGTON-ON-SEA DT2 9DJ (Tel & Fax: 01308 897232). Quality graded "very good" park. Fully serviced and equipped 4/6 berth caravans. Shop and launderette on site. Glorious sea views. Good country and seaside walks. One mile to beach. Personal attention. Holiday apartments with sea views and private garden. Pets most welcome. Colour brochure on request. [🐾]

Weymouth

Set in a beautiful bay, with fine beaches and a picturesque 17th-century harbour, Weymouth has a wide range of entertainment and leisure amenities.

ACE HOLIDAY FLATS, 48–50 SPA ROAD, WEYMOUTH DT3 5EW (01305 779393). Clean, comfy self-contained Flats. 2–8 persons and dogs. Ample car park and garden. Near local shops, pub, Radipole Lake. Easy access town and sea. [Pets £12 weekly.]

WEYMOUTH BAY HOLIDAY PARK, PRESTON. One 6-berth Caravan. Near sea. Dogs welcome. APPLY – MRS D. W. CANNON, 151 SANDSTONE ROAD, GROVE PARK, LONDON SE12 0UT (0181-857 7586). [🐾]

CO. DURHAM

Castleside

A suburb 2 miles south-west of Consett.

LIZ LAWSON, BEE COTTAGE FARM, CASTLESIDE, CONSETT DH8 9HW (01207 508224). Working farm in lovely surroundings. Visitors welcome to participate in all farm activities. Ideal for Metro Centre, Durham Cathedral, Beamish Museum etc. Bed and Breakfast; Evening Meal available. ETB 2 Crowns Highly Commended. *[🐾]*

Lanchester

Small town 7 miles north west of Durham. Site of Roman fort of Longovicium.

STOCKERLEY HOUSE, WOODSIDE, LANCHESTER DH8 7TQ. Bed and Breakfast accommodation in the Derwent Valley. Bring your four-legged friends too. Access to off-road tracks, for cyclists, horse riders and walkers. Ideally situated for Durham City, Dales and Scottish Borders, and shopping at the Metro Centre. Contact MRS HOLMES (01207 502588).

ESSEX

Saffron Walden

Unspoilt town dominated by 193' spire of Essex's largest church. Timber-framed 15th and 16th century buildings with elaborate plasterwork.

MRS D. FORSTER, PARSONAGE FARM, ARKESDEN, SAFFRON WALDEN CB11 4HB (01799 550306). Lovely Victorian farmhouse on busy arable farm with some resident pets; lots of "walkies" on "set aside" and footpaths for pets. For owners, en-suite facilities available; coffee/tea making and TV in rooms. Tennis and relaxing in large garden. Bed and Breakfast from £16 per person. 1 Crown. *[🐾]*

All the advertisers in PETS WELCOME! have an entry in the appropriate classified section and each classified entry may carry one or more of the following symbols:

🐾   This symbol indicates that pets are welcome free of charge.

£   The £ indicates that a charge is made for pets. We quote the amount where possible, either per night or per week.

pw!   This symbol shows that the establishment has some special provision for pets; perhaps an exercise facility or some special feeding or accommodation arrangements.

🏠   Indicates separate pets accommodation.

PLEASE NOTE that all the advertisers in PETS WELCOME! extend a welcome to pets and their owners but they may attach conditions. The interests of other guests have to be considered and it is usually assumed that pets will be well trained, obedient and under the control of their owner.

GLOUCESTERSHIRE

GLOUCESTERSHIRE *Lydney, Stow-on-the-Wold, Stroud*

SYMONDS YAT ROCK MOTEL   Hillersland, Near Coleford GL16 7NY
Telephone: Dean (01594) 836191

Small family run Motel. All rooms en suite with colour TV and central heating. Licensed restaurant. Situated near Symonds Yat East and the Wye Valley in a beautiful area of the Royal Forest of Dean. Dogs welcome. Brochure on request. Tourist Board Listed.

WELCOME COTTAGE HOLIDAYS. Hundreds of properties in wonderful locations at welcoming low prices. Pets, linen and fuel mostly included. For FREE colour brochure telephone 01756 702212.

POWELLS COTTAGE HOLIDAYS. Your choice of Cottage in Cornwall, Devon, Somerset, Avon, Cotswolds, Wye Valley, Gower and Pembrokeshire in our full colour brochure. *[Pets £10 per week.]* FREEPHONE 0800 378771 or apply: 61 High Street, Saundersfoot, Pembrokeshire SA69 9EJ or (24 hrs) 01834 813232.

Bourton-on-the-Water

Delightfully situated on the River Windrush, which is crossed by miniature stone bridges. Stow-on-the-Wold 4 miles.

CHESTER HOUSE HOTEL, VICTORIA STREET, BOURTON-ON-THE-WATER GL54 2BU (01451 820286). Personally supervised by proprietor Mr Julian Davies. All rooms en-suite, all with central heating, colour TV, radio, phone, tea/coffee making facilities. Ideal for touring Cotswolds. *[🐎]*

Coleford

Small town in Forest of Dean, 3 miles River Wye. Gloucester 19 miles, Chepstow 13, Monmouth 6.

MR L. E. CAPELL, SYMONDS YAT ROCK MOTEL, HILLERSLAND, NEAR COLEFORD GL16 7NY (01594 836191). Family-run Motel in Royal Forest of Dean near Wye Valley. All rooms en suite, colour TV, central heating. Licensed restaurant. Dogs welcome. Brochure on request. *[🐎]*

Lydney

Small town 8 miles north-east of Chepstow. Nearby Lydney Park has ruined 12th-century castle and remains of Roman temple, set amongst woodland, lakes, fine shrubs and trees.

PARKEND HOUSE HOTEL, PARKEND, NEAR LYDNEY GL15 4HL (01594 563666). Small country hotel surrounded by parkland. All rooms en suite. Good food and friendly service. Pets and children welcome. Ideal for Cheltenham, Bath and Bristol. *[Pets £1.50 per night.]*

Nailsworth

Hilly town 4 miles south of Stroud.

LESLEY WILLIAMS-ALLEN, THE LAURELS, INCHBROOK, NAILSWORTH GL5 5HA (01453 834021). 18th century house. En-suite bedrooms. Secure garden and parking. Swimming pool. Snooker. Licensed. Excellent food. No smoking. Three commons and excellent walks nearby. Brochure available. *[🐎]*

Painswick

Beautiful little Cotswold town with characteristic stone-built houses.

MISS E. COLLETT, HAMBUTTS MYND, EDGE ROAD, PAINSWICK GL6 6UP
(01452 812352). Bed and Breakfast. Old Cotswold house, very quiet. Close to
village. Central heating and open fire in winter months. One double room, one twin,
one single, all with TV. From £20 to £39.50 per night. RAC Acclaimed. *[🐕]*

Stow-on-the-Wold

*Charming Cotswold hill-top market town with several old inns and interesting buildings, including
the Church (Perp.) in which hundreds of prisoners were confined after a Civil War battle in 1646.
Birmingham 45 miles, Gloucester 26, Stratford-upon-Avon 21, Cheltenham 18, Evesham 16,
Chipping Norton 9.*

"THE LIMES", EVESHAM ROAD, STOW-ON-THE-WOLD GL54 1EN (01451
830034/831056). Large country house. Attractive garden, overlooking fields, 4
minutes town centre. Television lounge. Central heating. Car park. Bed and
Breakfast from £16 to £18.50. Children and pets welcome. AA, RAC, Les Routiers.
Twin, double or family rooms, some en suite.

Stroud

*Cotswold town on River Frome below picturesque Stroudwater Hills, formerly renowned for
cloth-making. Bristol 32 miles, Bath 29, Chippenham 25, Cheltenham 14, Gloucester 9.*

DOWNFIELD HOTEL, CAINSCROSS ROAD, STROUD GL5 4HN (01453 764496).
Washbasins in all rooms, central heating. Residents' bar. Ideal for touring Cotswolds.
Personal supervision, 5 miles M5. Ample parking. Children and pets welcome.
Evening Meal optional. ETB 3 Crowns; AA QQQ; RAC Acclaimed. *[🐕]*

HAMPSHIRE

HAMPSHIRE   *Hayling Island, Middle Wallop*

A LUXURY GEORGIAN COUNTRY HOUSE HOTEL

The Woodlands Lodge Hotel is a luxury hotel set in 4 acres of grounds opening onto the beautiful New Forest. Although the hotel is totally refurbished with a stunning interior it still offers the peace and tranquillity often only found in buildings of age and establishment. All bedrooms enjoy full ensuite facilities of jacuzzi bath, separate thermostatic shower, with some bathrooms also having bidets. The sumptuous kingsize pocket  sprung beds are possibly the most comfortable beds guests have slept on (this opinion is constantly being expressed by guests). All other amenities are present including 21" fast text television, writing desks, armchairs, hairdryer, trouser press, Teasmaid and telephone. At Woodlands Lodge the hotel service is extremely friendly and informal thus enabling guests to totally relax and feel at home. Our dinner menu is modestly priced at a maximum of £16.95 (incl. à la carte) for three courses and coffee. It offers

 succulent giant king prawns, garlic mushrooms and many more mouth-watering starters, with main courses ranging from fresh local rainbow trout, New Forest venison, poulet sauté Marengo (chicken flamed in brandy and cooked with marsala wine and tomatoes) or plain traditional Scotch sirloin steaks, etc. Modestly priced wine list from £6.95.

Something for absolutely everyone!

Terms: per person per night (incl. VAT).
Luxury doubles from £49.50; De luxe doubles from £59.50;
De luxe (with balcony) from £69.50.
All prices are inclusive of Full English Breakfast

THE WOODLANDS LODGE HOTEL
Bartley Road, Woodlands, New Forest, Hampshire SO40 2GN

AA***   **Reservations: (01703) 292257**   ETB ♥♥♥♥
Highly Commended

Ashurst

Three miles north-east of Lyndhurst.

WOODLANDS LODGE HOTEL, BARTLEY ROAD, WOODLANDS, NEW FOREST SO4 2GN (01703 292257). Luxury Hotel offering peace and tranquillity. 18 bedrooms, all en suite, with TV, hairdryer, telephone etc. Modestly priced dinner menu and wine list offering excellent value. ETB 4 Crowns Highly Commended. [🐕]

Basingstoke

Historic town in the South of England. Close by Heathrow and Gatwick airports. An ideal touring base.

Modern six-berth Caravan – two bedrooms, shower, toilet, colour TV. Indoor and outdoor pools, Jacuzzi, sauna, bars, entertainment, restaurant, takeaway, supermarket on site. PHONE (01256 55009) or SAE to MRS L. A. WESTON, 19 KNIGHT STREET, BASINGSTOKE RG21 1AX. [🐕]

Bramshaw

New Forest village surrounded by National Trust land. Golf course nearby. Southampton 10 miles. Lyndhurst 6.

BRAMBLE HILL HOTEL, BRAMSHAW, NEAR LYNDHURST SO43 7JG (01703 813165). Fully licensed country house hotel with own livery stables. Unique seclusion amidst glorious surroundings. Unlimited riding and walking territory. Dogs welcome. *[Pets £4 per night.]* DIY livery for horses.

Brockenhurst

Popular village attractively situated in New Forest. Golf course. Bournemouth 18 miles, Southampton 13, Lymington 5, Lyndhurst 4.

BALMER LAWN HOTEL, LYNDHURST ROAD, BROCKENHURST SO42 7ZB (01590 623116; Fax: 01590 623864). Country House Hotel set in the heart of the New Forest. Ideal for country walking. Indoor and outdoor leisure facilities. 55 Bedrooms, all en suite. Excellent cuisine. AA***, RAC. *[🐾]*

Hayling Island

Family resort with sandy beaches. Ferry to Portsmouth and Southsea. Linked by bridge to Havant (5 miles).

HAYLING HOLIDAYS LTD, 44A EASTOKE AVENUE, HAYLING ISLAND PO11 9QP (01705 467271). Book with confidence. Holiday homes and caravans all close to sea. Superbly equipped and very clean. Personal service. Telephone now for free colour brochure. *[Pets £10 per week.]*

Middle Wallop

Village 7 miles south-west of Andover.

FIFEHEAD MANOR HOTEL RESTAURANT, MIDDLE WALLOP, STOCKBRIDGE SO20 8EG (Tel: 01264 781565; Fax: 01264 781400). Beautiful historic manor house surrounded by three acres of lovely gardens. Divine food. Wonderful welcome for you and your dog. 4 Crowns Highly Commended, 3 Star RAC/AA, Egon Ronay, Good Hotel Guide. *[🐾 pw!]*

New Forest

Area of heath and woodland of nearly 150 square miles, formerly Royal hunting grounds. Home of ponies which roam freely through unspoilt countryside.

BARTLEY LODGE HOTEL, PIKES HILL, LYNDHURST, HAMPSHIRE SO43 7AS (01703 812248). Grade II Listed country house hotel set in 8 acres of gardens and parkland district. B&B from £79.00 for double room – special break rates. Pets welcome. *[Pets £3.00 per night.]*

THE CROWN HOTEL, LYNDHURST, NEW FOREST, HAMPSHIRE SO43 7NF (01703 28 29 22). 93,000 acres of "heritage" forest and heath – such walks for dogs; such good food for owners! 3 Star AA Rosette, 39 en suite bedrooms, all different, all pretty; privately owned/managed. *[Pets £5.]*

WHITLEY RIDGE COUNTRY HOUSE HOTEL, BEAULIEU ROAD, BROCK-ENHURST SO42 7QL (01590 622354; Fax: 01590 622856). Georgian Hotel set in 5 acres of secluded grounds. Twelve bedrooms, all en-suite, cosy bar and splendid dining room. Superb cuisine, friendly and efficient service. Ideally located for the New Forest. *[🐾]*

Readers are requested to mention this guidebook when seeking accommodation (and please enclose a stamped addressed envelope).

Portsmouth

Port and naval base with rich maritime heritage. Nelson's flagship HMS Victory lies in the harbour; of interest too are HMS Warrior and the Mary Rose.

MAYVILLE HOTEL, WAVERLEY ROAD, SOUTHSEA PO5 2PN (Freephone 0500 343494). Dogs. Car park for 20 cars on premises. Good food. Families catered for. Near beach. *[🐕]*

Ringwood

Busy market town on the River Avon, and a centre for trout fishing, trekking and rambling. There are some attractive old houses and inns, and a pretty Early English church. Bournemouth 13 miles, Lyndhurst 12.

MS S. P. STREET AND MS M. D. JENKINS, SUNEST PARK, 126 RINGWOOD ROAD, ST IVES, RINGWOOD BH24 2NT (01425 473750). New Forest: Bungalow/ Chalets, fully equipped, sleep 2/8. Small park, fenced gardens. Pets welcome. Local fishing, riding, walking, golf, sailing, coast 8 miles. *[Pets £10 per week.]*

MR AND MRS D. C. HAYLES, BURBUSH FARM, POUND LANE, BURLEY, NEAR RINGWOOD BE24 4EF (01425 403238). Character cottage delightfully situated in the heart of the New Forest close to Burley village. Equipped to highest standard with central heating. Each sleeps five. From £150 per week. *[Pets £10 per week.]*

Sway

Village in southern part of New Forest and within easy reach of sea. Lymington 4 miles SE.

THE NURSE'S COTTAGE, STATION ROAD, SWAY, LYMINGTON SO41 6BA (Tel/Fax: 01590 683402). Obedient pets and owners welcome! This popular licensed guest-house provides every possible comfort in cosy cottage surroundings. No smoking. Dinner, Bed & Breakfast from £40. *[🐕]*

GREEN PASTURES, PITMORE LANE, SWAY, LYMINGTON, HAMPSHIRE SO41 8LL (01590 682461). Situated close to the edge of the Forest this comfortable, modern family home in a rural setting is friendly and informal. Tea and coffee facilities and TV in room. B&B £14.50. *[🐕]*

MRS THELMA ROWE, 9 CRUSE CLOSE, SWAY, HANTS SO41 6AY (01590 683092). Ground floor accommodation. Bedroom, private bathroom and sitting room. Tea making facilities. TV. 3 minutes from open Forest. 4 miles from coast. Bed and Breakfast from £15. *[🐕]*

Winchester

Site of an old Roman town. Ancient capital of Wessex and of England. Notable Cathedral, famous boys' public school, a wealth of old and historic buildings.

ROYAL HOTEL, ST PETER STREET, WINCHESTER SO23 8BS (01962 840840. Fax: 01962 841582). Quality hotel of character quietly located in the heart of England's ancient capital. All rooms en suite with satellite TV, tea and coffee and telephone. ETB 5 Crowns Commended. *[🐕]*

Woodlands

Village on fringe of New Forest. Delightful scenery. Southampton 7 miles, Lyndhurst 4½.

BUSKETTS LAWN HOTEL, WOODLANDS, ASHURST, NEAR SOUTHAMPTON SO40 7GL (01703 292272 or 292077; Fax: 01703 292487). Comfortable Country House Hotel. Quiet surroundings, seasonal heated swimming pool, mini football/ cricket pitch, putting and croquet lawns. All rooms en suite. Open all year. *[Pets £3/£4 per night.]*

HEREFORDSHIRE

HEREFORDSHIRE   *Great Malvern, Hereford*

WELCOME COTTAGE HOLIDAYS. Hundreds of properties in wonderful locations at welcoming low prices. Pets, linen and fuel mostly included. For FREE colour brochure telephone 01756 702212.

Great Malvern

Fashionable spa town in last century with echoes of that period. Greatest treasure is the 11th-century church with 15th-century stained glass.

MR AND MRS D. BERISFORD, WHITEWELLS FARM COTTAGES, RIDGWAY CROSS, NEAR MALVERN WR13 5JS (01886 880607). Charming converted Cottages, sleep 2–6. Fully equipped with colour TV, fridge, iron, etc. Linen, towels also supplied. One cottage suitable for disabled guests. ETB 4 Keys Highly Commended. *[Pets £12 per week.]*

Hereford

Well-known touring centre on River Wye with several interesting old buildings, including Cathedral (Norm. and Dec.). Good sport and entertainment facilities including steeple-chasing. Cheltenham 37 miles, Gloucester 28, Worcester 26, Ludlow 24, Malvern 21, Monmouth 18, Ross-on-Wye 15.

MRS R. T. ANDREWS, WEBTON COURT, KINGSTONE, HEREFORD HR2 9NF (01981 250220). Georgian black and white farmhouse in heart of beautiful Wye Valley. All bedrooms with washbasins. Children and pets welcome. B&B or Evening Dinner, B&B. Large parties catered for. Long-term accommodation at reduced rates. Riding and riding lessons available.

NEW PRIORY HOTEL, STRETTON SUGWAS, HEREFORD (Tel and Fax: 01432 760264). The New Priory Hotel is situated just a short distance from the Hereford city limits in 3½ acre grounds. 10 bedrooms all with private bath or shower except for single rooms which have an adjacent shower. 3 Crowns. *[🐾]*

DIANA SINCLAIR, HOLLY HOUSE, ALLENSMORE, HEREFORD HR2 9BH (01432 277294). Escape with your horse or dog to our spacious luxury farmhouse. Bed and Breakfast from £16.

MARJORIE AND BRIAN ROBY, FELTON HOUSE, FELTON, NEAR HEREFORD HR1 3PH (01432 820366). Period-furnished stone-built Rectory in charming rural area. Double, single, twin-bedded rooms. Bed and Breakfast from £17.50. Vegetarian choice. Good Inns nearby for evening meals. Ideal locality for touring. *[🐾]*

Kington

Town on River Arrow, close to Welsh border 12 miles north of Leominster.

MRS C. D. WILLIAMS, RADNOR'S END, HUNTINGTON, KINGTON HR5 3NZ (01544 370 289). Detached cottage (sleeps 5) in lovely unspoiled Welsh border countryside, where rolling hills are home to Buzzard, Kestrel, Red Kite and a rich variety of other birds and wild flowers. Offa's Dyke footpath and Kilvert's Country nearby. Ample parking, lawn. *[🐾]*

**FREE and REDUCED RATE Holiday Visits!
Don't miss our Readers' Offer Vouchers on
pages 5 to 18.**

Ledbury

Pleasant town ideally situated for Ledbury Park, Market Hall, Cotswolds and Wye Valley. Buildings of note include Almshouses, Black and White Houses and Church (Norman to Perp.). Good centre for bowls, fishing, riding and tennis. Monmouth 23 miles, Leominster 22, Gloucester 17, Tewkesbury 14, Malvern 8.

MRS JANE WEST, CHURCH FARM, CODDINGTON, LEDBURY HR8 1JJ (01531 640271). Black and white 16th-century Farmhouse on a working farm close to the Malvern Hills – ideal for touring and walking. Three double bedrooms. Excellent home cooking. Bed and Breakfast from £19. Open all year. SAE for details. [🐾]

Leominster

Old wool town among rivers, hop-yards and orchards. Many lovely timbered buildings. Five miles north west is Croft Castle. Birmingham 45 miles, Gloucester 37, Hereford 13, Ludlow 11.

MRS P. W. BROOKE, NICHOLSON FARM, LEOMINSTER HR6 0SL (01568 760269). Cottage and two Bungalows sleeping 2–5. Open Easter to early October. Linen hire available. Attractive, peaceful area, good walking. Convenient Hereford and Worcester Cathedral Cities and for visits to Elan Valley Lakes north of A44. [🐾]

Llangarron

Picturesque village 5 miles north of Monmouth.

MRS P. AMOS, OAKLANDS, LLANGARRON, ROSS-ON-WYE HR9 6NZ (01989 770277). About 3 miles from Symonds Yat and Forest of Dean. Two cottages with large enclosed private gardens; sleep 2–7. Personally supervised. Three Keys Approved.

Much Birch

Village six miles south of Hereford.

POOLSPRINGE FARM COTTAGES. 5 delightfully converted cottages and a bungalow on secluded farm. Ideal for touring. Use of indoor swimming pool, sauna and solarium. Fully equipped incl. colour TV. Linen for hire on request. APPLY: DAVID AND VAL BEAUMONT, POOLSPRINGE FARM, MUCH BIRCH, HEREFORD HR2 8JJ (01981 540355). [Pets £15 weekly.]

Ross-on-Wye

An attractive town standing on a hill rising from the left bank on the Wye. Cardiff 47 miles, Gloucester 17.

YE HOSTELRIE, GOODRICH, ROSS-ON-WYE HR9 6HX (01600 890241). Enjoy seclusion, comfort and good food at this fully centrally heated 17th Century Inn. We have a reputation for quality food at a reasonable price.

THE KING'S HEAD HOTEL, 8 HIGH STREET, ROSS-ON-WYE, HEREFORDSHIRE HR9 5HL (Tel: 01989 763174; Fax: 01989 769578). Small coaching inn dating back to the 14th century with all bedrooms offering en suite bathrooms and a full range of modern amenities. A la carte menu offers home-cooked food which is served in a warm and friendly atmosphere. [🐾]

HEREFORDSHIRE

THE ARCHES COUNTRY HOUSE HOTEL, WALFORD ROAD, ROSS-ON-WYE HR9 5PT (01989 563348). Georgian Country House. Lovely rooms with all facilities; en-suite available. Centrally heated. Pets welcome. Bed and Breakfast or Half Board, weekly reductions available. AA, RAC, Les Routiers, Three Crowns.

GRAHAM WILLIAMS, THE SKAKES, GLEWSTONE, ROSS-ON-WYE H49 6AZ (01989 770456). 18th century farmhouse, orchard and garden setting, with superb views. Stone walls, open fireplace, licensed barn restaurant; well-equipped rooms, central heating. Parking. Bed and Breakfast from £17.00. [🐴]

ISLES OF SCILLY

St. Mary's

Largest of group of granite islands and islets off Cornish Coast. Terminus for air and sea services from mainland. Main income from flower-growing. Seabirds, dolphins and seals abound.

MRS PAMELA MUMFORD, SALLAKEE FARM, ST. MARY'S TR21 0NZ (01720 22391). Self catering farm cottage, available all year round. Sleeps 5. Children and pets welcome. Write or phone for details. Three Keys.

ISLE OF WIGHT

ISLE OF WIGHT   *Alum Bay, Bonchurch, Colwell Bay*

 **Holiday Apartments**

In acres of National Trust land with breathtaking views over the Needles. Lovely two-bedroom apartment – fully equipped for 4 including colour television.

Open all year. Dogs welcome.

Colour brochure: **Marion Smith, Headon Hall, Alum Bay, Isle of Wight PO39 0JD
Tel: (01983) 752123**

BONCHURCH MANOR

Bonchurch, Isle of Wight PO38 1NU Tel: 01983 852868
Bonchurch Manor is situated on the sheltered south coast of the Isle of Wight with spacious grounds overlooking the sea. All bedrooms with private facilities, colour TV, telephone and hair dryer. Five course table d'hôte and à la carte menu. 4 Crowns Highly Commended, RAC 2 Stars, Ashley Courtenay.

ONTARIO PRIVATE HOTEL

Colwell Common Road, Colwell Bay, Isle of Wight PO39 0DD Tel: (01983) 753237
Family run Hotel, offering a high standard of accommodation, excellent home-cooking and a warm welcome. En-suite bedrooms, licensed bar, private parking. Extensive grounds overlooking Colwell Common and central to National Trust Countryside. Only four minutes' walk to the beach. ♥ ♥

ISLE OF WIGHT   *Freshwater, Niton, Ryde, Shanklin*

 MOUNTFIELD **D**
HOLIDAY PARK
BHHPA
STB
FRESHWATER, ISLE OF WIGHT
Telephone: Freshwater (01983) 752993

Set in four acres of beautiful countryside, 2/6 berth Bungalows, 2/6 berth Chalets, 2/6 berth Caravans all with own toilet, bath or shower, TV. Licensed bar and club room with pool table. Good food. Table tennis room. Heated swimming pool. Play area for children with swings, etc. SAE please.

Proprietors: **The Roberts Family, Mountfield Holiday Park, Norton Green, Freshwater, Isle of Wight.**

WINDCLIFFE MANOR

 SANDROCK ROAD, NITON UNDERCLIFF PO38 2NG
(Tel: 01983 730215)

An historic Manor House set in wooded gardens on the southernmost part of the island
Bed, Breakfast and Evening Meal
We invite you to spend your holiday with us in our family run business.
We try to make you feel at home, because this is our home,
as well as our business! Trust us to do our best for you!
CHILDREN AND DOGS WELCOME

Heated pool ★ Colour television ★ Games room ★ No service charge ★ SAE for brochure
Under personal supervision of Proprietors: Mr & Mrs D. A. Heron

 # HILLGROVE PARK
Field Lane, St Helens, Ryde PO33 1UT

A secluded family-run holiday caravan park only minutes away from safe sandy beaches, beautiful countryside and places of interest. From 4 to 6/7 berth, we have a wide range of caravans and prices to suit all requirements. *Heated swimming pool, large play area, games room, self service shop with off-licence and laundry facilities.* Car ferries arranged on any route.
Pets welcome
Licensed Easter to October
For details ring I.O.W. (01983) 872802

BONDI HOTEL
Small friendly hotel. En-suite rooms with colour TV, tea-making and hairdryers. Choice of fine food. Licensed. Open all year. ETB Three Crowns Highly Commended, RAC Highly Acclaimed, AA QQQQ Selected. B&B from £18–£25; Optional Evening Dinner.
CLARENCE ROAD, SHANKLIN, ISLE OF WIGHT PO37 7BH TEL: 01983 862507

FHG PUBLICATIONS LIMITED publish a large range of well-known accommodation guides. We will be happy to send you details or you can use the order form at the back of this book.

Alum Bay

In extreme west of island, one mile from the Needles and lighthouse. Cliffs and multicoloured sands, Newport 13 miles, Yarmouth 5.

MARION SMITH, HEADON HALL, ALUM BAY PO39 0LD (01983 752123). Lovely two bedroom apartment, fully equipped for 4/6, including colour television. Breathtaking views. Dogs welcome. *[Pets £10 per week.]*

Bonchurch

Formerly a fishing and quarrying hamlet, during the last century Bonchurch became a magnet for many eminent literary figures. Its peace and beauty are as evident today as they were in days gone by.

BONCHURCH MANOR, BONCHURCH, ISLE OF WIGHT PO38 1NU (01983 852868). Bonchurch Manor combines elegance and comfort to provide a perfect setting for a holiday at any time of the year. Tastefully furnished bedrooms all with private facilities. Restaurant is regarded as one of the finest on the island. *[🐩]*

Chale

Pleasant village with sand and shingle beach. Several picturesque chines in the vicinity. Freshwater 11 miles, Newport 9, Ventnor 7.

JOHN AND JEAN BRADSHAW, THE CLARENDON HOTEL, CHALE PO38 2HA (01983 730431). 17th Century Coaching Inn, overlooking magnificent West Wight coast. Television lounge. First-class restaurant. Live entertainment nightly all year round. *[pw! £3 per night, £15 per week.]*

Colwell Bay

Small resort at western extremity of the island, excellent sands, cliff walks. Totland 2 miles, Yarmouth 2.

ONTARIO PRIVATE HOTEL, COLWELL COMMON ROAD, COLWELL BAY PO39 0DD (01983 753237). Family-run Hotel. Home cooking. En-suite bedrooms, licensed bar, private parking. Only four minutes' walk to the beach. Two Crowns. *[🐩]*

Cowes

Yachting centre with yearly regatta since 1814. Home of Royal Yacht Squadron. Victorian and Edwardian shops line narrow streets behind wide esplanade. 4 miles Newport.

SUNNYCOTT CARAVAN PARK, COWES PO31 8NN (01983 292859). 20 Deluxe and Luxury 4 and 6 berth caravans on quiet country park in rural surroundings. Laundry room and shop on site. Open from March to January. *[🐩]*

Freshwater

Pleasant and quiet resort on Freshwater Bay, near the start of the Tennyson Trail, Sandown 20 miles, Cowes 15, Newport 11, Yarmouth 4.

THE ROBERTS FAMILY, MOUNTFIELD HOLIDAY PARK, NORTON GREEN, FRESHWATER (01983 752993). 2/6-berth Bungalows, Chalets and Caravans, all set in beautiful countryside. Licensed bar. Television. Good food. ETB 3 ticks. *[Pets £10 per week.]*

Niton

Delightful village near sea at the southernmost part of the island. Several secluded chines nearby, cliff walks, Ventnor 5 miles.

MR AND MRS D. A. HERON, WINDCLIFFE MANOR, SANDROCK ROAD, NITON UNDERCLIFF PO38 2NG (01983 730215). Bed, Breakfast and Evening Meal in a historic Manor House set in wooded gardens. Heated pool. Colour television. Games room. Children and dogs welcome. 3 Crowns. *[pw!]*

Ryde

Popular resort and yachting centre, fine sands, pier. Shanklin 9 miles, Newport 7, Sandown 6.

HILLGROVE PARK, FIELD LANE, ST HELENS, NEAR RYDE PO33 1UT (01983 872802). Select site 10 minutes sea, 3 minutes bus stop. Self-service shop, heated swimming pool. Pets welcome. SAE brochure. *[Pets £10.00 per week.]*

Shanklin

Safe sandy beaches and traditional entertainments make this a family favourite. Cliff lift connects the beach to the cliff top.

THE CRESCENT HOTEL, HOPE ROAD, SHANKLIN, ISLE OF WIGHT PO37 6EA (01983 863140). This comfortable hotel now offers dog owners a walking package – IoW Strollers. This includes advance information and maps tailored to suit your interests and abilities. See our advertisement for hotel details. *[Pets £1.50 per night, £9 per week.]*

BONDI HOTEL, CLARENCE ROAD, SHANKLIN PO37 7BH (01983 862507). Small friendly hotel. En suite rooms with colour TV, tea making and hairdryers. Choice of fine food. Licensed. Open all year. B&B from £18; optional EM. ETB 3 Crowns Highly Commended, RAC Highly Acclaimed, AA QQQQ Selected. *[🐕]*

Totland

Little resort with good sands, safe bathing and high cliffs. Newport 13 miles, Yarmouth 3, Freshwater 2.

THE NODES COUNTRY HOTEL, TOTLAND BAY PO39 0HZ (01983 752859). Lovely Country House in extensive grounds. Children at reduced rates. Country cooking. Riding, fishing, sailing and golf nearby. *[🐕 pw!]*

COUNTRY GARDEN HOTEL, CHURCH HILL, TOTLAND BAY PO39 0ET (01983 754521: Fax: 01983 754421). Overlooking the sea, superb hotel; all rooms with bath and shower, TV, telephone, fridge, hairdryer etc. Telephone for brochure, tariff. Special spring and autumn rates.

SENTRY MEAD HOTEL, MADEIRA ROAD, TOTLAND BAY PO39 0BJ (01983 753212; Freephone 0500 131277). Get away from it all at this friendly and comfortable haven, just two minutes from sandy beach. Bedrooms have en suite bath or shower, colour TV and radio. Delicious table d'hôte dinners; lunchtime bar menu. *[Pets £1 per night.]*

Ventnor

Well-known resort with good sands, downs, popular as a winter holiday resort. Nearby is St Boniface Down, the highest point on the island. Ryde 13 miles, Newport 12, Sandown 7, Shanklin 4.

A. EVANS, "THE WATERFALL", SHORE ROAD, BONCHURCH, VENTNOR PO38 1RN (01983 852246). Spacious, self-contained Flats. Sleep up to 4. Colour TV. Sun verandah and garden. The beach, the sea and the downs nearby. [🐕]

RAVENSCOURT HOLIDAY BUNGALOWS, OCEAN VIEW ROAD, VENTNOR PO38 1AA (01983 852555). For self catering holidays for you and your pet on England's Sunshine Isle. Attractive bungalows, each accommodates up to six. Adjoins National Trust downland overlooking Ventnor. SAE or phone for brochure.

SEAGULLS HOTEL, BELLEVUE ROAD, VENTNOR, PO38 1DB (01983 852085). En-suite, centrally heated rooms with colour TV. Excellent home cooked menu. Hotel overlooks sea in quiet location. Close to Botanical Gardens, coastal paths and downs. Parking. licensed. ETB 3 Crowns Commended. Colour brochure.

WOODLYNCH HOLIDAY APARTMENTS, SHORE ROAD, BONCHURCH, VENTNOR PO38 1RF (01983 852513). Comfortable self-contained holiday apartments in picturesque seaside village from £75 per week. Pleasant seaside and country walks, gardens and private parking. Dogs welcome. Tourist Board Member. Please write or phone for brochure and tariff. [🐕]

Yarmouth

Coastal resort situated 9 miles west of Newport. Castle built by Henry VIII for coastal defence.

THE ORCHARDS HOLIDAY CARAVAN & CAMPING PARK, NEWBRIDGE, YARMOUTH, ISLE OF WIGHT PO41 0TS (Tel: 01983 531 331; Fax: 01983 531 666). Luxury caravans. Excellent camping facilities. Heated outdoor swimming pool, self service shop. Takeaway food bar. Coarse fishing. Complete ferry booking service. Five ticks. Rose Award. [Pets £1 per night, pw!]

"TUCKAWAY" – Holiday Chalet in private, secluded position. Sleeps six. Swimming pool. Dogs welcome. Large grassed area. Tourist Board Approved. APPLY – R. STEDMAN, FURZEBREAK, CRANMORE AVENUE, YARMOUTH PO41 0XR (01983 760082). [🐕]

KENT

KENT *Broadstairs*

HANSON HOTEL Licensed
Belvedere Road, Broadstairs. Tel: Thanet (01843) 868936
A small friendly Georgian hotel with relaxed atmosphere, centrally situated for beach, shops and transport.
Renowned for excellent food, we offer a 5-course Evening Dinner with choice of menu prepared by Chef/Proprietor.
* TV Lounge * Attractive Bar * Reading Room * Private Showers
Babies, children and pets welcome. Children reduced rates – one child per family free when sharing parents' room on weekly stays.
OPEN ALL YEAR   SPRING AND WINTER BREAKS
S.A.E. or telephone for brochure to Trevor and Jean Webb

Broadstairs

Quiet resort, once a favourite of Charles Dickens. Good sands and promenades.

TREVOR AND JEAN WEBB, HANSON HOTEL, BELVEDERE ROAD, BROAD-STAIRS (01843 868936). Small, friendly licensed Georgian Hotel. Home comforts; babies, children and pets welcome. Attractive bar. SAE. *[pw! 50p per night.]*

CASTLEMERE HOTEL, WESTERN ESPLANADE, BROADSTAIRS CT10 1TD (01843 861566; Fax: 01843 866379). 40 bedrooms, 31 with private bathrooms. Telephone and colour television in bedrooms. Television lounge. Licensed. Selective menus. Near beach, on seafront. Diets and children catered for. Dogs welcome. ETB 3 Crowns Commended, AA, RAC. *[Pets £2.00 per night.]*

Folkestone

Important cross-Channel port with good sandy beach and narrow old streets winding down to the harbour.

ABBEY HOUSE HOTEL, 5–6 WESTBOURNE GARDENS, OFF SANDGATE ROAD, FOLKESTONE CT20 2JA (01303 255514; Fax: 01303 245098). Friendly, Two Crown licensed Hotel, five minutes from Leas Promenade and Country Park. Convenient for Tunnel and Ferry. Bed and Breakfast from £18.00. *[Pets £1 per night.]*

THE HORSESHOE HOTEL, 29 WESTBOURNE GARDENS, FOLKESTONE CT20 2HY (01303 243433). Spacious Private Hotel close Promenade and town centre. All rooms colour TV, washbasins, tea/coffee making facilities; some en suite. Parking. Friendly hospitality and good home cooking. Mini Breaks. Details on request. Hotel and Catering Reg. ETB 2 Crowns. *[🐾]*

Herne Bay

Homely family resort on North Kent coast. Shingle beach with sand at low tide. Maidstone 32 miles, Faversham 13, Canterbury 9, Whitstable 5.

MR AND MRS N. EVANS, 156 BELTINGE ROAD, HERNE BAY CT6 6JE (01227 375750). A fully furnished detached bungalow for three people (double and single bedrooms). Car parking space and enclosed rear garden. Brochure on request. *[🐾]*

Hythe

Village on west bank of Southampton Water. Ferry connection for pedestrians. Urban expansion inland.

STADE COURT HOTEL, HYTHE, KENT CT21 6DT (01303 268263). Situated on the seafront close to parks and the beach, the hotel has comfortable well-equipped bedrooms with en suite facilities. Leisure and golf facilities available at our sister hotel close by. Phone for brochure and tariff. *[Pets "Doggie Dinner" £7.50 per night.]*

Margate

Most popular family resort with sands and harbour. Numerous attractions and entertainments. Maidstone 44 miles, Dover 22, Canterbury 16, Herne Bay 13, Sandwich 9, Ramsgate 5.

THE RAMBLERS, 19 ROYAL ESPLANADE, WESTBROOK, MARGATE CT9 5DX (01843 227306). Family-run licensed guest house overlooking the sea. All rooms have TV and tea making facilities. Open all year. Short breaks. Telephone for brochure. *[Pets 50p per night.]*

Ramsgate

Long-established family resort with sands, harbour and cliffs. Amusements, entertainments. Cross-Channel ferry. Maidstone 45 miles, Canterbury 18, Margate 5.

MR COSTIN, "SEASCAPE", 9 THE PARAGON, RAMSGATE CT11 9JX (01843 596829). Holiday flats on seafront; Promenade, shops/green close by. Colour TVs, own toilet/shower. H&C all rooms. Linen included. Personally supervised. Open May to September. *[🐕]*

LANCASHIRE

LANCASHIRE *Blackpool*

ASH-LEA GUEST HOUSE
76 LORD STREET, BLACKPOOL FY1 2DG TEL: 01253 28161
Good food and comfort assured. Tea making facilities and TV in all rooms. Some rooms with toilet en suite. Large TV lounge. Free showers. Close to all amenities. B&B from £11.00 Early Evening Meal optional extra. Open all year. Special rates for Senior Citizens, children and weekly bookings. No charge for pets.

SELECT HOLIDAY FLATLETS, ADJOINING QUEENS PROMENADE
COTSWOLD HOLIDAY FLAT/LETS, 2A HADDON ROAD, NORBRECK, BLACKPOOL FY2 9AH Tel: (01253) 352227
• Fully equipped including colour television and fridge • Select area North Shore
• Cross road to beach and trams • Short breaks early season and Illuminations
• Sleep up to seven. Rates from £56 per week. Details from Mrs C. Moore.
Open all year • S.A.E. for brochure stating dates plus number in party. Pets free

HAMPSON HOUSE
Hotel and Restaurant
AA**   RAC**   ETB 3 Crowns
Hampson Lane, Hampson Green, Nr Lancaster
Tel: 01524 751158 Fax: 01524 751779

A family run, fully licensed hotel with 14 bedrooms all with private facilities, radio, telephone, TV, and welcome tray. Set in two acres of mature gardens, the original house was built circa 1600 A.D. and was the home of the Welsh family from 1666 until 1973 when it was sold and converted into a hotel. Situated in an area known as "The Gateway to the Lakes" it is also an ideal base for the leisure traveller to use while touring the North West of England or halfway house for the traveller on his way North or South.

*   Manchester 40 miles   *   Blackpool 16 miles   *   The Lakes 30 miles   *
*   Morecambe 8 miles   *   Lancaster 4 miles   *   Glasson Park 4 miles   *

CRIMOND HOTEL ☙☙☙☙
Knowsley Road, Southport PR9 0HN *Tel: 01704 536456 Fax: 01704 548643*
The Crimond Hotel is situated close to the promenade and town centre. The 12 bedroom hotel has an indoor pool, sauna and jacuzzi. Open all year. All bedrooms en-suite with colour TV, radio, hair dryer and direct dial telephone.
Large car park.

THE AMBASSADOR HOTEL
13 Bath Street, Southport PR9 ODP Tel: 01704 543998 or 530459

Delightful small, quality Hotel centrally situated between Promenade and Lord Street. Noted for its warm welcome, good food and hospitality. Bedrooms en suite with colour TV and all facilities. Comfortable bar where lunchtime/late night snacks are available. Choice of menu; children's menu. Central heating. Car Park.

ETB ☙☙☙ Commended   **AA QQQ.**
Les Routiers   **British Tourist Authority Commended.**

Readers are requested to mention this guidebook when seeking accommodation (and please enclose a stamped addressed envelope).

Blackpool

Famous resort with fine sands and many attractions and vast variety of entertainments. Blackpool Tower (500ft). Three piers. Manchester 47 miles, Lancaster 26, Preston 17, Fleetwood 9.

ASH-LEA GUEST HOUSE, 76 LORD STREET, BLACKPOOL FY1 2DG (01253 28161). Good food and comfort assured. All rooms TV, some rooms toilet en suite. Free showers. Close to all amenities. B&B from £11.00, early Evening Meal optional extra. No charge for pets. *[🐕]*

MRS C. MOORE, COTSWOLD HOLIDAY FLATLETS, 2A HADDON ROAD, NOR-BRECK, BLACKPOOL FY2 9AH (01253 352227). Holiday Flatlets fully equipped. Cross road to beach and trams. Select area. Open all year. Short Breaks early season and Illuminations. SAE. *[🐕]*

Clitheroe

Pleasant market town, with ruined Norman keep standing on limestone cliff above grey roofs. Pendle Hill 4 miles to the east, from where there are spectacular views of the Forest of Bowland.

MRS FRANCES OLIVER, WYTHA FARM, RIMINGTON, CLITHEROE BB7 4EQ (01200 445295). Farmhouse accommodation in heart of countryside. Panoramic views. Warm welcome. Double and family rooms. Ideal touring centre. Bed and Breakfast from £14. Evening Meal £8. ETB LISTED. *[pw! Pets £1 per day.]*

Lancaster

For centuries the county town of Lancashire. Lancaster canal, which runs to north of Kendal, crosses the Lune on a fine aqueduct built in 1797 by Rennie. An impressive Norman Castle and fine Georgian houses around the area. Preston 20 miles.

HAMPSON HOUSE, HAMPSON LANE, HAMPSON GREEN, LANCASTER (Tel: 01524 751158; Fax: 01524 751779). A family-run, fully licensed hotel with 14 bedrooms all with private facilities, radio, telephone, TV and welcome tray. Set in two acres of mature gardens and situated in an area known as "The Gateway to the Lakes", it is also an ideal base for the leisure traveller.

Southport

Attractive and well-planned resort with sands and dunes. Many family attractions. Blackpool 34 miles, Liverpool 20, Preston 18.

SIDBROOK HOTEL, 14 TALBOT STREET, SOUTHPORT PR8 1HP (01704 530608; Fax: 01704 531198). Central and quiet comfortable accommodation. All rooms en suite. Run by two short, fat, mad Bassets, Agatha and Gemma. Bed and Breakfast from £17.50. ETB 4 Crowns Commended. RAC 1 Star. Brochure available.

THE AMBASSADOR HOTEL, 13 BATH STREET, SOUTHPORT PR9 0DP (01704 543998 or 530459). Delightful small, quality Hotel centrally situated between Promenade and Lord Street. Warm welcome, good food and hospitality. Bedrooms en suite with colour TV and all facilities. Bar where lunchtime/late night snacks are available. Car park. ETB 3 Crowns Commended, AA QQQ. Telephone call will bring you our brochure. Les Routiers. *[🐕]*

CRIMOND HOTEL & RESTAURANT, KNOWSLEY ROAD, SOUTHPORT PR9 0HN (Tel: 01704 536456; Fax: 01704 548643). Situated close to the town centre this 19 bedroom hotel can cater for all your needs with the luxury of an indoor Leisure Centre. Open all year. Table d'hôte service. Full central heating. *[🐕]*

LEICESTERSHIRE

LEICESTERSHIRE *Melton Mowbray*

SYSONBY KNOLL HOTEL **ASFORDBY ROAD** **MELTON MOWBRAY** **LEICESTERSHIRE LE13 0HP** **TEL: 01664-63563**	Traditional family-run Hotel with 24 bedrooms, all en-suite. All have TV, tea/coffee facilities and telephone. Ground floor rooms available. Restaurant serving à la carte menu, also set meals. Bar snacks served until 9pm. Large enclosed car park. Lovely gardens; outdoor swimming pool. 4 Crowns Commended RAC*** AA** Les Routiers

Melton Mowbray

Old market town, centre of hunting country. Noted for Stilton cheese and pork pies. Large cattle market. Church (E.E. and Perp.) and Anne of Cleves' House are of interest. Kettering 29 miles, Market Harborough 22, Nottingham 18, Grantham 16, Leicester 15.

MRS S. BOOTH, SYSONBY KNOLL HOTEL, ASFORDBY ROAD, MELTON MOWBRAY LE13 0HP (01664 63563). Set in two acres of grounds with outdoor swimming pool. Emphasis upon good food and the comfort of our guests. Central heating. TV and tea/coffee facilities in all our en-suite rooms. 2 lounges, cosy bar. [🐴]

Oakham

Small market town in vale of Catmose, 9 miles south east of Melton Mowbray. 12th century Great Hall survives from former fortified manor house. Market place with Butter Cross.

THE OLD RECTORY, BELTON IN RUTLAND, OAKHAM, RUTLAND LE15 9LE (01572 717279; Fax: 01572 717343). A country house on edge of this conservation village. Ground floor annexe rooms with en suite facilities. English or continental breakfast. Self Catering also available. Best pubs and restaurants in the country. Lots to see and do. ETB 2 Crowns. 3 Keys Commended. [🐴]

LINCOLNSHIRE

LINCOLNSHIRE *Rippingale*

TWO COTTAGES IN BEAUTIFUL LINCOLNSHIRE COUNTRYSIDE LARGE COTTAGE sleeps 8 in 4 bedrooms; sitting room, dining room, kitchen, toilet, bathroom. Comfortably furnished. 400-YEAR-OLD COTTAGE sleeps 4; open fires, dining room, sitting room, kitchen, bathroom. Both properties have fridge, colour TV, washing machine; linen supplied. £100 to £275 weekly. Apply: **Mrs V. Sanders, Barn Farm House, Station Street, Rippingale, Near Bourne, Lincs. PE10 0TD, or telephone (01778 440 666).**

Kirton in Lindsey

A small town 8 miles south of Scunthorpe, with an airfield to the south east.

KIRTON LODGE HOTEL, 13 DUNSTAN HILL, KIRTON IN LINDSEY DN21 4DU (01652 648994). Small, friendly Hotel, "Dog Mad" owners, all dogs welcome. Ideally situated for a multitude of "doggie" activities, i.e., beaches, woods, lakes. All rooms en suite with full services. Three Crowns Commended. *[🐶]*

Market Rasen

Market town and agricultural centre 14 miles north-east of Lincoln.

MRS M. E. DAWSON-MARGRAVE, THE WAVENEY GUEST HOUSE, WILLING-HAM ROAD, MARKET RASEN LN8 3DN (01673 843236). Very comfortable, smoke-free accommodation in small market town surrounded by woodland and close to golf and race courses, fishing and Lincolnshire Wolds. All rooms with private facilities, colour TV, tea-making equipment. Guests' own lounge and dining room. Excellent food. Brochure available. 2 Crowns Commended. *[🐶]*

Rippingale

Interesting Lincolnshire village 5 miles north of Bourne; Bourne noted as home town of Saxon hero Hereward the Wake, whose manor house stood in park where earthworks of 11th century castle remain.

Two delightful holiday cottages in rural situation. 400-year-old Cottage sleeps 4, larger Cottage sleeps 8. Both comfortably furnished, colour TV, fridge, washer, linen. From £100 to £275 weekly. Apply: MRS V. SANDERS, BARN FARM HOUSE, STATION STREET, RIPPINGALE, NEAR BOURNE PE10 0TD (01778 440 666). *[🐶]*

Skegness

Bright family resort with fine sands. Lincoln 42 miles, Grimsby 40, Boston 23, Mablethorpe 18.

SUE EVANS, WILLOW FARM, THORPE FENDYKES, SKEGNESS PE24 4QH (01754 830316). In fenland hamlet, 9 miles Skegness, a smallholding with ponies, goats, hens. Small pets welcome if safe around free range hens. Ponies by arrangement. *[🐶]*

Woodhall Spa

Spa town 6 miles south-west of Horncastle.

KIRKSTEAD MILL OLD COTTAGE, WOODHALL SPA. Sleeps 7–10 plus baby. Non-smokers only. Very well equipped – colour TV, washing machine, fridge/freezer, microwave etc. 4 Keys Highly Commended. £99–£400 per week. Membership of local leisure club. Beside river; rowing boat provided. Apply: MRS BARBARA HODGKINSON, "HODGES LODGES," 52 KELSO CLOSE, WORTH, CRAWLEY, WEST SUSSEX RH10 7XH (01293 882008; Fax: 01293 883352). *[Pets £10 per week.]*

LONDON

LONDON *Kingston-upon-Thames, London*

Kingston upon Thames

*Market town, Royal borough, and administrative centre of Surrey, Kingston is ideally placed for
London and environs.*

CHASE LODGE GUEST HOUSE, 10 PARK ROAD, HAMPTON WICK, KINGSTON-
UPON-THAMES KT1 4AS (0181-943 1862). Charming Guest House, recently
refurbished, situated in a quiet area close to Hampton Court and Bushy Park. All
rooms have telephone, TV, fridge, teamaking. Some four-poster rooms. Bed and
Breakfast, Evening Meals, Supper Trays. 4 Crowns. *[🐤]*

London

*Legislative Capital of UK and major port. Theatres, shops, museums, places of historic interest.
Airports at Heathrow and Gatwick.*

COLONNADE HOTEL, 2 WARRINGTON CRESCENT, LONDON W9 1ER (Tel:
0171-286 1052; Fax: 0171 286 1057). Family run, Grade 2 Listed Victorian building
encompassed by an award-winning garden. Rooms to suit all. Mouse, our cat, says
very handy for walkies. *[🐤]*

ST ATHANS HOTEL, 20 TAVISTOCK PLACE, RUSSELL SQUARE, LONDON
WC1H 9RE (0171-837 9140). Family Bed and Breakfast near British Museum,
shops, parks and theatres. Russell Square two blocks away; Euston and King's
Cross stations ten minutes. LTB LISTED. *[🐤]*

NORFOLK

NORFOLK *Bacton-on-Sea*

Peacock House

Old farmhouse. Lovely countryside with good walks. 3½ miles from Dereham, close for Norwich, N.T. houses, Sandringham, beaches. All rooms en suite, tea/coffee facilities. Own lounge, no smoking. Very warm welcome. B&B from £17 pp. Open all year.

ETB Listed Highly Commended

Mrs. Jenny Bell, Peacock Lane, Old Beetley, Dereham, Norfolk NR20 4DG. Tel: 01362 860371

THE HOSTE ARMS

The Green, Burnham Market,
Norfolk PE31 8HD Tel: 01328 738257; Fax: 01328 730103

🐾🐾🐾 Highly Commended

Contact: Fiona Graham.

17th century Hotel overlooking the village green in beautiful Georgian village. 15 elegantly furnished en suite bedrooms, colour TV and telephone. Two excellent menus featuring local produce, fish and game. Real ales and extensive wine list. AA**, RAC*** Inn. Ideal for golf, walking, water sports. *B&B from £40 pp per night; 2 nights from £58pp; DB&B – 2 nights from £78 pp, 3 nights from £116. Johansen's Inn of the Year '96. Egon Ronay Pub of the Year '96.*

Kings Chalet Park

Sleep 2 – 6
Open March to October

Pets welcome free of charge

Comfortable, well equipped chalets situated on beautiful landscaped quiet site. Ideally placed for walks to adjacent woods, cliffs and sandy beaches. 10 minutes' walk to town. Local shops nearby. Two bedrooms, bed/sofa in lounge, bathroom, colour TV, microwave, well equipped kitchenette. Children welcome.

Spring/Autumn 2 nights £20 per night
June – September £120–£200 per week

DETAILS FROM:
MRS I. SCOLTOCK, SHANGRI-LA, LT CAMBRIDGE,
DUTON HILL, DUNMOW, ESSEX (TEL: 01371 870482)

CROMER – SELF CATERING COTTAGES

Holiday Properties at Northrepps

Our cottages are very comfortably furnished, generously equipped and very carefully maintained. All are fully electric with cooker, water heater, fridge, colour television and electric fires.
Accommodation for four to six persons.
Cots available on request.
Pets always welcome!
Some of the cottages have their own enclosed garden, ideal for children and pets. Ample parking for cars.

As well as local wonderful sandy beaches we have golf, sailing, lake fishing, bird watching and miles of good walking in lovely surroundings. Cromer has a Cinema and Pier with first rate live shows.
Inclusive charges from £200 to £380 per week.

Detailed brochure and terms from
Northrepps Holiday Properties, Cromer, Norfolk NR27 0JW
Tel: (01263) 578196 and 512236

NORFOLK   *Cromer, Diss, Foxley, Great Yarmouth*

"BRECKWOOD"
Aylmerton, Near Cromer, Norwich NR11 8QG
One and a half miles from the sea; adjacent to Felbrigg Woods and Hall, also Roman Camp Woods. Self catering for 2–4 in property set in large woodland garden. B&B also available. Children and dogs welcome.
Mrs J. Stubbs   *Tel: 01263 837320*

"STRENNETH", Airfield Road, Fersfield, Diss, Norfolk IP22 2BP
Tel: 01379 688182 Fax: 01379 688260
Family run, fully renovated former farmhouse. Oak beams, log fires in winter. All rooms have en suite, colour TVs, tea/coffee-making facilities. Most of them are on the ground floor. Executive and four poster rooms for that special break. Open all year. Excellent food. Licensed. Pets welcome. Credit Cards accepted. Bed and Breakfast from £22.00; 3 Course Evening Meal £13.00.
Ladies and Gents HAIRDRESSING SALON now open.

Located on a working farm, a courtyard of seven 2/3 bedroomed SELF CATERING CHALETS. All fully equipped, and all with central heating which is included in the letting fee. Situated 20 miles from the coast and 15 miles from Norwich and the Broads. 365 acres of mature woodland adjoining owners' farm – ideal for walking. Fishing close by. Pets welcome at charge of £10. ETB 3 Keys Approved

MOOR FARM HOLIDAYS
FOXLEY, NORFOLK NR20 4QN Tel or Fax: 01362 688523

"ANCHOR" 21 North Denes Road, Great Yarmouth. Tel: 01493 844339
Holiday Flats pleasantly situated in select area. Close sea-front and Venetian Waterways. One and two bedroomed Flats. *Self-contained with own shower and toilet. *Kitchen/Diner/Lounge with sink unit. *Colour TV. *Electric fire. *All bed linen, crockery and utensils at no extra cost. *50p meter for electricity – hot water to sink units is free. *Reduced terms early and late season. *Children and Pets Welcome.
MRS PAULINE SMITH.

WINTERTON-ON-SEA
For a quiet, relaxing holiday – modern, personally maintained holiday chalets. Each sleeps 6 and is fully equipped for self catering, on a beautiful grassed site, close to sandy beach with marvellous sea views. Lovely valley area – this is a pets' paradise.

For further details contact:
Mrs J. S. Cooper, Silverlea, Mile Road, Carleton Rode, Norwich NR16 1NE Tel: 01953-789 407

NORFOLK   *Great Yarmouth, Horning, Hunstanton*

203

WELCOME COTTAGE HOLIDAYS. Hundreds of properties in wonderful locations at welcoming low prices. Pets, linen and fuel mostly included. For FREE colour brochure telephone 01756 702205.

Aylsham

Small market town on the River Bure 12 miles north of Norwich.

MRS K. D. EASY, CROPTON HALL, HEYDON, NORWICH NR11 6RX (Tel/Fax 01263 584159 or 01263 587869). Jacobean Hall in three acres, all rooms en-suite, log fires, pool, daily menu of home-cooked fresh produce, central for touring North Norfolk. From £14.95. EATB 3 Crowns Approved. *[🐕]*

Bacton-on-Sea

Village on coast, 5 miles from North Walsham.

CASTAWAYS HOLIDAY PARK, PASTON ROAD, BACTON-ON-SEA, NORFOLK NR12 0JB (01692 650436 and 650418). In peaceful village with direct access to sandy beach. Modern caravans with all amenities. Licensed club, entertainment, children's play area. Ideal for touring Norfolk. *[Pets £12 per week or £2.50 per night.]*

RED HOUSE CHALET AND CARAVAN PARK, PASTON ROAD, BACTON-ON-SEA NR12 0JB (01692 650815). Small family-run site, ideal for touring Broads. Chalets, caravans and flats, all with showers, fridges and colour TV. Some with sea views. Licensed. SAE for details, please. Open March–January. *[Pets £10 weekly.]*

Beetley

Village 4 miles/6 km north of East Dereham, which is notable for old buildings, inc. parish church, early 16c Cottages now Museum of local history.

MRS JENNY BELL, PEACOCK HOUSE, PEACOCK LANE, OLD BEETLEY, DEREHAM NR20 4DG (01362 860371). Old farmhouse in lovely countryside. All rooms en suite, tea/coffee facilities. Own lounge, B&B from £17 pp. Open all year. ETB Listed Highly Commended. *[🐕]*

Brooke

Attractive small village 8 miles south of Norwich; Lowestoft 20 miles, Great Yarmouth and Southwold 25 miles.

MRS D. VIVIAN-NEAL, WELBECK HOUSE, BROOKE, NEAR NORWICH NR15 1AT (01508 550292). Double, twin and single rooms, all with central heating and tea/coffee. Within easy reach of the coast, The Broads, nature reserves, gardens, nurseries, theatres; good dog walking. B&B £16–£20. Special diets. Non-smoking. Dogs welcome, owners tolerated. *[🐕]*

SYMBOLS

🐕   Indicates no charge for pets.
£   Indicates a charge for pets: nightly or weekly.
pw!   Indicates some special provision for pets: exercise, feeding etc.
🏠   Indicates separate pets accommodation.

Burnham Market

Village five miles west of Wells-next-the-Sea.

THE HOSTE ARMS, THE GREEN, BURNHAM MARKET PE31 8HD (01328 738257). 17th century Hotel overlooking village green. 15 bedrooms, elegantly furnished, all en suite with colour TV and telephone. Bar and restaurant menus. B&B from £32 pppn. *[🐕]*

Cromer

Attractive resort built round old fishing village. Norwich 21 miles

MRS J. STUBBS, "BRECKWOOD", AYLMERTON, NEAR CROMER, NORWICH NR11 8QG (01263 837320). 1½ miles from sea. Adjacent to Felbrigg Woods and Hall, also Roman Camp Woods. S/C for 2–4 in property set in large woodland garden. B&B also available. Children and dogs welcome. *[Pets £5 per week.]*

All-electric Holiday Cottages accommodating 4 to 6 persons in beautiful surroundings. Sandy beaches, sports facilities, Cinema and Pier (live shows). Parking. Children and pets welcome. *[pw! £12 weekly.]* Brochure: NORTHREPPS HOLIDAY PROPERTIES, CROMER, NORFOLK NR27 0JW (01263 578196 or 512236).

KINGS CHALET PARK. Comfortable well-equipped chalets on quiet site; ideally placed for woodland and beach walks. 10 minutes' walk to town; shops nearby. Details from MRS I. SCOLTOCK, SHANGRI-LA, LITTLE CAMBRIDGE, DUTON HILL, DUNMOW, ESSEX (01371 870482).

ROSEACRE COUNTRY HOUSE, WEST RUNTON, CROMER. Apartments sleeping 2–8. Colour TV. Large grounds and car park. Sea, shops, golf and riding facilities nearby. Beautiful woodland walks. Open all year. *[Pets £6 weekly.]* Joan and Rodney Sanders (01263 837221).

Dereham

Market town 16 miles west of Norwich.

PHOENIX HOTEL, CHURCH STREET, DEREHAM NR19 1DL (01362 692276; Fax: 01362 691752). Modern hotel situated in centre of market town. 23 en suite bedrooms; colour TV, radio, tea/coffee making facilities. Terms from £27.50 B&B. Write for colour brochure. AA/RAC 2 Stars, Egon Ronay Recommended. *[🐕]*

Diss

Twisting streets with Tudor, Georgian and Victorian architecture. 12th-century St. Mary's Church and 6 acre mere, haven for wildfowl.

BRENDA WEBB, STRENNETH, AIRFIELD ROAD, FERSFIELD, DISS IP22 2BP (01379 688182, Fax: 01379 699260). 17th C former farmhouse, fully renovated, full central heating. All rooms ensuite, some non-smoking, most on ground floor. 3 Course Evening Meal. Excellent food. Licensed. 2 Crowns Commended. *[🐕]*

Foxley

Village 6 miles east of East Dereham.

Self Catering Chalets (2/3 bedrooms) on working farm. All fully equipped, with central heating. 20 miles from coast, 15 from Broads. Mature woodland nearby – ideal for walking. Three Keys Approved. MOOR FARM HOLIDAYS, FOXLEY NR20 4QN (01362 688523). *[Pets £10]*

Great Yarmouth

Traditional lively seaside resort with a wide range of amusements, including the Marina Centre and Sealife Centre. Once one of Britain's wealthiest medieval towns, its buildings and walls retain many traces of the past.

Go BLUE RIBAND for quality inexpensive self-catering holidays where your dog is welcome – choice of locations all in the borough of Great Yarmouth. Detached 3 bedroom bungalows, Seafront bungalows, Detached Sea-Dell chalets and modern sea front caravans. Free colour brochure: DON WITHERIDGE, BLUE RIBAND HOUSE, PARKLANDS, HEMSBY, GREAT YARMOUTH NR29 4HA (01493 730445). *[Pets £6 per week.]*

MRS J. S. COOPER, SILVERLEA, MILE ROAD, CARLETON RODE, NORWICH NR16 1NE (01953 789 407). Modern holiday chalets at Winterton-on-Sea. Sleep six. Grassed site close to beach with marvellous sea views. A pets' paradise! *[pw! £5 per week.]*

CAREFREE HOLIDAYS, SOLITAIRE, PARKLAND ESTATE, NORTH ROAD, HEMSBY, GREAT YARMOUTH NR29 4HE (01493 732176). A wide selection of superior chalets for live-as-you-please holidays near Great Yarmouth and Norfolk Broads. All amenities on site. Sports facilities, parking. Children and pets welcome. *[pw! 1st pet free.]*

MRS PAULINE SMITH, "ANCHOR", 21 NORTH DENES ROAD, GREAT YARMOUTH NR30 4LW (01493 844339). Completely self-contained Flats with own shower and toilet. Fully equipped at no extra cost. Reduced terms early and late season. Close by public amenities. Children and pets welcome. *[pw!]*

Horning

Lovely riverside village ideally placed for exploring the Broads. In the vicinity are the remains of St Benet's Abbey. Cromer 19 miles, Great Yarmouth 17, Norwich 10, Wroxham 3.

SILVER BIRCHES HOLIDAYS, GREBE ISLAND, LOWER STREET, HORNING, NORFOLK NR12 8PF (Tel and Fax: 01692 630858). Five well-equipped houseboats and six all-weather motor day launches. All the comforts of a caravan afloat! Surrounded by lawns, adjacent parking. Ideal for families, fishermen and their pets. *[Pets £15 per week.]*

Hunstanton

Neat little resort which faces west across The Wash. Good sands, cliffs, play-green overlooking the sea. Norwich 47 miles, Cromer 38, Wells-next-the-Sea 17, King's Lynn 16.

MRS BROWN, MARINE HOTEL, HUNSTANTON PE36 5EH (01485 533310). Overlooking sea and green. Pets welcome, free of charge. Colour televisions. Open all year except Christmas period. SAE for terms and brochure. *[🐾]*

COBBLERS COTTAGE, 3 WODEHOUSE ROAD, OLD HUNSTANTON PE36 6UD (01485 534036). Near Royal Sandringham/Norfolk Lavender. All en suite twin/double rooms. Colour TV and tea-making. Near the beach, golf, bird-watching, pubs and restaurants. Sauna and jacuzzi available. [🐕]

King's Lynn

Ancient market town and port on the Wash with many beautiful medieval and Georgian buildings.

MRS JOAN BASTONE, MARANATHA GUEST HOUSE, 115 GAYWOOD ROAD, KING'S LYNN PE30 2PU (01553 774596). Large house, 10 minutes' walk from town centre. Direct road to Sandringham and the coast. Animal lovers and their pets welcomed. B&B from £13 per person. 2 Crowns Approved, AA QQ, RAC. *[Pets £1 per night. pw!]*

Mundesley-on-Sea

Small resort of character backed by low cliffs. Good sands and bathing. Norwich 20 miles, Cromer 7, North Walsham 5.

"WHINCLIFF", CROMER ROAD, MUNDESLEY NR11 8DU (01263 720961). Clifftop house, sea views and sandy beaches. Rooms with colour TV and tea-making. En suite family/twin room. Evening Meal optional. An abundance of coastal and woodland walks; many places of interest and local crafts. Well-behaved dogs welcome. *[🐕]*

Neatishead

Ideal for touring East Anglia. Close to Norwich. Lovely area. Aylsham 14 miles, Norwich 10, Wroxham 3.

ALAN AND SUE WRIGLEY, REGENCY GUEST HOUSE, THE STREET, NEATIS-HEAD, NORFOLK BROADS NR12 8AD (01692 630233). 17th century five-bedroom guest house, renowned for generous English breakfasts. Ideal East Anglian touring base. Accent on personal service. Tourist Board 2 Crowns Commended, AA QQQ. Dogs welcome. *[Pets £1.50 per night.]*

North Walsham

Market town 14 miles north of Norwich, traditional centre of the Norfolk reed thatching industry.

MRS V. O'HARA, GEOFFREY THE DYER'S HOUSE, CHURCH PLAIN, WOR-STEAD, NORTH WALSHAM, NORFOLK NR28 9AL (01692 536562). 17th century Listed weaver's house in centre of conservation village. Close to Broads, Coast, Norwich. Good walking and touring. All rooms en suite. Wholesome, well-cooked food. Dogs welcome. ETB 2 Crowns. *[🐕]*

TOLL BARN, OFF NORWICH ROAD (B1150). ONE MILE SOUTH OF NORTH WALSHAM (01692 403063). Charming converted 18th-century barn, all rooms ensuite with tea/coffee, fridge, TV. Breakfast in farmhouse or in the private dining area of your own room if preferred. Ideal for walking, close to coast, Norfolk Broads, North Norfolk and Norwich. *[pw! Pets £1.50 per night.]*

BEECHWOOD HOTEL, CROMER ROAD, NORTH WALSHAM NR28 0HD (01692 403231). This Georgian hotel is set in an acre of mature gardens. Ten en-suite bedrooms, small intimate bar, dining room and cosy residents' lounge. ETB 3 Crowns Commended. *[Pets £1 per night, pw!]*

Norwich

County town and Cathedral city with a daily open air market, medieval streets, a Norman castle and good shopping and leisure facilities.

SOUTHREPPS HOLIDAY COTTAGES. Five delightful cottages situated in the village of Southrepps, just 3 miles from the coast and safe, sandy beaches. 3 cottages with two bedrooms and 2 with three rooms. Each has a lounge with double bed settee and colour TV. Apply: MR CODLING, CHURCH FARM GUEST HOUSE, SOUTH-REPPS, NORWICH NR11 8NP (01263 833248). *[pw!🐾]*

THE GEORGIAN HOUSE HOTEL, 32/34 UNTHANK ROAD, NORWICH NR2 2RB (01603 615655 – 4 lines; Fax: 01603 765689). Ideal for sightseeing in Norwich or touring East Anglia. 27 bedrooms, all en-suite, with colour TV, radio, tea/coffee making facilities. Licensed. ETB 3 Crowns Commended. *[🐾]*

THE BROADS HOTEL, STATION ROAD, WROXHAM, NORWICH NR12 8UR (01603 782869; Fax: 01603 784066). Comfortable hotel renowned for its high standard cuisine. Owned and run by dog-loving family. Ideally situated for boating, fishing and exploring the beautiful Norfolk countryside and coastline. All rooms fully en suite with tea/coffee making, colour TV, etc. For brochure please telephone. *[🐾]*

Sheringham

Small, traditional resort which has grown around a flint-built fishing village. Sandy beaches and amusements.

ACHIMOTA, 31 NORTH STREET, SHERINGHAM NR26 8LW (01263 822379). Award-winning small guest house in quiet part of Sheringham. Beach, cliff, heath and National Trust woodland walks galore in this "Area of Outstanding Natural Beauty" Tourist Board rating "Two Crowns Commended". Council "Heartbeat Award". NO SMOKING. Brochure on request. *[🐾]*

Swaffham

Old market town. 15th-century church with angel carved roof. Palladian market cross. Norwich 28 miles, King's Lynn 15.

MRS GREEN, PAGET, LYNN ROAD, NARBOROUGH, KING'S LYNN PE32 1TE (01760 337734). Private house offering B&B. Lounge available, log fire. Televisions in bedrooms. Ample parking. Trout and coarse fishing lakes, pleasant rural walks. Situated between the old market town of Swaffham and King's Lynn. SAE please. *[🐾]*

Nar Valley Holiday Cottages, Norfolk. Choice of two charming cottages in the unspoilt Nar Valley. Winter weekends or Summer holidays. Telephone for brochure. NAR VALLEY HOLIDAYS, ESTATE OFFICE, WESTACRE, KING'S LYNN PE32 1UB (01760 755254; Fax: 01760 755444). *[🐾]*

Thetford

Town at confluence of River Thet and Little Ouse River, 12 miles north of Bury St Edmunds. Remains of castle and priory.

KEVIN AND YVONNE FICKLING, ROSE COTTAGE, BUTTERS HALL LANE, THOMPSON, THETFORD IP24 1QQ (01953 488104). Comfortable flint-walled house, situated in acre of garden, 3 miles south of Watton (off A1075). Colour TV, tea making facilities in spacious bedrooms. Delicious breakfasts served in oak-beamed dining room. Very peaceful, wonderful walks. Sorry, no smoking. EATB Listed and Commended. *[🐾]*

Wells-next-the-Sea

Lovely little resort with interesting harbour, famous for its cockles, whelks and shrimps. A winding creek leads to a beach of fine sands with dunes. Salt marshes: bird-watchers' paradise. Norwich 31 miles, King's Lynn 27, Cromer 19.

MRS J. M. COURT, EASTDENE, NORTHFIELD LANE, WELLS-NEXT-THE-SEA NR23 1LH (01328 710381). Homely Guest House offers warm welcome. Bed and Breakfast £17. One double, two twin rooms, one single, all en-suite; colour television lounge. Private parking. Les Routiers recommended. Tourist Board 2 Crowns Approved. *[Pets £1 per night.]*

Winterton-on-Sea

Good sands and bathing. Great Yarmouth 8 miles.

Self-contained ground floor of cottage in quiet seaside village. Broad sandy beach and pleasant walks. Close to Norfolk Broads. Secluded garden. Double, twin and single bedrooms, sleep 5 plus cot. Bed linen provided. Fully equipped for self-catering family holiday. £140–£300 per week. Full details from MR M. J. ISHERWOOD, 79 OAKLEIGH AVENUE, LONDON N20 9JG (01810-445 2192). *[Pets £5 per week.]*

NORTHAMPTONSHIRE

NORTHAMPTONSHIRE   *Weedon*

The Globe Hotel
High Street, Weedon, Northampton NN7 4QD
🏵 🏵 🏵 🏵 Commended   RAC**

While retaining its historic character, The Globe has been completely refurbished to a most comfortable standard. 18 en suite bedrooms. Within easy touring distance of Warwick, Leamington Spa, Stratford, Naseby Battlefield, and Silverstone. Close to Grand Union Canal. Comprehensive food operation OPEN ALL DAY features home fayre bar meals and à la carte menu. Special weekend Giveaway Breaks.

A Countryside Inn   **Tel: 01327 340336 Fax: 01327 349058**

Weedon

Village 4 miles south east of Daventry.

THE GLOBE HOTEL, HIGH STREET, WEEDON, NORTHAMPTON NN7 4QD (01327 340336; Fax: 01327 349058). Set in countryside close to Grand Union Canal. 18 en suite bedrooms. Comprehensive food operation. Convenient for Warwick, Stratford, Silverstone. Special Weekend Giveaway Breaks. Four Crowns Commended. *[🐾]*

NORTHUMBERLAND
Alnmouth, Alnwick, Corbridge, Ninebanks

Alnmouth

Quiet little resort with wide sands. Alnwick with its impressive Norman Castle is 5 miles N.W.

Alnwick

Situated in a historic area. Amongst the attractions are the Norman castle, Dunstanburgh Castle and Warkworth Castle. The Howick Hall Gardens and the fifteenth-century Church are also nearby. Saturday market. Nine-hole golf course, fishing, riding, tennis. Newcastle-upon-Tyne 34 miles, Berwick-upon-Tweed 30, Morpeth 19, Wooler 18.

VILLAGE FARM SELF CATERING, TOWN FOOT FARM, SHILBOTTLE, ALNWICK NE66 2HG (Tel/Fax: 01665 575591). Top quality accommodation with a choice of 17th century farmhouse or Scandinavian lodges and cottages. Indoor pool, games room, tennis court and award-winning beaches within 3 miles. Open all year. Short Breaks Autumn/Winter. Comprehensive brochure. *[Pets £10 per week.]*

Belsay

Village five miles north west of Ponteland. Belsay Hall is a Neo-Classical building resembling a Greek temple, has extensive gardens. 14th century castle.

MRS KATH FEARNS, BOUNDER HOUSE, BELSAY, NEWCASTLE-UPON-TYNE NE20 0JR (01661 881267). Stone farmhouse situated in beautiful Northumberland countryside, off A696 Newcastle/Edinburgh road. Two double (en suite), one family and one twin room from £15 p.p.p.n. Also self catering cottage, sleeps 4. ETB 4 Keys Highly Commended. Full central heating. Linen supplied. From £120 per week. Telephone for brochure.

Berwick-upon-Tweed

Historic border town on River Tweed encompassed by massive 13th century walls. Three great bridges span the river on which sailing, canoeing, water ski-ing and fishing are popular pastimes. Castle ruins may be seen adjacent to the railway station. Good resort facilities, fine sandy beaches. North Berwick 42 miles, Alnwick 29, Kelso 23, Wooler 17, Coldstream 14.

MRS M. MARTIN, FELKINGTON FARM, BERWICK-UPON-TWEED TD15 2NR (01289 387220). Comfortable farm holiday cottages close to coast and countryside. Sleep 6. Colour TV. Electric heaters and log fires, wood provided. Washing machine, microwave, shower & bath, playground, games room. Woodland walk. Children and pets welcome. ETB 3 Keys Approved. *[🐾]*

Corbridge

Small town on north bank of River Tyne, 3 miles east of Hexham. Nearby are remains of Roman military town of Corstopitum.

THE HAYES, NEWCASTLE ROAD, CORBRIDGE NE45 5LP (01434 632010). Superior flat for 4/5 and 3 ground floor cottages for 2/5 persons, available all year. Colour TV. Also luxury 6-berth caravan. Children and pets welcome. All properties, except flat, suitable for disabled. For details send SAE (ref. FHG). *[🐾]*

Embleton

Bayside town offering sand and solitude for walkers, and sport for golfers on links. Peel Tower incorporated into vicarage next to church.

C. M. MOORE, WEST FALLODON, EMBLETON, ALNWICK NE67 5EB (01665 579357). NTB 4 Keys Commended. Delightful 19th century "Storybook" cottages restored to very high standard offer comfortable, well-equipped accommodation in a superbly placed setting ideal for exploring Northumberland and its beautiful coastline. *[🐾]*

Hexham

Market town on bank of River Tyne, with medieval priory church. Racecourse 2 miles. Newcastle upon Tyne 20 miles.

RYE HILL FARM, SLALEY, NEAR HEXHAM NE47 0AH (01434 673259). Pleasant family atmosphere in cosy farmhouse. Bed and Breakfast and optional Evening Meal. Bedrooms with TV and tea/coffee facilities. All en-suite. Laundry facilities. Table licence. 3 Crowns Commended. *[pw! Pets £1 per night.]*

Ninebanks

Hamlet four miles south west of Allendale.

MRS MAVIS OSTLER, TAYLOR BURN, NINEBANKS, HEXHAM NE47 8DE (01434 345343). Bed and breakfast £14–£16; evening meal £9; special diets catered for. Guests encouraged to join in farm activities. Traditional farmhouse with all modern amenities. *[pw! £1 per night maximum.]*

Rothbury

Market town on steep bank of River Coquet, 11 miles south-west of Alnwick.

TERRY AND JANET CLUBLEY, WHITTON FARMHOUSE HOTEL, ROTHBURY, MORPETH NE65 7RL (Tel/Fax: 01699 620811). Charming country hotel in open country with en suite rooms (TV and hospitality tray), licensed lounge. Country house style dinners served each evening in attractive dining room. Riding from hotel's stables. Fishing and golf nearby. 14 miles from spectacular beaches.

Warkworth

Village on River Coquet near North Sea Coast north-west of Amble with several interesting historic remains.

WARKWORTH HOUSE HOTEL, BRIDGE STREET, WARKWORTH NE65 0XB (01665 711276; Fax: 01665 713323). Set in heart of small village, ideal for dog walking. Miles of open uncrowded beaches. Delicious evening meals. Phone for brochure. *[🐾]*

All the advertisers in PETS WELCOME! have an entry in the appropriate classified section and each classified entry may carry one or more of the following symbols:

🐾   This symbol indicates that pets are welcome free of charge.

£   The £ indicates that a charge is made for pets. We quote the amount where possible, either per night or per week.

pw!   This symbol shows that the establishment has some special provision for pets; perhaps an exercise facility or some special feeding or accommodation arrangements.

🏠   Indicates separate pets accommodation.

PLEASE NOTE that all the advertisers in PETS WELCOME! extend a welcome to pets and their owners but they may attach conditions. The interests of other guests have to be considered and it is usually assumed that pets will be well trained, obedient and under the control of their owner.

NOTTINGHAMSHIRE

NOTTINGHAMSHIRE *Southwell*

THE OLD FORGE

Burgage Lane, Southwell, Nottinghamshire NG25 0ER
Tel: 01636 812809/816302; Mobile 0850 237908

Quietly but centrally situated in this charming little town
known for its beautiful and historic Minster. Once an old
working forge, now a comfortable house with character. Attractive decorations
throughout and a secluded patio to relax on. Rooms are en suite with telephone,
tea/coffee making facilities and TV. Private parking. B&B from £20.
No smoking and pets by arrangement.
ETB 3 Crowns Highly Commended

Southwell

Home of beautiful cream-coloured Southwell Minster with splendid towers and spires, dating from 1108. Exquisite "Leaves of Southwell" stone carving in Chapter House.

THE OLD FORGE, BURGAGE LANE, SOUTHWELL NG25 0ER (01636 812809/816302). Quietly but centrally situated in this charming little town known for its beautiful and historic Minster. Once an old working forge, now a comfortable house with 3 twin rooms and 3 doubles (all private/en suite). [🐾]

OXFORDSHIRE

OXFORDSHIRE *Oxford, Thame*

Crown and Cushion Hotel and Leisure Centre 🐾🐾🐾🐾
High Street, Chipping Norton, Near Oxford OX7 5AD Commended

500-year-old Coaching Inn, tastefully modernised to provide 40 excellent en suite bedrooms; some four-poster suites. "Old World" bar, log fires, real ale, good food, Egon Ronay Recommended. Indoor pool, multi-gym, solarium etc. Modern conference centre. Located in picturesque Cotswolds town midway between Oxford and Stratford-upon-Avon. Convenient London, Heathrow, M40. Blenheim Palace, Bourton-on-the-Water, Stow-on-the-Wold, Shakespeare Country all nearby. Pets welcome.

Price Busters start at £19.50; DB&B at just £34.50.

Tel: 01608 642533 Fax: 01608 642926 Colour brochure Freephone 0800 585251

LITTLE ACRE
Tetsworth, Nr Thame, Oxford OX9 7AT Tel: 01844 281423

A charming secluded country house retreat with pretty landscaped garden and dining area overlooking spectacular waterfall, offering every comfort in 18 acres of private grounds. Single, twin and double rooms all with central heating, colour TV, tea/coffee making facilities, some en suite. A perfect place to relax and enjoy the local countryside in a quiet location. Pets allowed in bedrooms. Value for money from just £13 per night.

Ascott-Under-Wychwood

Village four miles west of Charlbury.

COTSWOLDS. Detached cottage, sleeps 2/4. Central heating, tennis court, garage. Lovely country views. Ideal for Cotswolds, Oxford, Stratford-upon-Avon. 3 Keys Commended. £150–£225 incl. weekly. *[🐕]* MRS P. GOODFORD, THE OLD VICARAGE, ASCOTT-UNDER-WYCHWOOD OX7 6AN (01993 830385; 01993 830966).

Oxford

Ancient university city on the Thames, here known as the Isis. Apart from the colleges there is a plethora of time-hallowed buildings, particularly churches and inns. Eights week is a well-known river spectacle held at the end of May. Numerous entertainment and sporting facilities. LONDON 56 miles, Stratford-upon-Avon 39, Windsor 39, Henley-on-Thames 24, Banbury 23, Chipping Norton 20, Burford 19, Wallingford 12.

MRS B. A. DOWNES, BRAVALLA GUEST HOUSE, 242 IFFLEY ROAD, OXFORD OX4 1SE (01865 241326 or 250511). Homely Guest House one mile south-east of centre. Majority of rooms en-suite with TV and beverage facilities. Parking. From £10 per person. 2 Crowns, AA/RAC Listed. *[Pets £1 per night.]*

CROWN & CUSHION HOTEL AND LEISURE CENTRE, HIGH STREET, CHIPPING NORTON, NEAR OXFORD OX7 5AD (01608 642533; Fax: 01608 642926; Colour Brochure Freephone 0800 585251). 500-year-old coaching inn, tastefully modernised. En suite bedrooms; some four-posters. Old World bar; indoor pool, solarium etc. Convenient Stratford, Oxford, London, Shakespeare Country. Price Busters from £19.50. *[🐕]*

Stanton Harcourt

Delightful village with thatched cottages spread out along winding country road. Parts of ruined manor date back to 12th century.

MRS MARGARET CLIFTON, STADDLE STONES, LINCH HILL, STANTON HARCOURT OX8 1BB (01865 882256). A welcome for dogs at the Chalet Bungalow, with four acres of grounds adjoining bridle paths. Bedrooms with en suite or private bathrooms. Disabled persons and children welcome. Bed and Breakfast from £16.50.

Thame

Town on River Thame 9 miles south west of Aylesbury. Airport at Haddenham.

MS. JULIA TANNER, LITTLE ACRE, TETSWORTH, NEAR THAME OX9 7AT (01844 281423). A charming secluded country house retreat offering every comfort in 20 acres of private grounds, nestling under Chilterns escarpment. Single/Twin/Double rooms, majority en suite, colour TV, beverage facilities. A perfect place to relax and enjoy the abundance of footpaths on our doorstep . . . your dog will love it. ONLY 3 mins. Junction 6 M40. *[🐕– Bring dog basket with you. 🏠]*

Woodstock

Old town 8 miles north-west of Oxford. Home to Oxford City and County Museum.

MRS B. JONES, GORSELANDS FARMHOUSE AUBERGE, NEAR LONG HANBOROUGH, WOODSTOCK OX8 6PU (01993 881895; Fax: 01993 882799). Old Cotswold Stone House with flagstone floors and oak beams situated in peaceful countryside. Convenient for many attractions. B&B from £15.00. En-suite rooms. Evening Meals from £9.95. 2 Crowns. RAC Listed. *[🐕]*

SHROPSHIRE

SHROPSHIRE   *Church Stretton, Cleobury Mortimer*

RYTON FARM HOLIDAY COTTAGES
Ryton, Dorrington, Shrewsbury SY5 7LY Tel/Fax: 01743 718449

Choose from a traditional country cottage sleeping six or a recently converted barn for either 2 or 4 persons. Some suitable for visitors with mobility difficulties. Ample parking, well-equipped kitchens, colour TV, fitted carpets, towels and linen. Pets especially welcome. Coarse fishing available. Quietly situated 6 miles south of Shrewsbury overlooking Shropshire Hills, convenient for Ironbridge, Ludlow and Shrewsbury.

Open all year   *Weekly bookings or Short Breaks*   *3 Keys Commended*

BOURTON MANOR
Hotel, Restaurant and Conference Centre

Set in a small hamlet nestling close to Wenlock Edge, Bourton Manor offers comfortable hotel facilities, with single, twin and double luxury bedrooms, each with radio, colour TV and direct-dial telephone.
Situated in its own private landscaped gardens, it is ideal for walking and riding;
within easy reach of Telford, Shrewsbury and many other historic places.
★ Traditional style dining room ★ Oak panelled bar ★ Cosy sitting room ★ Non-residents welcome in restaurant
★ Special Christmas and Easter packages. Also exciting activity weekends.
Bourton, Much Wenlock, Shropshire TF13 6QE Tel: (01746 785531)

Bishop's Castle

Small town in hills on Welsh border, eight miles north west of Craven Arms. Scanty remains of 12th century castle.

MRS P. ALLBUARY, THE GREEN FARM, WENTNOR, BISHOPS CASTLE SY9 5EF (01588 650394). En suite annexe sleeps two–four. B&B from £14.50. Two inns within 400 yards. Ideal walking country; riding available (extra). /🐾 pw!/

Church Stretton

Delightful little town and inland resort in lee of Shropshire Hills. Walking, riding country. Facilities for tennis, bowls, gliding and golf. Knighton 22 miles, Bridgnorth 19, Ludlow 15, Shrewsbury 12.

MYND HOUSE HOTEL, LITTLE STRETTON, CHURCH STRETTON SY6 6RB (01694 722212). Distinguished 8 bedroomed hotel and restaurant in rural hamlet at base of NT Long Mynd. Iron Bridge 15 miles. Award winning food and wine. Dogs free but contribution to Roden NCDL rescue centre appreciated. /🐾/

F. AND M. ALLISON, THE TRAVELLERS REST INN, UPPER AFFCOT, NEAR CHURCH STRETTON SY6 6RL (01694 781275). RAC Inn. Fully licensed Inn on main A49. Good base for touring. Ample parking space. Children and dogs welcome 2 Crowns Approved. SAE or phone for further details. /🐾/

MRS BRANDON-LODGE, NORTH HILL FARM, CARDINGTON, CHURCH STRETTON SY6 7LL (01694 771532). Rooms with a view. Farmhouse B&B in the Shropshire Hills. Ideal walking and riding country, situated on the Bridleway; ideal stop-off for Jack Mytton Way and the Long Mynd. No smoking. Horses and dogs welcome.

THE LONGMYND HOTEL, CHURCH STRETTON SY6 6AG (Tel: 01694 722244/8; Fax: 01694 722718). Situated overlooking the beautiful Welsh border this hotel has a subtle mixture of superb modern and period rooms equipped with every refinement demanded by the discerning guest of today. 4 Crowns.

BELVEDERE GUEST HOUSE, BURWAY RAOD, CHURCH STRETTON SY6 6DP (01694 722232). On slopes of Long Mynd, 200 yards from Church Stretton and 6000 acres of National Trust hill country. Central heating. Teasmaids. Two guest lounges. ETB 3 Crowns Commended. Routiers, AA QQQQ, RAC Acclaimed. Bed and Breakfast £21. Evening Meal £9.00. Reductions children, party, weekly. /🐾/

Cleobury Mortimer

Charming little town of timbered and Georgian houses, with very little building since the mid-nineteenth century, except Gilbert Scott's restoration of the church. There is fishing on the River Rea, and walking in the Wyre Forest or on Clee Hill, which rises to over 1,600 ft (500 m). Mawley Hall, a Georgian house, stands on a hill in a well-timbered park, with notable Roman Catholic chapel. Ludlow 10 miles.

THE REDFERN HOTEL, CLEOBURY MORTIMER DY14 8AA (01299 270395). Eleven well-equipped bedrooms, all with private facilities and some on the ground floor. Award-winning restaurant noted for fine food. ETB 4 Crowns Commended. No charge for pets to *PETS WELCOME!* readers. [🐴]

Craven Arms

Attractive little town with some interesting old half-timbered houses. Weekly cattle and sheep sales. Nearby is imposing Stokesay Castle (13th cent.) open regularly. Newtown 27 miles, Welshpool 24, Bridgnorth 21, Shrewsbury 20, Ludlow 8.

SUE TRUEMAN'S "B&B AT THE BELL", LEAMOOR COMMON, CRAVEN ARMS SY7 8DN (01694 781231; Fax: 01694 781461). Guests say "home from home". Quality accommodation in 12½ acres of natural beauty. Kids, pets, horses welcome. Exquisite countryside, historic towns. ETB Listed. From £14.50. [🐴]

MRS J. WILLIAMS, HURST HILL FARM, CLUNTON, CRAVEN ARMS SY7 0JA (01588 640224). Comfortable riverside farmhouse. Woodlands, riding ponies. Convenient for Offa's Dyke, Stiperstones. Bed and Breakfast from £15, Dinner, Bed and Breakfast from £23. 2 Crowns. AA Listed. Winner "Shropshire Breakfast Challenge".

Ironbridge

Situated on side of River Severn gorge and named after bridge spanning it, which was cast in 1778 and still used by pedestrians.

VIRGINIA AND ROBERT EVANS, CHURCH FARM, ROWTON, WELLINGTON, TELFORD TF6 6QY (01952 770381). Experience a true country holiday on our working farm in scenic Shropshire. En-suite rooms, tea/coffee making, four-poster bed. Also 2 self-catering cottages and 2 caravans for hire. Ideal touring area. 2 Crowns. [Pets £5 per week.]

Ludlow

Lovely and historic town on Rivers Teme and Corve with numerous old half-timbered houses and inns, particularly the "Feathers" and "Bull". Impressive Norman castle. River and woodland walks. Golf, tennis, bowls, steeplechase course. Worcester 29 miles, Shrewsbury 27, Hereford 24, Bridgnorth 19, Church Stretton 16.

MAURICE & GILLIAN PHILLIPS, THE CECIL GUEST HOUSE, SHEET ROAD, LUDLOW SY8 1LR (Tel and Fax: 01584 872442). Comfortable Guest House offers a relaxing atmosphere, freshly cooked food and spotlessly clean surroundings. Some en suite. All rooms have colour TV and tea makers. Licensed. Parking. 10% discount for five nights or more. ETB Two Crowns Commended, AA QQQ, RAC Acclaimed. [🐴]

Oswestry

Borderland Market town. Many old castles and fortifications including 13th century Chirk Castle, Whittington Castle, Oswestry's huge Iron Age hill fort, Offa's Dyke. Wales' highest waterfall close by. Llangollen 10 miles, Shrewsbury 16, Vyrnwy 18, Bala Lake 25.

PEN-Y-DYFFRYN COUNTRY HOUSE HOTEL, NEAR RHYDYCROESAU, OSWESTRY SY10 7DT (Tel. & Fax: 01691 653700). Georgian Rectory set in Shropshire/ Welsh Hills. Seven en-suite bedrooms, colour TV. Licensed Restaurant. 5-acre grounds. Very quiet and relaxed. Dinner, Bed and Breakfast from £39.00 per person. Pets free. 3 Crowns Highly Commended. *[🐶pw!]*

Shrewsbury

Fine Tudor Town with many beautiful black and white timber buildings, Abbey and Castle. Riverside walks, Quarry Park and Dingle flower garden. 39 miles north-west of Birmingham.

BRENDA AND DAVID COLLINGWOOD, TALBOT HOUSE HOTEL, CROSS HILL, SHREWSBURY SY1 1JH (01743 368889). ETB 3 Crowns Highly Commended. 17th century Grade II Listed. Highly recommended best Town Centre Hotel, but quiet area. See display advert. Everything you could wish for; comfort, relaxation, freedom, extra facilities, with friendly, helpful hosts. *[🐶]*

RYTON FARM HOLIDAY COTTAGES, RYTON, DORRINGTON, SHREWSBURY SY5 7LY (01743 718449). Traditional country cottage sleeping 6 or converted barn for 2 or 4 persons. Well-equipped kitchens, colour TV, fitted carpets, towels and linen. Pets especially welcome. 3 Keys Commended. *[Pets £17 per week pw!]*

Stiperstones

Situated beneath Stiperstones Ridge (1700 feet), and near to scenic Shropshire Hills and a nature reserve.

ROY AND SYLVIA ANDERSON, TANKERVILLE LODGE, STIPERSTONES, MINSTERLEY, SHREWSBURY SY5 0NB (01743 791401). Country Guest House next to a nature reserve in the dramatic Shropshire hills. Cats and small/medium dogs accepted and may share owners' rooms. Pleasant walks. B&B from £15.75. 1 Crown Commended. AA Recommended QQ. *[Pets £1 per night.]*

Telford

New town (1963). Ten miles east of Shrewsbury. Includes the south bank of the River Severn above and below Ironbridge, site of the world's first iron bridge (1777).

IRONBRIDGE RESTAURANT, 2 THE WHARFAGE, IRONBRIDGE, TELFORD TF8 7AW (01952 433993). Next door to the Museum Information Centre. Situated on The Wharfage. Open daily from 10 am. *[🐶]*

BOURTON MANOR, BOURTON, MUCH WENLOCK TF13 6QE (01746 785531). Set in small hamlet nestling close to Wenlock Edge. Single, twin and double luxury bedrooms, each with radio, colour TV etc. Ideal for walking and riding; Telford, Shrewsbury nearby. Dogs welcome. *[pw! Pets £2 per night.]*

SOMERSET

Draydon Cottages, Exmoor

Seven fabulous barn conversion cottages conveniently situated two miles north-west of Dulverton towards Tarr Steps in Exmoor National Park. The cottages offer outstanding and relaxing accommodation in a glorious tranquil setting with spectacular far-reaching views across the picturesque Barle Valley. All cottages are furnished and equipped to a very high standard and carefully maintained by the owner. All have modern kitchens and bathrooms, comfortable bedrooms and living rooms, heating throughout etc. Some have en suite facilities and whirlpool baths. There is a pleasant garden and adequate parking. A superb location and excellent base for walking, riding, wildlife and generally exploring Exmoor's beautiful countryside and coastline. Well behaved dogs welcome. Holidays/Short Breaks from March to January. Inclusive weekly terms from £135 – £370 according to cottage and season. Illustrated brochure from

**Katharine Harris, 6 Crabb Lane, Alphington,
Exeter, Devon EX2 9JD. Tel: 01392 433524**
4 Keys Highly Commended

HUNTERS MOON
Exford, Near Minehead, Somerset TA24 7PP
Cosy bungalow smallholding in the heart of Exmoor.
** Glorious views ** Good food ** Friendly atmosphere ** Open all year **
Dogs welcome free   Stabling available   Optional Evening Meal
Bryan and Jane Jackson   **Tel: 01643 831695**

Exmoor House Hotel
CHAPEL STREET, EXFORD TA24 7PY Tel: 01643 831304
Situated in the picturesque village of Exford, (central Exmoor), on village green. Comfortable accommodation, en suite rooms with colour TV, private bathroom, beverage facilities. Ideal for walking, riding, fishing etc. Bed and Breakfast from £18.00. Open all year.
For brochure contact Bev and Ges Dolman

All the advertisers in PETS WELCOME! have an entry in the appropriate classified section and each classified entry may carry one or more of the following symbols:
ħ   This symbol indicates that pets are welcome free of charge.
£   The £ indicates that a charge is made for pets. We quote the amount where possible, either per night or per week.
pw! This symbol shows that the establishment has some special provision for pets; perhaps an exercise facility or some special feeding or accommodation arrangements.
⌂   Indicates separate pets accommodation.

PLEASE NOTE that all the advertisers in PETS WELCOME! extend a welcome to pets and their owners but they may attach conditions. The interests of other guests have to be considered and it is usually assumed that pets will be well trained, obedient and under the control of their owner.

PETS STAY FREE

THE EXMOOR WHITE HORSE INN

Exford,
West Somerset
TA24 7PY

Tel: 01643 831229
Fax: 01643 831246

Managers: Peter and Linda Hendrie

INN: Situated in the delightful Exmoor village of Exford, overlooking the River Exe and surrounded by high moorland on almost every side, this family-run 16th Century Inn is an ideal spot for that well earned break. The public rooms are full of character with beams, log fires (Oct–Apr) and Exmoor stone throughout. There are 18 bedrooms, all of which have en suite facilities, colour TV, teamaking and central heating, and are furnished in keeping with the character of the Inn.

RESTAURANT: A variety of dishes to excite the palate served, including lobster, seafood platters, local venison & fish, whilst the bar has an extensive snack menu, with home made pies, local dishes and is renowned for its carvery. The menus change regularly with daily specials available.

NEARBY: Excellent walking country with a selection of circular walks from the Inn, plus many other local walks available. The village is also noted for its excellent riding facilities. Hunting, fishing & shooting can be arranged upon request. Open all year. Mini Breaks a speciality.

* Remember that your pets are free providing that you
return this advert with your booking *

THE PERFECT RETREAT FOR YOU AND YOUR DOG

WELCOME COTTAGE HOLIDAYS. Hundreds of properties in wonderful locations at
welcoming low prices. Pets, linen and fuel mostly included. For FREE colour
brochure telephone 01756 702218.

CLASSIC COTTAGES (25), HELSTON, CORNWALL (24 HOUR DIAL-A-
BROCHURE 01326 565555). Choose your cottage from 300 of the finest coastal and
country cottages throughout the West Country. *[Pets £9 weekly.]*

POWELLS COTTAGE HOLIDAYS. Your choice of Cottage in Cornwall, Devon,
Somerset, Avon, Cotswolds, Wye Valley, Gower and Pembrokeshire in our full colour
brochure. *[Pets £10 per week.]* FREEPHONE 0800 378771 or apply: 61 High Street,
Saundersfoot, Pembrokeshire SA69 9EJ or (24 hrs) 01834 813232.

Allerford

Village 1 mile east of Porlock.

THE PACK HORSE, ALLERFORD, NEAR MINEHEAD TA24 8HW (Tel & Fax:
01643 862475). Exmoor peace for both you and your dog. Charming self-
catering flatlets in glorious countryside. Open all year. Safe parking. Brochure
by return. *[Pets £8 per week.]*

Axbridge

Pleasant market town at foot of Mendips. Interesting Tudor houses. Bath 27 miles, Bristol 17, Bridgwater 16, Glastonbury 14, Wells 10, Cheddar 3.

L. F. DIMMOCK, MANOR FARM, CROSS, AXBRIDGE BS26 2ED (01934 732577). A working beef and sheep farm of 250 acres adjoining the beautiful Mendip Hills. Children and pets welcome. All rooms with tea/coffee making. B&B from £12.50–£13.75 pp, pn.

Brean

Coastal village with extensive sands. To the north is the promontory of Brean Down. Weston-super-Mare 9 miles, Burnham-on-Sea 5.

EMBELLE HOLIDAY PARK, COAST ROAD, BREAN, BURNHAM-ON-SEA TA8 2QZ (Freephone 0500 400 412). Chalets and Caravans on quiet park. Direct access to beach. Full facilities. Colour television. Pets welcome. Near entertainments. Club and restaurant. Free brochure. *[Pets £15.00 per week.]*

WESTWARD RISE HOLIDAY PARK, SOUTH ROAD, BREAN, NEAR BURNHAM-ON-SEA TA8 2RD (01278 751310). All-electric chalet bungalows on small site adjoining beach. 2 double bedrooms, shower, toilet. Colour TV, fridge, cooker. Shops, restaurants, clubs nearby. SAE for brochure. *[Pets £10 per week.]*

Burnham-on-Sea

Resort with sandy beaches and dunes. Bristol 27 miles, Taunton 20, Wells 18, Weston-super-Mare 11, Bridgwater 9.

JAGOVANS HOLIDAYS, RESTAWAY CARAVAN PARK, SOUTH ROAD, BREAN, BURNHAM-ON-SEA TA8 2RD (01278 751283). Accommodation designed for family holiday. Electricity, fridges, colour TVs, heaters, hot water, flush toilets and bathroom or shower in all units. Pets welcome. *[🐾]*

Crewkerne

Market town on a sheltered slope of the Blackdown Hills 8 miles west of Yeovil.

MRS G. SWANN, BROADVIEW, 43 EAST STREET, CREWKERNE TA18 7AG (01460 73424). Traditionally furnished bungalow in over an acre of gardens. Three en-suite bedrooms with colour TV, central heating etc. Bed and full English Breakfast £23. *[🐾 pw!]*

Draydon Cottages, Exmoor. 7 attractive s/c barn conversion cottages situated 2 miles north-west of Dulverton. Well equipped and maintained with heating throughout. Excellent base for exploring Exmoor. KATHARINE HARRIS, 6 CRABB LANE, ALPHINGTON, EXETER, DEVON EX2 9JD (01392 433524). *[Pets £2 p.d. or £12 weekly.]*

Dulverton

Attractively set between Exmoor and Brendon Hills. Good fishing. In vicinity, prehistoric Tarr Steps (A.M. and N.T.) Exeter 27 miles, Taunton 26, Lynton 23, Minehead 19, Tiverton 13.

EXMOOR – LOWER CHILCOTT FARM, DULVERTON TA22 9OQ (01398 323439). Self catering character cottages. Walks, adjacent riding school. Children, pets and mothers-in-law welcome. Sleep 2–9.

MR AND MRS F. A. HEYWOOD, SOUTH GREENSLADE FARMHOUSE, BROMP-TON REGIS, DULVERTON TA22 9NU (01398 371207). Keens Cottage, set in quiet countryside, suitable for 6 adults and 2 children. Small sitting-room with log fire (logs supplied), and oil Rayburn. Fully equipped. Ideal touring base. Terms from £175–£210 per week. 36-foot residential caravan also available. £120 per week.

Exford

Fine touring centre for Exmoor and North Devon, on River Exe. Dulverton 10 miles.

BRYAN & JANE JACKSON, HUNTERS MOON, EXFORD, NEAR MINEHEAD TA24 7PP (01643 831695). Cosy bungalow smallholding in the heart of Exmoor. Good food (optional Evening Meal), glorious views, friendly atmosphere. Pets welcome, free stabling available. Open all year. [🐴]

BEV AND GEOFF DOLMAN, EXMOOR HOUSE HOTEL, CHAPEL STREET, EXFORD TA24 7PY (01643 831304). Situated in picturesque village (middle of Exmoor). Comfortable accommodation, colour TV, private bathroom, beverage facilities available. B&B from £18.00. [🐴]

Exmoor

One of the country's smaller National Parks, with many beautiful sights and places of interest. Much of the moor remains untouched by modern life.

THE SHIP INN, HIGH STREET, PORLOCK TA24 8QT (01643 862507). Comfortable accommodation in famous old inn. Excellent English cooking, bar serving real ale and snacks. Car parking. [🐴]

THE ROYAL OAK INN, WITHYPOOL, EXMOOR NATIONAL PARK, SOMERSET TA24 7QP (Tel: 01643 831506/7; Fax: 01643 831659). The Royal Oak Inn has been renowned for its comfort and food for approximately three centuries and has many awards for the latter. It is an ideal base for riding, fishing or simply to walk and enjoy the calm and beauty of the moors. [🐴, 🏠]

CUTTHORNE, LUCKWELL BRIDGE, WHEDDON CROSS TA24 7EW (01643 831255). Enjoy a touch of sheer luxury at our 14th century country house in glorious Exmoor. En-suite facilities, log fires, candlelit dinners. Children's high teas. Stabling. 2 Crowns. Highly Commended. [🐴]

THE CROWN HOTEL, EXFORD TA24 7PP (01643 831554/5; Fax: 01643 831665). Situated in rural England. All bedroms with bath, colour television, hairdryer. Excellent cuisine and fine wines. Bargain Breaks. Superb dog holiday country. [pw! 🏠]

THE EXMOOR WHITE HORSE INN, EXFORD TA24 7PY (01643 831229. Fax: 01643 831246). Family-run 17th century inn situated in charming Exmoor village. 18 bedrooms all en-suite, with colour TV and tea making. Fully licensed. Restaurant with varied menu. [🐕]

MRS P. EDWARDS, WESTERMILL FARM, EXFORD TA24 7NJ (01643 831238; Fax: 01643 831660). Delightful Scandinavian pine log Cottages and a Cottage attached to farmhouse. Campsite for Tents/Dormobiles. Information centre and small shop. One/Three Keys Commended. [pw! £6 weekly S/C. Free when camping.]

JANE & BARRY STYLES, WINTERSHEAD FARM, SIMONSBATH, EXMOOR TA24 7LF (01643 831222; Fax: 01643 831628). Four tastefully furnished and well-equipped cottages plus small flat situated in the midst of beautiful Exmoor. Pets welcome, stables and grazing available. Colour brochure on request. [Dogs £12 per week, horses £7.]

Hillfarrance

4 miles west of Taunton with its 12th century castle. Situated in valley of Taunton Deane, famed for its apples and cider.

ANCHOR COTTAGES, THE ANCHOR INN, HILLFARRANCE, TAUNTON TA4 1AW (01823 461334). Three self-catering cottages, each sleeps up to 4. Full central heating, colour TV; tastefully furnished to high standard. Private gardens and ample parking. Anchor Inn renowned for good food. [🐕]

Ilminster

Market town founded in Saxon times, with charming Georgian houses and a 15th-century minster.

MRS GRACE BOND, GRADEN, PEASMARSH, near DONYATT, ILMINSTER TA19 0SG (01460 52371). Comfortable home in peaceful location within easy reach M5. Multi-screen cinema, ten-pin bowling, Cricket St Thomas (Crinkley Bottom), coast just 20 miles. Many local attractions, pubs serving good food. Bed and full English Breakfast from £15.00. Weekly terms available.

Minehead

Neat and stylish resort on Bristol Channel under the shelter of wooded North Hill. Small harbour, sandy bathing beach. Attractive gardens, golf course and good facilities for tennis, bowls and horse riding. Within easy reach of the beauties of Exmoor.

16th Century Cottage for two and Cottage with inglenook and beamed ceilings for 7/9. Fully furnished. Pets welcome. APPLY – MR T. STONE, TROYTES FARM-STEAD, TIVINGTON TA24 5RP (01643 704531). [🐕]

MERTON HOTEL, WESTERN LANE, THE PARKS, MINEHEAD TA24 8BZ (01643 702375). Pets and their families most welcome at this small, family hotel. 12 en suite rooms. Car park. Home cooking. [🐕]

HINDON FARM, NEAR MINEHEAD TA24 8SH (01643 705244). Lovely 18th century farmhouse on 500-acre working farm. B&B or Self Catering. Own horses and dogs welcome – kennel runs, stabling, grazing. Many animals kept. Relax and enjoy the countryside walks. Cross Country Jumps, Outdoor Arena, superb Bridleway and Moors. SAE or phone for brochure. [pw! Pets £2 per night.]

Porlock

Most attractive village beneath the tree-clad slopes of Exmoor. Picturesque cottages, old Ship Inn and interesting church (Perp). Good bathing from pebble beach at delightful Porlock Weir (2 miles). Several picture-book villages nearby. Lynton 11 miles, Minehead 6.

CASTLE HOTEL, PORLOCK TA24 8PY (01643 862504). Fully licensed, family-run hotel in centre of lovely Exmoor village. 11 en suite bedrooms, all with colour TV. Bar snacks and meals. Well-behaved children and pets welcome. 4 Crowns. *[★]*

MRS CHRISTINE FITZGERALD, "SEAPOINT", UPWAY, PORLOCK TA24 8QE (01643 862289). Spacious Edwardian house overlooking Porlock Bay. Open log fires. Coastal/moorland walks. Excellent traditional or vegetarian food. All bedrooms en-suite with tea/coffee facilities. 2 Crowns. *[★]*

Shipham

Pleasant village on edge of Mendip Hills, Cheddar 3½ miles, Axbridge 3.

PENSCOT FARMHOUSE HOTEL, SHIPHAM, WINSCOMBE BS25 1PW (01934 842659). Take a break in Somerset with your Pet! Quiet, country Hotel near Cheddar. Large attractive garden. Good farmhouse food. Log fires in winter. *[★]*

Taunton

County town, rich in historical associations. Good touring centre. Many sporting attractions. Notable links with the past include the Castle part of which is believed to be 12th century. Bristol 43 miles, Exeter 32, Weston-super-Mare 29, Yeovil 26, Chard 16, Bridgwater 11.

ANN TRUSLER R.G.N., THE SPINNEY, CURLAND, TAUNTON TA3 5SE (Tel and Fax: 01460 234362). Quality en suite accommodation in an Area of Outstanding Natural Beauty. Ideal for walking on the Blackdowns, Quantocks, and Somerset Levels. Delicious home cooking; Evening Meal available. Comfortable kennels for canines. Children welcome. Non-smoking. Open all year. Detailed brochure.

BEVERLEY AND VICTOR JENKINS, THE COTTAGE, FORDGATE, BRIDGWATER TA7 0AP (01278 691908). Cottage set in area of outstanding natural beauty; gardens offering tranquillity, privacy and comfort. Excellent food. Highly recommended. Stay while seeing Somerset.

Watchet

Small port and resort with rocks and sands. Good centre for Exmoor and the Quantocks. Bathing, boating, fishing, rambling. Tiverton 24 miles, Bridgwater 19, Taunton 17, Minehead 9, Dunster 6.

RALEGH'S CROSS INN, BRENDON HILLS, NEAR WATCHET TA23 0LN (01984 640343). Comfortable old inn set in own large grounds offers en suite rooms with colour TV. Extensive menu available in cosy bar area and restaurant. Families welcome.

LORNA DOONE CARAVAN PARK, WATCHET TA23 0BJ (01984 631206). Small quiet park with beautiful views of the coastline and Quantock Hills. Fully equipped luxury caravans. Rose Award Park. *[Pets £12 weekly.]*

SUNNY BANK HOLIDAY CARAVANS, DONIFORD, WATCHET TA23 0UD (01984 632237). Small picturesque family park on coast. All caravans with mains services. Colour TV. Showers. Heated swimming pool. Shop. Launderette. BHHPA 5 ticks. Also caravans for sale. Brochure. *[Pets £12 per week.]*

MR BEVAN, WEST BAY CARAVAN PARK, WATCHET TA28 0BJ (Tel. & Fax: 01984 631261). Small, quiet park on coast with superb views. Ideal for relaxing and touring Exmoor and Quantock Hills. 34 static caravans. Open March–October. √ √ √ √ √ Rose Award. Pets welcome. £81–£275 per caravan per week.

Waterrow

Picturesque village on the Devon/Somerset border. Wiveliscombe 3 miles.

RICHARD & PAM GROOME, TONE VALLEY PINE LODGES, WATERROW, NEAR WIVELISCOMBE TA4 2AU (01984 623322). Six pine lodges in secluded woodland setting. Sleep up to 6. Colour TV, fitted kitchens and bathrooms. Laundry, fitness suite etc. Bed, Breakfast & Evening Meal also available. *[Pets £15 weekly.]*

Weston-Super-Mare

Popular resort on the Bristol Channel with a wide range of entertainments and leisure facilities. An ideal base for touring the West Country.

MR AND MRS C. G. THOMAS, ARDNAVE CARAVAN PARK, KEWSTOKE, WESTON-SUPER-MARE BS22 9XJ (01934 622319. Caravans 4–6 berth, deluxe with colour TV, electric lighting, showers and toilets, 2–3 bedrooms. 4-Star two-bedroom caravans; all facilities, colour TV. Parking. Dogs allowed. Graded 4 ticks. *[🐕pw!]*

BRAESIDE HOTEL, 2 VICTORIA PARK, WESTON-SUPER-MARE BS23 2HZ (01934 626642). Delightful, family-run hotel, close to shops and sea front. All rooms en suite; colour TV; tea/coffee making. November to April THIRD NIGHT FREE. See display advertisement. *[🐕]*

Withypool

Delightful Exmoor village on River Barle. Dulverton 8 miles.

WESTERCLOSE COUNTRY HOUSE HOTEL AND RESTAURANT, WITHYPOOL, EXMOOR TA24 7QR (Tel and Fax: 01643 831302). Set in tranquillity of the National Park, ideal for a holiday with your horse and dog. Stabling and kennels available. 10 en suite bedrooms; excellent food and wines. 3 Crowns Highly Commended, AA and RAC**. *[🐕 🏠]*

Wootton Courtenay

Nestling in idyllic Exmoor countryside with fine views of Dunkery Beacon (1,705ft.). Within easy reach of sea. Minehead 5 miles.

DUNKERY BEACON HOTEL, WOOTTON COURTENAY TA24 8RH (01643 841241). Country House Hotel with superb views. Fully en suite rooms, colour TV. Lots of lovely "walkies". Special autumn and spring breaks. Write or phone Kenneth or Daphne Midwood for details. *[🐕]*

MRS N. E. COBB, BURROW FARM, WOOTTON COURTENAY, NEAR MINEHEAD TA24 7UD (01643 841361). Thatched period farmhouse in glorious countryside, 5 miles from Minehead and the coast. Self catering – weekly lets in summer, long/short lets in winter. Games room; large sheltered garden. Ideal for walkers; fishing, riding and golf locally. Children and pets very welcome. *[🐕]*

STAFFORDSHIRE

STAFFORDSHIRE   *Burton-on-Trent*

Burton-Upon-Trent

Historic brewing centre and shire horse stables are included among 400 years of brewing heritage in Bass Museum.

LITTLE PARK HOLIDAY HOMES, TUTBURY, BURTON-ON-TRENT DE13 9JH (01283 812654). Barn conversion chalets overlooking Dove Valley and Peak District next to medieval castle of Tutbury. Few minutes' walk to numerous shops, pubs, restaurants. *[✿pw!]*

SUFFOLK

SUFFOLK   *Kessingland*

WELCOME COTTAGE HOLIDAYS. Hundreds of properties in wonderful locations at welcoming low prices. Pets, linen and fuel mostly included. For FREE colour brochure telephone 01756 702205.

Aldeburgh

Coastal town 6 miles south-east of Saxmundham. Medieval Moot Hall now on beach. Annual music festival at Snape Maltings.

WENTWORTH HOTEL, ALDEBURGH IP15 5BD (01728 452312). Country House Hotel overlooking the sea. Immediate access to the beach and walks. Two comfortable lounges with log fires and antique furniture. Refurbished bedrooms with all facilities and many with sea views. Restaurant specialises in fresh produce and sea food.

Bury St. Edmunds

Town on River Lark 23 miles north west of Ipswich. Many old buildings, especially Georgian remains of abbey. 12th century flint and rubble building houses collections, including terrifying mantraps.

RAVENWOOD HALL COUNTRY HOUSE HOTEL AND RESTAURANT, ROUGHAM, BURY ST EDMUNDS IP30 9JA (01359 270345 Fax: 01359 270788). 16th century heavily beamed Tudor Hall set in seven acres of perfect dog walks. Beautifully furnished en suite bedrooms; renowned restaurant; relaxing inglenook fires. *[🐕pw!]*

Hadleigh

Historic town on River Brett with several old buildings of interest, including unusual 14th century church. Bury St Edmunds 20 miles, Harwich 20, Colchester 14, Sudbury 11, Ipswich 10.

EDGEHILL HOTEL, 2 HIGH STREET, HADLEIGH IP7 5AP (01473 822458). 16th-century property offering a warm welcome. Comfortable accommodation and good home-cooked food. Licensed. Pets welcome. SAE or telephone for details. ETB 3 Crowns Commended. *[🐕]*

Kessingland

Little seaside place with expansive sandy beach, safe bathing, wildlife park, lake fishing. To the south is Benacre Broad, a beauty spot. Norwich 26 miles, Aldeburgh 23, Saxmundham 19, Lowestoft 5.

Quality seaside Bungalows, all with colour television, refrigerator, parking, linen service. Children and pets welcome. Direct access to beach. APPLY – KNIGHTS HOLIDAY HOMES, 3 BERKELEY GARDENS, OULTON, LOWESTOFT NR32 4UF (01502 588533). *[Pets £18.50 per week.]*

Sudbury

Birthplace of painter, Thomas Gainsborough, with a museum illustrating his career. Colchester 13 miles.

Situated in small, picturesque village within 15 miles of Sudbury, Newmarket Racecourse and historic Bury St Edmunds. Bungalow well equipped to accommodate 4 people. All facilities. Car essential, parking. Children and pets welcome. Terms from £48 to £97 per week. For further details send SAE to MRS M. WINCH, PLOUGH HOUSE, STANSFIELD, SUDBURY, SUFFOLK CO10 8LT (01284 89253).

EAST SUSSEX

EAST SUSSEX   *Arlington, Battle, Brighton, Chiddingly*

Arlington

Village in valley of River Cuckmere below the South Downs. Hailsham 3 miles.

MRS P. BONIFACE, LAKESIDE FARM, ARLINGTON, POLEGATE BN26 6SB (01323 870111). Situated on the edge of Arlington Reservoir. Eastbourne within 15 miles. Accommodation sleeps 4–6 with two double rooms, lounge, dining area, kitchen, bathroom. Open April to October. Weekly from £155. *[🐾]*

Battle

Site of the famous victory of William the Conqueror; remains of an abbey mark the spot where Harold fell.

LITTLE HEMINGFOLD HOTEL, TELHAM, BATTLE TN33 0TT (01424 774338). In the heart of 1066 Country, 40 acres of bliss for you and your pets. Farmhouse hotel, all facilities. Fishing, boating, swimming, tennis. Special Breaks all year. Discounts for children. FREE accommodation for pets. *[🐾]*

Brighton

Famous resort with shingle beach and sand at low tide. Varied entertainment and nightlife; excellent shops and restaurants. Portsmouth 48 miles, Hastings 37, Tunbridge Wells 32, Horsham 23, Worthing 11, Newhaven 9.

GEOFF & MARION BURGESS, DIANA HOUSE, 25 ST GEORGE'S TERRACE, BRIGHTON BN2 1JJ (01273 605797). 100 yards seafront, close town, Lanes, marina and conference centre. All rooms with showers, colour TV, tea/coffee, CH, some ensuite. *[🐾]*

BEST OF BRIGHTON & SUSSEX COTTAGES, HORSESHOE COTTAGE, WHIPPING POST LANE, ROTTINGDEAN BN2 7HZ (Tel: 01273 308779 or Fax: 01273 300266). 4 Keys Commended, up to 5 Keys De Luxe. Good selection of self-catering quality apartments, houses and cottages in BRIGHTON, HOVE, and the country areas of East and West Sussex – many accepting pets. *[Pets £15 per week.]*

KEMPTON HOUSE HOTEL, 33/34 MARINE PARADE, BRIGHTON BN2 1TR (01273 570248). Private seafront Hotel, relaxed and friendly atmosphere, overlooking beach and Pier. En-suite rooms available, all modern facilities. Satellite TV. Choice of Breakfasts. Pets and children always welcome. *[🐾]*

Chiddingly

Charming village, 4 miles north-west of Hailsham. Off the A22 London–Eastbourne road.

Adorable small well-equipped cottage in grounds of Tudor Manor. Two bedrooms. Full central heating. Colour TV. Fridge, freezer, laundry facilities. Large safe garden. Use indoor heated swimming pool, sauna/jacuzzi and tennis. From £265 to £510 per week inclusive. 4 Keys Commended. Contact: EVA MORRIS, "PEKES", 124 ELM PARK MANSIONS, PARK WALK, LONDON SW10 0AR (0171-352 8088; Fax: 0171-352 8125). *[2 dogs free, extra dog £5 (max. 4) pw!]*

Hastings

Seaside resort with a famous past – the ruins of William the Conqueror's castle lie above the Old Town. Many places of historic interest in the area, plus entertainments for all the family.

MRS VICKI SAADE, "COPPERBEECHES", 41 CHAPEL PARK ROAD, ST LEONARDS-ON-SEA, HASTINGS TN37 6JB (01424 714026). Lovely Victorian Guest House with off-road parking. Friendly, relaxed atmosphere with pets most welcome. Rooms with colour TV, tea/coffee facilities and central heating. Close to BR Warrior Square. Good walks, ideal for touring 1066 Country. Terms £13–£17. Sorry no smokers. SEETB 2 Crowns Approved. *[*🐾pw!*]*

BEAUPORT PARK HOTEL, BATTLE ROAD, HASTINGS TN38 8EA (01424 851222). Georgian country mansion in 33 acres. All rooms private bath, colour television, trouser press, hairdryer, telephone. Country house breaks available all year. *[pw!]*

Herstmonceux

Small village four miles north-east of Hailsham. Royal Observatory at Herstmonceux Castle.

CLEAVERS LYNG 16th-CENTURY COUNTRY HOTEL, CHURCH ROAD, HERST-MONCEUX BN27 1QJ (01323 833131; Fax: 01323 833617). Small family-run Hotel in heart of rural East Sussex. Bedrooms en suite with tea making. Oak-beamed restaurant, bar, residents' lounge. Pets welcome. *[*🐾*]*

Polegate

Quiet position 5 miles from the popular seaside resort of Eastbourne. London 58 miles, Lewes 12.

MRS P. FIELD, 20 ST JOHN'S ROAD, POLEGATE BN26 5BP (01323 482691). Homely private house. Quiet location; large enclosed garden. Parking space. Ideally situated for walking on South Downs and Forestry Commission land. All rooms washbasins and tea/coffee facilities. Bed and Breakfast. Pets very welcome. *[pw!]*

Rye

Picturesque hill town with steep cobbled streets. Many fine buildings of historic interest. Hastings 12 miles, Tunbridge Wells 28.

MRS D. AVERY, "THACKER", OLD BRICKYARD, RYE TN31 7EE (01797 225870). Comfortable holiday home, quietly situated within easy walking distance of Rye's delightful "old town". Sleeps 2 to 3. Fully equipped including bed linen. Enclosed garden adjoining fields. Available all year – short breaks October to April. Dogs very welcome. *[*🐾*]*

FLACKLEY ASH HOTEL, PEASMARSH, RYE TN31 6HY (01797 230651; Fax: 01797 230510). Georgian Country House Hotel in beautiful grounds. Indoor swimming pool and Leisure Centre. AA Rosette for our food. Visit Rye and the castles and gardens of East Sussex and Kent. ETB 4 Crowns Highly Commended. *[Pets £5 per night.]*

JEAKE'S HOUSE, MERMAID STREET, RYE, EAST SUSSEX TN31 7ET (01797 222828; Fax: 01797 222623). Dating from 1689, this Listed Building has oak-beamed and panelled bedrooms overlooking the marsh. En suite facilities, TV, radio, telephone. Residential licence. £20.50–£29.50 per person. AA QQQQQ. *[*🐾*]*

South Heighton

Picturesque village 2 kilometres north of Newhaven.

CLIFF'S STATIC CARAVAN HIRE SERVICE, 19 THE HIGHWAY, HAMPDEN VALE, SOUTH HEIGHTON BN9 0HU (01273 514950 evenings). Situated one mile from Newhaven, Cliff's Static Caravans are all equipped to the highest standard. The park, a perfect sun trap, free from road traffic noise, is a haven for wildlife. Excellent facilities. Reasonable rates. Pets welcome. *[🐕]*

Telscombe

Tranquil Downland hamlet, close to South Downs Way. 4 miles south of Lewes and 2 miles from coast.

DUCK BARN HOLIDAYS, 51 SCHOOL ROAD, FIRLE, NEAR LEWES BN8 6LF (01273 858221). Beautiful converted Barn, sleeps 8/10; Coach House for 4/5; Cosy Cottage for 2/3. Central heating, woodburners. Exposed beams; pine furniture. Children and dogs welcome. Brochure. *[pw! £10 weekly.]*

WEST SUSSEX

WEST SUSSEX   *Bognor Regis*

Bognor Regis

Renowned for its wide sands and safe bathing, Bognor is ideal for family holidays, with a pier, promenade, gardens and a variety of entertainments.

BLACK MILL HOUSE HOTEL, PRINCESS AVENUE, BOGNOR REGIS (01243 821945). Children and dogs most welcome. Situated in the quieter West End of town, near sea and Marine Gardens, West End shops and bus routes. Attractive cocktail bar. Games room, colour television, private bathrooms, central heating throughout. Lift. Enclosed garden. Open all year. Mini-Breaks – 2 days D, B&B from £60 (October to March). Own car park. No service charge. Short summer breaks. *[Pets £1.50 per night.]*

JOAN AND ROGER TANN, ALANCOURT HOTEL, MARINE DRIVE WEST, BOGNOR REGIS (01243 864844). Fully licensed Hotel near Marine Park Gardens. All rooms colour TV, tea/coffee facilities; heating; many en-suite. Friendly atmosphere. Children and pets welcome. Goodwood and Fontwell racecourses nearby.

Eastergate

Village between the sea and South Downs. Fontwell Park steeplechase course is nearby. Bognor Regis 5 miles S.

WANDLEYS CARAVAN PARK, EASTERGATE PO20 6SE (01903 745831 evenings, weekends; 01243 543235 9am–5pm weekdays). Comfortable holiday caravans in tranquil little country park. All with internal WC and shower. Only 15 minutes from Sussex Downs, Bognor and Chichester. [🐾]

Pulborough

Popular fishing centre on the River Arun. Nearby South Downs Way makes it an ideal centre for walking. Arundel 8 miles.

THE BARN OWLS, LONDON ROAD, COLDWALTHAM, PULBOROUGH RH20 1LR (01798 872498). Small country Hotel specialising in gourmet breaks and holidays. 2 night breaks from £85. Bed and Breakfast (en suite) from £150 weekly. Gourmet Christmas and New Year breaks. Bed and Breakfast from £24 per night. Telephone for brochure. [pw! 🐾]

CHEQUERS HOTEL, PULBOROUGH RH20 1AD (01798 872486). Lovely Queen Anne house in village overlooking Arun Valley. Excellent food. Children and dogs welcome. AA and RAC 2 Star. ETB 4 Crowns Highly Commended. No charge for dogs belonging to readers of *Pets Welcome!* [pw! 🐾]

WARWICKSHIRE

WARWICKSHIRE   *Stratford-upon-Avon*

THE CROFT
Haseley Knob, Warwick CV35 7NL Tel: 01926 484447
This four acre smallholding has a friendly, family atmosphere and is situated in picturesque rural surroundings. Very comfortable accommodation. Bedrooms, most en suite, with colour TV, tea/coffee facilities. Ground floor en suite bedrooms available. Bed and Full English Breakfast from £20. Pets welcome.

WELCOME COTTAGE HOLIDAYS. Hundreds of properties in wonderful locations at welcoming low prices. Pets, linen and fuel mostly included. For FREE colour brochure telephone 01756 702212.

Stratford-upon-Avon

Historic town famous as Shakespeare's birthplace and home. Many interesting old buildings; rebuilt Shakespeare Memorial Theatre. There is a steeplechase course here. London 91 miles, Birmingham 24, Banbury 20, Coventry 19, Broadway 15, Evesham 14, Warwick 8.

JANE WELDON, BRIDGE HOUSE, ALDERMINSTER, NEAR STRATFORD-UPON-AVON CV37 8NY (01789 450521; 0850 065856 mobile). Charming Georgian house convenient for Stratford and the Cotswolds. Some rooms private facilities; all have colour TV and tea/coffee facilities. Fully enclosed garden. Licensed. Bed and Breakfast £18–£22. [🐾 pw!]

MRS J. M. EVERETT, NEWBOLD NURSERIES, NEWBOLD-ON-STOUR, STRATFORD-UPON-AVON CV37 8DP (01789 450285). Small farm and hydroponic tomato nursery close to Cotswolds, Stratford-upon-Avon, Warwick and Blenheim. Comfortable rooms with colour TV, tea/coffee. Local pub serves evening meals at budget prices. En suite available. Bed and Breakfast from £15. Children half price. [🐾]

MRS H. J. MELLOR, ARRANDALE, 208 EVESHAM ROAD, STRATFORD-UPON-AVON CV37 9AS (01789 267112). Guest House situated near River Avon, theatre, Shakespearen properties. Washbasins, tea making, TV, central heating, en-suite available. Children, pets welcome. Parking. Bed and Breakfast £14–16.50. Weekly terms £95–£110. Evening Meals £6. [🐾]

RAYFORD CARAVAN PARK, TIDDINGTON ROAD, STRATFORD-UPON-AVON (01789 293964). Luxury Caravans, sleep 6. Fully equipped kitchens, bathroom/shower/WC. Also two riverside Cottages, all modern facilities to first-class standards. Private fishing. On banks of River Avon. [£12 weekly.]

Warwick

Town on the River Avon, 9 miles south-west of Coventry, with medieval castle and many fine old buildings.

MR & MRS D. CLAPP, THE CROFT, HASELEY KNOB, WARWICK CV35 7NL (01926 484447). Smallholding with a friendly, family atmosphere and situated in picturesque rural surroundings. Very comfortable accommodation. Bedrooms, most en suite, with colour TV, tea/coffee facilities. Ground floor en suite bedrooms available. Bed and Full English Breakfast from £20. Pets welcome.

THE OLD RECTORY, STRATFORD ROAD, SHERBOURNE, WARWICK CV35 8AB (Tel and Fax: 01926 624562). Grade II Listed Georgian Country House offers Bed and Breakfast: en-suite bedrooms, brass beds; delicious home-cooked Breakfast. Beautiful surroundings. Half-mile M40 Junction 15. AA QQQQ Selected, ETB 2 Crowns Commended. [🐾]

WEST MIDLANDS

Birmingham

The second-largest city in Britain, with Art Galleries to rival London. The Bull Ring has been modernised and includes an impressive shopping centre, but there is still plenty of the old town to see; the town hall, the concert hall and the Cathedral Church of St Philip.

ANGELA AND IAN KERR, THE AWENTSBURY HOTEL, 21 SERPENTINE ROAD, SELLY PARK, BIRMINGHAM B29 7HU (0121-472 1258). Victorian Country House. Large gardens. All rooms have colour TV, telephones and tea/coffee making facilities. Some rooms en-suite, some with showers. All rooms central heating, wash-basins. Near BBC Pebble Mill, transport, University, City centre. Bed and Breakfast from £25 Single Room, from £39 Twin Room, inclusive of VAT.

WILTSHIRE

WILTSHIRE   *Coombe Bissett, Malmesbury*

Swaynes Firs Farm

Grimsdyke, Coombe Bissett, Salisbury, Wiltshire SP5 5RF
Small working farm with horses, cattle, poultry, geese and duck ponds. Spacious rooms, all en suite with colour TV and country views. Ideal for visiting the many historic sites in the area.

Mr A. Shering   AA QQ   ☛ Approved   *Tel: 01725 519240*

CRUDWELL COURT
HOTEL & RESTAURANT
Crudwell, Near Malmesbury, Wiltshire SN16 9EP
Tel: 01666 577194 Fax: 01666 577853

Restaurant and residential licence; 15 bedrooms, all with private bathrooms; Historic interest; children and dogs welcome; car park (45); Cheltenham 20 miles; Bath 18; Exit 17 M4 7 miles; Cirencester 5; Malmesbury 3; Tetbury 2.

17th Century rectory set in three acres of lovely Cotswold walled gardens with lily ponds, outdoor heated swimming pool. Recommended by recognised independent guides. The resident owners have created a relaxed and comfortable atmosphere with excellent cooking and extensive wine lists. The bedrooms have exceptionally good beds, are all individually decorated and have lovely views of the surrounding gardens leading to farm land. All cooking is freshly prepared to order and the panelled dining room overlooking the walled garden is open to non-residents for all meals and snack lunches.

Mini-breaks are available throughout the year by prior arrangement. Christmas and New Year packages.

Dairy Farm on the Wiltshire/Gloucestershire borders. Malmesbury 3 miles, 15 mins M4 (Junctions 16 or 17). **SELF CATERING:** The Bull Pen and Cow Byre each sleep 2/3 plus cot. Double bedded room, bathroom, kitchen, lounge. 3 KEYS COMMENDED. **B&B** in 15C farmhouse – three comfortable rooms, one en suite. Listed COMMENDED.

John & Edna Edwards, Stonehill Farm, Charlton, Malmesbury SN16 9DY Tel: 01666 823310

Castle Combe

Often hailed as England's prettiest village. Lies in hollow, approached through deep, tree-shaded valley.

CAROL ELLS, WOODMOUSE COTTAGE, EAST COMBE FARM, CASTLE COMBE SN14 7HH (Tel & Fax: 01249 783128). Enjoy country life in an idyllic village setting. East Combe Farm is in an outstanding situation on edge of village and conservation area. Sleeping 6/8. Central heating and log fire. Large private garden. Open all year. Ideal river and woodland walks. [🐕]

Coombe Bissett

Village on River Ebble 3 miles south west of Salisbury.

MR A. SHERING, SWAYNES FIRS FARM, GRIMSDYKE, COOMBE BISSETT, SALISBURY SP5 5RF (01725 519240). Small working farm with horses, poultry, geese and duck ponds. Spacious rooms, all en suite with colour TV. Ideal for visiting the many historic sites in the area.

Devizes

Market town with two 12th century churches, 15th century castle, 16th century buildings and elegant Georgian houses.

COLIN & CYNTHIA FLETCHER, LOWER FOXHANGERS FARM, ROWDE, DEVIZES SN10 1SS (Tel/Fax: 01380 828254). Tranquillity awaits you on our farm alongside the canal. Assist boats through locks, enjoy fishing, boating and scenic walks to pubs. Bed and Breakfast in family/double, twin rooms, twin-en-suite. Lounge with TV. Children, pets welcome. Also self-catering & small campsite. [🐕]

Malmesbury

Country town on river Avon with a late medieval market cross. Remains of medieval abbey.

MRS A. HILLIER, LOWER FARM, SHERSTON, MALMESBURY SN16 0PS (01666 840391). Self contained wing of farmhouse. Sleeps 3/5. Working farm. Large lawn and fields. Ideal for pets and children. Fishing. Half mile from shops, pubs/ restaurants. Wiltshire/Gloucestershire Borders, ideal for Bath, Cotswolds, etc. £95– £150 per week. Electricity 50p meter. [Pets £5 each per week.]

CRUDWELL COURT HOTEL AND RESTAURANT, CRUDWELL, NEAR MALMES- BURY SN16 9EP (01666 577194; Fax: 01666 577853). 17th century rectory in lovely gardens with outdoor heated pool. 15 bedrooms, all with private bathrooms. Excellent cooking and extensive wine list. [Pets £2 per night.]

JOHN AND EDNA EDWARDS, STONEHILL FARM, CHARLTON, MALMESBURY SN16 9DY (01666 823310). Family-run dairy farm, ideal for touring. 3 comfortable rooms, one en suite. Also 2 fully equipped bungalow-style barns, each sleeps 2/3 plus cot, self catering. [🐕]

WORCESTERSHIRE

Malvern

Famous inland resort on slopes of Malvern Hills. Spectacular views. The Priory Church dates from 1085. Numerous facilities for sport and entertainment including Festival Theatre. Good amenities for children. Many delightful open spaces and walks. Good touring centre for Shakespeare country and Wye Valley. Gloucester 20 miles, Hereford 19, Tewkesbury 13, Worcester 8.

ANN AND BRIAN PORTER, CROFT GUEST HOUSE, BRANSFORD, WORCESTER WR6 5JD (01886 832227). 16th–18th century country house, 10 minutes from Worcester, Malvern and M5. En suite rooms, tea/coffee trays, central heating. Dinners available; residential licence. Sauna and family jacuzzi. Dogs and children welcome; cot and baby listening service; family room. 2 Crowns. AA Listed. [🐕]

MALVERN HILLS HOTEL, WYNDS POINT, MALVERN WR13 6DW (01684 40237). Enchanting Hotel sitting atop the Malvern Hills. Magnificent views, prettily decorated en-suite rooms, oak-panelled lounge; friendly and efficient staff. Excellent walking country. Water dishes provided. Great animal lovers. [🐕]

EAST YORKSHIRE

EAST YORKSHIRE

WELCOME COTTAGE HOLIDAYS. Hundreds of properties in wonderful locations at welcoming low prices. Pets, linen and fuel mostly included. For FREE colour brochure telephone 01756 702209.

Bridlington

Traditional family holiday resort with picturesque harbour and a wide range of entertainments and leisure facilities. Ideal for exploring the Heritage coastline and the Wolds.

THE TENNYSON HOTEL, 19 TENNYSON AVENUE, BRIDLINGTON YO15 2EU (Tel & Fax: 01262 604382). 1994 Golden Bowl Award Winner for the Most Pet-Friendly Hotel in Yorkshire. Offering fine cuisine in attractive surroundings. Close to beach and cliff walks. AA QQQ, RAC 1 Star, 3 Crowns Commended. [🐕 pw!]

NORTH YORKSHIRE

NORTH YORKSHIRE   *Bentham, Brompton-by-Sawdon,*
Clapham, Easingwold

251

NORTH YORKSHIRE *Oldstead, Pickering, Scarborough, Skipton*

The Black Swan Inn
Oldstead
Coxwold, York YO6 4BL
Telephone: Coxwold 01347 868387

Charming family-run 18th century Inn set in the stunning
scenery of the North York Moors National Park.
Magnificent views – perfect dog walking country
2 miles Kilburn, 20 miles York. Superb chalet-style en suite
accommodation with colour TV, central heating and
tea/coffee making facilities.
* Hand-pumped real ale *
* Yorkshire farmhouse cooking *
* Bar Meals * A la carte Restaurant *
* Fine wines * Vegetarian meals a speciality *
Bed and Breakfast from £19.50
Bed, Breakfast and Evening Meal from £30.00

For bookings and brochures telephone 01347 868387

VIVERS MILL
Mill Lane, Pickering, North Yorkshire YO18 8DJ. Tel: 01751 473640

Ancient watermill in peaceful surroundings. Ideal for Moors, historic railway, interesting coastline, and York. Most of the original machinery preserved including waterwheel. Comfortable en suite bedrooms, with beamed ceilings. Tea making facilities. TV lounge.
Bed and Breakfast £22 per day (£135 weekly).   *Proprietors: Hilary and Stan Langton*

LUXURY BUNGALOW
2 miles from Filey, 4 miles from Scarborough

Enjoying magnificent setting in the Blue Dolphin parkland. Fully fitted kitchen. Bedrooms have quality beds. Bathroom. Separate toilet. Sleeps 4/6. CLEAN PETS WELCOME. Drive for two cars. Reduced terms April and October.
Please telephone 01709 815102 or SAE Mrs J. Holland, 32 Joan Lane, Rotherham S66 8PH

Near Skipton   **SELF CATERING COTTAGES**

in award-winning village surrounded by lovely walks. Equipped to a very high standard.
Convenient for Dales, Lakes, West Coast, Brontë Country.
Central heating, colour TV. Parking. Linen, towels and fuel inclusive. PET FREE.
**SUSAN STOTT, HIGH GABLES, THE FOLD, THORNTON-IN-CRAVEN, SKIPTON BD23 3TJ
TEL: 01282 843272**

FREE and REDUCED RATE Holiday Visits!
Don't miss our Readers' Offer Vouchers on
pages 5 to 18.

NORTH YORKSHIRE   *Wensleydale, York*

ST EDMUNDS COUNTRY COTTAGES
Cottages in Swaledale and Wensleydale
Properties sleeping two to seven persons plus cot. These recently renovated cottages are fully equipped and are an ideal base for exploring the Dales and Moors.

PETS WELCOME
For a brochure send SAE to:
Sue Cooper, St Edmunds, The Green, Crakehall, Bedale, North Yorkshire DL8 1HP

Tel: 01677 423584   **UP TO 4 KEYS COMMENDED**

ST. GEORGE'S HOUSE HOTEL, YORK YO2 2DR
♕♕♕ COMMENDED   **TEL: (01904) 625056**   RAC ACCLAIMED,
AA RECOMMENDED QQQ
Family run licensed Hotel in quiet cul-de-sac by racecourse. Perfect for doggy walking. Rooms en suite, colour TV, radio alarm, courtesy tray.
Private parking.

ASTORIA HOTEL
6 GROSVENOR TERRACE, BOOTHAM, YORK
Tel: 01904 659558
Near to Minster. This licensed Hotel has 15 centrally heated bedrooms, many with private bathrooms/showers, including ground-floor rooms. Private parking. Groups catered for. Dogs welcome.

Orillia House   89 The Village, Stockton-on-Forest, York YO3 9UP
Tel: 01904 400600 or 01904 738595

A warm welcome awaits you at Orillia House, conveniently situated in the centre of the village, 3 miles north-east of York, one mile from the A64. The house dates back to the 17th century and has been restored to offer a high standard of comfort with modern facilities, yet retaining its original charm and character. All rooms have private facilities, colour TV and tea/coffee making. Our local pub provides excellent evening meals. We have our own private car park. ETB Two Crowns.

YORK LAKESIDE LODGES
Moor Lane, York YO2 2QU
Tel: (01904) 702346 Mobile: (0831) 885824
Fax: (01904) 701631
Unique in a city! Luxurious Scandinavian lodges, and cottages in mature parkland overlooking large private fishing lake. Nearby superstore with coach to centre every 10 minutes. Easy access to ring road for touring. Open year round.

YORKSHIRE & HUMBERSIDE TOURIST BOARD WHITE ROSE AWARDS FOR TOURISM
WINNER

Award – British Holiday Home Parks Association

UP TO DELUXE

THREE SELF-CATERING CHOICES 12 MILES FROM YORK
Attractive self-catering on a farm. **WOODLEA** detached house with 3 bedrooms sleeping 5–6 with fully equipped kitchen, dining area, lounge, bathroom, extra toilet. **BUNGALOW** sleeping 2–4. Kitchen, bathroom, lounge/diner with double bed settee. Twin room with cot. **STUDIO** for 2. Kitchen, bathroom, lounge/diner. All with colour TV and parking. SAE for details.
Mrs M S A Woodliffe, Mill Farm, Yapham, Pocklington, York YO4 2PH. Tel: 01759 302172

WELCOME COTTAGE HOLIDAYS. Hundreds of properties in wonderful locations at welcoming low prices. Pets, linen and fuel mostly included. For FREE colour brochure telephone 01756 702209.

The North's Dales, Moors and Coast ... Over 500 superb, personally inspected, self-catering holiday properties from Yorkshire's "Bronte", "Herriot" and "Heartbeat" country to Northumberland's borders. Cottages for two to houses for 12. Contact PAT AMES, DALES HOLIDAY COTTAGES, CARLETON BUSINESS PARK, SKIPTON, NORTH YORKSHIRE BD23 2DG (01756 799821 & 01756 790919).

A wide choice of selected and personally inspected self-catering properties in most areas. APPLY – RECOMMENDED COTTAGES (01751 475547).

Askrigg

TV series based on popular "Vet" stories by James Herriot were filmed here. St Oswald's Church, "Cathedral of Wensleydale", dates from late 15th and early 16th centuries.

KATE EMPSALL, WHITFIELD, HELM, ASKRIGG, WENSLEYDALE DL8 3YF (Tel/ Fax: 01969 650565). Relax at 950 feet in peaceful surroundings with spectacular views in B&B (Two Crowns Commended) overlooking Upper Wensleydale. Cottages at Askrigg and Hawes (Three Keys Commended), sleep four persons. Non-smoking. *[🐕]*

Bentham

Quiet village amidst the fells. Good centre for rambling and fishing. Ingleton 5 miles N.E.

MRS L. J. STORY, HOLMES FARM, LOW BENTHAM, LANCASTER LA2 7DE (015242 61198). Cottage conversion in easy reach of Dales, Lake District and coast. Central heating, fridge, TV, washer, games room. 3 Keys Commended. *[🐕]*

Brompton-by-Sawdon

Quiet village on edge of North Yorkshire Moors. Close to Northallerton.

MRS D. PROCTOR, HEADON FARM, WYDALE, BROMPTON-BY-SAWDON, SCARBOROUGH YO13 9DG (01723 859019). Five spacious character cottages situated in a quiet wooded setting on edge of North York Moors. Open all year from £130 per week. Brochure available.

Clapham

Attractive village with caves and pot-holes in vicinity, including Gaping Ghyll. Nearby lofty peaks include Ingleborough (2,373ft.) to the north. Kendal 24 miles, Settle 6.

NEW INN HOTEL, CLAPHAM, NEAR SETTLE LA2 8HH (015242 51203; Fax: 015242 51496). Friendly 18th century coaching inn. Ideal centre for walking. All rooms en suite, with colour TV and tea/coffee facilities. Restaurant and bar meals. Dogs welcome.

NORTH YORKSHIRE

Coverdale

Small village set in Yorkshire Dales, in heart of Herriot Country.

MRS CAROLINE HARRISON, HILL TOP FARM & LIVERY YARD, YORKSHIRE
DALES NATIONAL PARK, WEST SCRAFTON, LEYBURN, COVERDALE DL8 4RU
(01969 640663). 3 Keys Highly Commended. Relax in our luxurious traditional stone
barns recently converted, modern en suite bathrooms, central heating, log fires,
dishwashers, etc. Panoramic views of open moorland. Take part in some of our
farming routines, pets' corner with pony. Ideal for children, walkers or relaxing. Livery
yard with qualified registered instructor. BHF Book of Bridling provided. Fishing,
shooting. Comprehensive brochure provided. *[pw!]*

**MRS JULIE CLARKE, MIDDLE FARM, WOODALE, COVERDALE, LEYBURN
DL8 4TY (01969 640271). Peacefully situated traditional Farmhouse offering
Bed and Breakfast, optional Evening Meal. Home cooking. Ideally positioned
for walking and touring the Dales *[ᛉ pw! ⌂]***

Easingwold

*Small market town with cobbled streets where weathered red brick dwellings are grouped around
a large green. 12 miles north-west of York.*

MRS R. RITCHIE, THE OLD RECTORY, THORMANBY, EASINGWOLD, YORK
YO6 3WN (01845 501417). Ideal for touring Herriot Country, Moors, Dales. TWO
SELF CONTAINED COTTAGES sleeping 4/6. Also Bed and Breakfast. 3 spacious
bedrooms, 2 en suite. SAE or phone for brochure. *[ᛉ]*

Filey

*Well-known resort with sandy beach. Off-shore is Filey Brig. Hull 40 miles, Bridlington 11,
Scarborough 7.*

MAYFIELD GUEST HOUSE, 2 BROOKLANDS, FILEY, NORTH YORKSHIRE YO14
9BA (01723 514557). Close to all amenities; five bedrooms (mostly en suite; one
ground floor). Ideal centre for touring. Bed and Breakfast from £16; Dinner £7. Open
all year. ETB 3 Crowns. *[ᛉ]*

Goathland

*Centre for moorland and woodland walks and waterfalls. Village of 19th century houses scattered
over several heaths.*

MRS MARION COCKREM, DALE END FARM, GREEN END, GOATHLAND, NEAR
WHITBY YO22 5LJ (01947 895371). 500-year-old stone-built farmhouse on 140-acre
working farm in North York Moors National Park. Rare breeds kept. Generous
portions home cooked food. Guest lounge with colour TV and log fire. Homely
olde-worlde interior. Many repeat bookings. SAE for brochure. *[ᛉ]*

Grassington

Wharfedale village in attractive moorland setting. Ripon 22 miles, Skipton 9.

GRASSINGTON HOUSE HOTEL, THE SQUARE, GRASSINGTON BD23 5AQ
(01756 752406; Fax: 01756 752135). A small hotel with a big reputation. Les
Routiers Newcomer of the Year! All rooms en suite, colour TV, tea making. AA
Rosette for food. Parking. 3 Crowns. *[ᛉ]*

NORTH YORKSHIRE

FORESTERS ARMS, MAIN STREET, GRASSINGTON, SKIPTON BD23 5AA (01756 752349). The Foresters Arms is situated in the heart of the Yorkshire Dales and provides an ideal centre for walking or touring. Within easy reach of York and Harrogate. *[🐕]*

Hackness

Village five miles west of Scarborough in National Park.

HACKNESS GRANGE HOTEL, HACKNESS, NEAR SCARBOROUGH YO13 0JW (01723 882345). Sensitively restored and idyllically tucked away in National Park. 26 superbly appointed rooms with en suite facilities. Kennels available. AA/RAC***. *[Pets £6 per night.]*

Harrogate

Charming and elegant spa town set amid some of Britain's most scenic countryside. Ideal for exploring Herriot Country and the moors and dales. Yorks 22 miles, Bradford 19, Leeds 16.

ABBATT & YOUNG'S HOTEL, 15 YORK ROAD (OFF SWAN ROAD), HARROGATE HG1 2QL (01423 567336). Licensed Hotel with attractive gardens. Colour television, tea/coffee making facilities in all rooms, all with en suite bathrooms. 4 Crowns Commended, AA 2 Stars. *[🐕]*

ROSEMARY HELME, HELME PASTURE, HARTWITH BANK, SUMMERBRIDGE, HARROGATE HG3 4DR (Tel: 01423 780279, Fax: 01423 780994). Country accommodation for dogs and numerous walks in unspoilt Nidderdale. Central for Harrogate. York, Herriot and Brontë country. National Trust area. Illustrated brochure available. ETB 3/4 Keys up to Highly Commended. *[pw! Pets £12 per week.]*

Luxury cottages and lodges sleeping two to ten people. All equipped to a high standard. Pool, licensed bar, golf and children's playground on estate. Illustrated brochure available. Three/Five Keys. RUDDING HOLIDAY PARK, FOLLIFOOT, HARROGATE HG3 1JH (01423 870439). *[🐕]*

SCOTIA HOUSE HOTEL, 66 KINGS ROAD, HARROGATE HG1 5JR (01423 504361). Owner-managed licensed Hotel five minutes' walk town centre. En suite bedrooms with colour TV, hospitality tray, telephone. Central heating throughout. On site parking. Pets and owners welcome. ETB 3 Crowns Commended, AA, RAC One Star. *[🐕]*

Hawes

Small town in Wensleydale. Situated 14 miles south-east of Kirkby Stephen.

CLOCK TOWER STUDIO, SIMONSTONE HALL, HAWES DL8 3LY (01969 667255). First-floor self-catering studio for two persons, combining living and sleeping areas. Separate kitchen and bathroom. In east wing of award-winning Country House Hotel. Open fire, central heating, well-equipped kitchen. Large garden. Dogs welcome.

GREEN DRAGON INN, HARDROW, HAWES DL8 3LZ (01969 667392). Family run licensed inn. Extended. 16 bedrooms all with private bathroom, colour TV and tea/coffee facilities. Central heating. Lift. Pets welcome.

COUNTRY COTTAGE HOLIDAYS, DRYDEN HOUSE, MARKET PLACE, HAWES DL8 3RA (01969 667654). 100 cottages in the lovely Yorkshire Dales. Colour TV, central heating, open fires. Gardens, private parking. Many allow pets. Rents £115–£295 per week. Sleep 2–8.

STONE HOUSE HOTEL, SEDBUSK, HAWES DL8 3PT (01969 667571; Fax: 01969 66720). This fine Edwardian country house has spectacular views and serves delicious Yorkshire cooking with fine wines. Comfortable en-suite bedrooms, some ground floor. Phone for details. *[🐕]*

MR AND MRS C. JEFFRYES, SIMONSTONE HALL, HAWES, WENSLEYDALE DL8 3LY (01969 667255). Facing south across picturesque Wensleydale. All rooms en-suite with colour TV. Fine cuisine. Extensive wine list. Off season bargain breaks. Self catering apartments also available. Personal attention. Resident owners.

Hawes near (Mallerstang)

12 miles north west on the Hawes to Kirkby Stephen road.

COCKLAKE HOUSE, MALLERSTANG CA17 4JT (017683 72080). Charming, High Pennine Country House. B&B in unique position above Pendragon Castle in Upper Mallerstang Dale offering good food and exceptional comfort to a small number of guests. Two double rooms with large private bathrooms. 3 acres riverside grounds. Dogs welcome.

Helmsley

A delightful stone-built town on River Rye with a large cobbled square. Thirsk 12 miles.

MRS ELIZABETH EASTON, LOCKTON HOUSE FARM, BILSDALE, HELMSLEY YO6 5NE (01439 798303). 16th century Farmhouse; oak beams, central heating. All rooms washbasins, tea/coffee facilities. Good home cooking. Panoramic views. Bed and Breakfast from £14; BB & EM from £22.

MRS SALLY ROBINSON, VALLEY VIEW FARM, OLD BYLAND, HELMSLEY, YORK YO6 5LG (01439 798221). Experience superb food, comfortable accommodation and outstanding hospitality on a farmhouse in the North York Moors National Park. Licensed. Traditional Bed and Breakfast £25, with Dinner £37. 2 Crowns Highly Commended. 3 Super Self Catering Cottages sleeping 2/4 or 6 also available. *[🐕]*

Scandinavian Pine Lodges, each sleeping up to five persons. Fully centrally heated and double glazed. Set in 60 acres, surrounded by pine forests. Open all year. CRIEF LODGE HOLIDAY HOMES, WASS, YORK YO6 4AY (01347 868207 or Fax: 01347 86822.) *[🐕]*

CROWN HOTEL, MARKET SQUARE, HELMSLEY YO6 5BJ (01439 770297). Fully residential old coaching inn. Bedrooms are very well appointed, all have tea and coffee-making facilities, colour TV, radio and telephones. Traditional country cooking. AA and RAC 2 Stars. *[🐕]*

Horton-in-Ribblesdale

Moorland village in the Craven country in the shadow of Pen-y-Ghent (2273 ft.). Many caves and potholes in the vicinity. Settle 6 miles.

COLIN AND JOAN HORSFALL, STUDFOLD HOUSE, HORTON-IN-RIBBLESDALE, NEAR SETTLE BD24 0ER (01729 860200). Georgian house standing in one acre of beautiful gardens. All rooms have central heating, washbasins, colour TVs and tea/coffee making facilities. Vegetarians, children and pets also welcome. Bed and Breakfast £15. Evening Meal £7.50. Self-catering £95–£195. SAE please.

Huby

Small village 9 miles north of York. Ideal as base for exploring Dales, Moors and coast.

THE NEW INN MOTEL, MAIN STREET, HUBY, YORK YO6 1HQ (01347 810219). Ideal base for Yorkshire attractions. Ground floor rooms, en suite, colour TVs etc. Bed and Breakfast from £20 pp,pn (EM available). Pets welcome. Special 3 day breaks. Telephone for brochure. AA Listed. *[🐕]*

Kilburn

Village to south of Hambleton Hills. Nearby is White Horse carved into hillside. Helmesley 9 miles, Thirsk 6.

CLAIRE STRAFFORD, CHAPEL COTTAGE, KILBURN, YORK YO6 4AH (01347 868383). Converted farm buildings in excellent area for touring Moors, Dales and coast. Range of sports facilities and restaurants in area. ALL PETS VERY WELCOME.

Kirkbymoorside

Small town below North Yorkshire Moors, 7 miles west of Pickering. Traces of a medieval castle.

MRS F. WILES, SINNINGTON COMMON FARM, KIRKBYMOORSIDE, YORK YO6 6NX (01751 431719). Newly converted cottages, tastefully furnished and well equipped, on working family farm. Sleep 2/4 from £100 per week including linen and heating. Also spacious ground floor accommodation (teamakers, colour TV, radio alarms). Disabled facilities, separate entrances. B&B from £16. *[🐕]*

Leeming Bar

Small, pretty village two miles north-east of Bedale.

THE WHITE ROSE HOTEL, LEEMING BAR, NORTHALLERTON DL7 9AY (01677 422707; Fax: 01677 425123). Eighteen bedroom, two-star private Hotel situated in village on A684, half a mile from A1 motorway. Ideal base for touring North Yorks Moors, Dales and coastal resorts. Licensed; Restaurant. 3 Crowns Commended. *[🐕]*

Leyburn

Small market town, 8 miles south-west of Richmond, standing above the River Ure in Wensleydale.

PEN VIEW FARMHOUSE, THORALBY, LEYBURN DL8 3SU (01969 663319). Fully centrally heated with one single, one twin, one double and one family room, two en-suite. Licensed. Ideal for walking or touring Dales. Children and pets welcome. 2 Crowns.

PARK GRANGE FARM, HARMBY, LEYBURN DL8 5HJ (01969 640258). Three-bedroomed farmhouse, approximately one mile from Leyburn in the heart of Wensleydale. Horses and dogs welcome. Competitive rates for stabling or grazing. Trail riding routes available. *[🐕, horses £3 per night. 🏠]*

BARBARA & BARRIE MARTIN, THE OLD STAR, WEST WITTON, LEYBURN DL8 4LU (01969 622949). Former 17th century Coaching Inn now run as a guest house. Oak beams, log fire, home cooking. En suite from £15. ETB 2 Crowns. *[🐕]*

Malham

In picturesque Craven District with spectacular Malham Cove (300ft.) and Gordale Scar with waterfalls. Malham Tarn (N.T.) is 4 miles N., Skipton 12 miles.

MRS V. SHARP, MIRESFIELD FARM, MALHAM, SKIPTON BD23 4DA (01729 830414). In beautiful gardens bordering village green and stream. Well known for excellent food. 14 bedrooms, 12 with private facilities. Full central heating. Two well-furnished lounges and conservatory for guests' use.

Malton

17 miles north-east of York. Site of a Roman camp; market square has church dating from Norman times. Castle Howard, designed by Sir John Vanbrugh, lies 4½ miles to the south-west.

BEANSHEAF HOTEL, MALTON ROAD, KIRBY MISPERTON, MALTON YO17 0UE (01653 668614). RAC Merit Award for Comfort. Impressive menus. Gateway to North York Moors. Half an hour from coast resorts, York, Helmsley. Good value for money. AA and RAC 2 Stars *[🐾]*.

Myton-on-Swale

Beautiful, rural surroundings. Very peaceful. Brafferton 2 miles.

MRS R. W. HALL, THE HADDOCKS, MYTON-ON-SWALE, HELPERBY, YORK YO6 2RB (01423 360224). 2 three-bedroom farm cottages. Sleep 5/6 plus cot. Fridge/freezer, colour TV, open fire, ample parking. Quiet rural surroundings central for all Yorkshire. *[pw! 🐾]*

Oldstead

Hamlet 7 miles east of Thirsk in beautiful North Yorkshire Moors.

THE BLACK SWAN INN, OLDSTEAD, COXWOLD, YORK YO6 4BL (01347 868387). 18th-century Country Freehouse offers Chalet-style accommodation, en suite, colour TV, central heating, tea/coffee facilities. Real ale. A la Carte Restaurant. Fine wines. No charge for pets. Brochure available. *[pw!🐾]*

Pateley Bridge

Picturesque and friendly small town in the heart of beautiful Nidderdale, bordering the Dales National Park. Excellent walking country and a good centre for touring the Dales, Moors, Herriot Country etc.

RIVULET COURT, PATELEY BRIDGE ETB rating 5 Keys Highly Commended. Spacious 18th century cottage, comfortable accommodation for six or more. Central heating, fully equipped for self catering with laundry, dishwasher, fridge freezer etc, and situated close to village amenities. Fully enclosed courtyard. Weekly rates £180–£350 incl. For colour brochure contact: ANNE RACK, BLAZEFIELD, BEWERLEY, HARROGATE HG3 5BS (01423 711001). *[🐾]*

Pickering

Pleasant market town on southern fringe of North Yorkshire Moors National Park with moated Castle (Norm.). Bridlington 31 miles, Whitby 20, Scarborough 16, Helmsley 13, Malton 8.

VIVERS MILL, MILL LANE, PICKERING YO18 8DJ (01751 473640). Bed and Breakfast in ancient Watermill in peaceful surroundings. Comfortable en-suite rooms with beamed ceilings. Tea making facilities. Ideal for Moors, coastline, and York. Bed and Breakfast £22 per day, £135 weekly. *[🐾]*

Richmond

One of Yorkshire's most attractive towns, with fine views across the dales to the Vale of York. The Theatre Royal in Friar's Wynd, built in 1788, is one of the oldest surviving theatres in England. Kendal 53 miles, Penrith 52, York 45, Barnard Castle 15, Darlington 12.

THE KING'S HEAD HOTEL, MARKET PLACE, RICHMOND DL10 4HS (01748 850220; Fax: 01748 850635). Tastefully refurbished Georgian coaching hotel. Comfortable en suite accommodation, convivial bars, real ale, log fires; excellent bar and restaurant food. Not to be missed.

Scarborough

Very popular family resort with fine coast scenery, good sands. Of interest is the ruined 12th century Castle. Wood End Museum and Oliver's Mount (viewpoint). York 41 miles, Whitby 20, Bridlington 17, Filey 7.

PARADE HOTEL, 29 ESPLANADE, SCARBOROUGH YO11 2AQ (01723 361285). Splendidly situated Victorian Hotel; superb views of sea and coastline; 17 comfortable bedrooms, all en-suite, with colour TV and tea/coffee trays. Emphasis on preparation of fresh food "home-style". Easy parking. ETB 2 Crowns Approved. RAC Acclaimed. [🐾]

SCARBOROUGH near. One luxury detached Bungalow, sleeps 2–6, on 170-acre park enjoying wonderful views. APPLY – MRS J. HOLLAND, 32 JOAN LANE, HOOTON LEVITT, ROTHERHAM, SOUTH YORKSHIRE S66 8PH (01709 815102) with SAE. [pw!]

THE PREMIER HOTEL, ESPLANADE, SCARBOROUGH YO11 2UZ (01723 501062/501038). The Premier Hotel is situated on the Esplanade. All rooms have private bath/shower and toilet en suite, colour TV, radio, tea/coffee facilities and full central heating. [Pets £2 per night.]

Skipton

Airedale market town, centre for picturesque Craven district. Fine Castle (14th cent). York 43 miles, Manchester 42, Leeds 26, Harrogate 22, Settle 16.

The North's Dales, Moors and Coast ... Over 500 superb, personally inspected, self-catering holiday properties from Yorkshire's "Bronte", "Herriot" and "Heartbeat" country to Northumberland's borders. Cottages for two to houses for 12. Contact PAT AMES, DALES HOLIDAY COTTAGES, CARLETON BUSINESS PARK, SKIPTON, NORTH YORKSHIRE BD23 2DG (01756 799821 & 01756 790919).

NEAR SKIPTON. Self Catering Cottages equipped to high standard. Central heating, colour TV. Parking. Linen, towels and fuel inclusive. Convenient for Lakes and Dales. APPLY: SUSAN STOTT, HIGH GABLES, THE FOLD, THORNTON IN CRAVEN, SKIPTON BD23 3TJ (01282 843272).

Over 200 super self-catering Cottages, Houses and Flats throughout Yorkshire Dales, York, Moors, Coast, Peak and Lake District. Telephone for free illustrated brochure. APPLY – HOLIDAY COTTAGES (YORKSHIRE) LTD, WATER STREET, SKIPTON (18) BD23 1PB (01756 700872). [🐾]

Sleights

Village running down to River Esk, 3 miles south-west of Whitby.

WHITE ROSE HOLIDAY COTTAGES, SLEIGHTS, NEAR WHITBY. Superior stone village cottages situated near Sleights Bridge. Available all year, including Christmas and New Year. 3 Keys Commended. APPLY – MRS J. ROBERTS (PW), 5 BROOK PARK, SLEIGHTS, NEAR WHITBY YO21 1RT. Telephone 01947 810763 *[pw! £5 per week.]*

MRS M. CANA, PARTRIDGE NEST FARM, ESKDALESIDE, SLEIGHTS, WHITBY YO22 5ES (01947 810450). Six caravans on secluded site, five miles from Whitby and sea. Ideal touring centre. All have mains electricity, colour TV, fridge, gas cooker. SAE or phone please. *[Pets £5 per week.]*

Staithes

Fishing village surrounded by high cliffs on north sea coast, 9 miles north-west of Whitby.

THE FOX INN, ROXBY, STAITHES, SALTBURN TS13 5EB (01947 840335). Family run village inn; all rooms colour TV, tea/coffee making. Open all year for B&B from £16; Evening Meals on request. Also caravan for hire. *[🐕pw!]*

Thirsk

Market town with attractive square. Excellent touring area. Northallerton 8 miles.

FOXHILLS HIDEAWAYS, FELIXKIRK, THIRSK YO7 2DS (01845 537575). Scandinavian designed, heated throughout; linen provided. A supremely relaxed atmosphere on the edge of the North Yorkshire Moors National Park. Open all year. Secluded site with miles of forest tracks to explore. *[🐕]*

HAYWOOD, BARLEY GARTH, BALK, THIRSK YO7 2AJ (01845 597524). 18th century mill house. Excellent dog walks. B&B from £15, 3 rooms, colour TV. Also S/C 4-roomed flat. From £130 per week. *[Pets £1 each per night.]*

Wensleydale

Possibly the most picturesque of all the Dales, ideal for touring some of the most beautiful parts of Yorkshire and the nearby Herriot Country. Kendal 25 miles, Kirkby Stephen 15.

ANNE & KNIGHTON BUTTERWORTH, "GREYSTONE", PRESTON-UNDER-SCAR, NEAR LEYBURN DL8 4AQ (01969 622042). Small, comfortable guesthouse in peaceful little village between Wensley and Castle Bolton. Ideal for walks or drives to many nearby dales, offering flowers, birds and history. Panoramic views from both bedrooms. Optional evening meal. Weekly terms available. No smoking please. *[🐕]*

THE WENSLEYDALE HEIFER, WEST WITTON, WENSLEYDALE DL8 4LS (01969 622322; Fax: 01969 624183). A 17th Century Inn of character and style offering 20 en suite bedrooms and 3 Four Posters. Real Ales with Bistro and Bar Food. Home cooking specialising in Fish and Seafood. 3 Crowns Commended.

MRS SUE COOPER, ST EDMUNDS, CRAKEHALL, BEDALE DL8 1HP (01677 423584). Set in Swaledale and Wensleydale, these recently renovated cottages are fully equipped and are an ideal base for exploring the Dales and Moors. Sleep 2–7 plus cot. Up to 4 Keys Commended. Brochure available. *[🐕]*

Whitby

Charming resort with harbour and sands. Cliffs and moors. Of note is the 13th-century Abbey (ruins). Stockton-on-Tees 34 miles, Scarborough 20, Saltburn-by-the-Sea 19.

MRS K. E. NOBLE, SUMMERFIELD FARM, HAWSKER, WHITBY YO22 4LA (01947 601216). Between Whitby/Robin Hood's Bay. Six berth caravan. Private farm site. Beach one mile. "Cleveland Way" footpath nearby. Set in secluded safe grassy area. SAE for details. *[pw! £10 per week.]*

SNEATON HALL HOTEL, SNEATON, WHITBY YO22 5HP (Tel and Fax: 01947 605929). Small, friendly 2 Star country hotel, three miles south of Whitby. All rooms en suite; tea making facilities, TV. Good food, pleasant gardens, ample car parking. Fully licensed; open to non-residents. Pets most welcome. [🐾]

MRS R. B. O'DONNELL, "KINGSWOOD", THE AVENUE, SLEIGHTS, NEAR WHITBY YO2 5BS (01947 810280). Charming Edwardian house in own grounds on edge of moors/sea. Centrally heated. Double room en suite, twin bedroom with private bathroom. Lounge and bedrooms with colour TV. Private parking. B&B from £17.50. Brochure on request. *[🐾,pw!]*

York

Historic cathedral city and former Roman Station on River Ouse. Magnificent Minster (E.E. to Perp.) and 3 miles of ancient walls. Many interesting old churches and other notable buildings, including Palace Chapel, St William's College (15th–17th cent), Merchant Adventurers Hall, St. Anthony's Hall (15th cent.) and Treasurer's House (17th cent); also old inns, museums. Facilities for a wide range of sports and entertainments. Horse-racing on Knavesmire. Bridlington 41 miles, Filey 41, Helmsley 24, Leeds 24, Harrogate 22, Malton 18, Selby 13.

ASTORIA HOTEL, 6 GROSVENOR TERRACE, BOOTHAM, YORK (01904 659558). Licensed Hotel, 15 bedrooms, many with private bathroom. Dogs welcome. Private parking. *[🐾]*

MRS S. JACKSON, VICTORIA VILLA GUEST HOUSE, 72 HESLINGTON ROAD, YORK YO1 5AU (01904 631647). Ten minutes' walk from city centre. Comfortable double, twin, single and family bedrooms, all with TV. Children and pets welcome. Open all year. B&B from £13 to £18. *[pw!🐾]*

EMMA SWIERS, FIR TREE FARM HOUSE, THORMANBY, EASINGWOLD, YORK YO6 3NN (01845 501201 and 501220). Attractive farmhouse with two double rooms and one family room, one en suite. Sittingroom with open fire and colour TV. Good home cooking and friendly welcome. Ideally located for visits to York, the North Yorks Moors and Dales. Pets and children welcome. B&B from £14; B, B & Dinner from £22. ETB *[🐾]*

YORK LAKESIDE LODGES, MOOR LANE, YORK YO2 2QU (01904 702346 or 0831 885824; Fax: 01904 701631). Self-catering pine lodges. Mature parkland setting. Large fishing lake. Nearby superstore with coach to centre every 10 mins. ETB 4 Keys up to De Luxe. *[Pets £12 per visit.]*

PEGGY SWANN, SOUTH NEWLANDS FARM, SELBY ROAD, RICCALL, YORK YO4 6QR (01757 248203). Friendliness, comfort, and good traditional cooking are always on offer to our guests. The kettle's always on the boil in our kitchen, and a comfortable lounge is yours to relax in at any time. Easy access to York and the Dales and Moors. No smoking please. Day kennelling available. (Pets £1 per night.)

PETER & JUDITH JONES, FOURPOSTER LODGE HOTEL, 68/70 HESLINGTON ROAD, YORK YO1 5AU (01904 651170). Enjoy the relaxing luxury of a four-poster bed and hearty English breakfast at this Victorian villa, convenient for York with all its fascinations. Bed and Breakfast from £24.50. ETB 3 Crowns Commended.

CLIFTON VIEW GUEST HOUSE, 118/120 CLIFTON, YORK YO3 6BQ (01904 625047). Victorian family-run guest house 12 minutes' walk from City Centre. All rooms have colour TV, tea/coffee facilities; most have shower. Private car park. ETB One Crown. *[🐾]*

3 attractive self-catering choices. 12 miles from York. WOODLEA detached house, sleeping 5–6, with kitchen, dining area, large lounge and colour TV, bathroom, cloakroom, 3 bedrooms. BUNGALOW adjacent to farmhouse sleeps 2–4. Kitchen, bathroom, lounge/dining room with colour TV and double bed settee. Twin room with cot. STUDIO adjacent to farmhouse, sleeping 2. Kitchen, lounge/dining room with colour TV, twin bedroom, bathroom/toilet. SAE for details: MRS M. S. A. WOOD-LIFFE, MILL FARM, YAPHAM, POCKLINGTON, YORK YO4 2PH (01759 302172).

ST GEORGE'S HOUSE HOTEL, 6 ST GEORGE'S PLACE, YORK YO2 2DR (01904 625056). Family-run licensed Hotel in quiet cul-de-sac near racecourse. All rooms with colour TV, radio. Tea/coffee facilities. Private parking. Pets welcome. 3 Crowns Commended. RAC, AA. *[🐾]*

ORILLIA HOUSE, 89 THE VILLAGE, STOCKTON-ON-FOREST, YORK YO3 9UP (01904 400600 or 01904 738595). Conveniently situated in centre of village 3 miles from York. All rooms with private facilities etc. Bed and Breakfast from £16. Telephone for brochure. *[Pets £1 per night.]*

Yorkshire Dales

Scenic area stretching from Ilkley in the south to Ingleton in the west, Langthwaite in the north and Kirkby Malzeard in the east. Peaceful, unspoilt villages, wooded valleys with waterfalls and limestone caves.

The North's Dales, Moors and Coast . . . Over 500 superb, personally inspected, self-catering holiday properties from Yorkshire's "Bronte", "Herriot" and "Heartbeat" country to Northumberland's borders. Cottages for two to houses for 12. Contact PAT AMES, DALES HOLIDAY COTTAGES, CARLETON BUSINESS PARK, SKIPTON, NORTH YORKSHIRE BD23 2DG (01756 799821 & 01756 790919).

WEST YORKSHIRE

WEST YORKSHIRE   *Calderdale*

ASHENHURST COTTAGE
Todmorden, in Calderdale, West Yorkshire

Our stone cottage is warm, quiet and comfortable. It lies behind our house on a south-facing Pennine hillside, convenient for the town, yet footpaths from the door lead directly onto the hillside. Ideal for walkers, and for touring Yorkshire and Lancashire. Good opportunities for eating out. Prices are based on provision for two with twin bedroom and separate bathroom with bath and shower. At extra cost up to two additional children or adults can be accommodated, with modern double bed settee in living room. Cot also available. Well behaved pets are welcome. Modern gas central heating, instant hot water, linen, towels, colour TV, parking, all inclusive. Open all year. Prices £118–£175. Please write or ring for brochure:

Mrs Heather M. Grieve, Ashenhurst House, Todmorden, Lancs OL14 8DS.
ᵖᵖᵖ **Commended**   **Tel: (01706) 812086**

Calderdale

Administrative district of West Yorkshire. Industrial museum in town.

ASHENHURST COTTAGE. Convenient for town, yet footpaths lead directly to the Moors. Sleeps up to four. Central heating, linen, towels, colour TV all inclusive. Open all year. Well-behaved pets welcome. Brochure from MRS H. M. GRIEVE, ASHENHURST HOUSE, TODMORDEN, LANCS OL14 8DS (01706 812086). *[Pets £5 per week.]*

Haworth

Town situated above the River Worth Valley. Of interest is the parsonage, one-time home of the Brontë Family, now a museum; the revived Worth Valley Railway runs from Keighley to Oxenhope. Keighley 2 miles.

Superb small moorland Cottage, one mile Haworth. Sleeps 4–6. Luxuriously equipped, sunny lounge, patio garden, central heating. Breathtaking moorland views. Children welcome. Available all year round. Price £200 to £285 throughout the year, includes sheets and heating. Tourist Board Category 3. APPLY – MRS P. M. SEABROOK, 30 NEWCOMBE STREET, MARKET HARBOROUGH, LEICESTER-SHIRE LE16 9PB (01858 463723).

CHANNEL ISLANDS

CHANNEL ISLANDS *Jersey*

SOUTHERN HOTELS

BEAUSITE HOTEL, GROUVILLE

Situated on the South East coast of Jersey, looking over the Royal Golf Course and Grouville Bay beyond. Tastefully furnished en-suite bedrooms and excellent cuisine make this hotel the ideal spot for a relaxing break. Gardens surround the new indoor leisure complex and lovely coastal walks are just around the corner.

BERGERAC HOTEL & APARTMENTS, PORTELET BAY

A lovely complex comprising of both hotel rooms and S/C apartments. An ideal place for pets as lovely coastal walks surround the Hotel. Work out in the indoor leisure complex or take it easy in the restaurant where we are proud of our excellent cuisine.

For brochure and tariff details please tick the boxes below and forward to:

SOUTHERN HOTELS, LA MOTTE ST, ST. HELIER, JERSEY JE2 4SY or telephone 01534 23243.

BEAUSITE HOTEL ☐   BERGERAC HOTEL & APTS ☐

Jersey

The Island of flowers and friendliness. Marvellous coastline and enchanting, unspoilt countryside. Island's capital, St. Helier, includes Jersey Museum amongst its many attractions.

SOUTHERN HOTELS: The BEAUSITE HOTEL and the BERGERAC HOTEL AND APARTMENTS are situated on the beautiful island of Jersey and are an ideal place for pets. Both feature indoor leisure complexes and are close to lovely coastal walks. For brochure and tariff contact: SOUTHERN HOTELS, LA MOTTE ST. ST HELIER, JERSEY JE2 4SY (01534 23243). *[🐕]*

274

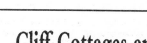
Beaumaris

Elegant little town dominated by castle built by Edward I in 13th century. Museum of Childhood has Victorian toys and music boxes.

Dulas Bay

On north-east coast of Anglesey, between Amlwch and Moelfre.

MRS G. McCREADIE, DERI ISAF, DULAS BAY LL70 9DX (01248 410536). Beautiful Victorian country house standing in 20 acres of woodland, gardens and fields. High standard of accommodation in two family rooms and one double with en suite. Pets welcome; stabling available. 3 Crowns. *[🐴]*

Gaerwen

Village on A5 Holyhead road. Good touring centre for island. Holyhead 18 miles. Bangor 6.

MRS D. WILLIAMS, FRON, STATION ROAD, GAERWEN, ANGLESEY LL60 6DP (01248 421670/722012). Self catering Cottage, sleeps 5, plus cot. Half a mile from A5, four and a half miles from Menai Bridge. 15 minutes' drive to sandy beach. Pets welcome. Available from May – October. *[🐴]*

Llanddaniel

Village just off the A5, Menai Bridge 5 miles E.

MRS M. E. WILLIAMS, TYDDYN GOBLET, BRYNSIENCYN, ANGLESEY LL61 6TZ (01248 430296). Secluded farmhouse, uninterrupted views Snowdonia. 3 bedrooms, bathroom, kitchen, living & sitting rooms. Telephone. Modern 34 ft 3 bedroomed caravan very pleasantly and privately situated on smallholding. Shower etc. Also en-suite B&B. Ground floor bedrooms. *[🐴]*

Llanddona

Village on Anglesey 3 miles north west of Beaumaris.

MR P. W. REES, "QUALITY COTTAGES", CERBID, SOLVA, HAVERFORDWEST, PEMBROKESHIRE SA62 6YE (01348 837871). Cottages set in all coastal areas, unashamed luxury; highest residential standards. Dishwashers, microwaves, washing machines. Log fires. Linen supplied. Pets welcome. *[pw!]*

Llanerchymedd

Pretty village on Anglesey. 6 miles south of Amlwch.

MRS J. THOMAS, GLEGIR FARM, BODAFON MOUNTAIN, LLANERCHYMEDD (01248 470244). Luxury Caravan (33' Pemberton) with all amenities, shower, colour TV, fridge. On secluded farm site with idyllic views. Also lovely farmhouse cottage. Lligwy beach three miles, Moelfre Bay four miles. Pets and children welcome. *[🐴]*

Llangaffo

Peaceful village 7 miles west of Menai Bridge.

ANN LAMB, PLAS LLANGAFFO, ANGLESEY LL60 6LR (01248 440452). Peaceful location near Newborough Forest and Llandwyn Bay with its miles of golden sands. Sheep, horses and hens kept. Free-range eggs and home-made marmalade for breakfast. Dinner optional. Tea/coffee making facilities. Horse riding available. *[🐴]*

Pentraeth

Picturesque village on Anglesey 5 miles north of Menai Bridge.

TAN Y GRAIG FARM COTTAGES, PENTRAETH, ANGLESEY LL75 8UR (01248 450223). Choice of 12 luxury cottages all with microwave, colour TV and video on a small quiet complex with 20 acres of grass. Heated swimming pool. *[Pets £10 per week, pw!]*

Red Wharf Bay

Deep curving bay with vast expanse of sand, very popular for sailing and swimming.

MR P. W. REES, "QUALITY COTTAGES", CERBID, SOLVA, HAVERFORDWEST, PEMBROKESHIRE SA62 6YE (01348 837871). Cottages set in all coastal areas, unashamed luxury; highest residential standards. Dishwashers, microwaves, washing machines. Log fires. Linen supplied. Pets welcome. *[pw!]*

MIN-Y-DON HOTEL, RED WHARF BAY, ISLE OF ANGLESEY LL75 8RJ (01248 852596). Fully residential, licensed Free House, noted for hospitality and relaxing atmosphere. Beautifully situated on sandy beach. Extensive meals choice, bar entertainment. Reductions for children. Open all year round. *[pw! £1.75 per night.]*

Trearddur Bay

Attractive holiday spot set amongst low cliffs on Holy Island, near Holyhead. Golf, sailing, fishing, swimming.

CLIFF COTTAGES AND PLAS DARIEN APARTMENTS, TREARDDUR BAY LL63 3LD (01407 860789). Fully equipped holiday Cottages, sleeping 4/8 plus cot. Near sea. Children's playground. Indoor and outdoor heated pools. Colour television. Choice of centrally heated apartments or stone-built cottages. Own private leisure complex with bowls, sauna, snooker, table tennis etc. Also tennis, croquet. Adjacent golf course. *[🐕]*

CLWYD

CLWYD *Colwyn Bay, Llandyrnog, Rhos-on-Sea*

COLWYN BAY
NANT-Y-GLYN LEISURE HOLIDAY HOMES
Garden Cottages   Cedarwood Chalets
Situated in exceptionally pretty sheltered valley only 15
minutes' walk to beach and town centre
Pets welcome   Comfort and Cleanliness assured
Please send SAE for illustrated brochure to:
Mrs J. Macey, Nant-y-Glyn Leisure, Colwyn Bay, Clwyd LL29 7RD
Tel: Colwyn Bay (01492) 531316

EDELWEISS HOTEL
off LAWSON ROAD, COLWYN BAY, NORTH WALES LL29 8HD
Comfortable 3 Crown Commended Country House Hotel set in own wooded grounds close to open
parkland, ideal for dog owners. Superb bargain breaks in quiet setting, just a short stroll from
promenade, beach and town centre. All rooms with en suite facilities, television, inhouse movies (in
rooms), telephones (in rooms), tea/coffee makers, baby listening service and solarium. Well-behaved
dogs welcome in all parts of the hotel except in the dining room.   **Brochure: (01492) 532314**

ASHMOUNT HOTEL
College Avenue, Rhos-on-Sea, Colwyn Bay, Clwyd LL28 4NT
Tel: 01492 544582 Fax: 01492 545479
Situated close to the picturesque harbour and village of Rhos-on-Sea and
ideal for touring Snowdonia and the North Wales coast. Small beautiful
hotel with elegant restaurant renowned for its cuisine, vegetarian and
special diets. All bedrooms en suite and suitable for the disabled; dogs
most welcome and car parking available.
4 Crowns Highly Commended   **AA/RAC★★**

Bring your four-legged friends to stay at our 18th century Georgian farmhouse, set
in 200 acres of peaceful countryside. Spacious comfortable bedrooms with
private/en suite facilities. B&B from £17.00pp; BB&EM from £30.00pp.

For further information please contact Marie or Graham at:
Pentre Bach, Llandyrnog, Near Denbigh, Clwyd LL16 4LA
Tel and Fax: 01824 790725

SUNNYDOWNS HOTEL
66 Abbey Road, Rhos-on-Sea, Near Llandudno LL28 4NU
Tel: 01492 544256 Fax: 01492 543223
Proprietors: Mr & Mrs Mike Willington

A 4-Crown luxury family-run hotel just 2 minutes' walk to beach & shops with lots of nice
walks for you and your dog close by. All rooms en suite with colour TV, video and satellite
channels, clock radio, tea/coffee facilities, hair dryers, mini-bar refrigerator, direct dial
telephone and central heating. Hotel facilities; bar, pool room, restaurant, sauna and car
park. Only five minutes' drive to Llandudno and Colwyn Bay and 10 minutes' to the
mountains and castles of Snowdonia. Dog sitting available. By arrangement meals can be
taken in the bar with your dog. Open all year. Telephone for brochure.

279

Pen-y-Dyffryn

Country House Hotel

*Rhydycroesau, Near Oswestry,
Shropshire SY10 7DT*

AA** *Ashley Courtenay Recommended*
WTB Highly Commended

**Tel & Fax: 01691 653700
(Miles and Audrey Hunter)**

Comfort, warmth and hospitality abound in this peaceful Georgian former rectory, beautifully set in the Shropshire/Welsh hill country. Right on the border and **Offa's Dyke**, close **Llangollen, Bala, Vyrnwy, Shrewsbury, Chester.** Ideal walking country
* Eight en-suite bedrooms (one on ground floor)
* Colour TVs
* Magnificent views
* Licensed Restaurant
* Safe for dogs
* 5-acre grounds
Dinner, Bed and Breakfast from £39.00 per person. Pets free.

Colwyn Bay

Lively seaside resort with promenade amusements. Attractions include Mountain Zoo, Eirias Park; golf, tennis, riding and other sports. Good touring centre for Snowdonia. The quieter resort of Rhos-on-Sea lies at the western end of the bay.

Popular seafront holiday flats from £59, some discounts. Dogs welcome if house trained and well behaved. Please send SAE for brochure to THE CONTINENTAL, WEST PROMENADE, COLWYN BAY LL28 4BY (01492 531516). *[Pets £9 per week.]*

CLWYD

EDELWEISS HOTEL, OFF LAWSON ROAD, COLWYN BAY LL29 8HD (01492 532314). Comfortable Country House Hotel set in own wooded grounds close to open parkland; ideal for dog owners. All rooms with en-suite facilities. Well-behaved dogs welcome. 3 Crowns Commended. [🐾]

MRS J. MACEY, NANT-Y-GLYN LEISURE, NANT-Y-GLYN ROAD, COLWYN BAY LL29 7RD (01492 531316). Set in a sheltered valley these garden cottages and cedarwood chalets are 15 minutes' walk to the beach and town centre. All pets welcome. SAE for illustrated colour Brochure. [Pets £5 weekly.]

ASHMOUNT HOTEL, COLLEGE AVENUE, RHOS-ON-SEA, COLWYN BAY LL28 4NT (Tel: 01492 544582; Fax: 01492 545479). Situated close to the picturesque harbour and village of Rhos-on-Sea. Ideal for touring Snowdonia and the North Wales coast. Small, beautiful hotel with elegant restaurant renowned for its cuisine, vegetarian and special diets. 4 Crowns Highly Commended, AA/RAC Two Stars. [Pets £1.50 per night.]

Llangollen

Famous for International Music Eisteddfod held in July. Plas Newydd, Valle Crucis Abbey nearby. Standard gauge steam railway; canal cruises; ideal for golf and walking.

BRYN DERWEN HOTEL, ABBEY ROAD, LLANGOLLEN LL20 8EF (01978 860583). Warm, friendly welcome for your pet in well-appointed hotel in picturesque Dee Valley. Super walking country, many tourist attractions including Llangollen Steam Railway. Special discounts for Pets Welcome! readers.

PEN-Y-DYFFRYN COUNTRY HOUSE HOTEL, NEAR RHYDYCROESAU, OSWESTRY SY10 7DT (Tel. & Fax: 01691 653700). Georgian Rectory set in Shropshire/Welsh Hills. Seven en-suite bedrooms, colour TV. Licensed restaurant. Very quiet and relaxed. 5-acre grounds. Dinner, Bed and Breakfast from £39.00 per person. 3 Crowns. [🐾 pw!]

Rhos-on-Sea

Popular resort at east end of Penrhyn Bay, adjoining Colwyn Bay to the north-west.

SUNNYDOWNS HOTEL, 66 ABBEY ROAD, RHOS ON SEA, NEAR LLANDUDNO LL28 4NU (01492 544256; Fax: 01492 543223). A 4 Crown luxury family hotel just 2 minutes' walk to beach & shops. All rooms en suite with colour TV, video & satellite channels, tea/coffee facilities and central heating. Hotel has bar, pool room and car park. [🐾 pw!]

Ruthin

On hill above River Clwyd, with many interesting buildings and modern craft centre producing glass, leather, ceramics and jewellery.

MARIE CARRINGTON-SYKES, PENTRE BACH, LLANDYRNOG LL16 4LA (Tel and Fax: 01824 790725). 18th century Georgian farmhouse set in 200 acres of peaceful countryside. Spacious comfortable bedrooms with private/en suite facilities. B&B from £17.00. [🐾]

MRS B. QUINN, BERLLAN BACH, FFORDD LAS, LLANDYRNOG LL16 4LR (01824 790732). Meg and Nell, our lovely collies, are delighted to welcome your four-legged friends to their lovely home. En suite rooms with french windows opening into the orchard. Bed and Breakfast from £17.50. 3 Crowns. [🐾]

GILFACH HOLIDAY VILLAGE
THE HOLIDAY VILLAGE ON THE COAST MID-WAY
BETWEEN NEW QUAY AND ABERAERON
HORSE AND PONY RIDING
TENNIS COURT ON THE ESTATE

Gilfach is set in lovely unspoiled countryside on the coast midway between the resorts of New Quay and Aberaeron, not far from Aberystwyth, Devil's Bridge and other attractions. There is a choice of modern Bungalows, accommodating up to 6 persons and luxury 2/3 person Apartments set in 36 acres of ground. Horse riding to suit all ages is available on the Estate and you can fish from the beach. River fishing is also available nearby. The Estate has its own licensed club and local traders deliver bread, meat, papers, etc. The children have a den and playground and pets are welcome. All the accommodation is fully equipped and includes colour TV, and bed linen is available. For our colour Brochure Pack, write or phone the MANAGER, at:

GILFACH HOLIDAY VILLAGE,
LLWYNCELYN, Nr ABERAERON, DYFED SA46 0NN
TEL: LLANARTH (01545) 580288

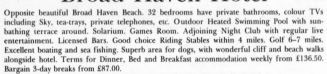

TYGLYN HOLIDAY ESTATE (Dept. PW)

CILIAU AERON, NEAR LAMPETER, DYFED SA48 8DD

Telephone: (01570) 470684

Tyglyn Holiday Estate nestles in the heart of rural Wales and yet is only four miles from the pretty little seaside town of Aberaeron.

From your holiday bungalow the views up and down the Aeron Valley are awe-inspiring. Beautiful rolling hills rise from the valley through which the river Aeron flows. It passes through the estate for almost a mile and its outfall is at Aberaeron where day or fishing trips can be taken.

The bungalows take pride of place overlooking most of the 120-acre farm and in sight of some of the woodland.

Buzzards nest on the farm, Ravens are regular visitors, Dippers can be seen on the river, Kestrels and the rare Red Kite can be seen in the air. We have Badgers and Foxes breeding on the estate, Otters have been seen in the river, and there are rare butterflies and an abundance of wild flowers.

There is an adjacent pub and restaurant.

Riding can be arranged locally, bowling, tennis, golf and swimming can all be found within a few miles.

While at Tyglyn your accommodation will be provided by one of only 20 award-winning brick-built semi-detached two-bedroom bungalows which include all modern facilities and colour TV. Milk, newspapers and grocery deliveries daily if required. Your pets are welcomed as warmly as you. For further details contact Nigel Edkins on 01570 470684 for a free colour brochure.

4/6 Berth
£107–£220

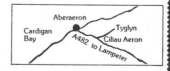

DYFED   *Nolton Haven, Saundersfoot*

NOLTON HAVEN FARM
QUALITY BEACHFRONT COTTAGES/FARM GUESTHOUSE

Quality Beachfront Cottages. The stone, slate and pine constructed Cottages occupy a unique position just 30 yards from Nolton Haven's sandy beach, with extensive lawns leading to the beach which they overlook. The Cottages are equipped with double oven cookers, colour television, steam iron, fridge/freezer, toasters, auto kettles, microwave ovens and fixed heating. The Cottages, fully carpeted and sleeping 4/6, are open all year including Winter Breaks.

Farm Guesthouse. ★ 50 yards sandy beach ★ Colour television lounge ★ Children and pets welcome ★ Babysitting ★ Use of house all day ★ Children's ponies, donkey, chickens, ducks ★ Pub/Restaurant 75 yards ★ Dinner, Bed and Breakfast. En suite rooms available.

J. CANTON, NOLTON HAVEN FARM, Nolton Haven, Haverfordwest, Pembrokeshire, Dyfed SA62 6NH. Tel: (01437) 710263

Folkeston Hill Holiday Bungalows
A small group of bungalows in a sheltered valley which winds down to the sea at Nolton Haven. WTB Graded. Pets welcome (no charge). Brochure from: John & Ceri Price, St Brides Bay Cottages, Nine Wells, Solva, Haverfordwest, Pembrokeshire SA62 6UH (Tel: 01437 720027).

SAUNDERSFOOT, Mrs Joy Holgate, Carne Mountain Farm, Reynalton, Kilgetty SA68 0PD Tel: 01834 860 546
A warm welcome awaits you at our lovely 200-year-old farmhouse set amidst the peace and tranquillity of the beautiful Pembrokeshire countryside. Pretty, picturesque bedrooms with colour TV, washbasins, tea/coffee tray and central heating. Vegetarians very welcome. Bed and Breakfast from £13.50. Wales Tourist Board Commended. Farmhouse Award. Quality 6 berth caravan also available from £85 per week. SAE please.

VINE FARM
The Ridgeway, Saundersfoot SA69 9LA
Tel: 01834 813543
Situated half mile from the village centre and beaches this delightful former farmhouse has been sympathetically modernised whilst retaining its charm. Centrally heated throughout, licensed; ample parking and an exercise paddock for dogs. All five bedrooms are en suite with colour TV, tea/coffee tray and clock/radio. We take great pride in the quality of our food, with choices on all menus, including a 5 course dinner, using local produce and vegetables from our own garden in season.   B&B from £20 pp. Dinner, B&B from £180 weekly pp.

AA Listed QQQ — Special 3–day breaks throughout the season. Bargain 4–day breaks late May/early June and late August. Also 1–bedroom s/c flat for 2 from £120 per week. — RAC Acclaimed

286

DYFED *St Davids*

"LLYSNEWYDD" – Pembrokeshire National Park

Delightful farmhouse, 6 miles from St David's and near safe, sandy beaches and coastal path. Sleeps six in one family bedroom, one double bedroom and an attic suitable for an agile person. Fully equipped dining kitchen, new automatic washing machine; TV room and spacious lounge. Bathroom with toilet, also downstairs toilet. Storage heating and radiators. Electricity by coin meters. No linen. One pet free, £15 weekly for second pet. Terms from £105 to £285 weekly. SAE for prompt reply.

Mrs C. E. Skeel Jones, Arosfyr Farm, Dolgellau, Gwynedd LL40 2YP (01341 422 355)

POWELLS COTTAGE HOLIDAYS. Your choice of Cottage in Cornwall, Devon, Somerset, Avon, Cotswolds, Wye Valley, Gower and Pembrokeshire in our full colour brochure. *[Pets £10 per week.]* FREEPHONE 0800 378771 or apply: 61 High Street, Saundersfoot, Pembrokeshire SA69 9EJ or (24 hrs) 01834 813232.

Aberaeron

Attractive little town on Cardigan Bay, good touring centre for coast and inland. The Aeron Express Aerial Ferry offers an exciting trip across the harbour. Marine aquarium; Aberarth Leisure Park nearby.

GILFACH HOLIDAY VILLAGE, LLWYNCELYN, NEAR ABERAERON SA46 0NN (01545 580288). Choice of modern Bungalows (6 persons) or luxury 2/3 person apartments. Fully equipped, linen, colour TV. Horse and pony riding. Tennis. Write or phone for brochure pack to the Manager. *[Pets £10 per week.]*

Aberporth

Popular seaside village offering safe swimming and good sea fishing. Good base for exploring Cardigan Bay coastline.

MR P. W. REES, "QUALITY COTTAGES", CERBID, SOLVA, HAVERFORDWEST, PEMBROKESHIRE SA62 6YE (01348 837871). Cottages set in all coastal areas, unashamed luxury; highest residential standards. Dishwashers, microwaves, washing machines. Log fires. Linen supplied. Pets welcome. *[pw!]*

Boncath

Hamlet 5 miles south of Cardigan.

MRS K. S. LEWIS, PENLANFEIGAN, BONCATH SA37 0JE (01239 841499). 10 minutes from Cardigan, Preseli Hills and coast. Small family stables, B&B and mobile home. Dogs and horses welcome. 20 acres and gardens. B&B from £15. *[🐎 🏠]*

Bosherston

Village 4 miles south of Pembroke, bordered by 3 man-made lakes, a haven for wildlife and covered in waterlilies in early summer.

MR P. W. REES, "QUALITY COTTAGES", CERBID, SOLVA, HAVERFORDWEST, PEMBROKESHIRE SA62 6YE (01348 837871). Cottages set in all coastal areas; unashamed luxury; dishwashers, microwaves, washing machines – highest residential standards. Log fires. Linen provided. Pets welcome. *[pw!]*

Broad Haven

Attractive little resort on St Bride's Bay in the Pembrokeshire Coast National Park. Superb sandy beach; National Park Information Centre.

DAVID & SHEILA TATTERSALL, ROSEHILL CARAVAN PARK, ROSEHILL, NEAR BROADHAVEN, HAVERFORDWEST SA62 3LU (01437 781245). WTB 4 ticks. Luxury caravans from £100 per week. Situated on quiet woodland park with attractive gardens yet close to several sandy beaches. *[Pets £10.00 per week.]*

MILLMOOR FARM COTTAGES AND ROCKSDRIFT APARTMENTS. Enjoy a relaxing and peaceful holiday only yards from safe sandy beaches and woodland walks. Personal supervision. Microwaves, fridge freezers, colour TV. Full central heating. Children's play areas; cots, high chairs. Brochure from HELEN MOCK, MILLMOOR, BROAD HAVEN, HAVERFORDWEST SA62 3JB (01437 781507; Fax: 01437 781002). *[Pets £12 per week.]*

BROAD HAVEN HOTEL, ENFIELD ROAD, BROAD HAVEN, NEAR HAVERFORD-WEST SA62 3JN (Tel: 01437 781366 or Fax: 01437 781070). On sea-front. Heated swimming pool. Games room. Colour television in bedrooms. Quiet, well-behaved dogs welcome. Please send for colour brochure. *[Pets £3.00 per day, £21 weekly.]*

PEMBROKESHIRE NATIONAL PARK. Three-bedroom fully furnished holiday house, sleeps 6. Walking distance sandy beaches and coastal footpath. £90 to £220 per week. MRS L. P. ASHTON, 10 ST LEONARDS ROAD, THAMES DITTON, SURREY KT7 0RJ (0181-398 6349). *[🐕]*

Brynberian

Village among Prescelly Hills. Numerous quiet seaside places within easy reach. Cardigan 12 miles, Newport 9.

GLAN YR AFON ISAF. Holiday cottage at foot of Preseli Hills, 7 miles from Cardigan. Sleeps up to 6. Living room, kitchen, bathroom, two bedrooms. Electricity by £1 meter. APPLY: MRS F. RUTHERFOORD, ALVESTOKE FARM, SHEEP-DROVE ROAD, LAMBOURN, BERKSHIRE RG17 7XA (01488 71737).

Cardigan

Town on River Teifi estuary 34 miles south west of Aberystwyth across Cardigan Bay. Remains of 12th-century castle.

CROFT FARM GUESTHOUSE & COTTAGES, LLANTOOD, CARDIGAN SA43 3NT (Tel/Fax: 01239 615179). Welcome to our charming cottages. Help feed Tabitha (pig) and Pearl (goat). Near coastal paths, National Park and beaches. Garden, playground and barbecue. *[Pets £15 per week.]*

Carmarthen

Town on a bluff above the Tywi, dominated by ruined Norman castle. Site of Roman amphitheatre off Priory Street, and Roman relics in Carmarthen Museum, east of town.

PENDINE SANDS HOLIDAY PARK, NEAR CARMARTHEN (01345 443 443). Heated indoor pool. Live family evening entertainment. Bar, snack food, barbecues and supermarket. Horse riding, bike hire and tennis nearby. Tourers welcome. Call now for a free colour brochure.

Ciliau Aeron

Village in undulating country just inland from the charming Cardigan Bay resorts of New Quay and Aberaeron. New Quay 12 miles, Aberaeron 6.

TYGLYN HOLIDAY ESTATE, CILIAU AERON, NEAR LAMPETER SA48 8DD (01570 470684). In the heart of rural Wales and only four miles from the seaside town of Aberaeron. Twenty award-winning brick-built semi-detached two-bedroom Bungalows with all modern facilities and colour TV. Range of outdoor activities locally. £107–£220 per week.

Fishguard

Picturesque Lower Town clusters round the old quayside; Upper Town is spread out on a hill above the harbour. Many craft workshops in the area; ferry to Ireland from nearby Goodwick.

MRS C. JAMES, HENDREWEN, MANOROWEN, FISHGUARD SA65 9QD (01348 891242). Spacious modernised self-contained wing of farmhouse. Four bedrooms, bed linen provided. Sleeps 12 people. Full central heating, double glazing, lounge with log fire, colour TV, games room. Modern kitchen with electric cooking. Garden with barbecue. Open all year. Near many beaches. WCTB Grade 3.

Haverfordwest

Administrative and shopping centre for the area; ideal base for exploring National Park. Historic town of narrow streets; museum in castle grounds; many fine buildings.

CLARE HALLETT, KEESTON KITCHEN, KEESTON, HAVERFORDWEST SA62 6EJ (01437 710440). Two fully equipped comfortable Flats, sleeping 4/5, in beautifully converted Cottage with large garden. One suitable for wheelchair. Close to our first-class restaurant. Open all year; short breaks available. Central heating, electricity and linen included. WTB 4 Dragons. *[£5 per pet per week.]*

Little Haven

Village on St Bride's Bay 10 miles from Haverfordwest.

HAVEN COTTAGES, WHITEGATES, LITTLE HAVEN, HAVERFORDWEST, PEM-BROKESHIRE SA62 3LA (01437 781552). Cottages sleep two to twelve. On Coastal Path, 200 yards beach. Linen provided. B&B in fishing village. WTB Four Dragons. *[Pets £12 per week.]*

Llandovery

Little town on Rivers Tywi and Bran, with ruins of Norman Castle. Picturesque Tywi Valley to the north. Swansea 35 miles, Carmarthen 28, Builth Wells 24, Brecon 21, Lampeter 19.

THE ROYAL OAK INN, RHANDIRMWYN, LLANDOVERY SA20 0NY (01550 760201; Fax: 01550 760332). Spacious, attractively decorated bedrooms, friendly service and good food can all be found at this free and easy establishment, situated 6 miles from Llandovery.

Llangrannog

Pretty little seaside village overlooking a sandy beach. Superb cliff walk to NT Ynys Lochtyn, a secluded promontory.

MR P. W. REES, "QUALITY COTTAGES", CERBID, SOLVA, HAVERFORDWEST, PEMBROKESHIRE SA62 6YE (01348 837871). Cottages set in all coastal areas; unashamed luxury. All equipped to highest residential standards with washing machines, dishwashers, microwaves. Log fires. Linen supplied. Pets welcome. *[pw!]*

Llwyndrain

Village 5 miles south-west of Newcastle Emlyn.

CWMBACH GUEST HOUSE, LLWYNDRAIN, PEMBROKESHIRE SA35 0AU (01239 698225). B&B in idyllic setting. Double en suite rooms, colour TV, tea making. Beach and leisure activities within easy motoring distance. £13.50 pppn. Free use of kennel (8' 6" × 6' 6"). [🐾 🏠 pw!]

Manorbier

Unspoiled village on South Pembrokeshire coast near Tenby. Sandy bay and fine coastal walks. Impressive 12th century moated castle overlooks bay.

AQUARIUM COTTAGE, MANORBIER. Delightful detached country cottage. Two bedrooms. Sleeps 6. Also THE LOBSTER POT, MANORBIER. Pleasant modern ground floor flat. Two bedrooms, Sleeps 4. Both properties ½ mile sea. Pets welcome. Ample parking. Electricity and bed linen included in price. Brochure from: MRS J. HUGHES, ROSE COTTAGE, MANORBIER, PEMBROKESHIRE SA70 7ST (01834 871408). [🐾]

Newgale

On St Bride's Bay 3 miles east of Solva. Long beach where at exceptionally low tide the stumps of a submerged forest may be seen.

MR P. W. REES, "QUALITY COTTAGES", CERBID, SOLVA, HAVERFORDWEST, PEMBROKESHIRE SA62 6YE (01348 837871). Cottages set in all coastal areas, unashamed luxury; equipped to highest residential standards with dishwashers, washing machines, microwave ovens. Log fires. Linen provided. Pets welcome. [pw!]

Newport

Small town at mouth of the River Nyfer, 9 miles south west of Cardigan. Remains of 13th-century castle.

MR P. W. REES, "QUALITY COTTAGES", CERBID, SOLVA, HAVERFORDWEST, PEMBROKESHIRE SA62 6YE (01348 837871). Cottages set in all coastal areas, unashamed luxury; highest residential standards. Dishwashers, washing machines, microwaves. Log fires. Linen supplied. Pets welcome. [pw!]

Nolton Haven

Hamlet at head of inlet on St Bride's Bay. Fine coastal views.

Quality beachfront Cottages 30 yards from Nolton Haven's sandy beach. Fully equipped, sleeping 4/6. Also nearby Farm Guest House offering Dinner, Bed and Breakfast. APPLY – J. CANTON, NOLTON HAVEN FARM, NOLTON HAVEN, HAVERFORDWEST SA62 6NH (01437 710263).

FOLKESTON HILL HOLIDAY BUNGALOWS. A small group of bungalows in a sheltered valley which winds down to the sea. WTB Graded. Pets welcome – no charge. Brochure from JOHN & CERI PRICE, ST BRIDES BAY COTTAGES, NINE WELLS, SOLVA, HAVERFORDWEST, PEMBROKESHIRE SA62 6UH (01437 720027).

Saundersfoot

Popular resort and sailing centre with picturesque harbour and sandy beach. Tenby 3 miles.

VINE FARM, THE RIDGEWAY, SAUNDERSFOOT SA69 9LA (01834 813543). Former Farmhouse close to village and beaches. Central heating, log fires. All rooms en-suite. Pets welcome – garden and paddock. AA Listed QQQ. *[pw!* Pets £1.00 per night.*]* Also available, one-bedroomed Self Catering flat for 2.

MRS JOY HOLGATE, CARNE MOUNTAIN FARM, REYNALTON, KILGETTY SA68 0PD (01834 860 546). A warm welcome awaits you at our lovely 200-year-old farmhouse set amidst the peace and tranquillity of the beautiful Pembrokeshire countryside. Bedrooms have colour TV and all facilities. B&B from £13.50. *[Second pet £1.00 per night.]*

Solva

Picturesque coastal village with sheltered harbour and excellent craft shops. Sailing and watersports; sea fishing; long sandy beach.

MRS M. J. PROBERT, YNYS DAWEL, SOLVA, HAVERFORDWEST SA62 6UF (01437 721491). Quality Cottages in Solva near safe, sandy beaches. Highest standards. Enclosed rear gardens. Modern central heating. Resident owners. Particularly warm welcome to Boxer dogs (and others) and their owners. *[Pets £7/£10 per week.]*

MR P. W. REES, "QUALITY COTTAGES", CERBID, SOLVA, HAVERFORDWEST, PEMBROKESHIRE SA62 6YE (01348 837871). Cottages set in all coastal areas; unashamed luxury; dishwashers, microwaves, washing machines – highest residential standards. Log fires. Linen provided. Pets welcome. *[pw!]*

MRS M. JONES, LOCHMEYLER FARM, PEN-Y-CWM, NR SOLVA, HAVERFORDWEST SA62 6LL (01348 837724; Fax: 01348 837622). Modernised farmhouse on 220-acre dairy farm retains all its old character. Smokers' lounge, video library. Choice of menus including traditional farmhouse and vegetarian. Children over 10 welcome. Open all year. From £15 B&B. From £20 B&B, ED. *[pw!🐾]*

UPPER VANLEY, LLANDELOY, NEAR SOLVA, PEMBROKESHIRE SA62 6LJ (01348 831418). Old farmhouse, near coast and beaches, castles, Solva Harbour and St David's. All rooms en-suite, colour TV, teamaking facilities. Traditional food. Dining room. Lounge. Garden. Licensed. Bed and Breakfast from £16; Bed, Breakfast and Evening Meal £26. *[🐾pw!]*

St David's

Smallest cathedral city in Britain, shrine of Wales' patron saint. Magnificent ruins of Bishop's Palace. Craft shops, farm parks and museums; boat trips to Ramsey Island.

MR P. W. REES, "QUALITY COTTAGES", CERBID, SOLVA, HAVERFORDWEST, PEMBROKESHIRE SA62 6YE (01348 837871). Cottages set in all coastal areas, unashamed luxury; highest residential standards. Dishwashers, microwaves, washing machines. Log fires. Linen supplied, pets welcome. *[pw!]*

JILL AND ROBIN MOORE, IDYLLIC COTTAGES, TREVINE, NEAR ST DAVID'S SA62 5AG (01348 837865). Beautiful coast and country locations in Pembrokeshire. Our specialist agency can offer you a selection of warm, comfortable cottages sleeping from 2 to 9. Most welcome a pet. *[Pets £10 per week, or free with Senior Citizens.]*

MAC AND SANDRA THOMPSON, RAMSEY HOUSE, LOWER MOOR, ST DAVID'S SA62 6RP (01437 720321). Mac and Sandra Thompson offer quiet relaxation exclusively for non-smoking adults. Superior en suite rooms with central heating, TV and tea makers. Traditional Welsh cuisine. Licensed bar. Parking. Open all year. Superb beaches and walks nearby – DOGS' PARADISE! 3 Crowns Highly Commended, RAC Highly Acclaimed, AA QQQQ. [🐾]

Delightful farmhouse 6 miles from St David's. 3 bedrooms sleeping 6. Fully equipped except linen. New automatic washing machine. Electricity by coin meter. APPLY: MRS C. E. SKEEL JONES, AROSFYR FARM, DOLGELLAU LL40 2YP (01341 422 355). [First pet free, £15 per week for second pet.]

TREVACCOON FARM, ST DAVID'S, HAVERFORDWEST SA62 6DP (01348 831438). Large comfortable farmhouse; four family rooms and one double, all en suite. TV lounge; dinner licence; play area. Children welcome; pets welcome by arrangement. Self catering cottages also available. [Pets £1 per night.]

Tenby

Popular resort with two wide beaches. Fishing trips, craft shops, museum. Medieval castle ruins, 13th-century church. Golf, fishing and watersports; boat trips to nearby Caldy Island with monastery and medieval church.

MR P. W. REES, "QUALITY COTTAGES", CERBID, SOLVA, HAVERFORDWEST, PEMBROKESHIRE SA62 6YE (01348 837871). Cottages set in all coastal areas, unashamed luxury; highest residential standards. Dishwashers, microwaves, washing machines. Log fires. Linen provided, pets welcome. [pw!]

MRS J. N. FRAZER, HIGHLANDS FARM, MANORBIER-NEWTON, TENBY SA70 8PX (01834 871446). Spacious six-berth caravan situated in quiet three-acre meadow. Caravan has electric lighting and TV, gas cooker and heater. Two separate bedrooms, shower, kitchen/diner and lounge. Car essential. Peaceful setting, ideal for children or well-behaved pet. Please write or phone for details.

Whitland

Village 6 miles east of Narberth. Scanty ruins of 12th century Cistercian house remain.

WATKINS, PARC-Y-FFYNNON, CWMFELIN MYNACH, WHITLAND SA34 0DJ (01994 448341). Well appointed six-berth caravan in owner's large garden. Mains services, CTV. Situated in a quiet rural area, within easy travelling distance to beaches. Ideally placed for exploring Carmarthenshire, Pembrokeshire and Cardiganshire. Prices £100–£150 per week inclusive. Brochure on request. [🐾]

WEST GLAMORGAN

WEST GLAMORGAN *Llanmadoc*

Located near the splendid Gower coastline, surrounded by beautiful countryside, "Tallizmand" has tastefully furnished en suite bedrooms with tea/coffee making facilities. Home cooking (vegetarians catered for); packed lunches. Pets welcome.

♔ ♔ ♔ Highly Commended

Mrs A. Main, Tallizmand, Llanmadoc, Gower SA3 1DE (01792 386373)

Gower

Britain's first designated Area of Outstanding Natural Beauty with numerous sandy beaches and lovely countryside to explore.

MRS D. A. STILL, CULVER HOUSE, PORT EYNON, GOWER SA3 1NN (01792 390755). Small, friendly hotel with fabulous food and quality service. Peacefully situated, with superb coast and countryside. En suite, sea views. DB&B from £30.00. WTB 3 Crowns Highly Commended. *[Pets £2 per night.]*

Llanmadoc

Village on Gower Peninsula, a secluded area with unspoilt beaches and many bird reserves.

MRS A. MAIN, TALLIZMAND, LLANMADOC, GOWER SA3 1DE (01792 386373). Located near the splendid Gower coastline, surrounded by beautiful countryside, Tallizmand has tastefully furnished en suite bedrooms with tea/coffee facilities. Home cooking, packed lunches. Pets welcome. 3 Crowns Highly Commended. *[🐕]*

Mumbles

Seaside resort of Swansea to west and north west of Mumbles Head.

MUMBLES & SWANSEA holiday homes, some with sea views. Flat locations. Well equipped, modern conveniences; carpets throughout. Convenient for beaches, countryside and town's amenities. Personally supervised. WTB Graded Three Ticks. Cottage, maisonette, flat and town house available. MRS JEAN GRIERSON, 112 MUMBLES ROAD, BLACKPILL, SWANSEA SA3 5AS (01792 402278). *[🐕]*

GWENT

Abergavenny

Historic market town at south-eastern gateway to Brecon Beacons Natinal Park. Pony trekking, leisure centre; excellent touring base for Vale of Usk.

CHRISTINE SMITH, THE HALF MOON, LLANTHONY, NEAR ABERGAVENNY NP7 7NN (01873 890611). Friendly 17th-century inn. Serves good food and real ale. Enjoy wonderful scenery of Black Mountains. Good base. Walking, pony trekking. Dogs welcome. *[🐕]*

Pontypool

Town 8 miles north of Newport-Valley Inheritance exhibition centre in former Georgian stable of Pontypool Park House tells story of the valleys.

MRS S. ARMITAGE, TY'RYWEN FARM, TREVETHIN, PONTYPOOL NP4 8TT (Tel & Fax: 01495 785200). A very remote 16th Century Longhouse high in the Brecon Beacons National Park. Spacious en suite rooms, colour TV and beverage tray. Some four-posters. One room with jacuzzi. No smoking. No children. Light supper available. Two nights B&B £35.00 per person. *[🐕]*

Wye Valley

Scenic area, ideal for relaxation.

MR & MRS J. LLEWELLYN, CWRT-Y-GAER, WOLVESNEWTON, CHEPSTOW NP6 6PR (01291 650700). 1, 4 or more dogs welcome free. Self catering, attractively converted stone buildings of Welsh Longhouse. 20 acres, super views of Usk Vale. Brochure. Three units (one suitable for disabled). Four Dragons Award. *[🐕pw!]*

GWYNEDD *Llandudno, Porthmadog, Pwllheli, Tywyn*

SUNNYDOWNS HOTEL
66 Abbey Road, Rhos-on-Sea, Near Llandudno LL28 4NU
Tel: 01492 544256 Fax: 01492 543223
☻☻☻ Proprietors: Mr & Mrs Mike Willington

A 4-Crown luxury family-run hotel just 2 minutes' walk to beach & shops with lots of nice walks for you and your dog close by. All rooms en suite with colour TV, video and satellite channels, clock radio, tea/coffee facilities, hair dryers, mini-bar refrigerator, direct dial telephone and central heating. Hotel facilities; bar, pool room, restaurant, sauna and car park. Only five minutes' drive to Llandudno and Colwyn Bay and 10 minutes' to the mountains and castles of Snowdonia. Dog sitting available. By arrangement meals can be taken in the bar with your dog. Open all year. Telephone for brochure.

TYDDYN DU FARM HOLIDAYS (PW),
Gellilydan, Near Ffestiniog, Porthmadog, Gwynedd LL41 4RB
Tel: 01766 590281 ☻ ☻ ☻ Highly Commended

This enchanting historic 17th century farmhouse is situated amidst spectacular scenery in the **heart of the Snowdonia National Park.** It is an excellent centrally located base for the numerous attractions, beaches and walks of North Wales. The old world farmhouse has a relaxed homely atmosphere, charm and character with a massive stone inglenook fireplace, antique furniture, exposed beams and stonework. We also have a superb private ground floor cottage suite with a solid fuel stove, which sleeps up to four (meals served in farmhouse). All rooms have remote-control colour TV, tea/coffee/drinking chocolate trays; most are en suite. Payphone for guests' use. Candlelight dinners are served using fresh local produce with home-made soups and buns; vegetarians welcome. Packed lunches available. Breakfast menu with seven choices, plus porridge! Non-smoking area in farmhouse. You are welcome to bottle-feed pet lambs, collect the eggs, feed the ducks on our mill pond and fuss over Polly the pony. We are easy to find, 300 yards off the A470, near the village of Gellilydan. Open all year. Bed and Breakfast from £16–£20, Dinner £10.00.
Weekly Dinner, Bed and Breakfast from £160. Stamp for brochure please to Mrs Paula Williams.

Stuart & Barbara White invite you to their comfortable, informal, family run hotel. Spacious gardens, peaceful location, magnificent views across Cardigan Bay to Snowdonia. Tasteful en suite bedrooms, excellent cuisine, restaurant and bar meals. Golf packages. Short breaks. Xmas package. AA/RAC**. Ashley Courtenay Recommended. Open all year round. Pets welcome at management's discretion.

DEUCOCH HOTEL
Abersoch,
Pwllheli,
Gwynedd LL53 7LD **Tel: 01758 712680 Fax: 01758 712670**

COASTAL HOUSE TYWYN GWYNEDD
**3 bedrooms
Sleeps five
£130–£199
per week**

* 2 minutes' walk to sandy beach
* 2 minutes' walk to pub/bar meals
* Fully equipped as own home
* Garden front and rear. * Garage
* 8 doors from the home bakery
* Tal-y-Llyn Steam Railway walking distance
* Pets welcome FREE OF CHARGE

Enquiries: **Mr and Mrs Ian Weston, 18 Elizabeth Road,
Basingstoke, Hampshire RG22 6AX Tel: 01256 52364**

300

GWYNEDD   *Trefriw*

Crafnant Guest House

WTB ☜ ☜ Commended
**Trefriw, Gwynedd,
N. Wales LL27 0JH
Tel: 01492 640809**

A non-smoking Guest House situated in the Conwy Valley, renowned for its beautiful lakes and forests. Superbly positioned for tourist attractions. 5 homely guest rooms have TV, drinks; most have en suite facilities. Private car park. Children/groups special rates. Bed and Breakfast £15–£17 per person; traditional/vegetarian meals £8.50. 5% discount on a week's B&B booking. Open all year.
Dogs welcome by arrangement £2 per night.

SEASIDE COTTAGES, MANN'S HOLIDAYS (01758 701 702). Large selection of self catering seaside and country cottages, bungalows, farmhouses, caravans etc. offering superb, reasonably priced accommodation for owners and their pets. Please telephone for brochure.

WELCOME COTTAGE HOLIDAYS. Hundreds of properties in wonderful locations at welcoming low prices. Pets, linen and fuel mostly included. For FREE colour brochure telephone 01756 702206.

Aberdovey

Small resort on North shore of River Dovey estuary near mouth, 9 miles west of Machynlleth.

THE HARBOUR HOTEL, ABERDOVEY LL35 0EB (01654 767250; Fax: 01654 767078). Three Crowns Highly Commended. Wonderful seafront location in picturesque and very doggy village. Children welcome. Family restaurant. Basement wine bar. Easy access to many local attractions. *[Pets £3 per night.]*

Abersoch

Dinghy sailing and windsurfing centre with safe sandy beaches. Pony trekking, golf, fishing and sea trips.

MR P. W. REES, "QUALITY COTTAGES", CERBID, SOLVA, HAVERFORDWEST, PEMBROKESHIRE SA62 6YE (01348 837871). Cottages set in all coastal areas, unashamed luxury; highest residential standards. Dishwashers, microwaves, washing machines. Log fires. Linen supplied. Pets welcome. *[pw!]*

MRS C. A. JONES, RHEDYN, MYNYTHO, PWLLHELI LL53 7PS (01758 740669). Country Cottage available for self catering holidays. Sleeps four people. All modern conveniences. Bed linen provided. Large garden. Rabbit hutch, separate pets' accommodation. *[🐕 🏠]*

Bala

Natural touring centre for Snowdonia. Narrow-gauge railway runs along side of Bala Lake, the largest natural lake in Wales. Golf, sailing, fishing, canoeing.

MRS ANN SKINNER, TALYBONT ISA, RHYDUCHAF, BALA LL23 7SD (01678 520234). Bed and Breakfast, optional Evening Meal, on the farm. Also two 6/8 berth Caravans with all modern conveniences. Just two miles from Bala Lake. Ideal for walking, sailing, fishing, golfing. *[🐕]*

Barmouth

Modern seaside resort with two miles of sandy beaches. Surrounding hills full of interesting archaeological remains.

LAWRENNY LODGE HOTEL, BARMOUTH LL42 1SU (01341 280466). Quiet, family-run hotel overlooking harbour and estuary but only 5 minutes from town. Most rooms en-suite, all with TV, tea/coffee making facilities and clock/radio alarms. Restaurant menu includes vegetarian dishes. Residential licence. Large car park. 3 Crowns. *[🐾]*

Beddgelert

Delightfully picturesque village in scenic landscape 4 miles south of Snowdon.

COLWYN, BEDDGELERT, GWYNEDD (01766 890276). Joan Williams. Old stone cottage overlooking river in centre of picturesque village right at the foot of Snowdon. Self-catering 6/8 in 3/4 en suite bedrooms with white linen towels, electric blankets, central heating. Inns, shops and good food all within 100 yds. Elec./std. rate. Parking adjacent. No garden. Walkers muddy boots and wet dogs welcome. Unsuitable for small children or the infirm. Sleep 6, £390; 8, £480. Winter Breaks £180 and £240. Also: Cottage for 2, £160.

Betws-y-Coed

Popular mountain resort in picturesque setting where three rivers meet. Trout fishing, craft shops, golf, railway and motor museums, Snowdonia National Park Visitor Centre. Nearby Swallow Falls are famous beauty spot.

SUMMER HILL NON-SMOKERS' GUEST HOUSE, BETWS-Y-COED LL24 0BL (01690 710306). Quiet location, overlooking river. 150 yards from main road, shops. En suite and standard rooms, tea-making. Residents' lounge. TV. Singles, children welcome. EM available. B&B from £14.00. *[Pets £1 per night.]*

Caernarvon

Historic walled town and resort, ideal for touring Snowdonia. Museums, Segontium Roman Fort, magnificent 13th century castle. Old harbour, sailing trips.

Cherished, crafted, comfortable, family mountain cottages, sleep 4/6. Posture beds, patchworked; cots. Fitted kitchens, washing machines; luxury conservatories. Stone-walled peaceful gardens, magnificent views. £125–£299: REVD & MRS E. J. S. PLAXTON, THE VICARAGE, VICARAGE ROAD, LINGFIELD, SURREY RH7 6HA (01342 832021). *[🐾]*

OUR WORLD BY THE SEA. Executive Beach Bungalows. Villa Chalets and Luxury Caravans with your own beach moments from your door. Fully equipped. Ideal base for touring. BEACH HOLIDAY, WEST POINT, THE BEACH, PONTLLYFNI, CAER-NARVON LL54 5ET (01286 660400). *[Pets £2/£5 nightly.]*

MRS B. CARTWRIGHT, TAN DINAS, LLANDDEINIOLEN, CAERNARVON LL55 3AR (01248 670098). Comfortable friendly farmhouse. Large grounds. Ideal touring, set between mountains and sea. TV lounge, separate dining room and tables. Open March to October. Evening Meal, Bed and Breakfast £17, Bed and Breakfast £15. WTB LISTED. *[🐾pw!]*

302

Conwy

One of the best preserved medieval fortified towns in Britain on dramatic estuary setting. Telford Suspension Bridge, many historic buildings, lively quayside (site of smallest house in Britain). Golf, pony trekking, pleasure cruises.

PINEWOOD TOWERS COUNTRY GUEST HOUSE, SYCHNANT PASS ROAD, CONWY LL32 8BZ (01492 592459). Dogs, cats. One of the few Guest Houses catering for animal lovers and their pets, being fully equipped in the right surroundings. 10 acres of gardens and paddocks, with own stream and woods. *[pw! 75p per night* 🏠*]*

THE LODGE, TAL-Y-BONT, CONWY LL32 8YX (01492 660766; Fax: 01492 660534). Family-run Hotel with lovely en suite bedrooms. Enjoy peace and quiet, superb food and attention from friendly and efficient staff. B&B from £25 to £35; 2 days DB&B from £59.50 to £79.50. Pets welcome.

Crafnant

Peaceful scenic area in North Wales with mountains and lakes.

Secluded cottage with log fire and beams. Dogs will love it. Plenty of walks around mountains and lakes. For up to 5 people plus their pet. MRS WILLIAMS, LOW RISBY HOUSE, LOW RISBY, SCUNTHORPE, S. HUMBERSIDE DN15 0BX (01724 733990 or 0831 298448). *[*🐾*]*

Criccieth

Popular family resort with safe beaches divided by ruins of 13th century castle. Salmon and sea trout fishing; Festival of Music & Arts in summer.

WERNOL CARAVAN PARK, CHWILOG FAWR, CHWILOG, PWLLHELI LL53 6SW (Tel & Fax: 01766 810506). Family run park in elevated position offers accommodation in superior detached chalets with colour TV, microwave, etc. Luxury Farmhouse also available. Convenient for beach, touring, etc. *[Pets £10 weekly.]*

ABEREISTEDD HOTEL, WEST PARADE, CRICCIETH LL52 0EN (01766 522710). Overlooking Cardigan Bay, most rooms en suite. Ideal base for walking, climbing or simply relaxing. Special rates for short breaks. WTB 3 Crowns, AA/RAC*. *[*🐾*]*

MR P. W. REES, "QUALITY COTTAGES", CERBID, SOLVA, HAVERFORDWEST, PEMBROKESHIRE SA62 6YE (01348 837871). Cottages set in all coastal areas, unashamed luxury; equipped to highest residential standards with dishwashers, washing machines, microwaves. Log fires. Linen provided. Pets welcome. *[pw!]*

MRS M. JONES, YNYS GRAIANOG, YNYS, CRICCIETH LL52 0NT (01766 530234). Two stone cottages, 3 & 4 bedrooms. Quiet rural area. Convenient for Lleyn Peninsula and Snowdonia. Also annexe, ideal for two. Plenty of parking space. *[pw!]*

MRS A. M. JONES, BETWS-BACH, YNYS, CRICCIETH LL52 0PB (Tel. and Fax: 01758 720 047/01766 810 295). Traditional, stone-built Farm Cottages. Situated in peaceful secluded grounds amidst fine walking countryside. Sleep 2–6. All home comforts. Full heating – open all year. WTB Grade 5. *[*🐾*]*

Fairbourne

Bright little resort facing Barmouth across the Mawddach estuary. Safe spacious sands. A short distance inland is Cader Idris. Dolgellau 9 miles.

THE FAIRBOURNE HOTEL, FAIRBOURNE LL38 2HQ (01341 250203). Views of Cardigan Bay from own grounds. Licensed. Private bathrooms. Bowls green. Games room. Car park. Open all year. Pets welcome. WTB 3 Crowns Highly Commended. *[🐕]*

Garndolbenmaen

Village 4 miles north of Criccieth.

CEFN UCHAF FARM GUEST HOUSE, GARNDOLBENMAEN, PORTHMADOG, GWYNEDD LL51 9PJ (01766 530239). Spacious, comfortable farmhouse. All rooms H&C, beverage making, some en suite. Excellent cooking including vegetarian. Meet our own friendly animals. B&B from £16.00 pppn. 2 Crowns Highly Commended. *[🐕]*

Harlech

Small stone-built town dominated by remains of 13th century castle. Golf, theatre, swimming pool, fine stretch of sands.

CAE NÈST HALL COUNTRY HOUSE HOTEL, LLANBEDR LL45 2NL (01341 241349). Delightful 15th century manor house in 3 acres of secluded grounds. Restaurant, bar, lounge. All bedrooms en suite with colour TV, tea/coffee making. AA**, 3 Crowns Highly Commended. *[🐕]*

MR P. W. REES, "QUALITY COTTAGES", CERBID, SOLVA, HAVERFORDWEST, PEMBROKESHIRE SA62 6YE (01348 837871). Cottages set in all coastal areas, unashamed luxury; highest residential standards. Dishwashers, microwaves, washing machines. Log fires. Linen supplied. Pets welcome. *[pw!]*

FRON DEG GUEST HOUSE, LLANFAIR, HARLECH LL46 2RE (01766 780448). Small Georgian cottage overlooking beach at Harlech. Pretty bedrooms. Central for unspoiled beaches and countryside; within easy reach of Porthmadog. Reasonable terms for Bed and Breakfast, also Dinner.

Llandudno

Premier holiday resort of North Wales coast flanked by Great Orme and Little Orme headlands. Wide promenade, pier, two beaches; water ski-ing, sailing, fishing trips from jetty. Excellent sports facilities: golf, indoor pool, tennis, pony trekking, Leisure Centre. Summer variety shows, Alice in Wonderland Visitor Centre.

MR AND MRS C. WATTS, HEN DŶ HOTEL, 10 NORTH PARADE, LLANDUDNO LL30 2LP (01492 876184). Experience the warm welcome extended by the proprietors of this charming Hotel, set opposite the Pier, with panoramic views. All rooms with central heating, TV, radio, teamakers; some en suite. Good food. Cosy bar. From £17.50 per night. 3 Crowns Highly Commended. *[🐕]*

SUNNYDOWNS HOTEL, 66 ABBEY ROAD, RHOS ON SEA, NEAR LLANDUDNO LL28 4NU (01492 544256; Fax: 01492 543223). A 4 Crown luxury family hotel just 2 minutes' walk to beach & shops. All rooms en suite with colour TV, video & satellite channels, tea/coffee facilities and central heating. Hotel has bar, pool room and car park. *[🐕 pw!]*

MR AND MRS J. WILLIAMS, "DEVA", 34 TRINITY AVENUE, LLANDUDNO LL30 2TQ (01492 877059). Holiday Flats for 2/4 adults. House-trained pets welcome. Car parking. Colour television. Bed linen provided. Park opposite to walk your dog. Stamp please for brochure. [🐾]

HEADLANDS HOTEL, HILL TERRACE, LLANDUDNO LL30 2LS (01492 877485). Personal service and comfort at this AA, RAC, Ashley Courtenay recommended Hotel. Adjoining Snowdonia. All rooms with TV, Teasmaid; most with private facilities. Telephone for brochure. [🐾]

Llanfairfechan

Small resort on Conway Bay midway between Bangor and Conway.

BARBARA & TERRY ALLIX, YENTON, PROMENADE, LLANFAIRFECHAN LL33 0BU (01248 680075). Warm, comfortable, well-equipped self-contained family apartments. Sleep 2/6. Bedlinen and central heating included. Sandy beach, scenic views, easy seaside or mountain walks, good touring position. [Pets £6.00 per week.]

Morfa Nefyn

Picturesque village 2 miles west of Nefyn.

MR P. W. REES, "QUALITY COTTAGES", CERBID, SOLVA, HAVERFORDWEST, PEMBROKESHIRE SA62 6YE (01348 837871). Cottages set in all coastal areas, unashamed luxury; highest residential standards. Dishwashers, microwaves, washing machines. Log fires. Linen supplied. Pets welcome. [pw!]

Porthmadog

Harbour town with mile-long Cob embankment, along which runs Ffestiniog Narrow Gauge Steam Railway to Blaenau Ffestiniog. Pottery, maritime museum, car museum. Good beaches nearby.

MR P. W. REES, "QUALITY COTTAGES", CERBID, SOLVA, HAVERFORDWEST, PEMBROKESHIRE SA62 6YE (01348 837871). Cottages set in all coastal areas, unashamed luxury; highest residential standards. Dishwashers, microwaves, washing machines. Log fires. Linen supplied. Pets welcome. [[pw!]

TYDDYN FARM, GELLILYDAN, NEAR FFESTINIOG LL41 4RB (01766 590281). Beautiful historic 17th century farmhouse situated in the heart of Snowdonia National Park. All rooms have colour TV, tea/coffee and most are en suite.

BLACK ROCK SANDS, PORTHMADOG. Private site, beach 150 yards. 14 Caravans only. Fully equipped 6 berths. Own flush toilets. Showers and televisions. Shop and tavern near. APPLY – M. HUMPHRIES, 251 HEDNESFORD ROAD, NORTON CANES, CANNOCK, STAFFORDSHIRE WS11 3RZ (01543 279583).

Pwllheli

Popular sailing centre with harbour and long sandy beach. Golf, leisure centre, river and sea fishing.

MRS M. PARRY ROBERTS, "TY FRY", ABERDARON, PWLLHELI LL53 8BY (01758 760274). Modernised, fully furnished Cottage with views over Aberdaron Bay. Two bedrooms sleeping 5, cot; bathroom; large lounge, TV; kitchen/diner, cooker, fridge; metered electricity. Ample parking. Sandy beaches and coves, mountain walks nearby. Pets welcome. Booking March–October; SAE please.

DEUCOCH HOTEL, ABERSOCH, PWLLHELI, GWYNEDD LL53 7LD (Tel: 01758 712680; Fax: 01758 712670). Stuart & Barbara White invite you to their comfortable, informal, family run hotel. Spacious gardens with magnificent views across Cardigan Bay to Snowdonia. Open all year. [🐾]

Trefriw

Hillside village, popular as spa in Victorian times. Local beauty spots at Llyn Crafnant and Llyn Geironnydd. Woollen mill demonstrating traditional techniques.

CRAFNANT GUEST HOUSE, TREFRIW LL27 0JH (01492 640809). Non-smoking Guest House in beautiful Conwy Valley, superbly positioned for touring. 5 rooms, all with TV and drinks facility; most en suite. B&B from £15–£16.50. Special rates Senior Citizens. Open all year. *[Pets £2 per night.]*

MRS B. COLE, GLANDWR, TREFRIW, NEAR LLANRWST LL27 0JP (01492 640431). Large country house on outskirts of Trefriw village. Good touring area with Llanrwst, Betws-y-Coed and Swallow Falls five miles away. Fishing, walking, golf, pony trekking close by. Comfortable bedrooms, lounge with TV, dining room. Good home cooking. Parking. Bed and Breakfast from £15, Dinner if required.

Tywyn

Pleasant seaside resort, start of Talyllyn Narrow Gauge Railway. Sea and river fishing, golf.

Fully equipped coastal house, close to sandy beach. Sleeps five. Gardens; garage. Pets welcome free of charge. APPLY – MR AND MRS WESTON, 18 ELIZABETH ROAD, BASINGSTOKE, HAMPSHIRE RG22 6AX (01256 52364). *[🐕]*

POWYS

POWYS   *Brecon, Builth Wells*

MAES-Y-COED FARM, LLANDEFALLE, BRECON LD3 0WD

Three Crowns. Comfortable, friendly, 17th century farmhouse with oak beams offers you a warm welcome. Ideal centre for walking and touring. One family and one double bedded room en suite. All rooms have tea-making facilities.

Bed and Breakfast from £16; Evening Dinner by arrangement.

Mrs Sue Morgan   *Tel: 01874 754211*

Lane Farm
Painscastle, Builth Wells, Powys LD2 3JS
Tel: 01497 851605
Fax: 01497 851617

In the heart of Kilvert Country, close to Hay-on-Wye (famous for books). Wonderful walking and riding area.

Two self-contained self-catering flats;

THE OLD STABLES - 2 bedrooms, 2 bathrooms, large living room, well equipped kitchen. Additional sofa bed in living room.

THE GRANARY - 2 bedrooms, landing bedroom, bathroom, large living room and well equipped kitchen. Sofa bed in living room.

Visitors have use of washing machine and tumble dryer. All bed linen and towels provided; cot and high chair available. Electricity and logs included.

PETS WELCOME   **WTB 4 Dragons**

MID-WALES

PENLLWYN LODGES

Self catering luxury in beautiful two, three and four bedroomed Log Cabins set in 30 acres of unspoilt woodlands and meadows teeming with wildlife around the Montgomery Canal and our own lake.

Each cabin is set in half-an-acre of its own woodland with central heating, colour television, microwave, full kitchen and bath/shower room. Pets welcome.

From £200 - £550 per week Including VAT

Telephone for colour brochure:

01686 640269

PENLLWYN LODGES
GARTHMYL POWYS SY15 6SB

Brecon

Main touring centre for National Park. Busy market, Jazz Festival in summer. Brecknock Museum, ruined castle, cathedral of interest. Golf, walking, fishing, canal cruising, pony trekking.

MRS SUE MORGAN, MAES-Y-COED FARM, LLANDEFALLE, BRECON LD3 0WD (01874 754211). Comfortable, friendly 17th century farmhouse offers you a warm welcome. One family and one double room en suite. Bed and Breakfast from £16; Evening Dinner by arrangement. Three Crowns.

MRS ANN PHILLIPS, TYLEBRYTHOS FARM, CANTREF, BRECON LD3 8LR (01874 665329). Well equipped self catering bungalow, farmhouse and apartments situated amongst spectacular scenery in the Brecon Beacons National Park. Sleep 2–15 persons. Well maintained grounds. Children's play area. Ample parking. Personally supervised with cleanliness assured. Short breaks available. Pets by arrangement. WTB Grade 4. *[Pets £10 per week.]*

Builth Wells

Old country town in lovely setting on River Wye amid beautiful hills. Lively sheep and cattle markets; host to Royal Welsh Agricultural Show.

MRS LINDA WILLIAMS, OLD VICARAGE, ERWOOD, BUILTH WELLS LD2 3SZ (01982 560680). Beautiful situation just off A470 near Erwood. Spacious rooms with full central heating, beverage trays and washbasins; views over Wye Valley to Black Mountains. Private lounge with games, maps, literature. Bathroom and separate WC. Secluded grounds. B&B £13–£13.50; EM by arrangement, own produce. WTB One Crown. *[🐾]*

THE OLD STABLES & THE GRANARY: two self catering cottages set in wonderful walking and riding country. Each has 2 bedrooms (additional sofa bed in lounge); well equipped kitchen, large lounge. Use of laundry facilities; bed linen and towels provided. APPLY: MRS E. BALLY, LANE FARM, PAINSCASTLE, BUILTH WELLS LD2 3JS (01497 851605; Fax: 01497 851617).

R. I. AND M. C. WILTSHIRE, BRON WYE GUEST HOUSE, 5 CHURCH STREET, BUILTH WELLS LD2 3BS (01982 553587). Bed and Breakfast. Evening Meals by prior arrangement. Snacks, home cooking. Licensed. TV Lounge. Tea/coffee making all rooms, en suites available. Car park. Children and pets welcome. Bed and Breakfast from £13, en suite £16 per person. Evening Meal £7 per person by arrangement. WTB Three Crowns Commended. *[🐾]*

Corris

Peaceful village 4 miles north of Machynlleth.

BRAICH GOCH HOTEL & RESTAURANT, CORRIS, NEAR MACHYNLLETH SY20 9RD (01654 761229). Set in beautiful surroundings, in area rich in mountain walks. Ideal for train enthusiasts and birdwatchers; activity holidays can be arranged. Fully licensed restaurant and friendly bar. Pets most welcome.

Crickhowell

Pleasant village in the Usk Valley at foot of Black Mountains. 16th-cent. bridge, fine Georgian houses, fragments of a castle, gateway of a long-vanished manor house, and 14th-cent. church with elaborate tombs and memorials.

PRISCILLA LLEWELYN, WHITE HALL, GLANGRWYNEY, CRICKHOWELL NP8 1EW (01873 811155 or 840267). Comfortably furnished and well placed for exploring Black Mountains, Brecon Beacons etc. Double and twin rooms with TV and tea-making. Terms on request. Pets welcome. WTB 2 Crowns. *[🐾]*

Dinas Mawddwy

Hamlet 8 miles east of Dolgellau.

BUCKLEY PINES HOTEL, DINAS MAWDDWY, NEAR MACHYNLLETH SY20 9LP (01650 531261). Comfortable family-run hotel set in Snowdonia National Park. All rooms with TV and tea/coffee; some en suite. Dogs free of charge and welcome in rooms and bar. Special terms for 3-day breaks. WTB Three Crowns, AA/RAC**. *[🐾]*

Garthmyl

Situated on A483 between Welshpool and Newtown in unspoiled countryside.

Self-catering luxury in beautiful log cabins set in 30 acres of unspoilt woodland. Central heating, colour TV, microwave, etc. Pets welcome. From £175 to £535 per week. APPLY – PENLLWYN LODGES, GARTHMYL SY15 6SB (01686 640 269).

Hay-on-Wye

Small market town at north end of Black Mountains, 15 miles north-east of Brecon.

PETER & OLWEN ROBERTS, YORK HOUSE, CUSOP, HAY-ON-WYE HR3 5QX (01497 820705). RAC Acclaimed, AA QQQ. Enjoy a relaxing holiday in this elegant Victorian guest house quietly situated on the edge of Hay, "Town of Books". Excellent walking country for pets. *[Pets £3.50 per visit.]*

Llandrindod Wells

Popular inland resort, Victorian spa town, excellent touring centre. Golf, fishing, bowling, boating and tennis. Visitors can still take the waters at Rock Park Gardens.

THE PARK MOTEL, CROSSGATES, LLANDRINDOD WELLS LD1 6RF (01597 851201). In three acres, amidst beautiful countryside near Elan Valley. Luxury, self-contained, centrally heated Chalets. Licensed restaurant open all day. Swimming pool. Children's play area. Pets welcome. *[Pets £1 per night, £5 per week.]*

Llangurig

Village on River Wye 4 miles south-west of Llanidloes. Craft centre and monastic 14th century church. Ideal walking countryside.

THE OLD VICARAGE COUNTRY GUEST HOUSE, LLANGURIG, MONTGOMERY-SHIRE SY18 6RN (01686 440280). Charming Victorian house, ideal base for exploring the mountains and valleys of this unspoiled area. All bedrooms en suite. Two guest lounges; licensed dining room. WTB 3 Crowns Highly Commended. *[🐾]*

Machynlleth

Set in enchanting position on the Dovey Valley, this spot has been inhabited since the Iron Age and was made capital of Wales by Owen Glendower, who was proclaimed king at a parliament in 1404. Four 19th century inns cluster round the old clock tower which marks the centre of the town. LONDON 203 miles, Welshpool 38, Newtown 28, Aberystwyth 18, Dolgellau 18, Aberdovey 11.

WYNNSTAY ARMS HOTEL, MAENGWYN STREET, MACHYNLLETH SY20 8AE (01654 702941; Fax: 01654 703884). Traditional coaching inn on edge Snowdonia. Comfortable en suite rooms, cosy bars with traditional ales; excellent bar and restaurant food. Experience the warmest of welcomes.

Presteigne

An attractive old town with half-timbered houses. Ideal for hillside rambles and pony trekking.

MRS R. L. JONES, UPPER HOUSE, KINNERTON, NEAR PRESTEIGNE LD8 2PE (01547 560207). Charming Tudor cottage in lovely Border countryside. 2 miles from Offa's Dyke. Children and pets welcome. Storage heaters, washing machine, microwave, colour TV, log fire. Linen hire optional. Sleeps 5 plus 2 cots. Ample parking. Sun trap garden. On working farm in peaceful hamlet. WTB Grade 3. *[🐾]*

Welshpool

Lively market town with medieval streets. Narrow gauge Welshpool and Llanfair Light Railway runs along restored 8-mile track. Shrewsbury 17 miles.

LORDS BUILDINGS FARM, LEIGHTON, NEAR WELSHPOOL. Set in 73 acres with panoramic views. Sleeps 7 plus cot. Everything provided except linen. Ideal touring base. Children and pets welcome. WTB 2 Dragons. MR G. R. EDWARDS, WINDMILL FARM, HALFWAY HOUSE, NEAR SHREWSBURY, SHROPSHIRE SY5 9EJ (01743 884 356). *[🐾]*

SCOTLAND

SCOTLAND *Ballachulish, Ballindalloch, Beattock, Biggar,*
Blairgawrie, Burnhouse

- **HOUSE IN THE WOOD HOLIDAYS**
Glenachulish, Ballachulish, Argyll PA39 4JZ Telephone: 01855 811379
Cottage and Chalets in natural woodland sleeping 4 to 6 people.
From £140–£250
GOOD AREA FOR WALKING – AND NATURE LOVERS
PETS WELCOME *BROCHURE AVAILABLE* *NO VAT*

♨♨♨♨ Commended **BEECHGROVE COTTAGES, TOMNAVOULIN & GLENLIVET**
Traditional Highland Cottages near the Rivers Livet and Avon, in very scenic area. Each sleeps 2
to 6 persons; 2 double bedrooms, bathroom/shower; fully equipped dining/kitchen, livingroom
with colour TV. All electric. Linen supplied. Central for Coast, Spey Valley, Aviemore, Dee Valley,
Balmoral. Skiing at Lecht Ski Centre 20 minutes, Glen Shee 45 minutes. Open all year. Car
essential. Children and pets welcome. Terms £180 to £260.

Apply: **MRS J. WHITE, BEECHGROVE, TOMNAVOULIN, BALLINDALLOCH AB3 9JA (01807 590220)**

♨♨♨   **BEATTOCK HOUSE HOTEL & CARAVAN PARK**   AA/▶▶
This 2 Star hotel is an ideal place to rest from the busy A74 from Glasgow to the South. Restaurant and
bar (full day licence) 11am to 11pm. Unrivalled as a touring base for Galloway, Burns Country and the
Lake District. Free fishing on River Evan in grounds, permits available for parts of the Annan, stalking and
rough shooting can be arranged. Golf, tennis and riding nearby. Caravan Park has toilets and showers with
H&C, and electric hook-ups for touring vans. Patrons welcome in Hotel restaurant and bars.
Beattock, Dumfriesshire DG10 9QB Tel: 01683 300403

CARMICHAEL COUNTRY COTTAGES
CARMICHAEL ESTATE, BY BIGGAR, LANARKSHIRE ML12 6PG
Tel: 01899 308336 Fax: 01899 308481 *3 Crowns Commended–5 Crowns Highly Commended*
Our stone cottages nestle in the woods and fields of our historic family-run
estate. Ideal homes for families, pets and particularly dogs. Walking trails, private
tennis, fishing, restaurant/farm shop. 12 cottages, 25 bedrooms. Open all year.
Central location. £160 to £430 per week.

PERTHSHIRE AND CENTRAL HIGHLANDS

* A choice of 1–3 bedroom self-catering
Scandinavian-style chalets in 2 acres parkland,
only 5 minutes' walk from shops and town centre.
* OPEN ALL YEAR. Spring/Autumn short
breaks welcome in warm, fully-equipped,
comfortable accommodation. Colour TV. Tennis.
Children's amenities on site.
* Ideal centre for touring in all directions. Golf (40 courses within an hour's drive), walking and
fishing holidays.   Credit Cards Accepted.   ♨♨/♨♨♨♨ Commended
For detailed brochure and bookings, please write or telephone:
ALTAMOUNT CHALETS, BLAIRGOWRIE, PERTHSHIRE PH10 6JN
Tel: (01250) 873324 Fax: (01250) 872464

Manor Farm Hotel
Burnhouse, By Beith, Ayrshire KA15 1LJ
Tel: 01560 484006

En suite accommodation within a farmhouse setting provides an ideal "home"
for a tranquil holiday with a few added luxuries – without the added price!
We are situated 50 yards from the A736 Glasgow to Irvine road, making us
the perfect base for touring Burns Country, the South West coastline, the
Trossachs and Glasgow, with plenty of things to see and do for the whole family e.g. Magnum Leisure
Centre, Kelburn Country Park, Culzean Castle.
9 rooms (some family), most en suite, all with washbasin, colour TV, tea making facilities and central heating.

Personally run by the Robertson family.   **Brochure on request.**

NETHYBRIDGE – STRATHSPEY

Choice of very comfortable modern cottages or converted smithy of unique character, set individually in this quiet Highland village. Fenced gardens. Sleep 2–9. Linen, towels, visitor laundry, winter central heating included. Good walking and touring centre. Close to RSPB reserve with river and forest walks at your doorstep.

Write or phone for brochure to:

STB ♕ ♕ ♕ ♕ Highly Commended   **Mr and Mrs P.W. Patrick, Chapelton Place,**
Forres, Moray IV36 0NL

Member of THE ASSOCIATION OF SCOTLAND'S SELF CATERERS   **Tel/Fax: (01309) 672505**

Modern cottages in an elevated position on edge of attractive Highland village with glorious views. Excellent walking country. Golf, tennis and fishing nearby. Famous Loch Garten ospreys 4 miles. Furnished to a very high standard – carpeted throughout, colour television and washing machine. Equipped for 4–8. Children and pets welcome. Car essential. Shops ½ mile, Aviemore 12 miles. Whisky Trail nearby. Scottish Tourist Board 4 Crowns De Luxe.
Mrs M. Fraser, 36 Lynstock Crescent, Nethybridge, Inverness-shire PH25 3DX
Tel: 01479 821312 *(24 hour answering service)*

ELERAIG HIGHLAND CHALETS

Near OBAN, ARGYLL
Gateway to the
Highlands and Islands
STB Two/Three Crowns Commended
Fully equipped
Norwegian chalets on
secluded Eleraig Estate
12 miles from Oban.
PERFECT FOR PETS

In the breathtaking scenery of a private glen within 1800-acre working sheep farm the chalets are ideal for a holiday with dogs (& cats). Widely spaced, sleeping four to seven. Parking by each chalet. Cots and high chairs available. By Loch Tralaig. Free fishing and boating. Peace and tranquillity are features of this walkers' and birdwatchers' paradise. Riding, golf, watersports and evening entertainment available locally. Open March to October.

**From £190 weekly per chalet, including electricity. Colour brochure from resident owners: Gill and Andrew Stevens, Eleraig Highland Chalets, Kilninver, by Oban, Argyll PA34 4UX.
Tel: 01852 200225**

SYMBOLS

🐕 Indicates no charge for pets.
£ Indicates a charge for pets: nightly or weekly.
pw! Indicates some special provision for pets: exercise, feeding etc.
🏠 Indicates separate pets accommodation.

MRS C. M. KILPATRICK

Slipperfield House
West Linton EH46 7AA

Tel and Fax: 01968 660401

Two Commended Cottages a mile from West Linton at the foot of the Pentland Hills, set in 100 acres of lochs and woodlands.

AMERICA COTTAGE, which sleeps 6 people in 3 bedrooms, is secluded and has been completely modernised.

♕♕♕♕ Commended.

LOCH COTTAGE, which sleeps 4 people in 2 bedrooms, is attached to the owners' house and has magnificent views over a seven acre loch.

♕♕♕♕ Commended.

Both Cottages have sittingrooms with dining areas and colour TV; modern bathrooms and excellently equipped Schreiber kitchens with washing and drying machines, microwave oven and telephone. SAE please for terms.

**Controlled pets welcomed **Ample parking ** Car essential ** Edinburgh 19 miles ** Golf and private fishing ** Available all year.

Your pets are welcomed as part of the family at an especially attractive selection of holiday cottages all over Scotland. Please write or phone for our 30-page colour brochure by return of post. ECOSSE UNIQUE LTD, THORNCROFT, LILLIESLEAF, MELROSE TD6 9JD (Tel: 01835 870779; Fax: 01835 870417). *[🐾 or £6 p.n.]*

WELCOME COTTAGE HOLIDAYS. Hundreds of properties in wonderful locations at welcoming low prices. Pets, linen and fuel mostly included. For FREE colour brochure telephone 01756 702213.

Aberdour (Fife)

Small resort on north shore of Firth of Forth 3 miles west of Burntisland. Remains of 17th century castle.

THE WOODSIDE HOTEL, HIGH STREET, ABERDOUR KY3 0SW (01383 860328). You will be made welcome in newly refurbished 3 star comfort. Enjoy the good restaurant, or the tasty food in the bar. You will find the hotel ideally situated for walking your dog. Easy reach to Edinburgh. B&B from £26.50 each. *[🐾]*

Aberfeldy (Perthshire)

Small town standing on both sides of Urlar Burn near its confluence with the River Tay. Pitlochry 8 miles.

LOCH TAY LODGES, REMONY, ACHARN, ABERFELDY PH15 2HR (01887 830 209). STB 4 Crowns Highly Commended. Self catering in village close to Loch. Enjoy hill walking, golf, sailing or touring. Salmon and trout fishing available. Log fires. Pets welcome. Walks along loch shore from house. For brochure, contact MRS G. DUNCAN MILLAR at above address. *[🐾]*

Acharacle (Argyll)

Picturesque village in Lochaber district, 2 miles north of Salen.

This is a modern bungalow situated in quiet surroundings overlooking Loch Shiel and Moidart Hills. We have three letting bedrooms (two double and one twin) with washbasins; bathroom and shower facilities; TV lounge. Ample parking. Ideal for touring West Highlands. B&B only. R. BREMNER, "ACHNESS", ACHARACLE, BY FORT WILLIAM PH36 4JY (01967 431239).

Appin (Argyll)

Mountainous area bounded by Loch Linnhe, Glen Creran, and Glen Coe, partly in Strathclyde and partly in Highland region.

MRS J. PERY, ARDTUR, APPIN, ARGYLL PA38 4DD (01631 730223). Two adjacent cottages sleeping six or eight people in secluded farmland surroundings on shores of Loch Linnhe. Magnificent views. Ideal centre for hillwalking, Glencoe and Ben Nevis nearby. *[🐾]*

Ardbeg (Isle of Bute)

Popular resort reached by ferry from Wemyss Bay. Overlooked by ruined castle; nearby Ardencraig Gardens are noted for magnificent floral displays; another attraction is Mount Stuart.

ARDMORY HOUSE HOTEL, ARDMORY ROAD, ARDBEG, ISLE OF BUTE PA20 0PG (01700 502346). Nero (black Labrador) invites friends to share his country retreat of 3/4 acre mature grounds (great sniffs), overlooking Rothesay Bay. 5 well appointed en suite bedrooms. Restaurant, Bar. Open all year. Bed and Breakfast from £25.00. Bedrooms and Restaurant are NON-SMOKING. STB 3 Crowns Commended, RAC 2 Stars, Guild of Master Craftsmen Award.

Aviemore (Inverness-shire)

Scotland's leading ski resort in Spey valley with superb sport and entertainment facilities. All-weather holiday centre with accommodation to suit all pockets. Ice-rink. Excellent fishing. Centre for exploring Cairngorms. Edinburgh 129 miles, Grantown-on-Spey 14, Kingussie 12, Carrbridge 7.

PINE BANK CHALETS, DALFABER ROAD, AVIEMORE PH22 1PX (01479 81000; Fax: 01479 811469). Cosy Log Cabins and Quality Chalets, situated in a secluded area near the River Spey. Superb Family/Activity Holidays by Mountains. Ideal ski-ing, walking, fishing and golf. Sky TV, mountain bikes. Short breaks available. Pets welcome. Open all year. ASSC Member. Brochure. *[Pets £15 per week.]*

CAIRNGORM HIGHLAND BUNGALOWS. Beautifully furnished and equipped bungalows ranging from 2–4 bedrooms sleeping up to 8. All have a wide range of facilities including colour TV, fridge, cooker and microwave. Ideal base for families and pet owners. Prices from £180 per week. CONTACT LINDA MURRAY (Tel: 01479 810653; Fax: 01479 810262). *[🐾]*

Ballachulish (Argyll)

Impressively placed village at entrance to Glencoe and on Loch Leven. Magnificent mountain scenery including Sgorr Dhearg (3362 ft). Good centre for boating, climbing and sailing. Glasgow 89 miles, Oban 38, Fort William 14, Kinlochleven 9.

BALLACHULISH HOTEL, BALLACHULISH, NEAR FORT WILLIAM PA39 4JY (Tel: 0185 582 1582; Fax: 0185 582 1463. Escape to the magnificent West Highlands and enjoy a stylish, high value break. Luxurious accommodation and warm, friendly service. Set above Loch Linnhe, ideal base for touring. *[pw! £2.50 per night.]*

THE ISLES OF GLENCOE HOTEL AND LEISURE CENTRE, BALLACHULISH, ARGYLL, PA39 4HL (0185 582 1582; Fax: 0185 582 1463). Almost afloat! Scotland's wonderful new Hotel, tiered down a hillside. Stylish bedrooms, breathtaking views. Superb Restaurant, 40 acres surrounding parkland. Swimming pool. Pets welcome. *[pw! £2.50 per night.]*

Cottages and Chalets in natural woodland sleeping 4 to 6 people. The Glencoe area is lovely for walking and perfect for nature lovers too. Pets welcome. No VAT. Brochure available. APPLY – HOUSE IN THE WOOD HOLIDAYS, GLENACHULISH, BALLACHULISH, ARGYLL PA39 4JZ (01855 811379). *[🐾]*

Ballindalloch (Banffshire)

Baronial Castle with modern additions and alterations is the most noteworthy building in this area; set on right bank of River Avon near its confluence with River Spey 7 miles south-west of Charleston of Aberlour.

MRS J. WHITE, BEECHGROVE COTTAGES, TOMNAVOULIN, BALLINDALLOCH AB3 9JA (01807 590220). Traditional Highland Cottages in scenic area. Each sleeps 6 maximum; two double bedrooms, fully equipped dining/kitchen, living room, colour TV. All electric. Linen supplied. Central for coast and ski slopes. Open all year. Car essential. Children and pets welcome.

Beattock (Dumfriesshire)

Picturesque Dumfriesshire village, ideally placed for touring Borders region and Upper Clyde Valley.

BEATTOCK HOUSE HOTEL AND CARAVAN PARK, BEATTOCK DG10 9QB (01683 300403). Ideally situated Hotel and Caravan Park for travellers wishing to rest awhile from the busy A74 or to tour the lovely Borders country, Burns Country and the Lake District. Fishing, stalking and rough shooting available. Restaurant; all-day bar licence. AA, RAC.

Biggar (Lanarkshire)

Small town set round broad main street. Gasworks museum, puppet theatre seating 100, street museum displaying old shopfronts and interiors. Peebles 13 miles.

CARMICHAEL COUNTRY COTTAGES, CARMICHAEL ESTATE, BY BIGGAR ML12 6PG (01899 308336; Fax: 01899 308481). Our stone cottages nestle in the woods and fields of our historic family-run estate. Ideal homes for families, pets and dogs. 12 Cottages, 25 bedrooms. Open all year. £160 to £430 per week. *[🐾]*

MRS MARGARET KIRBY, WALSTON MANSIONS FARMHOUSE, WALSTON, CARNWATH, LANARK ML11 8NF (0189-981 0338). Friendly and relaxed atmosphere. Good home cooking with home-produced meat, eggs and organic vegetables. Guest lounge with log fire, TV and video. Bedrooms with colour TV. Cot and high chair available. Biggar 5 miles. Edinburgh 24 miles. B&B £13.00, en suite £15.00; Evening Meal £7.00. FHB member. 3 Crowns Commended. *[🐾]*

Blairgowrie (Perthshire)

Town in picturesque situation near Ericht Gorge. Fine touring centre. Several castles in vicinity. Pitlochry 23 miles, Dundee 20, Forfar 20, Perth 15.

ALTAMOUNT CHALETS, COUPAR ANGUS ROAD, BLAIRGOWRIE PH10 6JN (01250 873324). Modern, fully equipped 1, 2 and 3 bedroom Scandinavian-style Chalets. Colour television. Centrally situated for touring Highlands. Children's amenities on site. Pets welcome. *[Pets £2.00 per night.]*

Bridge of Cally (Perthshire)

Village on River Ardle 5 miles north-west of Blairgowrie.

MRS JOSEPHINE MACLAREN, BLACKCRAIG CASTLE, BRIDGE OF CALLY PH10 7PX (01250 886251 or 0131-551 1863). Beautiful castle of architectural interest situated in spacious grounds. Ideal centre for touring, walking, golf. Free fishing. Dogs most welcome. B&B £19.50 reductions for children. Open July to early September. *[🐕]*

Burnhouse (Ayrshire)

In the heart of Ayrshire. Ideal for touring Burns country. Many wonderful golf courses nearby.

MANOR FARM HOTEL, BURNHOUSE, BY BEITH KA15 1LJ (01560 484006). Situated 50 yards from A736 Glasgow to Irvine, a perfect base for touring Burns country, Trossachs and Glasgow. Nine rooms, most en suite, all with washbasin, colour TV and central heating.

Callander (Perthshire)

Holiday resort and base for walks and drives around the Trossachs and Loch Katrine. Stirling 14 miles.

E. L. MACLEOD, CRAIGROYSTON, 4 BRIDGE STREET, CALLANDER FK17 8AA (01877 331395). Family run Guest House. Warm welcome, home cooking. Comfortable rooms, all en suite with tea/coffee facilities, colour TV, central heating. Pets welcome. Prices from £17.50. 2 Crowns Commended. *[🐕]*

LYNNE AND ALISTAIR FERGUSON, ROSLIN COTTAGE GUEST HOUSE, LAGRANNOCH, CALLANDER FK17 8LE (01877 330638). Bed and good Scottish Breakfast from £13.50 per person. Evening Meal optional. Comfortable accommodation in 18th century Cottage, historic features. Good "walkies" area – dogs are especially welcome. *[🐕pw!]*

Carr-Bridge (Inverness-shire)

Village on River Dulnain in Badenoch and Strathspey district. 7 miles north of Aviemore. Landmark Visitor Centre has exhibition explaining history of local environment.

LIZ AND IAN BISHOP, SLOCHD COTTAGES, BY CARR-BRIDGE PH23 3AY (Tel: 01479 841 666; Fax: 01479 841 699). Cottage sleeping 6, ideal for touring; close to ski-ing, sailing, windsurfing and golfing. Mountain bike hire and wonderful forest and mountain trails on the doorstep. SAE for further details please. *[🐕]*

Castle Douglas (Kirkcudbrightshire)

Old market town northern end of Carlingwalk Loch, good touring centre for Galloway. Nearby Threave House surrounded by woodland walks and wildfowl refuge.

MR P. W. BALL, BARNCROSH FARM, CASTLE DOUGLAS, KIRKCUDBRIGHT-SHIRE DG7 1TX (01556 680216). Comfortable Cottages and flats for 2/4/6/8. Fully equipped, including linen. Colour TV. Children and dogs welcome. Beautiful rural surroundings. Brochure on request. *[Pets £10 weekly.]*

MRS CELIA PICKUP, "CRAIGADAM", CASTLE DOUGLAS DG7 3HU (Tel and Fax: 01556 650233). Working farm. Family-run 18th century farmhouse. All bedrooms en suite. Lovely oak-panelled dining room offering Cordon Bleu cooking using local produce such as venison, pheasant and salmon. Trout fishing, walking, and golfing available. Well-behaved dogs £1 per night.

Contin (Ross-shire)

Village in Ross and Cromarty district two miles south-west of Strathpeffer.

COUL HOUSE HOTEL, CONTIN, BY STRATHPEFFER IV14 9EY (01997 421487; Fax: 01997 421945). Skye and Raasay, our lovable labradors look forward to welcoming you. "Taste of Scotland" food, log fires, well-equipped bedrooms. Miles of wonderful walks. 4 Crowns Highly Commended. *[🐾pw!]*

Dalbeattie (Kirkcudbrightshire)

Small granite town on Kirgunzeon Lane (or Burn), 13 miles south-west of Dumfries.

BAREND HOLIDAY VILLAGE AND RIVER VIEW PARK, DALBEATTIE (01387 780663; Fax: 01387 780283). Two peaceful sites with Scandinavian-style/timber-built lodges. Accommodation superbly equipped. Facilities at Barend available to both include heated pool, restaurant, riding, fishing. Brochure on request.

KIRKLAND FARMHOUSE AND COTTAGES. 3/4 Crowns Commended & Highly Commended. One mile safe sandy beach; surrounded by owner's fields. Superbly equipped and comfortable; private gardens. Sleep 6/8, 5/6, 2/3 persons plus cots. Forestry and seaside walks. Bicycle hire; golf, sailing, fishing. Terms from £75; special rates for couples only. Mid-week breaks available. *[Pets £15 weekly.]* MRS K. SINCLAIR, ROCKCLIFFE, DALBEATTIE DG5 4QC (01556 630205).

Daviot (Inverness-shire)

Village 5 miles south-east of Inverness, the Highland "capital".

TORGUISH HOUSE & HOLIDAY HOMES, DAVIOT, INVERNESS IV1 2XQ (01463 772208; Fax: 01463 772308). Homely Guest House with generous rooms, some en suite, all with TV, tea/coffee. Large garden. Also, The Steading (self catering cottages sleeping 2–4). Fully equipped kitchen and bathroom. *[🐾]*

Dunoon (Argyll)

Lively resort reached by car ferry from Gourock. Cowal Highland Gathering held at end of August.

ASHGROVE GUEST HOUSE, WYNDHAM ROAD, INNELLAN, DUNOON PA23 7SH (Tel: 01369 830306; Fax: 01369 830776). Situated in the village of Innellan this guest house is ideal for an energetic or restful holiday with golf, tennis, bowls and fishing all nearby. Relax in the secluded gardens with outstanding views over the Firth of Clyde. *[🐾]*

ENMORE HOTEL, MARINE PARADE, DUNOON PA23 8HH (01369 702230; Fax: 01369 702148). Small luxury Hotel with well-tended garden, situated overlooking the beautiful Firth of Clyde. Own shingle beach. Promenade and superb walking in the hills and forests within five minutes' drive. Owners have retriever and standard poodle. STB 4 Crowns Highly Commended. [pw! Pets £3.95 per night.]

Duns (Berwickshire)

Picturesque Borders town with nearby ancient fort, castle, and Covenanters stone to commemorate the army's encampment here in 1639. Excellent touring centre. Berwick-upon-Tweed 13 miles.

BARNIKEN HOUSE HOTEL, MURRAY STREET, DUNS TD11 3DE (01361 882466). Dogs most welcome, colour TV and tea/coffee facilities in all rooms. Luxurious bar, sun lounge, large garden and car park. Central heating. Near spectacular scenery and ideal for walks for dogs. 2 Crowns Commended. [🐾]

Easdale Island (Argyll)

Take the A816 from Oban towards Lochgilphead for 16 miles, turn west at Kilninver and cross the Clachan Bridge – 'the bridge over the Atlantic' – to Ellenan Ellenanbeich – Easdale, then by passenger-ferry to car-free Easdale Island in the Firth of Lorn.

41 EASDALE ISLAND, BY OBAN PA34 4TB. Terraced cottage with harbour views, sleeps 2. Double bedroom, all-electric kitchen, lounge, bathroom, front porch/sun lounge, rear garden. Bed linen provided. Leave your car (and troubles!) on the mainland; ferry details supplied. Open all year. £100–£220 per week, including electricity. Contact MRS R. A. SAMPSON, 22 BUXTON LANE, CATERHAM, SURREY CR3 5HD (01883 341534). [🐾]

Fort William (Inverness-shire)

Small town at foot of Ben Nevis, ideal base for climbers and hillwalkers. West Highland Museum, Scottish crafts.

WELCOME COTTAGE HOLIDAYS. Hundreds of properties in wonderful locations at welcoming low prices. Pets, linen and fuel mostly included. For FREE colour brochure telephone 01756 702213.

MRS M. MATHESON, THISTLE COTTAGE, TORLUNDY, FORT WILLIAM (01397 702428). Central for touring Highlands; 3½ miles Fort William, 2 miles Nevis Range. One double and one family bedroom. Large parking area. B&B from £11.00 per night, reductions for children.

LINNHE CARAVAN PARK, DEPT PW, CORPACH, FORT WILLIAM PH33 7NL (01397 772376). One of the best and most beautiful lochside parks in Scotland. Thistle Award caravans for hire. Graded "Excellent". Private beach, free fishing. Prices from £160; Breaks from £50. [pw! Pets £1 per night, £5 weekly.]

Grantown-on-Spey (Inverness-shire)

Popular ski resort and market town. Excellent trout and salmon fishing in Spey and Dulnain rivers.

MR AND MRS J. R. TAYLOR, MILTON OF CROMDALE, GRANTOWN-ON-SPEY, MORAYSHIRE PH26 3PH (01479 872415). Fully modernised Cottage with large garden and views of River Spey and Cromdale Hills. Golf, tennis and trekking within easy reach. Fully equipped except linen. Two double bedrooms. Shower, refrigerator, electric cooker, colour television. Car desirable. Children and pets welcome. Available Easter to October. [🐾]

Haddington (East Lothian)

Historic town on River Tyne 16 miles east of Edinburgh. Birthplace of John Knox, 1505. Renovated Church of St Mary, 14c–15c; St Martin's Church, AM.

THE MONKS' MUIR, HADDINGTON EH41 3SB (Tel and Fax: 01620 860340). Secluded and tranquil amidst beautiful countryside, only 25 minutes from Edinburgh. Tourers, tents and luxury hire caravans. Award winning, lovely facilities, totally "green," very friendly. Open all year. √ √ √ √ √ EXCELLENT. [🐾]

Innerleithen (Peeblesshire)

An old woollen-manufacturing town set in beautiful Borders countryside. Peebles 6 miles.

MRS JENNIFER CAIRD, TRAQUAIR BANK, INNERLEITHEN EH44 6PS (01896 830425). Stone House with rambling garden, overlooks Tweed. Walking, fishing, riding. Help on farm. Edinburgh ¾ hour. Animals welcome. Bed and Breakfast; Evening Meals by arrangement. STB LISTED COMMENDED. [🐾]

Invergordon (Ross-shire)

On north shore of Cromarty Firth, 11 miles from Dingwall.

KINCRAIG HOUSE HOTEL, INVERGORDON IV18 0LF (01349 852587; Fax: 01349 852193). Country house hotel in its own grounds with 18 bedrooms all en suite with tea/coffee makers, telephone and TV. A la carte dining, cocktail bar. Resident proprietors Sandra and Harry Dixon.

John O'Groats (Caithness)

Mainland Britain's most northerly village, named after founder of ferry service to Orkney in 1496, Jan de Groot. Two miles west of Duncansby.

CELTIC FIRS, SCARFSKERRY, THURSO KW14 8XW (01847 851 616). Secluded Bed and Breakfast accommodation in one acre grounds. Shop and Tea Room. John O'Groats eight miles. All rooms with TV/Video. All pets most welcome. [🐾]

Kingscross (Isle of Arran)

Located near east coast of Island, at end of Lamlash Bay. Kingscross Point is site of Viking burial ground.

JEAN S. PATERSON, WHITEFIELD FARM, KINGSCROSS, ISLE OF ARRAN KA27 8RB (01770 700291). This small south-facing farm has beautiful sea views overlooking Holy Isle and Firth of Clyde. Three properties, each sleeping two, adjoin main farmhouse. All well equipped and with separate gardens. Excellent local walking. Further details on request. [🐾]

Kinross (Kinross-shire)

Town and resort on west side of Loch Leven, nine miles north of Dunfermline. Angling on Loch Leven. Formal gardens at Kinross House.

THE GREEN HOTEL, 2 THE MUIRS, KINROSS KY13 7AS (01577 863467; Fax: 01577 863180). Independently owned hotel with well-appointed bedrooms and family suites. Restaurant, bar meals. Leisure facilities include indoor pool, golf courses, tennis and fishing. M90 five minutes.

Langholm (Dumfriesshire)

Small mill town at the junction of 3 rivers. Common Riding held in July.

THE ESKDALE HOTEL, LANGHOLM DG13 0JH (Tel & Fax: 013873 80357). Former Coaching Inn. All rooms with central heating, colour TV, radio. En-suite available. Licensed. Two bars. Restaurant. Games room. Golf, shooting, fishing. AA 2 STAR. 3 Crowns Commended. [🐕]

Lauder (Berwickshire)

Historic small town 9 miles north of Melrose. Nearby are Thirlestane Castle and Border Country Life Museum.

THE CARFRAEMILL HOTEL, BY LAUDER TD2 6RA (01578 750200; Fax: 01578 750640). Experience the freedom of the beautiful Scottish Borders in this friendly hotel, situated in the heart of the countryside, yet only 35 minutes from Edinburgh. From £40–£50 per night for a double room. Bargain Breaks. Delicious food. Well-behaved pets welcome.

Lochearnhead (Perthshire)

Popular little touring centre on wooded Loch Earn, dominated by Ben Vorlich (3,244 ft). EDINBURGH 65 miles, Glasgow 50, Aberfeldy 30, Crieff 19, Crianlarich 16, Callander 14.

CLACHAN COTTAGE HOTEL, LOCHSIDE, LOCHEARNHEAD FK19 8PU (01567 830247; Fax: 01567 830300). Ideal holiday venue for pets and their owners. Spectacular Highland scenery, walking, fishing, watersports. Open fires, wonderful food. Three Day, Golf and Off-Season Breaks. [🐕]

MR ANGUS CAMERON, LOCHEARNHEAD HOTEL, LOCHEARNHEAD FK19 8PU (01567 830229). Small family-run hotel (3 Crowns Commended), restaurant and self-catering chalets (4 Crowns Highly Commended) at the west end of Loch Earn with lovely views across the loch. Excellent golf and touring centre with water ski-ing, sailing and windsurfing on our doorstep. Ample hill walking. AA One Star. [🐕]

Loch Goil (Argyll)

Peaceful loch running from Lochgoilhead to Loch Long.

Five self catering Chalets on the shores of Loch Goil in the heart of Argyll Forest Park. Fully equipped except linen. Colour TV, fitted kitchen, carpeted. Pets welcome. Open all year. DARROCH MHOR, CARRICK CASTLE, LOCH GOIL PA24 8AF (01301 703249/703432).

Lochgoilhead (Argyll)

Village at head of Loch Goil in Argyll.

MRS ROSEMARY DOLAN, THE SHOREHOUSE INN, LOCHGOILHEAD PA24 8AJ (01301 703 340). The Shorehouse Inn has seven letting rooms, central heating and double glazing. There is a bar, lounge and licensed restaurant. Local amenities include water sports, fishing, tennis, bowls, golf, swimming pool; good area for walking. Rates from £13.50 B&B. Well trained dogs welcome.

Loch Lomond (Dunbartonshire)

Largest loch in Scotland – 23 miles long, up to 5 miles wide, and 630 ft at deepest point – with 30 islands. Pleasure boats and paddle steamer offer rides. Surrounded by beautiful woodland areas.

MRS SALLY MACDONELL, MARDELLA FARMHOUSE, OLD SCHOOL ROAD, GARTOCHARN, LOCH LOMOND, DUNBARTONSHIRE G83 8SD (01389 830428). Set on a quiet country lane, surrounded by fields. Friendly and comfortable, where the kettle's always boiling. AA QQQQ, RAC Listed, AA "Landlady of the Year" 1995 Finalist. *[🐾]*

Loch Maree (Ross-shire)

Narrow, very deep loch running from Kinlochewe to near Poolewe in dramatic and unspoiled countryside.

THE SHEILING. Secluded Bungalow in wooded grounds, amidst spectacular scenery. Sleeps 5/6, with coal fire in lounge; equipped to high standard. All pets are welcome. Terms from £140 to £295; electricity by coin meter. APPLY: MR & MRS A. ALLAN, TORGUISH, DAVIOT, INVERNESS IV1 2XQ (01463 772208; Fax: 01463 772308). *[🐾]*

Lockerbie (Dumfriesshire)

Annandale town noted as the scene of a battle in 1593 which ended one of the last great Border feuds. This and the surrounding area comprised the lands of Robert Bruce. Ecclefechan six miles south was the birthplace of Thomas Carlyle. Gretna 15 miles.

LOCKERBIE MANOR COUNTRY HOTEL, LOCKERBIE DG11 2RG (01576 202610). Splendid Georgian mansion house set in 78 acres of beautiful grounds. Ideal base for exploring countryside. Single, twin, double and family rooms, all en suite, and equipped with colour TV, tea-making etc. *[🐾]*

Longformacus (Berwickshire)

Village on Dye Water 6 miles west of Duns.

RATHBURNE, LONGFORMACUS TD11 3PG (0191 268 0788) Well-equipped self catering cottages in beautiful secluded setting. Large enclosed gardens. Lovely area for wildlife and walking. Pets welcome. *[Pets £5 per week.]*

Melrose (Roxburghshire)

Picturesque village ideal for touring scenic Borders country. Famous for its medieval abbey. Edinburgh 37 miles, Galashiels 5.

Your pets are welcomed as part of the family at an especially attractive selection of holiday cottages all over Scotland. Please write or phone for our 30-page colour brochure. ECOSSE UNIQUE LTD, THORNCROFT, LILLIESLEAF, MELROSE, ROXBURGHSHIRE TD6 9JD (01835 870779; Fax: 01835 870417). *[🐾 or £6 p.n.]*

Moffat (Dumfriesshire)

At head of lovely Annandale, grand mountain scenery. Good centre for rambling, climbing, angling and golf. The 'Devil's Beef Tub' is 5 miles N. EDINBURGH 52 miles, Peebles 33, Dumfries 21, Beattock 2.

BUCCLEUCH ARMS HOTEL, MOFFAT DG10 9ET (01683 220003; Fax: 01683 221291). Renowned for its excellent food, this elegant Georgian hotel has welcomed man and beast for over 230 years. All rooms en-suite with central heating etc. B&B £29 per person. Taste of Scotland. 3 Crowns Commended. Awarded "Best Eating-out Place in Area" 1994. *[🐾]*

Nethybridge (Inverness-shire)

Popular Strathspey resort on River Nethy with extensive Abernethy Forest to the south. Impressive mountain scenery. Grantown-on-Spey 5 miles N.

MRS M. FRASER, 36 LYNSTOCK CRESCENT, NETHYBRIDGE, INVERNESS-SHIRE PH25 3DX (01479 821312). Modern Cottages set in an idyllic spot in Speyside. Fully equipped for 4–8 persons. Car essential. Children and pets welcome. Aviemore 12 miles. STB 4 Crowns De Luxe.

NETHYBRIDGE, STRATHSPEY. Choice of modern cottages or converted smithy. Linen and visitor laundry included. Central heating included in winter. Good walking and touring area. STB 4 Crowns Highly Commended. Write or phone for brochure. MR AND MRS P. W. PATRICK, CHAPELTON PLACE, FORRES, MORAY IV35 0NL (01309 672505). [One dog free, thereafter £10 per week.]

Newcastleton (Roxburghshire)

Borders town on Liddel Water, 17 miles south of Hawick. Newcastleton Forest to east forms part of Border Forest Park.

PAMELA COPELAND, BAILEY MILL, BAILEY, NEWCASTLETON TD9 0TR (01697 748617). Enjoy Northern hospitality in Courtyard Apartments. Tranquil walks through surrounding forests and country lanes. Sauna, solarium, gym, toning table, and games rooms; baby-sitting, laundry and meal services.

Oban (Argyll)

Popular Highland resort and port, yachting centre; ferry services to Inner and Outer Hebrides. Sandy bathing beach at Ganavan Bay. McCaig's Tower above town in Colosseum replica built in 1890s.

J. AND F. TURNBULL, LAG-NA-KEIL CHALETS, LERAGS, BY OBAN PA34 4SE (01631 562746). One, two or three bedroomed Bungalows or Chalets; fully equipped including linen, colour TV. Free fishing; boat hire. Deer stalking by arrangement. Pets welcome. Up to 4 Crowns Commended.

WELCOME COTTAGE HOLIDAYS. Hundreds of properties in wonderful locations at welcoming low prices. Pets, linen and fuel mostly included. For FREE colour brochure telephone 01756 702213.

Fully equipped Scandinavian chalets in breathtaking scenery near Oban. Chalets sleep 4–7, are widely spaced and close to Loch Tralaig. Car parking. From £190 per week per chalet. Available March to October. APPLY – GILL AND ANDREW STEVENS, ELERAIG HIGHLAND CHALETS, KILNINVER, BY OBAN PA34 4UX (01852 200225). [🐕]

MR HENRY P. WOODMAN, COLOGIN HOMES LTD, LERAGS, BY OBAN PA34 4SE (01631 564501); Fax: 01631 566925). Modern centrally heated timber bungalows, sleep 2–6, all conveniences. Situated on farm, wildlife abundant. Games room, licensed bar with all-day bar meals. Cycle hire, fishing. Live entertainment. [🐕pw!]

D. R. KILPATRICK, KILNINVER, BY OBAN PA34 4UT (01852 316272). Five self-catering houses on coastal estate near Oban. Sleep 4–8. All fully equipped; electricity, newspapers, trout fishing included in rental. From £220 including VAT. 4 Crowns. [🐕pw!]

Onich (Inverness-shire)

On shores of Loch Linnhe, near entrance to Loch Leven. Good boating, fishing. Fort William 10 miles N.E.

INCHREE CHALETS, ONICH, FORT WILLIAM PH33 6SD (01855 821287). Comfortable chalets sleeping up to 6; all facilities. Restaurant and lounge bar adjacent. Forest walks from site. Midway between Ben Nevis and Glencoe. Discount for couples. [🐕]

THE LODGE ON THE LOCH, CREAG DHU, ONICH, BY FORT WILLIAM PH33 6RY (0185 582 1582; Fax: 0185 582 1463). Enjoying one of the finest panoramas in Scotland, a spell-binding blend of gentle elegance and a delightful, informal atmosphere. Taste of Scotland cuisine.

MRS N. McKAY, "GLENDEVIN", INCHREE, ONICH PH33 6SE (01855 821 330). Bed and Breakfast accommodation, in a quiet location 300 metres from main A82 between Fort William and Glencoe. Enjoy forest walks. TV lounge. Private parking. Non-smoking. 2 Crowns Commended. Bed and Breakfast £12.50–£18; Dinner (optional) £9/£10.

CREAG MHOR HOTEL, ONICH, BY GLENCOE, FORT WILLIAM PH33 6RY (Tel: 01855 821379; Fax: 01855 821579). Enjoy our famed Highland hospitality in Hotel with en-suite rooms (phones, Sky TV), cheery bar, fine home cooking; Bed and Breakfast from £25 per person. Ideal for a host of outdoor activities. [Pets £3.]

MRS K. A. McCALLUM, TIGH-A-RIGH GUEST HOUSE, ONICH, FORT WILLIAM PH33 6SE (01855 281255). Well-equipped, comfortable accommodation in licensed Guest House. Ideal touring centre. Pets and children welcome. Open all year. Bed, Breakfast and Dinner reasonable terms. En suite rooms available. [🐕]

MRS J. MACLEAN, FORESTERS BUNGALOW, INCHREE, ONICH, FORT WILLIAM PH33 6SE (01855 821285). Quarter-mile from A82, quiet, peaceful; perfect for touring North-West Highlands; 9 miles Fort William. Good home cooking. One family, two twin rooms. Parking. Children, dogs welcome. D, B & B from £20; B & B from £13. Weekly reductions.

Peebles (Peeblesshire)

Town on River Tweed (noted for salmon). Renowned for knitwear and tweeds. Cross Kirk ruin dates from 13th c.

GLENRATH HOLIDAY HOMES. Country cottages and farmhouses offering the highest standards of comfort. Three peaceful locations, all within 10 miles of Peebles. Ideal for children; pets welcome under control. Brochure with full details from MRS J. CAMPBELL, GLENRATH FARM, KIRKTON MANOR, PEEBLES EH45 9JW (01721 740265; Fax: 01968 676957).

Pitlochry (Perthshire)

Popular resort on River Tummel in beautiful Perthshire Highlands. Excellent golf, loch and river fishing. Famous for summer Festival Theatre; distillery, Highland Games.

THE MOULIN HOTEL, PITLOCHRY, PERTHSHIRE PH16 5EW (01796 472196). 17th Century Inn extended to the present 16 en suite bedroomed Hotel overlooking the village square. This hotel offers real hospitality in its restaurant and two bars.

KILLIECRANKIE HOTEL, KILLIECRANKIE, BY PITLOCHRY PH16 5LG (01796 473220; Fax: 01796 472451). Charming small Hotel set in 4 acres. Wonderful views. Superb food, high standard of comfort. Open Christmas and New Year. 4 Crowns Commended. AA 2 Star Rosette. [🐕 pw!]

JACKY & MALCOLM CATTERALL, "TULLOCH", ENOCHDHU, BY KIRKMICHAEL, STRATHARDLE PH10 7PW (01250 881404). STB Approved. Former farmhouse offers comfortable accommodation and good food. One family room with washbasin, one twin with washbasin; one en suite double room. All have tea/coffee facilities and face open country to mountains beyond. Peace and quiet guaranteed. Haven for wildlife and dogs. B&B £14 to £16; optional Dinner £8. [pw! 🐕]

MRS BARBARA M. BRIGHT, CRAIG DUBH COTTAGE, MANSE ROAD, MOULIN, PITLOCHRY PH16 5EP (01796 472058). Pets and guests are welcomed to our family home in a rural setting, one mile from Pitlochry. B&B accommodation, one twin en suite, one double, two singles. All tea/coffee, electric blankets. £13.50/£14.50. [🐕]

Port William (Wigtownshire)

Small resort with quay, on east shore of Luce Bay, seven miles south-west of Wigtown.

3 Crown Commended self-catering cottage opposite sea. Sleeps 6. 400 yards from shops. Post Office and pubs with restaurants. Touring, fishing, golf, walking. £120 weekly, £100 only out of season or £20 per night. Brochure from: MRS WRIGHT, SHORE COTTAGE, 49 SOUTH STREET, PORT WILLIAM, NEWTON STEWART, WIGTOWNSHIRE DG8 9SH (Tel & Fax: 01988 700831). [🐕]

Rockcliffe (Kirkcudbrightshire)

Quiet resort on wooded Rough Firth; sandy and rocky bays. Bird sanctuary on Rough Island (N.T. Scot.). Dumfries 20 miles.

TORBAY GUEST HOUSE, TORBAY FARMHOUSE, ROCKCLIFFE, BY DALBEATTIE DG5 4QE (01556 630403). Our Galloway farmhouse stands in beautiful gardens overlooking the sea. Imaginative cooking and baking using our garden produce and tastefully appointed en suite rooms. Well-behaved dogs welcome. STB 3 Crowns DE LUXE. B&B & EM from £28; weekly terms. [Pets £1 per night.]

BARON'S CRAIG HOTEL, ROCKCLIFFE, BY DALBEATTIE, KIRKCUDBRIGHTSHIRE DG5 4QF (01556 630 225). This 19th-century structure stands in two acres of wooded country overlooking the expanse of the Solway Firth. 22 en suite bedrooms with full heating. Tempting and interesting menus complemented with selected wines from the wine list. [🐕]

Roy Bridge (Inverness-shire)

Located in Glen Spean at foot of Glen Roy in Lochaber, 3 miles east of Spean Bridge.

STRONLOSSIT HOTEL, ROY BRIDGE PH31 4AG (01397 712253). Quiet Village Hotel which has nine fully appointed bedrooms with en suite facilities. Lounge bar with log fire, meals service. Excellent food. Ideal location for touring.

Skipness (Argyll)

Picturesque coastal haven on Mull of Kintyre, overlooking Kilbrannan Sound and Isle of Arran.

Peaceful, unspoiled West Highland estate. Traditional cottages, well equipped including TV, dinghy (not winter) and open fires. Sleep 4–10. Children and pets welcome. Walks, pony trekking, golf nearby. APPLY SOPHIE JAMES, SKIPNESS CASTLE, BY TARBERT PA29 6XU (01880 760207; Fax: 01880 760208). [🐕]

Skirling (Lanarkshire)

Borders village 2 miles east of Biggar.

MRS MARION McINTYRE, FOREST EDGE, MUIRBURN FARM, SKIRLING, Near BIGGAR ML12 6HL (01899 860284). Set half a mile from road in beautiful surroundings. Dog walking in adjacent forest. Good home cooking. Lounge with log fire. Ample parking. Convenient for Glasgow and Edinburgh. [🐕]

Spean Bridge (Inverness-shire)

At western end of Glen Spean amidst grand mountain scenery. Bridge built by Telford, Commando memorial nearby. Fort William 10 miles S.W.

MRS M. H. CAIRNS, INVERGLOY HOUSE, SPEAN BRIDGE PH34 4DY (01397 712681). Two spacious 5-berth luxury caravans, highest standard (fridge, shower). 50 acre wooded estate, beautifully secluded overlooking Loch Lochy, beach, fishing, rowing boats, bird watching, lovely walks. Free gas and electricity. Discounts for two occupancy and two-week bookings. Controlled dog welcome. £165–£235 per week. Fort William & Lochaber Tourist Board, British Graded Holiday Parks inspected. SAE for details [🐕]

Staffin (Isle of Skye)

Crofting and fishing town on rocky coast around Staffin Bay. Reached by narrow road crossing Stenscholl River.

C. M. BOOTH, GLENVIEW INN & RESTAURANT, CULNACNOC, STAFFIN IV51 9JH (0147062 248). Traditional island house, ideally situated for exploring north east Skye. Comfortable en suite bedrooms. Restaurant renowned for traditional seafood, ethnic and vegetarian specialities. Dogs most welcome. 3 Crowns Commended. [🐕]

Stanley (Perthshire)

Pretty village on River Tay 8 miles south-east of Dunkeld and 6 miles north of Perth.

MRS A. GUTHRIE, NEWMILL FARM, STANLEY PH1 4QD (01738 828281). On A9, six miles north of Perth. Lounge, sitting room. Twin, double, family rooms, most en suite. Bed and Breakfast from £15. Evening meal on request. Reductions for children. Ideal for touring, fishing, golf. 3 Crowns Commended.

St Andrews (Fife)

Home of golf – new British Golf Museum has memorabilia dating back to the origins of the game. Remains of castle and cathedral. Sealife Centre and beach Leisure Centre. Excellent sands. Ideal base for exploring the picturesque East Neuk of Fife.

MRS M. MANSELL, EDENSIDE HOUSE, EDENSIDE, ST ANDREWS KY16 9SQ (Tel: 01334 838108 or Fax: 01334 838493). Waterfront location. St Andrews only 2½ miles. Listed pre-1775 building. Non-smoking, well appointed double/twin en suite rooms. Some ground floor. Colour TV's, beverage trays. Extensive breakfast menu. Ample private parking. Golf a speciality. Adjacent bird sanctuary, stables. 2 Crowns Commended. AA QQQQ Selected. [🐕pw!]

MRS A. WEDDERBURN, MOUNTQUHANIE HOLIDAY HOMES, MOUNTQUHANIE, CUPAR KY15 4QJ (Tel: 01382 330 252; Fax: 01382 330 480). Good quality self-catering houses, flats or cottages in tranquil, rural countryside. Central heating, modern kitchens, fitted carpets, colour TV, telephone. STB 4 Crowns Commended to 5 Crowns De Luxe. *[🐾]*

Stirling (Stirlingshire)

Historic town dominated by castle standing on 250 ft high rock; nearby are Wallace Monument and Bannockburn Memorial. Excellent road and rail links to Glasgow and Edinburgh.

MRS A. AGNEW, BRAES OF BOQUHAPPLE FARM, THORNHILL, NR STIRLING FK8 3QH (01786 850484). This farm is situated on B822 between Thornhill and Callander. It has splendid panoramic views. There are two en suite family rooms. Evening Meals provided by arrangement. Grazing and stabling available for horses, and all well-behaved pets are welcome.

Strathyre (Perthshire)

Village set in middle of Strathyre Forest, just off A84 north of Callander. Information centre and picnic area to south of village.

ARDOCH LODGE, STRATHYRE (01877 384666). Log cabins and cottage in wonderful mountain scenery. Comfortably furnished and fully equipped. Country house accommodation also available. Phone for brochure. Open all year. Pets most welcome. 3 Crowns Highly Commended. *[🐾]*

Strontian (Argyll)

Beautifully situated at head of Loch Sunart which stretches 20 miles to the sea. In the glen to the north are deserted lead mines. Fort William (ferry) 23 miles.

SEAVIEW GRAZINGS HOLIDAYS, STRONTIAN PH36 4HZ (01967 402191). Quality self catering in Scandinavian log houses overlooking Loch Sunart. Sleep up to 8. TV, washer/dryer etc. Pubs/hotels 5 minutes. Pets welcome. Ideal touring centre. Send for colour brochure. *[🐾]*

Tain (Ross-shire)

Small town in Ross and Cromarty district on south shore of Dornoch Firth. 10 miles north-east of Invergordon.

MRS SHIRLEY ROSS, DUNBIUS, MORANGIE ROAD, TAIN IV19 1PY (01862 893010). Comfortable bedrooms, all en-suite, colour TV, tea/coffee. Off road parking. Good golfing area, horse riding, forest walks. Prices from £16 per person. Tourist Board registered. *[🐾]*

West Linton (Peeblesshire)

Village on east side of Pentland Hills, 7 miles south-west of Penicuik. Edinburgh 18 miles.

MRS C. M. KILPATRICK, SLIPPERFIELD HOUSE, WEST LINTON EH46 7AA (Tel/Fax: 01968 660401). Two excellently equipped converted cottages set in 100 acres of lochs and woodlands. America Cottage sleeps 6, Loch Cottage sleeps 4. Car essential. *[🐾]*

KENNELS AND CATTERIES

Are you having difficulty locating a boarding kennel/cattery in an area other than your own? Have you words of praise (or criticism) for a kennel/cattery you have used? Perhaps you're even thinking of opening an Animal Boarding Establishment? The Boarding Kennels Advisory Bureau is a free service for the general public and monitors progress within the industry. Please write with your enquiry (enclosing SAE) or comments: The Boarding Kennels Advisory Bureau, c/o Blue Grass Animal Hotel, Little Leigh, Near Northwich, Cheshire CW8 4RJ. Tel: 01606 891303.

CORNWALL

Buckinghamshire
BEAUMONT KENNELS AND CAT'S INN, UPHILL FARM, THE HALE, WENDOVER, NEAR AYLESBURY HP22 6QR
(Tel: 01296 623344; Fax: 01296 624333)

Dogs and cats; solid brick and tile kennels; individual cat houses with large runs. All animals must have full inoculations including Intrac for dogs. Extensive exercise facilities on large country estate. Established quarter of a century. Full time residential staff to look after small number of "guests".

Cambridgeshire
FIELDS VIEW KENNELS AND CATTERY, FENSTANTON ROAD, HILTON, HUNTINGDON PE18 9JA
(Tel: 01480 830215)

Dogs and Cats; individual kennels and outside runs for both; cats also have beautiful garden and pond feature to look at; dogs walked individually daily; all inoculations must be up to date; pampered pets section and grooming parlour for all breeds – Member of Pet Groomers Association; collection and delivery service available; pets with special diets catered for. Run by professionally qualified staff.

Devon
THREE ACRE BOARDING KENNELS, THE MOUNT, TOTNES TQ9 5ES
(Tel: 01803 862127)

Dogs, cats and other small domestic pets; dogs have own individual kennels and runs, heated; cats have individual pens in centrally heated catteries. Up-to-date inoculations required. Special needs and diets catered for e.g. diabetics. Veterinary attention daily if necessary. Open for inspection 7 days a week 9 am–6 pm.

Essex
SOUTH VIEW CENTRE, MARSH FOOT ROAD, CHADWELL ST MARY RM16 4LU
(Tel: 01375 842698)

Send your pet on holiday to be cared for by our trained staff, tempted by our à la carte menu, and entertained by daily country walks. Reservations taken all year, with central heating for the colder months. Inoculations required. Open for viewing. Member of BARK (Bureau of Approved Residential Kennels).

KAHN-ROHAN KENNELS, TUDWICK ROAD, LITTLE TOTHAM, NEAR MALDON CM9 8LR
(Tel: 01621 815344)

Dogs and cats; both have large sleeping quarters and individual outside runs. Full up-to-date vaccination certificates required. Animal rescue unit.

ROSE COTTAGE CATTERY, COLLIER ROW ROAD, ROMFORD RM5 2BH
(Tel: 0181-590 2278)

Cats only; brick-built rooms. Must be fully vaccinated. Single or family rooms available. Pleasant country site close to London. Special diets available. F.A.B. Member.

Gloucestershire
AVONLEY KENNELS AND CATTERY, MOOREND ROAD, ELDERSFIELD GL19 4NS
(Tel: 01452 840247)

Dogs and Cats; large individual kennels with attached concrete runs for dogs and large pens for cats, both heated in winter; all animals must have up-to-date inoculations and boosters; delivery and collection service available; inspection welcome; problem and temperamental dogs a speciality; full grooming service available.

Kent
THE ANIMAL INN, DOVER ROAD, RINGWOULD, NEAR DEAL CT14 8HH
(Tel: 01304 373597; Fax: 01304 380305)

Dogs (110), Cats (40); daily vet visit as also quarantine. Dogs in individual kennels, all with own covered runs; cats in individual pens; kennels and pens have optional heating. Vaccination cards with proof of vaccination within previous 12 months must be produced. Kennels approx 5 minutes from Dover Docks. Open all year 8 am–6 pm; closed Bank Holidays and Sunday afternoons.

Lancashire
MERESANDS KENNELS AND CATTERY MERESANDS WOOD, HOLMESWOOD ROAD, RUFFORD L40 1TG
(Tel/Fax: 01704 822779)

Set in 5 acres natural woodland, no traffic fumes or neighbours. Cleanliness second to none. Dogs and cats housed in large heated individual sleeping areas with own attached runs. Cats have natural log scratching post and sunbathing balcony; dogs are lead walked and groomed daily. Access to runs 7 am to 11 pm. Family-run and caring; lots of "hands on" attention.

London
CHINGFORD BOARDING KENNELS AND CATTERY 160 CHINGFORD MOUNT ROAD, CHINGFORD E4 9BS
(Tel: 0181-529 0979; Fax: 0181-529 2563)

Dogs, cats, birds, rabbits and other children's pets. Individual kennels; dogs walked in runs individually; cats have own runs. Dogs and cats must be fully vaccinated. Collection and delivery arranged; exports world-wide; quarantine for cats and dogs. Vets' surgery on site.

Nottinghamshire
HILLBANKS KENNELS AND CATTERY, COMMONSIDE, SELSTON NG16 6FL
(Tel: 01773 860586)

Dogs, cats and most other pets (not tarantulas!) boarded in small, personally managed establishment. Large kennels with covered runs; dogs played with individually on extending leads in our own fields/gardens. Cats have 8' indoor cubicles. Comfortable beds provided, or bring pets' own. Vet on call. Vaccination boosters required at least 28 days prior to arrival and within past 12 months. Elderly and convalescent pets welcome. Any diet can be matched – we try to feed as if at home. Heating and insurance included. Grooming available to highest standards. Emergency kennelling available. Daily rates.

West Midlands
KAMA KENNELS, SPRINGFIELD ROAD, WALMLEY, SUTTON COLDFIELD B76 2SL
(Tel: 0121-378 0911)

Dogs (50), cats (50); dogs in individual or family kennels, large exercise areas; cats in individual pens with heating when necessary; must have current inoculations – dogs against hard pad, distemper, hepatitis, leptospirosis, parvovirus, kennel cough; cats against flu and enteritis. Rabbits and guinea pigs also boarded. Open all year. Tattooist for National Dog Tattoo Register. PTIA Member. Inspection welcome.

HOLIDAYS WITH HORSES

For the horse-lover, there is a wide selection of accommodation available where horse and owner/rider can be put up at the same address – if not actually under the same roof! Such accommodation and any accompanying facilities are useful when in transit, when travelling to and from events and competitions and, of course, for holidays. The following few addresses are a first attempt by *PETS WELCOME!* to make descriptions and contact details of providers accessible to our readership and to a wider public. We hope that this Supplement will grow in time to offer fuller choice.

Some of the entries listed here also have a Display advert under their appropriate county heading in the main holiday accommodation section.

We would be grateful if readers who make enquiries and/or bookings from this Supplement would mention *PETS WEL-COME!*

Berkshire/Lambourn
MRS F. RUTHERFOORD
ALVESTOKE, SHEEPDROVE ROAD, LAMBOURN RG17 7XA
(Tel: 01488 71737)
Four acres grazing, one acre paddock with shelter; other divisible into half-acres via slip rails; lock-up, tack room; manège (grass) with things to jump; three stables; B&B or self-catering accommodation.

Cumbria/Ousby
THE FOX INN
OUSBY, PENRITH CA10 1QA
(Tel/Fax: 01768 881374)
17th century village inn at foot of Pennines; home-cooked food, real ales; B&B £15; camping also available; 6 clean block-built stables; superb area for walking and riding.

Devon/Aylesbeare
MRS H. BALE
GREAT HOUNDBEARE FARM, AYLESBEARE, EXETER EX5 2DB
(Tel: 01404 822771)
Secure stabling and grazing with hay, straw and shavings on arable farm only minutes from Exeter, M5 and coast; B&B or self catering cottage; games room and coarse fishing.

MRS JACOBINA LANGLEY
THE STABLES, HYDE CROOK, FRAMPTON, DORCHESTER DT2 9NW
(Tel: 01300 320075)
Comfortable equestrian property in 20 acres grounds close to bridleways; grazing and stabling available; en suite accommodation with TV lounge for owners.

MISS F. J. SOLLEY
WHATCOMBE HOUSE, LONG BREDY, DORCHESTER DT2 9HN
(Tel: 01308 482275)
Comfortable stabling and grazing; varied hacking in lovely countryside with copious bridleways; room to park lorry or trailer; close to sea and good local pubs; pets by arrangement.

MRS HOLMES
STOCKERLEY HOUSE, WOODSIDE, LANCHESTER DH8 7TQ
(Tel: 01207 502588)
Bring your four-legged friends on holiday too; direct access to off-road tracks for cyclists, horse riders and walkers; ideal for Dales and Scottish Borders; B&B accommodation in beautiful Derwent Valley.

JUDITH SHANKS
YOUNGWOODS FARM, WHITEHOUSE ROAD, PORCHFIELD, NEWPORT PO30 4LJ
(Tel/Fax: 01983 522170)
Stabling available on grassland farm set in open countryside. Four miles from Cowes, beaches within 15 minutes' drive. Accommodation for owners in 3 bedrooms; non-smokers welcome. Open all year.

THE OLD RECTORY
BELTON IN RUTLAND, OAKHAM LE15 9LE
(Tel: 01572 717279; Fax: 01572 717343)
Stabling and grazing; 20' × 40'' manège; members of BHS and Bridle Rides; 20 minutes from Burghley Horse Trials; excellent hunting box; B&B or self catering accommodation.

SUE EVANS
WILLOW FARM, THORPE FENDYKES, SKEGNESS PE24 4QH
(Tel: 01754 830316)
Horses/ponies taken for overnight stops; current vaccination certificates to be shown on arrival; outdoor manège; feed, hay, straw, shavings available; fenced paddock; B&B for owners.

MRS MAVIS OSTLER
TAYLOR BURN, NINEBANKS, HEXHAM NE47 8DE
(Tel: 01434 345343)
Large traditional stabling; excellent hill farm grazing with spring water, straw, feed; safe parking for horse transport; wonderful moorland rides; equine references available!

MRS BRANDON-LODGE
NORTH HILL FARM, CARDINGTON, CHURCH STRETTON SY6 7LL
(Tel: 01694 771532)
Farmhouse B&B in the Shropshire Hills; ideal walking and riding country; on Bridleway, good stop-off on Jack Mytton Way and Long Mynd; horses and dogs welcome.

Wiltshire/Coombe Bissett
MR A. SHERING
SWAYNES FIRS FARM, GRIMSDYKE, COOMBE BISSETT, SALISBURY SP5 5RF
(Tel: 01725 519240)
Small working farm with cattle, horses and poultry; access to bridleways and footpaths; ideal for ramblers and horse riders; en suite accommodation available; 7 miles from Salisbury; ample parking.

Clwyd/Ruthin
MARIE CARRINGTON-SYKES, PENTRE BACH, LLANDYRNOG, NEAR RUTHIN LL16 4LA
(Tel and Fax: 01824 790725)
DIY Horse and Pony Livery available in 18th century stable block adjacent to house. Set in 200 acres of peaceful countryside; accommodation for owners in spacious private/en suite bedrooms.

Dyfed/Boncath
MRS K. S. LEWIS
PENLANFEIGAN, BONCATH SA39 0JE
(Tel: 01239 841499)
Escorted riding, sand school, stabling and grazing, beach and mountain riding; B&B and mobile home in 20 acres and gardens; 10 minutes from Cardigan and coast.

Dyfed/Brynberian
GLAN YR AFON ISAF (MRS F. RUTHERFOORD)
ALVESTOKE FARM, SHEEPDROVE ROAD, LAMBOURN, BERKSHIRE RG16 7YU
(Tel: 01488 71737)
Self catering cottage at foot of Preseli Hills; one acre sheltered paddock adjoining; direct access to the moor from gate; superb walking/riding country; Cardigan 7 miles.

Powys/Builth Wells
MRS E. BALLY
LANE FARM, PAINSCASTLE, BUILTH WELLS LD2 3JS
(Tel: 01497 851605; Fax: 01497 851617)
Six large stables available, also grazing; ample parking for lorries etc; hunter trial course and UK chasers course on farm; accommodation in two self catering flats.

Kirkcudbrightshire/Dalbeattie
BAREND HOLIDAY VILLAGE
SANDYHILLS, DALBEATTIE DG5 4NU
(Tel: 01387 780663; Fax: 01387 780283)
BHS Approved riding centre with facilities for keeping horses at livery; instruction provided; cross-country course available; trekking centre offering rides through beautiful surrounding countryside.

Stirlingshire/Stirling
MRS A. AGNEW
BRAES OF BOQUHAPPLE FARM, THORNHILL, STIRLING FK8 3QH
(01786 850484)
Grazing and stabling available on farm situated between Thornhill and Callander; all well-behaved pets welcome; accommodation for owners in two en suite family rooms; splendid panoramic views.

Are you ready to take the place of her mum?

Leaving mum can be scary for a small puppy. But if you feed Beta Puppy at least the food's as good as mum's was. For details on the full Beta range call the Beta Petcare Advice Service on 0638 552266 or write to PO Box 53, Newmarket, Suffolk CB8 8QF.

BETA
petfoods
Food for Life

The Golden Bowl Supplement for Pet-Friendly Pubs

BETA
petfoods

When Beta Petfoods launched its search for Britain's warmest pet welcome, in the form of the Beta Petfoods Golden Bowl Awards Scheme, the response was staggering. Hundreds wrote nominating their pubs for a Golden Bowl award and the chance to be recognisd as kind-hearted publicans for their willingness to provide a bowl of water for their canine customers also.

The pick of the pet pubs (and hotels) have gone into this Supplement to enable owners travelling, holidaying or just walking their dogs to find a warm welcome for *everyone* in the party when they stop for refreshment. We only wish we had room to include more!

BETA PETFOODS has combined sound nutritional expertise with first class innovation to provide a range which has established itself over the last twenty years as a leading brand in complete dog foods, sold nationally through specialist outlets, pet shops, vets and country stores.

Particularly renowned for their life cycle feeding programme Beta provide all the necessary nutrients to help keep dogs healthy and fit throughout life. Understanding that every dog is different, Beta has created a range of foods suitable for the demands of all dogs whatever their age and lifestyle: *Beta Puppy* for the vital early growth stage; *Beta Junior* for young, growing dogs; *Beta Recipe* for active pets: *Beta Pet* for less active and older dogs; *Beta Field* for active, working dogs and *Beta Champion* for highly active and breeding dogs.

All manufactured to the highest quality providing excellent palatability and maximum enjoyment.

For further advice on what to feed your pet, please write to: **Spillers Beta Petcare Advice Service, Moulton Road, Kennett, near Newmarket, Suffolk CB8 8QU.**

The Golden Bowl Supplement
for Pet-Friendly Pubs

BERKSHIRE

THE GREYHOUND (known locally as 'The Dog')
The Walk, Eton Wick, Berkshire (01753 863925).

Dogs allowed throughout the pub.

Pet Regulars: Include Lady (GSD), at one o'clock sharp she howls for her hot dog; Trevor (Labrador/Retriever), who does nothing; Skipper (Jack Russell), the local postman's dog and Natasha (GSD) who simply enjoys the ambience.

THE QUEEN
Harts Lane, Burghclere, near Newbury, Berkshire (01635 278350).

Dogs allowed throughout the pub.

Pet Regulars: Sam (Border Terrier), makes solo visits to the pub to play with resident long-haired Dachshund Gypsy.

NOTE

A few abbreviations and 'pet' descriptions have been used in this section which deserve mention and, where necessary, explanation as follows: *GSD:* German Shepherd Dog. *. . . -cross:* a cross-breed where one breed appears identifiable. *57:* richly varied origin. You will also enounter *'mongrel'*, *'Bitsa'* and *'???!'* which are self-evident and generally affectionate.

THE SWAN
9 Mill Lane, Clewer, Windsor, Berkshire (01753 862069).

Dogs allowed throughout the pub.

Pet Regulars: Include Luke (Samoyed), enjoys a glass of Tiger beer.

THE TWO BREWERS
Park Street, Windsor, Berkshire (01753 855426).

Dogs allowed, public and saloon bars.

Pet Regulars: Missy and Worthey (Huskies), prefer to remain outside; Sam (Golden Retriever), will retrieve any food and eat it while owner is not looking; Bumble (Highland Terrier), better known as the Highland Hooverer.

BUCKINGHAMSHIRE

WHITE HORSE
Village Lane, Hedgerley, Buckinghamshire SL2 3UY (01753 643225).

Dogs allowed at tables on pub frontage, beer garden (on leads), public bar.

Pet Regulars: Digby (Labrador), the entertainer; Cooper (Boxer), tries hard to better himself – also drinks!

CAMBRIDGESHIRE

YE OLD WHITE HART
Main Street, Ufford, Peterborough (01780 740250).

Dogs allowed in non-food areas.

Pet Regulars: Henry and Robotham (Springer Spaniels), 'pub dog' duties include inspection of all customers and their dogs and, on occasion, seeing them home after last orders.

CHESHIRE

JACKSONS BOAT
Rifle Road, Sale, Cheshire (0161 973 3208).

Dogs allowed throughout with the exception of the dining area.

Pet Regulars: Bix (Labrador), will share pork scratchings with pub cat, chases beer garden squirrels on solo missions; hamburger scrounging a speciality.

CLEVELAND

TAP AND SPILE
27 Front Street, Framwellgate Moor, Durham DH1 5EE (0191 386 5451).

Dogs allowed throughout the pub.

Pet Regulars: These include Smutty (Labrador) who brings her own beer bowl and is definitely *not* a lager Lab – traditional brews only.

CORNWALL

THE WHITE HART
Chilsworthy, near Gunnislake, Cornwall (01822 832307).

Dogs allowed in non-food bar, car park tables, beer garden.

Pet Regulars: Joe (Terrier-cross), sleeps on back under bar stools; Max (Staffordshire-cross), lager drinker; Tatler (Cocker Spaniel), pork cracklings fan; Sheba (GSD), welcoming committee.

CUMBRIA

BRITANNIA INN
Elterwater, Ambleside, Cumbria (015394 37210).

Dogs allowed throughout (except dining area).

Pet Regulars: Bonnie (sheepdog/Retriever), beer-mat catching, scrounging, has own chair.

THE MORTAL MAN HOTEL
Troutbeck, Windermere, Cumbria LA23 1PL (015394 33193).

Dogs allowed throughout and in guest rooms.

Pet Regulars: Include James (Labrador) who will take dogs for walks if they are on a lead and Snip (Border Collie), makes solo visits.

STAG INN
Dufton, Appleby, Cumbria (017683 51608).

Dogs allowed in non-food bar, beer garden, village green plus B&B.

Pet Regulars: Bacchus (Newfoundland), enjoys a good sprawl; Kirk (Dachshund), carries out tour of inspection unaccompanied – but wearing lead; Kim (Weimaraner), best bitter drinker; Buster (Jack Russell), enjoys a quiet evening.

WATERMILL INN

School Lane, Ings, near Staveley, Kendal, Cumbria (01539 821309).

Dogs allowed in beer garden, Wrynose bottom bar.

Pet Regulars: Smudge (sheepdog); Gowan (Westie) and Scruffy (mongrel). All enjoy a range of crisps and snacks. Scruffy regularly drinks Theakstons XB. Pub dogs Misty (Beardie) and Thatcher (Lakeland Terrier).

DERBYSHIRE

DOG AND PARTRIDGE COUNTRY INN & MOTEL

Swinscoe, Ashbourne, Derbyshire (01335 343183).

Dogs allowed throughout, except restaurant.

Pet Regulars: Include Mitsy (57); Rusty (Cairn); Spider (Collie/GSD) and Rex (GSD).

RIFLE VOLUNTEER

Birchwood Lane, Somercotes, Derbyshire DE55 4ND (01773 602584).

Dogs allowed in non-food bar, car park tables, beer garden.

Pet Regulars: Flossy (Border Collie), bar stool inhabitant; Pepper (Border Collie), has made a study of beer mat aerodynamics; Tara (GSD), pub piggyback specialist.

WHITE HART

Station Road, West Hallam, Derbyshire DE7 6GW.

Dogs allowed in all non-food areas.

Pet Regulars: Ben and Oliver (Golden Retrievers), drinking halves of mixed; Sid (Greyhound), plays with cats.

DEVON

BRENDON HOUSE HOTEL

Brendon, Lynton, North Devon EX35 6PS (01598 741206).

Dogs very welcome and allowed in tea gardens, guest bedrooms.

Pet Regulars: Mutley (mongrel), cat chasing; Pie (Border Terrier), unusual 'yellow stripe', was once chased – by a sheep! Farthing (cat), 20 years old, self appointed cream tea receptionist. Years of practice have perfected dirty looks at visiting dogs.

THE BULLERS ARMS

Chagford, Newton Abbot, Devon (01647 432348).

Dogs allowed throughout pub, except dining room/kitchen.

Pet Regulars: Miffin & Sally (Cavalier King Charles Spaniels), celebrated Miffin's 14th birthday with a party at The Bullers.

CROWN AND SCEPTRE

2 Petitor Road, Torquay, Devon TQ1 4QA (01803 328290).

Dogs allowed in non-food bar, family room, lounge.

Pet Regulars: Samantha (Labrador), opens, consumes and returns empties when offered crisp packets; Toby & Rory (Irish Setters), general daftness; Buddy & Jessie (Collies), beer-mat frisbee experts; Cassie (Collie), scrounging.

THE DEVONSHIRE INN

Sticklepath, near Okehampton, Devon EX20 2NW (01837 840626).

Dogs allowed in non-food bar, car park, beer garden, family room, guest rooms.

Pet Regulars: Bess (Labrador), 'minds' owner; Annie (Shihtzu), snoring a speciality; Daisy (Collie), accompanies folk singers; Duke (GSD) and Ben (Collie-cross), general attention seeking.

THE JOURNEY'S END INN

Ringmore, near Kingsbridge, South Devon TQ7 4HL (01548 810205).

Dogs allowed throughout the pub.

Pet Regulars: Lager, Cider, Scrumpy and Whiskey (all Terriers) – a pint of real ale at lunchtime between them.

THE ROYAL OAK INN

Dunsford, near Exeter, Devon EX6 7DA (01647 252256).

Dogs allowed in non-food bars, beer garden, accommodation for guests with dogs.

Pet Regulars: Tom Thumb (Jack Russell), pub bouncer – doesn't throw people out, just bounces.

THE SEA TROUT INN

Staverton, near Totnes, Devon TQ9 6PA (01803 762274).

Dogs allowed in non-food bar, car park tables, beer garden, owners' rooms (but not on beds).

Pet Regulars: Billy (Labrador-cross), partial to drip trays; Curnow (Poodle), brings a blanket.

THE WHITE HART HOTEL

Moretonhampstead, Newton Abbot, Devon TQ13 8NF (01647 440406).

Dogs allowed throughout, except restaurant.

Pet Regulars: Poppie, Rosie (Standard Poodles) and Bobby (Collie).

ESSEX

THE OLD SHIP

Heybridge Basin, Heybridge, Maldon, Essex (01621 854150).

Dogs allowed throughout pub.

Pet Regulars: Toby (57), monopolising bar stools; Tag (Spaniel), nipping behind the bar for biscuits; Toto (57), nipping behind the bar to 'beat up' owners' Great Dane; Happy (terrier), drinking beer and looking miserable.

THE WINGED HORSE

Luncies Road, Vange, Basildon, Essex SS14 1SB (01268 552338).

Dogs allowed throughout pub.

Pet Regulars: Gina (Newfoundland), visits solo daily for a pub lunch – biscuits and a beer; Roxy (Bull Terrier), fond of making a complete mess with crisps and loves a glass of beer. There are 14 canine regulars in all, not including the pub dog Tinka.

THE WOODEN FENDER

Harwich Road, Ardleigh, Essex CO7 7PA (01206 230466).

Dogs allowed in non-food bar, car park tables, beer garden.

Pet Regulars: Holly (Labrador), part-time door stop and vacuum cleaner (paid in marrow-bones); Busty (Labrador), when not eating crisps, thinks/dreams of eating crisps.

GREATER LONDON

THE PHOENIX
28 Thames Street, Sunbury on Thames, Middlesex (01932 789163).

Dogs allowed in non-food bar, beer garden, family room.

Pet Regulars: Pepe (57), fire hog; Cromwell (King Charles), often accompanied by small, balled-up sock. Drinks Websters, once seen with a hangover. Fred (Labrador), would be a fire hog if Pepe wasn't always there first; Oliver (Standard Poodle), still a pup, pub visits are character-building!

THE TIDE END COTTAGE
Ferry Road, Teddington, Middlesex (0181 977 7762).

Dogs allowed throughout the pub.

Pet Regulars: Angus (Setter), "mine's a half of Guinness"; Dina (GSD), guide dog, beautiful, loyal and clever; Harry (Beagle), partial to sausages, a greeter and meeter; Lady (cross), likes a game of tug o' war with Angus.

HAMPSHIRE

THE CHEQUERS
Ridgeway Lane, Lower Pennington, Lymington (01590 673415).

Dogs allowed in non-food bar, outdoor barbecue area (away from food).

Pet Regulars: Otto (Hungarian Vizsla), eats beer-mats and paper napkins. Likes beer but not often indulged.

FLYING BULL
London Road Rake, near Petersfield, Hampshire GU33 7JB (01730 892285).

Dogs allowed throughout the pub.

Pet Regulars: Flippy (Labrador/Old English Sheepdog), partial to the biscuits served with coffee. Status as 'pub dog' questionable as will visit The Sun over the road for a packet of cheese snips.

THE VICTORY

High Street, Hamble-le-Rice, Southampton (01703 453105).

Dogs allowed throughout the pub.

Pet Regulars: Sefton (Labrador), his 'usual' chew bars are kept especially.

HERTFORDSHIRE

THE BLACK HORSE

Chorly Wood Common, Dog Kennel Lane, Rickmansworth, Hertfordshire (01923 282252).

Dogs very welcome and allowed throughout the pub.

Pet Regulars: Spritzy (mongrel), pub hooligan, former Battersea Dogs' Home resident.

THE FOX

496 Luton Road, Kinsbourne Green, near Harpenden, Hertfordshire (01582 713817).

Dogs allowed in non-food bar, car park tables, beer garden.

Pet Regulars: A tightly knit core of regulars which includes assorted Collies, German Shepherd Dogs and Retrievers. Much competition for dropped bar snacks.

THE ROBIN HOOD AND LITTLE JOHN

Rabley Heath, near Codicote, Hertfordshire (01438 812361).

Dogs allowed in non-food bar, car park tables, beer garden, pitch and putt.

Pet Regulars: Willow (Labrador), beer-mat catcher. The locals of the pub have close to 50 dogs between them, most of which visit from time to time. The team includes a two Labrador search squad dispatched by one regular's wife to indicate time's up. When they arrive he has five minutes' drinking up time before all three leave together.

NOTE

A few abbreviations and 'pet' descriptions have been used in this section which deserve mention and, where necessary, explanation as follows: **GSD:** German Shepherd Dog. **. . . -cross:** a cross-breed where one breed appears identifiable. **57:** richly varied origin. You will also enounter **'mongrel', 'Bitsa' and '???!'** which are self-evident and generally affectionate.

HUMBERSIDE

BARNES WALLIS INN

North Howden, Howden, North Humberside (01430 430639).

Dogs allowed throughout the pub.

Pet Regulars: A healthy cross-section of mongrels, Collies and Labradors. One of the most popular pastimes is giving the pub cat a bit of a run for his money.

BLACK SWAN

Asselby, Goole, North Humberside (01904 625236).

Dogs allowed in non-food bar.

Pet Regulars: A variety of canine customers.

KINGS HEAD INN

Barmby on the Marsh, North Humberside DN14 7HL (01757 638357).

Dogs allowed in non-food bar.

Pet Regulars: Many and varied!

ISLE OF WIGHT

THE CLARENDON HOTEL AND WIGHT MOUSE INN

Chale, Isle of Wight (01983 730431).

Dogs allowed in pub but not hotel diningroom.

Pet Regulars: Guy (mongrel), calls in for daily sausages. Known to escape from house to visit solo. Hotel dog is Gizmo (Spoodle – Toy Poodle-cross King Charles Spaniel), child entertainer.

KENT

KENTISH HORSE

Cow Lane, Mark Beech, Edenbridge, Kent (01342 850493).

Dogs allowed throughout.

Pet Regulars: Include Boozer (Greyhound), who enjoys a beer and Kylin (Shihtzu), socialising. Pub grounds also permanent residence to goats, sheep, lambs, a horse and geese.

THE OLD NEPTUNE

Marine Terrace, Whitstable, Kent CT5 1EJ (01227 272262).

Dogs allowed in non-food bar and beach frontage.

Pet Regulars: Josh (mongrel), solo visits, serves himself from pub water-bowl; Bear (GSD), insists on people throwing stones on beach to chase, will drop stones on feet as quick reminder; Trigger (mongrel), accompanied by toys; Poppy & Fred (mongrel and GSD), soft touch and dedicated vocalist – barks at anything that runs away!

PRINCE ALBERT

38 High Street, Broadstairs, Kent CT10 1LH (01843 861937).

Dogs allowed in non-food bar.

Pet Regulars: Buster (King Charles), a health freak who likes to nibble on raw carrots and any fresh veg; Suki (Jack Russell), Saturday-night roast beef sampler; Sally (Airedale), official rug; Bruno (Boxer), particularly fond of pepperami sausage.

THE SWANN INN

Little Chart, Kent TN27 0QB (01233 840702).

Dogs allowed – everywhere except restaurant.

Pet Regulars: Rambo (Leonbergers), knocks on the door and orders pork scratchings; Duster (Retriever), places his order – for crisps – with one soft bark for the landlady; Ben (GSD), big licks; Josh (Papillon), hind-legged dancer.

UNCLE TOM'S CABIN

Lavender Hill, Tonbridge, Kent (01628 483339).

Dogs allowed in non-food bar, beer garden.

Pet Regulars: Bob Minor (Lurcher); Tug (mongrel); Bitsy (mongrel); Tilly (Spaniel): 10pm is dog biscuit time!

LANCASHIRE

ABBEYLEE

Abbeyhills Road, Oldham, Lancashire (0161 678 8795).

Dogs allowed throughout.

Pet Regulars: Include Susie (Boxer), so fond of pork scratchings they are now used by her owners as a reward in the show ring.

MALT'N HOPS

50 Friday Street, Chorley, Lancashire PR6 0AH (01257 260967).

Dogs allowed throughout pub.

Pet Regulars: Freya (GSD), greets everyone by rolling over to allow tummy tickle; Abbie (GSD), under-seat sleeper; Brandy (Rhodesian Ridgeback), at the sound of a bag of crisps opening will lean on eater until guest's legs go numb or he is offered a share; Toby (Labrador), valued customer in his own right, due to amount of crisps he eats, also retrieves empty bags.

LEICESTERSHIRE

CHEQUERS INN

1 Gilmorton Road, Ashby Magna, near Lutterworth, Leicestershire (01455 209523).

Dogs allowed throughout the pub.

Pet Regulars: Bracken (Labrador), barmaid; Jessie (Labrador), socialite; Blue (English Setter), 'fuss' seeker.

LINCOLNSHIRE

THE BLUE DOG INN

Main Street, Sewstern, Grantham NG33 5QR (01476 860097).

Dogs allowed in non-food bar, beer garden. Dog-hitching rail outside.

Pet Regulars: The Guv'nor (Great Dane), best draught-excluder in history; Jenny (Westie) shares biscuits with pub cats; Jemma (98% Collie), atmosphere lapper-upper; JoJo (Cavalier King Charles), enjoys a drop of Murphys.

MERSEYSIDE

AMBASSADOR PRIVATE HOTEL

13 Bath Street, Southport PR9 0DP (01704 543998).

Dogs allowed in non-food bar, lounge, guest bedrooms.

THE SCOTCH PIPER

Southport Road, Lydiate, Merseyside (0151 5260503).

Dogs allowed throughout the pub.

Pet Regulars: Pippa (Rescued Russell), one dog welcoming committee, hearth rug, scrounger. Landlord's dogs very much second fiddle.

MIDLANDS

AWENTSBURY HOTEL

21 Serpentine Road, Selly Park, Birmingham B29 7HU (0121 4721258).

Dogs allowed in non-food bar, car park tables, beer garden.

Pet Regulars: Well-behaved dogs welcome.

TALBOT HOTEL

Colley Gate, Halesowen, West Midlands.

Dogs are allowed throughout the pub.

Pet Regulars: Include Inga, Gil, Jack and Red, all Border Collies. Every Christmas canine customers are treated to gift-wrapped dog chews.

NORFOLK

MARINE HOTEL

10 St Edmunds Terrace, Hunstanton, Norfolk PE36 5EH (01485 533310).

Dogs allowed throughout, except dining room.

Pet Regulars: Many dogs have returned with their owners year after year to stay at The Marine Bar.

THE OLD RAILWAY TAVERN

Eccles Road, Quidenham, Norwich, Norfolk NR16 2JG (01953 888223).

Dogs allowed in non-food bar, beer garden.

Pet Regulars: Maggie (Clumber Spaniel); Indi (GSD), Soshie (GSD) and pub dogs Elsa (GSD) & Vell (Springer). Elsa is so fond of sitting, motionless, on her own window ledge that new customers often think she's stuffed!

THE ROSE AND CROWN

Nethergate Street, Harpley, King's Lynn, Norfolk (01485 520577).

Dogs allowed in non-food bar, car park tables.

Pet Regulars: A merry bunch with shared interests – Duffy (mongrel); Tammy (Airedale); Bertie & Pru (Standard Poodles), all enjoy pub garden romps during summer and fireside seats in winter.

OXFORDSHIRE

THE BELL INN
High Street, Adderbury, Oxon (01295 810338).

Dogs allowed throughout the pub.

Pet Regulars: Include Wilf (mongrel), supplies full cabaret including talking to people and singing.

SHROPSHIRE

LONGMYND HOTEL
Cunnery Road, Church Stretton, Shropshire SY6 6AG (01694 722244).

Dogs allowed in owners' hotel bedrooms but not in public areas.

Pet Regulars: Sox (Collie/Labrador), occasional drinker and regular customer greeter; Kurt (GSD), entertainments manager; Sadie (Retriever), self appointed fire-guard.

REDFERN HOTEL
Cleobury Mortimer, Shropshire CY14 8AA (01299 270395).

Dogs allowed throughout and in guests' bedrooms.

SOMERSET

THE BUTCHERS ARMS
Carhampton, Somerset TA 24 (01643 821333).

Dogs allowed throughout the pub.

Pet Regulars: Lobo and Chera (Samoyeds), eating ice cubes and drinking; Emma (Spaniel), a whisky drinker; Benji (Spaniel-cross), self-appointed rug. Jimmy, a pony, also occasionally drops in for a drink.

HALFWAY HOUSE
Pitney, Langport, Somerset TA10 9AB (01458 252513).

Dogs allowed throughout (except kitchen!)

Pet Regulars: Pip (Lurcher), enjoys bitter, cider and G&T; Bulawayo (Ridgeback-cross), the advance party, sometimes three hours in advance of owner; Potter (57), sits at the bar.

THE SHIP INN

High Street, Porlock, Somerset (01643 862507).

Dogs allowed throughout and in guests' rooms.

Pet Regulars: Include Buster, Hardy and Crackers (Jack Russells), terrorists from London; Bijoux (Peke), while on holiday at The Ship enjoys Chicken Supreme cooked to order every evening.

SURREY

THE CRICKETERS

12 Oxenden Road, Tongham, Farnham, Surrey (01252 331340).

Dogs allowed in non-food bar, beer garden.

Pet Regulars: Include Lucy (a 'Bitsa'), surreptitious beer drinker and Chocolate Labradors Marston – after the beer – and Tullamore Dew – after the whisky.

SUSSEX

CHARCOAL BURNER

Weald Drive, Furnace Green, Crawley, West Sussex RH10 6NY (01293 526174).

Dogs allowed in non-food bar areas and front and back patios.

Pet Regulars: Lucy (Irish Setter), dedicated to cheese snips.

THE FORESTERS ARMS

High Street, Fairwarp, near Uckfield, Sussex TN22 3BP (01825 712808).

Dogs allowed in the beer garden and at car park tables, also inside.

Pet Regulars: Include Scampi (Jack Russell) who enjoys a social interlude with fellow canine guests.

THE INN IN THE PARK (CHEF & BREWER)

Tilgate Park, Tilgate, Crawley, West Sussex RH10 5PQ (01293 545324).

Dogs allowed in non-food bar, beer garden, upstairs lounge and balcony.

Pet Regulars: Tuffy (Staffordshire Bull Terrier) leans, on hind legs, on bar awaiting beer and nibbles; Ted (Weimaraner), a 'watcher'; Jacko (Dalmatian), a crisp howler who, once given a pack, opens them himself; Meg (Border Collie), hoovers fallen bar snacks.

THE PLOUGH

Crowhurst, near Battle, Sussex TN33 9AY (01424 830310).

Dogs allowed in non-food bar, car park tables, beer garden.

Pet Regulars: Kai (Belgian Shepherd), drinks halves of Websters; Poppy and Cassie (Springer Spaniels), divided between the lure of crisps and fireside.

THE PRESTONVILLE ARMS

64 Hamilton Road, Brighton, East Sussex (01273 701007).

Dogs allowed in beer garden, throughout the pub (no food served).

Pet Regulars: These include Katie and Susie, a Yorkie and a ???!, who have been known to jump onto the pool table and help out by picking up the balls.

QUEENS HEAD

Village Green, Sedlescombe, East Sussex (01424 870228).

Dogs allowed throughout the pub.

Pet Regulars: Misty (Whippet) partial to Guinness and Bacardi and Coke. Hogs the dog biscuits kept especially for guests' dogs – proceeds to Guide Dogs for the Blind.

THE SLOOP INN

Freshfield Lock, Haywards Heath, Sussex RH17 7NP (01444 831219).

Dogs allowed in non-food bar, at car park tables, beer garden, family room, public bar.

Pet Regulars: Pub dogs are Staffordshire Bull Terriers Rosie and Chutney. Customers include Solo (Labrador), crisp burglar, beer drinker; Tania (Rottweiller), sleeping giant. All bedraggled gun-dogs are especially welcome to dry out by the fire.

THE SMUGGLERS' ROOST

125 Sea Lane, Rustington, West Sussex BN16 25G (01903 785714).

Dogs allowed in non-food bar, at car park tables, in beer garden, family room.

Pet Regulars: Moffat (Border Terrier), beer makes him sneeze; Leo (Border Terrier), forms instant affections with anyone who notices him; Max (Cocker Spaniel), eats crisps only if they are 'plain'; Tim (King Charles Spaniel), quite prepared to guard his corner when food appears. The landlord owns a Great Dane.

THE SPORTSMAN'S ARMS
Rackham Road, Amberley, near Arundel BN18 9NR (01798 831787).

Dogs allowed throughout the pub.

Pet Regulars: Ramsden (Labrador), likes pickled onions. Landlord's dogs will not venture into the cellar which is haunted by the ghost of a young girl.

WELLDIGGERS ARMS
Lowheath, Petworth, West Sussex GU28 0HG (01798 342287).

Dogs allowed throughout the pub.

Pet Regulars: Angus (Labrador), crisp snaffler; Benji (Cavalier King Charles), hearth rug.

THE WYNDHAM ARMS
Rogate, West Sussex GU31 5HG (01730 821315).

Dogs allowed in non-food bar and at outside tables.

Pet Regulars: Henry (wire-haired Dachshund), hooked on Bristol Cream Sherry; Blot (Labrador), welcoming-committee and food fancier; Scruffy (Beardie), completely mad; Oscar (Labrador), floor hog.

WILTSHIRE

ARTICHOKE
The Nursery, Devizes, Wiltshire SN10 2AA (01380 723400).

Dogs allowed throughout pub.

Pet Regulars: Heidi (mongrel), pub tart; Monty (Dalmatian), trifle fixated; Rosie (Boxer), customer 'kissing'; Triffle (Airedale) and Shandy (mongrel) pub welcoming-committee.

THE PETERBOROUGH ARMS
Dauntsey Lock, near Chippenham, Wiltshire SN15 4HD (01249 890409).

Dogs allowed in non-food bar, at car park tables, in beer garden, family room (when non-food).

Pet Regulars: Include Winston (Jack Russell), will wait for command before eating a biscuit placed on his nose; Waddi (GSD), can grab a bowling ball before it hits the skittle pins; Harry 4 Legs (GSD), always wins the Christmas prize draw.

THE THREE HORSESHOES
High Street, Chapmanslade, near Westbury, Wiltshire (01373 832280).

Dogs allowed in non-food bar and beer garden.

Pet Regulars: Include Clieo (Golden Retriever), possibly the youngest 'regular' in the land – his first trip to the pub was at eight weeks. Westbury and District Canine Society repair to the Three Horseshoes after training nights (Monday/Wednesday). The pub boasts six cats and two dogs in residence.

WAGGON AND HORSES
High Street, Wootton Bassett, Swindon, Wiltshire (01793 852326).

Dogs allowed in non-food bar.

Pet Regulars: Include Gemma, a very irregular Whippet/Border collie-cross. She likes to balance beer-mats on her nose, then flip them over and catch them, opens and shuts doors on command, walks on her hind legs and returns empty crisp bags. She is limited to one glass of Guinness a night.

YORKSHIRE

THE FORESTERS ARMS
Kilburn, North Yorkshire YO6 4AH (01347 868386).

Dogs allowed throughout, except restaurant.

Pet Regulars: Ebony (Labrador) and Jess (Labrador), eating ice cubes off the bar and protecting customers from getting any heat from the fire.

FOX INN
Roxby Staithes, Whitby, North Yorkshire (01947 840335).

Dogs allowed throughout including guests' bedrooms, but not in bar.

Pet Regulars: B&B guests include Lucy and Mouse (Jack Russell & Dachshund); Mattie & Sally (Spaniels) and Meg and George (Bassetts); Lady (57) and another Lady, also a Heinz 57.

THE GOLDEN FLEECE
Lindley Road, Blackley, near Huddersfield (01422 372704).

Dogs allowed in non-food bar, at outside tables.

Pet Regulars: Ellie & Meara (Rhodesian Ridgebacks), starving dog impressions, animated hearthrugs.

THE GREENE DRAGON INN

Hardraw, Hawes, North Yorkshire DL8 3LZ (01969 667392).

Dogs allowed in bar, at car park tables, in beer garden, family room but not dining room or restaurant.

THE HALL

High Street, Thornton Le Dale, Pickering, North Yorkshire YO18 7RR

Dogs allowed usually throughout the pub.

Pet Regulars: Include Lucy (Jack Russell), she has her own beer glass at the bar, drinks only Newcastle Brown and Floss (mongrel), partial to Carlsberg.

NEW INN HOTEL

Clapham, near Settle, Yorkshire LA2 8HH (015242 51203).

Dogs allowed in non-food bar, beer garden, family room.

Pet Regulars: Ben (Collie-cross), a model customer.

PREMIER HOTEL

66 Esplanade, South Cliff, Scarborough, Yorkshire YO11 2UZ (01723 501062).

Dogs allowed throughout in non-food areas of hotel.

Pet Regulars: enjoy sharing their owners' rooms at no extra cost. There is a walking service available for pets with disabled owners.

THE SHIP

6 Main Street, Greasbrough, Rotherham S61 4PX (01709 551020).

Dogs allowed throughout the pub.

Pet Regulars: Include Hans (Guide Dog), reverts to puppy behaviour when 'off duty' and Ben (Border Terrier), 'frisks' customers for tit-bits.

SIMONSTONE HALL

Hawes, North Yorkshire DL8 3LY (01969 667255).

Dogs allowed throughout hotel except dining area.

Pet Regulars: account for 2,000 nights per annum. More than 50% of guests are accompanied by their dogs, from Pekes to an Anatolian Shepherd (the size of a small Shetland pony!) Two dogs have stayed, with their owners, on 23 separate occasions.

THE SPINNEY

Forest Rise, Balby, Doncaster, South Yorkshire DN4 9HQ (01302 852033).

Dogs allowed throughout the pub.

Pet Regulars: Shamus (Irish Setter), pub thief. Fair game includes pool balls, beer mats, crisps, beer, coats, hats. Recently jumped 15 feet off pub roof with no ill effect. Yan (Labrador), a dedicated guide dog; Sam (Boxer), black pudding devotee.

THE ROCKINGHAM ARMS

8 Main Street, Wentworth, Rotherham, South Yorkshire S62 7LO (01226 742075).

Dogs allowed throughout pub.

Pet Regulars: Tilly (Beardie), does nothing but has adopted the quote of actor Kenneth Williams – "Sometimes I feel so unutterably superior to those around me that I marvel at my ability to live among them"; Sasha & Penny (Terriers), enjoy a social coffee; Kate & Rags (Airedale and cross-breed), prefer lager to coffee; Holly (terrier and pub dog), dubbed 'the flying squirrel', likes everyone, whether they like it or not!

ROTHERHAM COMPANIONS CLUB

The Fairways, Wickersley, Rotherham, South Yorkshire (01709 548192).

Dogs on leads allowed throughout the pub (some restrictions if wedding party booked).

Pet Regulars: All chocolate fanatics who receive their favourite treat on arrival include Viking (Springer), Duke (Chow), Max (Border Collie) and Willie (Yorkshire Terrier). Viking keeps a box of toys and a ball behind the bar.

WALES

ANGLESEY

THE BUCKLEY HOTEL

Castle Street, Beaumaris, Isle of Anglesey LL58 8AW (01248 810415).

Dogs allowed throughout the pub, except in the dining room.

Pet Regulars: Cassie (Springer Spaniel) and Rex (mongrel), dedicated 'companion' dogs.

DYFED

THE ANGEL HOTEL

Rhosmaen Street, Llandeilo, Dyfed (01558 822765).

Dogs allowed throughout the pub.

Pet Regulars: Skip (Spaniel/Collie), a Baileys devotee; Crumble (GSD), a devotee of anything edible.

SCOTLAND

ARGYLL

THE BALLACHULISH HOTEL

Ballachulish, Argyll PA39 4JY (01855 811606).

Dogs allowed in the lounge, beer garden and guests' bedrooms, but not in bar.

Pet Regulars: Thumper (Border Collie/GSD-cross), devoted to his owner and follows him everywhere.

DUMFRIES & GALLOWAY

CULGRUFF HOUSE HOTEL

Crossmichael, Castle Douglas, Dumfries & Galloway DG7 3BB (01556 670230).

Dogs allowed in family room, guest bedrooms, but must be kept on leads outside.

Pet Regulars: A cross-section of canine visitors.

MORAYSHIRE

THE CLIFTON BAR

Clifton Road, Lossiemouth, Morayshire (01343 812100).

Dogs allowed throughout pub.

Pet Regulars: Include Zoe (Westie), has her own seat and is served coffee with two lumps and Rhona (Labrador) who makes solo visits.

ROYAL OAK

Station Road, Urquhart, Elgin, Moray (01343 842607).

Dogs allowed throughout pub.

Pet Regulars: Murphy (Staffordshire Bull Terrier) – food bin. Biscuits (from the landlady), Maltesers (from the landlord), sausages and burgers (from the barbecue).

PERTHSHIRE

CLACHAN COTTAGE HOTEL

Lochside, Lochearnhead, Perthshire (01567 830247).

Dogs allowed in all non-food areas.

Pet Regulars: Regulars are few but passing trade frequent and welcome. Previous owner's dog was a renowned water-skier.

CHANNEL ISLANDS   *JERSEY*

LA PULENTE INN

La Pulente, St Brelade, Jersey (01534 41760).

Dogs allowed throughout the pub.

Pet Regulars: Include Bridie (Border Collie), darts, pool, watching TV, beer-mat skiing, stone shoving. Also responsible for fly catching. Drinks Bass and Guinness.

ONE FOR YOUR FRIEND 1996

FHG Publications have a large range of attractive holiday accommodation guides for all kinds of holiday opportunities throughout Britain. They also make useful gifts at any time of year. Our guides are available in most bookshops and larger newsagents but we will be happy to post you a copy direct if you have any difficulty. We will also post abroad but have to charge separately for post or freight.

The inclusive cost of posting and packing the guides to you or your friends in the UK is as follows:

Farm Holiday Guide
ENGLAND, WALES and IRELAND
Board, Self-catering, Caravans/Camping,
Activity Holidays.   **£4.80**

Farm Holiday Guide SCOTLAND
All kinds of holiday accommodation.   **£3.60**

SELF-CATERING HOLIDAYS IN BRITAIN
Over 1000 addresses throughout for
Self-catering and caravans in Britain.   **£4.60**

BRITAIN'S BEST HOLIDAYS
A quick-reference general guide
for all kinds of holidays.   **£3.60**

The FHG Guide to CARAVAN & CAMPING HOLIDAYS
Caravans for hire, sites and
holiday parks and centres.   **£3.60**

BED AND BREAKFAST STOPS
Over 1000 friendly and comfortable
overnight stops. Non-smoking, The
Disabled and Special Diets
Supplements.   **£4.80**

CHILDREN WELCOME! FAMILY HOLIDAY & ATTRACTIONS GUIDE
Family holidays with details of
amenities for children and babies.   **£4.60**

SCOTTISH WELCOME
Introduced by Katie Wood. A new
guide to holiday accommodation
and attractions in Scotland.   **£4.50**

Recommended SHORT BREAK HOLIDAYS IN BRITAIN
'Approved' accommodation for
quality bargain breaks. Introduced by
John Carter.   **£4.50**

Recommended COUNTRY HOTELS OF BRITAIN
Including Country Houses, for
the discriminating.   **£4.50**

Recommended WAYSIDE & COUNTRY INNS OF BRITAIN
Pubs, Inns and small hotels.   **£4.50**

PGA GOLF GUIDE
Where to play. Where to stay
Over 2000 golf courses in Britain with
convenient accommodation. Endorsed
by the PGA. Holiday Golf in France,
Portugal, Spain and USA.   **£9.80**

PETS WELCOME!
The unique guide for holidays for
pet owners and their pets.   **£5.20**

BED AND BREAKFAST IN BRITAIN
Over 1000 choices for touring and
holidays throughout Britain.
Airports and Ferries Supplement.   **£3.60**

THE FRENCH FARM AND VILLAGE HOLIDAY GUIDE
The official guide to self-catering
holidays in the 'Gîtes de France'.   **£9.80**

Tick your choice and send your order and payment to FHG PUBLICATIONS, ABBEY MILL BUSINESS CENTRE, SEEDHILL, PAISLEY PA1 1TJ (TEL: 0141-887 0428. FAX: 0141-889 7204). **Deduct** 10% for 2/3 titles or copies; 20% for 4 or more.

Send to: NAME ....

ADDRESS ....

....

.... POST CODE ....

I enclose Cheque/Postal Order for £ ....

SIGNATURE .... DATE ....

Please complete the following to help us improve the service we provide. How did you find out about our guides:

☐ Press   ☐ Magazines   ☐ TV   ☐ Radio   ☐ Family/Friend   ☐ Other.